Cognitive Social Mining Applications in Data Analytics and Forensics

Anandakumar Haldorai
Sri Eshwar College of Engineering, India

Arulmurugan Ramu
Presidency University, India

A volume in the Advances in Social Networking
and Online Communities (ASNOC) Book Series

Published in the United States of America by
  IGI Global
  Information Science Reference (an imprint of IGI Global)
  701 E. Chocolate Avenue
  Hershey PA, USA 17033
  Tel: 717-533-8845
  Fax: 717-533-8661
  E-mail: cust@igi-global.com
  Web site: http://www.igi-global.com

Library of Congress Cataloging-in-Publication Data

Names: Haldorai, Anandakumar, 1983- editor. | Ramu, Arulmurugan, 1985- editor.
Title: Cognitive social mining applications in data analytics and forensics /
  Anandakumar Haldorai and Arulmurugan Ramu, editors.
Description: Hershey, PA : Information Science Reference, [2019] | Includes
  bibliographical references and index.
Identifiers: LCCN 2018029253| ISBN 9781522575221 (h/c) | ISBN 9781522575238
  (eISBN)
Subjects: LCSH: Data mining. | Online social networks--Data processing.
Classification: LCC QA76.9.D343 C477 2019 | DDC 006.3/12--dc23 LC record available at https://lccn.loc.gov/2018029253

This book is published in the IGI Global book series Advances in Social Networking and Online Communities (ASNOC) (ISSN: 2328-1405; eISSN: 2328-1413)

British Cataloguing in Publication Data
A Cataloguing in Publication record for this book is available from the British Library.

All work contributed to this book is new, previously-unpublished material. The views expressed in this book are those of the authors, but not necessarily of the publisher.

For electronic access to this publication, please contact: eresources@igi-global.com.

Advances in Social Networking and Online Communities (ASNOC) Book Series

Hakikur Rahman
Institute of Computer Management and Science,
Bangladesh

ISSN:2328-1405
EISSN:2328-1413

MISSION

The advancements of internet technologies and the creation of various social networks provide a new channel of knowledge development processes that's dependent on social networking and online communities. This emerging concept of social innovation is comprised of ideas and strategies designed to improve society.

The **Advances in Social Networking and Online Communities** book series serves as a forum for scholars and practitioners to present comprehensive research on the social, cultural, organizational, and human issues related to the use of virtual communities and social networking. This series will provide an analytical approach to the holistic and newly emerging concepts of online knowledge communities and social networks.

COVERAGE

- Knowledge Chains
- Introduction to Mobile Computing
- Information and Data Management
- Citizens' E-participation in Local Decision-Making Processes
- Knowledge Communication and the Role of Communities and Social Networks
- Knowledge as a Symbol/Model of Development
- Conceptual Role of ICTs in Knowledge Communication and Management
- Current State and Future Development of the Institutional Knowledge Management
- Advanced Researches in Knowledge Communities
- Organizational Knowledge Communication and Knowledge Transfer as the Focal Point of Knowledge Management

IGI Global is currently accepting manuscripts for publication within this series. To submit a proposal for a volume in this series, please contact our Acquisition Editors at Acquisitions@igi-global.com or visit: http://www.igi-global.com/publish/.

Titles in this Series

For a list of additional titles in this series, please visit: www.igi-global.com/book-series

Exploring the Role of Social Media in Transnational Advocacy
Floribert Patrick C. Endong (University of Calabar, Nigeria)
Information Science Reference • copyright 2018 • 307pp • H/C (ISBN: 9781522528548) • US $195.00 (our price)

Online Communities as Agents of Change and Social Movements
Steven Gordon (Babson College, USA)
Information Science Reference • copyright 2017 • 338pp • H/C (ISBN: 9781522524953) • US $195.00 (our price)

Social Media Performance Evaluation and Success Measurements
Michael A. Brown Sr. (Florida International University, USA)
Information Science Reference • copyright 2017 • 294pp • H/C (ISBN: 9781522519638) • US $185.00 (our price)

Political Scandal, Corruption, and Legitimacy in the Age of Social Media
Kamil Demirhan (Bülent Ecevit University, Turkey) and Derya Çakır-Demirhan (Bülent Ecevit University, Turkey)
Information Science Reference • copyright 2017 • 295pp • H/C (ISBN: 9781522520191) • US $190.00 (our price)

Power, Surveillance, and Culture in YouTube™'s Digital Sphere
Matthew Crick (William Paterson University, USA)
Information Science Reference • copyright 2016 • 317pp • H/C (ISBN: 9781466698550) • US $185.00 (our price)

Social Media and the Transformation of Interaction in Society
John P. Sahlin (The George Washington University, USA)
Information Science Reference • copyright 2015 • 300pp • H/C (ISBN: 9781466685567) • US $200.00 (our price)

New Opportunities for Artistic Practice in Virtual Worlds
Denise Doyle (University of Wolverhampton, UK)
Information Science Reference • copyright 2015 • 322pp • H/C (ISBN: 9781466683846) • US $185.00 (our price)

Cases on Strategic Social Media Utilization in the Nonprofit Sector
Hugo Asencio (California State University – Dominguez Hills, USA) and Rui Sun (California State University – Dominguez Hills, USA)
Information Science Reference • copyright 2015 • 375pp • H/C (ISBN: 9781466681880) • US $195.00 (our price)

701 East Chocolate Avenue, Hershey, PA 17033, USA
Tel: 717-533-8845 x100 • Fax: 717-533-8661
E-Mail: cust@igi-global.com • www.igi-global.com

Dedicated to our friends and families for their constant support during the course of this book

Editorial Advisory Board

Table of Contents

Detailed Table of Contents

Chapter 1

    S. Uma, Hindusthan Institute of Technology, India
    SenthilKumar T, Hindusthan Institute of Technology, India

Using social media has become an integral part of life for people of different demographics for information exchange, searching, maintaining contact networks, marketing, locating job opportunities etc. Social networking is used for education, research, business, advertisements and entertainment. Social media platforms are prone to cybercrime, which is a threat not only for the individual user but for national and international security according to the National Security Council Report. With the advent of big data storage and analytics abilities, decision making is a potential problem and requires smarter machines to organize data faster, make better sense of it, discover insights, learn, adapt and improve over time without direct programming. Cognitive computing makes it easy to unveil the patterns hidden in unstructured data and make more informed decision on consequential matters. In this chapter is a discussion of the challenges and opportunities in social mining services and the applications of cognitive technology towards national security.

Chapter 2

    Vijayaganth V., Bannari Amman Institute of Technology, India

Social networks have increased momentously in the last decade. Individuals are depending on interpersonal organizations for data, news, and the assessment of different clients on various topics. These issues often make social network data very complex to analyze manually, resulting in the persistent use of computational means for analyzing them. Data mining gives a variety of systems for identifying helpful learning from huge datasets and a wide range of techniques for detecting useful knowledge from massive datasets like trends, patterns and rules. This chapter discusses different data mining techniques used in mining social networks.

Chapter 3

Logeswari Shanmugam, Bannari Amman Institute of Technology, India

Premalatha K., Bannari Amman Institute of Technology, India

Biomedical literature is the primary repository of biomedical knowledge in which PubMed is the most absolute database for collecting, organizing and analyzing textual knowledge. The high dimensionality of the natural language text makes the text data quite noisy and sparse in the vector space. Hence, the data preprocessing and feature selection are important processes for the text processing issues. Ontologies select the meaningful terms semantically associated with the concepts from a document to reduce the dimensionality of the original text. In this chapter, semantic-based indexing approaches are proposed with cognitive search which makes use of domain ontology to extract relevant information from big and diverse data sets for users.

Chapter 4

Suriya Murugan, Bannari Amman Institute of Technology, India

Sumithra M. G., Bannari Amman Institute of Technology, India

The future of space communications has evolved towards being cognitive in order to improve energy and spectrum efficiency. Nowadays, near-Earth space satellites for weather, civil defense, and public commercial sectors are rapidly increasing, thereby resulting in congestion. Cognitive digital radio is a form of dynamic wireless communication in which a transceiver can intelligently detect the parts of communication channels that are currently not in use and instantly move into vacant channels while avoiding occupied ones. A challenge for communication between satellites and ground terminals involves calibrating both the time and frequency channels during rapid relative movement. A more dynamic and highly-precise algorithm for enhancing communication between satellites and base station terminals such as deep learning in cognitive radios is proposed that enables significant degree of automation in the space communication networks where spectrum interference is a key issue.

Chapter 5

Ramanujam Elangovan, Thiagarajar College of Engineering, India

Prianga M., Thiagarajar College of Engineering, India

Cloud computing is used for storing and managing information using the remote servers, which is hosted on the internet instead of storing it in a normal server or personal computer. The main purpose of why most of the companies use the cloud for storing and managing data is to not have to pay money for storing data. The main aim is to allow users to benefit from all technologies. Virtualization is considered to be the main technology of cloud computing. Several privacy concerns are caused by the cloud because the service provider can access the data at any time. Cloud providers can also share the information for the purpose of law and order. The information gathered from the physical implementation is called a side channel attack. Some technical knowledge is required for side channel attacks and these attacks are based on statistical methods. It works by monitoring the security critical operations. The side channel attack is based on the information which is leaking and the information which is kept secret.

Chapter 6

Dharmpal Singh, JIS College of Engineering, India

Social media are based on computer-mediated technologies that smooth the progress of the creation and distribution of information, thoughts, idea, career benefits and other forms of expression via implicit communities and networks. The social network analysis (SNA) has emerged with the increasing popularity of social networking services like Facebook, Twitter, etc. Therefore, information about group cohesion, contribution in activities, and associations among subjects can be obtained from the analysis of the blogs. The analysis of the blogs required well-known knowledge discovery tools to help the administrator to discover participant collaborative activities or patterns with inferences to improve the learning and sharing process. Therefore, the goal of this chapter is to provide the data mining tools for information retrieval, statistical modelling and machine learning to employ data pre-processing, data analysis, and data interpretation processes to support the use of social network analysis (SNA) to improve the collaborative activities for better performance.

Chapter 7

Suriya Murugan, Bannari Amman Institute of Technology, India
Sumithra M. G., Bannari Amman Institute of Technology, India
Logeswari Shanmugam, Bannari Amman Institute of Technology, India

This chapter examines the exploratory data analytics that require statistical techniques on data sets which are in the form of object-attribute-time format and referred to as three-dimensional data sets. It is very difficult to cluster and hence a subspace clustering method is used. Existing algorithms like CATSeeker are not actionable and its 3D structure complicates the clustering process, hence they are inadequate to solve this clustering problem. To cluster these three-dimensional data sets, a new centroid-based concept is introduced in the proposed system called clustering using particle swarm optimization (CPSO). This CPSO framework can be applied to financial and stock domain datasets through the unique combination of (1) singular value decomposition (SVD), (2) particle swarm optimization (PSO), and (3) 3D frequent item set mining which results in efficient performance. CPSO framework prunes the entire search space to identify the significant subspaces and clusters the datasets based on optimal centroid value.

Chapter 8

Deivanathan R., VIT Chennai, India

Bridging the design, planning and manufacturing departments of a production enterprise is not a conclusive effort for the implementation of computer integrated manufacturing. Continuous interaction and seamless exchange of information among these functions is needed and requires the maintenance of a large database and user-friendly search and optimization techniques. Among several artificial intelligence techniques capable of the above task, four important and popular ones are, expert systems, artificial neural networks, fuzzy logic and genetic algorithms. In this chapter, these four techniques have been conceptually studied in detail and exemplified by reviewing an application in the manufacturing domain. Successful implementations of artificial intelligence that are recently reported in machining domain are also reviewed, suggesting potential applications in the future.

Many different areas of computer science have been developed for many years in the world. Data mining is one of the fields which many algorithms, methods, and models have been built and applied to many commercial applications and research successfully. Many social networks have been invested and developed in the strongest way for the recent years in the world because they have had many big benefits as follows: they have been used by lots of users in the world and they have been applied to many business fields successfully. Thus, a lot of different techniques for the social networks have been generated. Unsurprisingly, the social network analysis is crucial at the present time in the world. To support this process, in this book chapter we have presented many simple concepts about data mining and social networking. In addition, we have also displayed a novel model of the data mining for the social network analysis using a CLIQUE algorithm successfully.

Chapter 10

Online social networks, such as Facebook are increasingly used by many users and these networks allow people to publish and share their data to their friends. The problem is user privacy information can be inferred via social relations. This chapter makes a study and performs research on managing those confidential information leakages which is a challenging issue in social networks. It is possible to use learning methods on user released data to predict private information. Since the main goal is to distribute social network data while preventing sensitive data disclosure, it can be achieved through sanitization techniques. Then the effectiveness of those techniques is explored, and the methods of collective inference are used to discover sensitive attributes of the user profile data set. Hence, sanitization methods can be used efficiently to decrease the accuracy of both local and relational classifiers and allow secure information sharing by maintaining user privacy.

Chapter 11

Hybrid networks are next generation of wireless networks that are increasingly used in wireless communications that highly support real time transmission with a limited quality of service. The study proves that existing systems use QoS-oriented distributed routing protocols to enhance the QoS support capability of hybrid networks and it transforms the packet routing problem to a resource scheduling problem which has five algorithms. They are (1) QoS-guaranteed neighbor election algorithm, (2) distributed packet scheduling algorithm, (3) mobility-based segment resizing algorithm, (4) traffic redundant elimination algorithm, and (5) data redundancy elimination-based transmission algorithm. To increase the performance of hybrid networks in a real mobility model, this chapter analyses and devises a method to authenticate data streams for transmission. Data transparent authentication without communication overhead is an approach which reduces breakdown of original data or sends out-of-band authentication information.

Chapter 12

Rajamohana S. P., PSG College of Technology, India
Dharani A., PSG College of Technology, India
Anushree P., PSG College of Technology, India
Santhiya B., PSG College of Technology, India
Umamaheswari K., PSG College of Technology, India

Autism spectrum disorder (ASD) is one of the common disorders in brain. Early detection of ASD improves the overall mental health, which is very important for the future of the child. ASD affects social coordination, emotions, and motor activity of an individual. This is due to the difficulties in getting self-evaluation results and expressive experiences. In the first case study in this chapter, an efficient method to automatically detect the expressive states of individuals with the help of physiological signals is explored. In the second case study of the chapter, the authors explore breast cancer prediction using SMO and IBK. Breast cancer is the second leading cause of cancer deaths in women worldwide and occurs in nearly one out of eight. In this proposed system, the tumor is the feature that is used to identify the breast cancer presence in women. Tumors are basically of two types (i.e., benign or malignant). In order to provide appropriate treatment to the patients, symptoms must be studied properly, and an automatic prediction system is required that will classify the tumor into benign or malignant using SMO and IBK.

Chapter 13

M. Manikandakumar, Thiagarajar College of Engineering, India
Sri Subarnaa D. K., Thiagarajar College of Engineering, India
Monica Grace R., Thiagarajar College of Engineering, India

Wireless ad hoc networks are dynamic networks in which nodes can move freely in the network. A new type of Vehicular Ad Hoc Network (VANET) that allows smart transport system to provide road security and reduces traffic jams through automobile-to-automobile and automobile-to-roadside communication. In this, vehicles rely on the integrity of received data for deciding when to present alerts to drivers. Because of wireless network the VANET messages are vulnerable to many attacks and the security concerns are also major issues. So, with respect to these methods, this article will discuss the Denial of Service (DoS) attack, masquerading, and their vulnerabilities. Also, it classifies the securities and their prevention mechanisms in overcoming these security issues in VANET and Cognitive Radio VANET perspectives.

Cognitive systems mimic the functions of the human brain and improves decision-making to harness the power of big data in multiple application areas. It generates a model that reacts by sensing, understanding natural language, and providing a response to stimulus naturally rather than traditional programmable systems. Cognitive computing is trained to process large unstructured datasets imposing machine learning techniques to adapt to different context and derive value from big data. Using a custom chat box or search assistant to interact with human in natural language which can understand queries and explains data insights. This chapter also touches on the challenges of cognitive computing to demonstrate insights that are similar to those of humans.

This book chapter presents the role of telecommunications network in voice and data transmission. Switching, signaling and transmission are the technologies used to carry out this process. In landline call establishment, calls are routed from subscriber handset to a remote switching unit (RSU), a main switching unit (MSU), and to the internet protocol trunk automated exchange (IPTAX). Then, it is directed to the National Internet Backbone (NIB). On the receiver side, the IPTAX receives this signal from the NIB and directs to it to the MSU and RSU, respectively. The receiver side RSU delivers the information to the destination subscriber. In order to transmit the information from one place to other, it undergoes various process like modulation, demodulation, line coding, equalization, error control, bit synchronization and multiplexing, digitizing an analog message signal, and compression. This chapter also discusses the various services provided by BSNL and agencies governing the internet. Finally, it focuses on the National Internet Backbone facility of BSNL, India.

Preface

INTRODUCTION

The rapid proliferation of wireless technologies is expected to increase the demand for the radio spectrum by orders of magnitude over the next decade. This problem must be addressed via technology and regulatory innovations for significant improvements in spectrum efficiency and increased robustness and performance of wireless devices.

Emerging cognitive radio technology has been identified as a high impact disruptive technology innovation that could provide solutions to the radio energy problem and provide a path to scaling wireless systems for the next 25 years. Significant new research is required to address the many technical challenges of cognitive radio networking. These include dynamic spectrum allocation methods, spectrum sensing, cooperative communications, incentive mechanisms, cognitive network architecture and protocol design, cognitive network security, cognitive system adaptation algorithms and emergent system behavior. A major hurdle to the continued progress in the field is the inability to conclusively test, evaluate, and demonstrate cognitive networking technology, at scale and in real-world deployment scenarios.

Cognitive radios are expected to play a major role towards meeting the exploding traffic demand over social networks. A cognitive radio node senses the environment, analyzes the outdoor parameters, and then makes decisions for dynamic time, frequency, space, resource allocation and management to improve the utilization of mining the social data. For efficient real-time processes, the cognitive radio is usually combined with artificial intelligence and machine-learning techniques so that an adaptive and intelligent mining is achieved. Recently there has been a rapid increase in interest regarding social network analysis in the data mining community so in this book we briefly review the basic concepts underlying cognitive radio, and examine their applications to social mining in machine learning approach.

OBJECTIVE OF THE BOOK

This book deliberates the methods of implementing cognitive social mining applications in data analytics and forensics are cognitive radio communication, data mining for social network analysis, supervised machine learning techniques, social mining for cognitive radio networks, real-time ubiquitous social mining services, platform for privacy preserving social mining, internet-based social platform, challenges in space communication, social relationship ranking on internet, social platforms cognitive databases, applications of cognitive social mining services and future advancements in data analytics and forensics.

ORGANIZATION OF THE BOOK

The book consists of 15 chapters that are organized as shown below.

Chapter 1

In this chapter the author covers about the advances in information and communication technology that have made the world a global village. The chapter highlights about Cognitive computation and intelligence as the enrichment layer on top of this digital village is very much helpful in providing much deeper and rapid global national and international security insights out of the services and massive data produced in social media. This chapter makes a research study how IBM institute of business value has reported that nearly 60% of security professionals believe that cognitive security systems can slow down cybercrimes significantly. Finally, the chapter concludes there will be a threefold increase i.e., 7% to 21% in the percentage of companies implementing cognitive security systems by 2020.

Chapter 2

This chapter studies about different data mining techniques that have been used in social network analysis. The chapter elaborates about unsupervised to semi-supervised and supervised learning methods and how successes were achieved either with solitary or combined techniques. The chapter shows how the experiments conducted on social network analysis is believed to have shed more light on the structure and activities of social network and experimental results have also confirmed the relevance of data mining techniques in retrieving valuable information and contents from huge data generated on social network. The author also compared similar data mining tools and recommends the most suitable tool(s) for the dataset to be analyzed.

Chapter 3

In this chapter author makes a survey of cognitive healthcare assessment support for improving patient health and reducing the costs of missed diagnoses and optimal treatment plans. Also explains the purpose of cognitive computing in healthcare for producing better, best-practice, decision-relevant information for everyone in the health system. This chapter states the concept of indexing and smoothing that are employed for indexing the medical documents. The concept weights are assigned based on the semantic relations that are derived from the MeSH ontology through concept mapping and implemented as the mixture models of two components namely the simple concept translation model and the multiword phrase translation model. The chapter states that the phrases within the documents are considered using tri-gram techniques where both the terms and the phrases are given equal importance in this smoothing process.

Chapter 4

This chapter focuses over the importance of cognitive radio for satellite communications. The chapter explains about importance of space communication networks as the Earth Observation Satellite-based (EOS) sensors have emerged into a rapid source of multi-sensor, multi-resolution and multispectral geospatial information for decision making in varying application domains. The author uses spectrum sensing, dynamic spectrum allocation, and spectrum databases in-order to alleviate issues like (i) spectrum interference (ii) minimize communication delay between inter- satellite and satellite – terrestrial system (iii) increase network speed and coverage and (iv) optimize battery consumption. The chapter shows how all these factors can be improved for the single link connectivity and cognitive networking techniques for the multiple link connectivity by adapting cognitive radio communication for space satellites using deep learning algorithms.

Chapter 5

This chapter explores about side-channel attacks like micro architectural attacks (MA), which form the correlation between the higher-level functionalities of the software and the underlying hardware phenomena. This chapter has surveyed cache side-channel attacks and the way they gain from multi-tenancy and virtualization in cloud computing to explain safety of cryptographic algorithms. This chapter proposed a generic method to cache side-channel attack on preventing these attacks without affecting the cache and CPU efficiencies.

Chapter 6

This chapter uncovers how social sites provide privilege for the users to access the uncensored information post by them in real time for the broadcast and also provides the platform to the use to express their views, opinions on products and services of the organizations to know their interest. Author explains how data mining techniques will filter, categories, organize and scan the social network contents to perform the automated information processing to analyze the data within a reasonable time the chapter shows how data mining techniques enable the advanced search results in search engines to help in better understanding of social data for research and organizational functions.

Chapter 7

In this chapter the author presents a technique for mining actionable 3D subspace clusters from continuous valued 3D (object-attribute- time) data that is useful for various domains ranging from finance to biology. A technique called CPSO is an optimization and parallel methodology which is used to obtain the best clustering results was proposed. This chapter implements CPSO for saying how (1) clustering is done based on centroid value and (2) CPSO is used to find optimal centroids based on the velocity of particle. Finally, the chapter concludes how CPSO framework can be applied to data with increasing sizes and achieves high cluster quality with minimal time and space requirements.

Chapter 8

This chapter presents the problems in manufacturing engineering and states how knowledge intensive and unavoidably involve in decision making by experts at various levels. Further this chapter reviews that soft computing techniques are preferred to physics-based methods for modeling and optimizing manufacturing systems which are characterized by complexity, uncertainty and lack of accuracy and precision. It explains how intelligent manufacturing can be achieved by utilizing the proven technologies of AI (fuzzy logic, neural networks, etc.) to monitor and control the manufacturing functions such as production planning, scheduling and shop floor operations. The author has presented four key technologies of AI domain, viz., expert system, neural network, fuzzy logic and genetic algorithms have been studied and are seen to be taking semantic and Evolutionary approach to model the machining process. It shows how knowledge-based systems should be preferably integrated with the manufacturing system to increase their usage. Finally, the chapter concludes how AI techniques like fuzzy expert systems, neuro fuzzy systems and hybrid genetic algorithms can be used in implementation of process monitoring and control.

Chapter 9

This chapter presents the simple concepts of the DM, the SN, the SNG, and the SNA and also displayed the importance of the DM and the SNA in the world. This chapter has stated a novel model using the CLA of the DM with the MULTDIMVECTs according to the OPL of the SC through the GSE and the CPNE. This chapter proposed a model, for the SNA that can process billions of the documents in English of the semantic mining in a big data. This is very significant for many organizations, economies, governments, countries, companies, and research in the world.

Chapter 10

This chapter addresses the problem of protect private information leakage using friendship links in social networks. This chapter analyses privacy issues in social networking and explores various data mining techniques for preventing privacy issues. Finally, the chapter concludes by combining the results from the collective inference implications with the individual results, by removing details and friendship links together is the best way to reduce classifier accuracy and also show how filter the commenting text in a wall can greatly reduce the accuracy of local and relational classifiers.

Chapter 11

This chapter reviews how data streams have been used in many internet applications, such as grid computing and streaming media. This chapter presents how more and more applications demand a reliable and effective authentication mechanism to ensure the genuineness of data streams transferred over the internet. It has proposed a distributed block authentication coding technique to increase the performance of hybrid networks in real mobility model to authenticate data streams for transmission. Finally, the chapter concludes how data transparent authentication without communication overhead reduces the breakdown of original data or sends out-of-band authentication information.

Chapter 12

This chapter highlights various data mining techniques can be applied for identification and prevention of breast cancer among patients. This chapter proposes the use of two different data mining classification methods for the prediction of breast cancer SMO and IBK. The chapter makes comparison based on the different parameters for predicting the breast cancer and based on the selected classifier algorithm the accuracy of classification techniques is evaluated. Finally, the chapter concludes how the performance of SMO is efficient when compared with other classifiers to get better results with accuracy, low error rate and performance.

Chapter 13

This chapter outlines about Vehicular Adhoc Networks (VANETs) and states how the security hazards in these types of networks need to be integrated with the upcoming automobile technology. Finally, the chapter concludes how VANET securities via digital certificate secure the network against the most common form of network attacks like DOS and Masquerade.

Chapter 14

This chapter explains how the patient need to be alerted with signs of heart attack using pulse rate recorded by HB-heartbeat sensor, the client movement (with a PIR sensor) and location (with a microwave sensor). This chapter introduces how artificial neural networks provide higher accuracy in classifying the pulse rate on exceeding the given threshold value. The chapter created a model when the pulse rate is above or below the given threshold limit, a notification message is sent to the registered mobile number. It can be sent to multiple mobile numbers, like a guardian, doctor, or hospital helpline. Finally, the chapter concludes how this work can be extended to detect few more disorder occurrences in the human body.

Chapter 15

This chapter presents how a telecommunication switching system provides an electrical path between a sending and a receiving device. This chapter outlines how circuit switching and packet switching techniques are used for transmitting voice and data and describe landline call establishment procedures through the National Internet Backbone (NIB).

Anandakumar Haldorai
Sri Eshwar College of Engineering, India

Arulmurugan Ramu
Presidency University, India

Acknowledgment

The editors would like to acknowledge the help of all the people involved in this project and, more specifically, to the authors and reviewers that took part in the review process.

The editors would like to thank each one of the authors for their contributions. Our sincere gratitude goes to the chapter's authors who contributed their time and expertise to this book. We believe that the team of authors provides the perfect blend of knowledge and skills that went into authorizing this book. We thank each of the authors for developing their time, patience, perseverance and effort towards this book.

A special thanks to the publisher team, who showed the editors, ropes to start and continue. The editors would like to express their gratitude to all the people support, share, talked things over, read, wrote, offered comments, allowed us to quote their remarks and assisted in editing, proofreading, and design through the book journey.

Chapter 1

The Potential of Cognitive Social Mining Applications in Data Analytics for Protecting Social Media Users for National and International Security

S. Uma
Hindusthan Institute of Technology, India

SenthilKumar T
Hindusthan Institute of Technology, India

ABSTRACT

Using social media has become an integral part of life for people of different demographics for information exchange, searching, maintaining contact networks, marketing, locating job opportunities etc. Social networking is used for education, research, business, advertisements and entertainment. Social media platforms are prone to cybercrime, which is a threat not only for the individual user but for national and international security according to the National Security Council Report. With the advent of big data storage and analytics abilities, decision making is a potential problem and requires smarter machines to organize data faster, make better sense of it, discover insights, learn, adapt and improve over time without direct programming. Cognitive computing makes it easy to unveil the patterns hidden in unstructured data and make more informed decision on consequential matters. In this chapter is a discussion of the challenges and opportunities in social mining services and the applications of cognitive technology towards national security.

DOI: 10.4018/978-1-5225-7522-1.ch001

INTRODUCTION

The emergence of social media and its tremendous growth has influenced the change in information and technology over the past two decades. The increase in development of mobile technology has a major role in shaping the impact of social media. Social networking accounts for 28% of all media time spent online. It is used for a wide variety of reasons like socializing, communicating, sharing of information, etc. Social media which was once considered as an unofficial tool has now turned out to become more essential and occupies the board rooms for business discussions. For many organizations, social media is the backbone for creating brand awareness, marketing their products and services and conversions. The commercial value of the social media could not be ignored, and the online presence of organizations and constant nurturing is of prime importance for increasing the online sales and sustainability. It has become a potential digital marketing tool for all range of businesses and entrepreneurs to leverage social advertising, boost brand awareness, for lead generation, to increase the sales, to engage, to increase the user traffic on a web site, increase inbound traffic, improve search engine optimization, increase conversion rates, satisfy customers, etc. Social media platforms are used by retail companies, investors and traders of the financial markets, public health and sociology departments, public and government officials, media startups, etc.

Cybercrime is a threat for the individual users as well as for the nation. One of the major reasons behind is that, the social media user groups fail to follow the ethics to be followed. The ethics of identity and community on social networking services, anonymity and commitment are not followed among the social media users and become victims of cybercrimes (Anandakumar, 2014). Identifying the offender and eradicating cybercrimes is a challenging task for the cyber security force. Security threats are identified in the form of Viruses that can infect millions of computers using malicious links, Attacker with access to account ids could masquerade as that user and post malicious content, Social Engineering Attacks, Identity Thefts, Third party applications, Business Data, Professional Reputation, etc.

With the increasing dependency of a nation's economic and financial institutions on information technology, a cyber-attack against them will lead to an irreparable collapse of the country's economic structures. The reciprocation events are ineffective or sometimes alternative arrangements are not available which makes it difficult to think of the adverse situations it will lead to the Nation. The sectors like Income Tax, Police, Judiciary and Travel, Passports, Visa are already brought under the realm of e-governance in many nations. The E-commerce and e-banking sectors could also be affected more seriously which will have adverse effects on a nation's economic and financial positions. Such damages are more catastrophic and are irreversible. New technologies and approaches have to be identified for maintaining and securing the welfare of the individuals and the nation from the ill effects of cyber-attacks emanating from social networking sites.

The challenges in mining the big data is that it contains data and metadata which cannot be readily treated using traditional analysis tools, combining data from different sources like micro blogs, blogs, real-time markets, customer data and reviews to get meaningful insights. The correctness of the end result is based on the quality and quantity of the data. Restrictions in collecting data from websites, sampling and filtering data streams by providers, spread of unsubstantiated rumors, changing human behaviors, non-humans/robots, replication of data and dynamic data size are some of the challenges in mining social data.

Data mining, artificial intelligence and machine learning are some of the techniques used in social media analytics which makes it difficult to handle unstructured data from social networking sites and overcome the challenges mentioned above. Cognitive computing makes it easy to unveil the patterns hidden in unstructured data and make more informed decision on consequential matters. The advantage of these systems is that they could interpret and weigh the information from multiple sources, organize it with explanations along with the rationale for conclusions though they cannot provide definite answers. It attaches a confidence level for each potential insight. The ability of cognitive systems to read text, see images and hear natural speech in addition, has made their application in social media analysis more meaningful. Cognitive computing brings in smart automation that is capable of solving problems without the need for human assistance and also reduces manual errors thus changing the way information technology and industries will work. A discussion of the challenges and opportunities in social mining services and the applications of cognitive technology towards national and international security is presented in this chapter.

BACKGROUND

With reference to "We Are Social" and "Hootsuite" 2018 Global Digital suite of reports, more than 4 billion people around the world are using the Internet (Kemp, 2018). It implies that half of the world's population is online. The amazing fact is that nearly a quarter of a billion new users came online for the first time in 2017. The number of new users using the top most social platform in each country has increased by 1 million every day in the last 12 months. Social media is used by more than 3billion users every month. The number of social media, internet and mobile phone users in 2018 has increased by 13%, 7% and 4% respectively year-on-year. The online interactions are spontaneous and complex. The online users are members of several communities/groups and involved in multiple conversations (Graffigna & Riva, 2015). They are involved in multiple relationships and potential influencers of ideas, products and services. As a result, a rich new set of social network data is created through social media tools like message boards, web blogs, micro blogs, wikis, location based social networks, discussion forums, podcast networks, ratings and reviewing committees, social bookmarking sites, friend and contact networks, activity streams and file, photo and video shares and avatar based virtual reality spaces (Smith et al., 2009; Sharma et al., 2017).

Social media sites have become a common place for its users to express their sentiments, opinions and feedback. The large volumes of data generated out of social networking sites has promoted the analysis of this data to get the real insight of the feedback given by the users for arriving at better decision-making abilities. Social media mining is the process of representing, analyzing and extracting actionable patterns and trends from raw social media data (Social Media Mining, 2018). It has both advantages and limitations (Kulkarni, 2018). Social network analysis has a significant following in anthropology, biology, demography, communication studies, economics, geography, history, information science, organizational studies, political science, social psychology, development studies, sociolinguistics and computer science (Social Network Analysis Practical Applications, 2018).

An analysis of social network analysis is aimed at a variety of tasks which are listed down (Tang & Liu, 2010).

- **Social Network Influencers:** Identifying the most important actors in a social network, to understand the social influence and power in a network.
- **Community Identification:** It is concerned with identifying communities through network structures and topologies.
- **Position/Role Analysis:** It is concerned with the analyzing the Position/Role of a user during network interaction.
- **Simulation:** Simulating the real-world network through network modeling which is used for capturing the patterns presented in large scale complex networks.
- **Information Diffusion:** Studying information propagation in a network, which is useful in understanding the cultural dynamics and infection blocking.
- **Network Classification and Outlier Detection:** For example, to identify the abnormal behavior of users who are likely to be terrorists.
- **Viral Marketing and Link Prediction:** For example, the adoption of a small set of users can influence other members in the network which will maximize the benefits.

Data aggregation and mining, network propagation modeling, network modeling and sampling, user attribute and behavior analysis, community-maintained resource support, location-based interaction analysis, social sharing and filtering, recommender systems development, and link prediction and entity resolution are some of the common network analysis applications (Social network analysis Practical Applications, 2018). Private sectors use social network analysis for businesses to support customer interaction and analysis, information system development analysis, marketing and business intelligence requirements. Predictive analysis, lowering costs and improving revenue, enforcing governmental regulations and creating awareness in case of misconduct are the benefits of mining social data (Haldorai & Ramu, 2018). On the other hand, public sectors use social network analysis for activities such as leader engagement strategies, analysis of individual and group engagement, media use and community-based problem-solving (Social Network Analysis Practical Applications, 2018). Yet individuals are prone to social attacks like identity theft, defamation, stalking, injures to personal dignity and cyber bulling. False profiles and personalities or brands are mimicked to damaging the reputation in a network of friends (Gharibi & Shaabi, 2012). The limitations of using social data for analysis affects the privacy and security of the users, higher initial installation costs, incorrect information, evaluation dilemma, sampling bias, noise removal fallacy, studying distrust in social media and deception detection (Liu, 2014).

Sentiment analysis is broader and powerful and is used by organizations across the world for extracting insights from social data. Sentiment analysis or opinion mining is the process of determining the emotional tone behind a series of words which is used to gain an insight of the attitudes, opinions and emotions expressed in an online mention (Bannister, 2015). It is used for a variety of applications like stock market, where a shift in the sentiments has correlated the shifts in stock market. To gauge the public opinion to policy announcements and campaign messages, the Obama administration used sentiment analysis ahead of 2012 presidential elections, to quickly understand customer attitudes and react accordingly. For example, Expedia Canada used sentiment analysis to correct the negative feedbacks it received in one of its television adverts. Like any other automated process, sentiment analysis is also error prone due to the fact that the human language is complex. It is difficult to analyze the grammatical nuances, cultural variations, slang and misspellings that occur in online mentions as well as to teach a machine to understand the same with respect to the context (Bannister, 2015). For example, the comment "My flight's delayed, Brilliant" should not be taken literally but as a feel of frustration that the flight is delayed.

One of the potential applications of social network analysis is in intelligence, counter intelligence and law enforcement activities. The clandestine mass electronic surveillance programs are used by the National Security Agency (NSA) to generate the data needed to perform an analysis of terrorist's cells and other networks deemed relevant to national security (Wheaton & Richey, 2014). One of the issues with social network analysis is it contains a lot of white noise or extraneous information. Though social network analysis is a mathematical tool, it is very much useful in decision making on visualizing the networks. It is used to identify the flow of money and information throughout the networks. National insecurity is realized globally since the terrorists struck in September 11, 2001 on the World Trade Centre in the United States of America (Nsude & Onwe, 2017).

Potential operations across the globe and the awareness for their cause are inspired through social media (Nsude & Onwe, 2017). Many African Countries have also experienced security issues that led to the death of many people. Alakali et al. (2013) have indicated the fight between government forces and militant groups in Sudan which has claimed many lives and rendered several thousands homeless (Alakali et al., 2013). Terrorist groups use chat rooms, dedicated servers, websites and social networking tools to propagate for recruiting and for fund raising through cybercrime. For example, it is seen that international terrorists use specific codes in the social media which will be understood by their groups only to organize their attacks or devise ways to escape security agencies in order to carry out their attacks.

Chat rooms and emails are used by Hamas activists of middle east to plan their operations to coordinate actions across Gaza, the West Bank, Lebanon and Israel (Nsude & Onwe, 2017). Steganography is used by these terrorists to give instructions in the form of maps, photographs and directions. Terrorists also spread misinformation to deliver threats to instill fear and disseminate horrific images of recent actions.

IMPACT OF SOCIAL NETWORKS

As more and more social websites and applications proliferate, the usage of social media has become an integral part of online life for people of all demographics and backgrounds. It is used in various fields of science and research like education, business, medicine, and agriculture. As social media users create communication, collaborate, reviews and opinions, monitor brands, entertainment, media sharing political activity, report on news, use artificial intelligence and allow machine learning are the positive impacts of social media (Anandakumar & Umamaheswari, 2018).

While there are a lot of good reasons for using social media as mentioned above, it is not free from the ill effects it produces and is a threat to national and international security. Some of them are listed down.

- Spamming is the most common scenario seen in the social networks. Spam messages are seen in messages, status updates, comments on videos, contact requests, etc. Sometimes multiple messages are delivered on different channels. For example, a user may get a friend request notification in the form of a notification message within Facebook and email notification, unless the user has explicitly disabled the notification emails.
- Social engineering threats in the form of placing baits in social networks, follower scams, impersonation of celebrities, friends, malware attacks, phishing and advanced fee scams.
- Information attacks like creating false information, manipulating information, inserting malicious, logic-based weapons in the space based globally shared infrastructures for telecommunication and computing.

- Terrorist threats like gaining access to the nation's utilities, power grids, nuclear power plants, air traffic control systems and aircrafts.
- Cyber humiliation and cyber bullying.
- Promotion and distribution of drugs.

ISSUES AND DIMENSIONS OF CYBER TERRORISM

The "dark side of surfing the Internet", "Deep Web" or "Dark net" is the topic of interest that has captured the expert minds in recent years (Vilic, 2017). The "digital underground" is much bigger in size than the internet. Hackers, terrorists and criminals use the cyber space for terrorist activities and operations for communication since it is cheaper and secure. Usually the attack is of three basic methods – physical, electronic and computer networks. The extent of activities of the deep web users ranges from buying and selling drugs, forged money and documents, weapons, ammunition and explosives, order and pay to murder someone, sell and buy human organs (Vilic, 2017). The means for online payment without concealing the identity has enriched the criminality in the cyber space.

Information conflict plays a major role in social media and is considered to be an application of information warfare in both military and civilian contexts (Niekerk, 2013). Information warfare is defined as,"all actions taken to defend the military's information-based processes, information systems and communications networks and to destroy, neutralize or exploit the enemy's capabilities within the physical, information and cognitive domains"(Brazzoli, 2007). The major topics of interest in information warfare are listed below (Niekerk, 2013):

- **Network Warfare**: It is concerned with the offensive and defensive actions in relations to information, communications, computer networks and infrastructure.
- **Command and Control Warfare**: Actions taken to manage, direct and coordinate the movements and actions of various forces are considered. It seeks to protect this ability in friendly forces and disrupt the ability of an adversary.
- **Intelligence Based Warfare**: It is concerned with the actions to degrade an adversary's intelligence cycle while protecting one's growth.
- **Psychological Operations**: It intended to alter the perceptions of a target audience to be favorable to one's objectives.

Facebook has reported that for 2015, up to 2% of its monthly average users i.e., 31 million accounts are false. While Twitter estimates the figures as 5% LinkedIn has stated that they don't have a reliable system for identifying and counting duplicate or fraudulent accounts. More than 45,000 ransomware cyber-attacks were recorded in 99 countries by the security researchers at Kaspersky lab spreading across countries like UK, Russia, Ukraine, India, China, Italy, Egypt, etc. (Wong. & Solon, 2017).

CHALLENGES IN CYBER TERRORISM

Most of the terrorist activities are based on using Internet as a tool for engaging in a number of malpractices. It could be curtailed to some extent by removing their ability to access the internet (Anandakumar,

Umamaheswari & Arulmurugan, 2018). But they are spread across the globe and removing internet access may backfire as it prevents the people in that region to communicate with the external world. Sometimes the ISPs are privately owned by the terrorists.

The websites accessed by the terrorists could not be blocked as it is used publicly by a huge number of users. Identifying the genuineness of the individual users is quite difficult and genuine users are brain washed to become terrorists. Internet has become a cheaper and faster tool for information dissemination amongst the terrorists. Terrorist insurgencies have a fairly low barrier to entry and don't require a lot of manpower to operate efficiently.

Though law enforcement could intercept these messages, due to the sophistication of the network and tools used by the terrorist group, the messages might not contain any actionable intelligence (Miller, 2015). Terrorists do not own host servers, large databases and information or complex services for their operations like a government does. They piggy-back their services to use internet and don't worry about defense. Identifying the individuals planning to indulge in violence and taking action against them may lead to collateral damage and damage the regime's legitimacy (Miller, 2015).

APPROACHES IN MINING SOCIAL NETWORK DATA

Social network data are mined using four different approaches namely, structural, resource, regulatory and dynamic (Lyudmyla et al., 2017). It is used to investigate the relative position of the vertices, center and transitive interactions. Statistical analysis, clustering and classification algorithms are used to analyze the behavior of connections.

Structural Approach

This approach focuses on the geometric shape of the network and intensity of interactions. It is used to study the behavior of vertices while clustering and typical temporal characteristics of the social networks. Detection of phishing attacks, tracking malicious activity (Anandakumar & Umamaheswari, 2017), changes in network structure in the process of growth or behavior and distribution of connected components of the graph, identifying regions of active interaction are some of the activities that could be carried out using this approach (Lyudmyla et al., 2017).

Resource Approach

This approach considers the possibility of participants in attracting individual resources and network resources or achieving some goals and differentiates participants (Lyudmyla et al., 2017) who are in identical structural positions of the social network according to their resources. Knowledge, prestige, wealth, race, gender, etc., are some of the individual resources and status, information, fund is some of the network resources. Determining the significance and the attitude of the members of a social network as a political platform, importance of individual users, communities, topics, events, etc., are analyzed using this approach.

Normative Approach

This approach is used to study the level of trust among the participants and the rules, regulations that influences the behavior of the participants and their interactions. The normative approach is used in identifying the individuals who indulge in illegal actions and analyze the relationship between the manager and the subordinate, friendships or family connections. It is used to determine the functional roles of the participants which is essential to measure the effectiveness and sustainability of the social network (Lyudmyla et al., 2017). Identifying experts of a particular domain is a topic of interest in all fields of science and engineering. This approach is useful in identifying the experts of a domain using the ant colony optimization algorithm.

CHALLENGES IN MINING SOCIAL NETWORK DATA

Social network datasets are prone to noise, voluminous and dynamic in nature. Hence, it requires automated information processing mechanisms for analyzing it within a reasonable time (Olowe, 2013). The comments and reviews are complex and sometimes colloquial. It is difficult for an automated or machine learning process to easily learn the grammatical variations, cultural variations, slang and misspellings in the online mentions to get potential insights.

Data mining techniques require huge datasets to mine remarkable patterns from data and for advanced search results in the search engines to provide potential insights for research and organizational functions (Olowe, 2013). Characterization, classification, regression, association, clustering change detection, deviation detection, link analysis and sequential pattern mining are the various data mining techniques used (Sharma et al., 2017). Though it is used to analyze data to identify anomalies, predict the future trends and helps in decision making, it has a number of limitations in its usage which is listed below (Flair, 2018).

- **Skilled Person for Data Mining:** For example, it requires special expertise to prepare the data and understand the output. The patterns and relationships generated, significance, and validity should be made by the user.
- **Privacy Issues:** The sample data sets for data mining are collected from the social networking websites based on several factors using marketing and information technology techniques with or without the knowledge of the users involved. Due to this the privacy of the users are violated in terms of safety and security which leads to miscommunication between the users.
- **Security Issues:** Huge data sets collected for data mining may sometimes include critical data which might be hacked by hackers. For example, the websites of SsangYong Motors, Kawasaki Heavy Industries, Ford Motor Company (NYSE: F), KIA Motors, Subaru, Suzuki Motors and Toyota Motor Corporation was hacked and defaced by Q8 spy (Waqas, 2012).
- **Additional Irrelevant Information Gathered:** Some of the data collected may contain additional irrelevant information which will not be useful. Identifying what data to be collected towards data mining is essential.
- **Misuse of Information:** The sample data collected could be misused and faces the risk of being secure and safe.

The rich set of data and meta data generated by the social media are not treated systematically by the data and text mining literature (Sharma et al., 2017). David et al. (2010) proposed a GraphCT SNA algorithm to analyze public data from Twitter, a micro blogging network. The limitation of the work is that the focus is on a much smaller data subset and more work on sampling is needed (Pak & Paroubek, 2010). Raju & Sravanthi (2012) have reported that though web mining techniques like clustering and association rule mining are applied for the analysis of social networks, data sampling is identified as a big issue. Selecting suitable samples as representative of the real social network, finding communities and patterns in overlapping communities are cited as the major challenges in using these techniques. Beig (2015) has pointed out that a hybrid approach using content mining will be better than using traditional data mining techniques due to the unstructured and dynamic behavior of the web data. Mathur (2016) has mentioned that it becomes more challenging to mine social network data when the text information is not structured according to the grammatical convention (Mathur, 2016). Similarly, Pawar and Solapur (2016) have mentioned that mining rules from semi and unstructured data is a challenging task.

Machine learning is used for predictive analysis/classification by building a model based on the patterns of historical data/available patterns. The machine learning approach uses the training and testing learning mode for the new task. The learning mode in turn depends entirely on the machine's performance and the learning algorithms used (Zheng et al., 2017). Using machine learning for dealing with complex, unstructured data is difficult. Since machine learning is dependent on the learning rules, it may result in poor portability and scalability. Thus, it can work only in environments with tight constraints and limited objectives (Zheng et al., 2017). Machine learning cannot be fully relied on for completion of a task, especially to process data which involves unstructured human data from social media. It requires human intervention in the form of supervision, interaction and participation, for accurate decision making for critical tasks like economic decision making, medical problem solving and email processing, etc. (Zheng et al., 2017).

Getting meaningful insights out of the social network data collected from a variety of sources like micro blogs, real time markets and customer reviews depends on the quality and quantity of data. Rumors of data being collected for analytics may change the human behavior in the social networks. Since social networks are powerful in influencing the society to a greater extent, the need for organizing data faster to make better sense of it, discover insights, learn, adapt and improve over time without direct programming is realized.

The limitations in the usage of social media sites like 140 characters in Tweets in Twitter has transformed the way users communicate, which in turn has led to the evolution of languages. Hence, a more sophisticated multidimensional scale of emotions are required to capture the broad range of emotions that users express. Since the number of such emotions available online are larger in number, a manual analysis of the sentiments will not be sufficient. Hence, we need a computing technology that will simulate the human thought process into a computerized model which is cognitive computing.

NEED FOR COGNITIVE COMPUTING

The enormous size complexity of social network data, adaptive nature of intelligent adversaries, lack of ground truth to assess performance, the increasing number of false alarms presented by automated alerting systems by organizations and technology are considered as the problems in understanding the human needs (Mcneese, 2012). Due to the challenges mentioned above in using the traditional techniques, cognitive computing which could easily learn and unveil the hidden patterns from unstructured data with respect to the context is used for social network analysis. It involves self-learning systems that use data mining, pattern recognition and natural language processing to mimic the way the human brains work.

IBM's qadar advisor with Watson applies artificial intelligence to automatically investigate indicators of compromise. It utilizes cognitive reasoning to provide critical insights from large volumes of structured and unstructured data. The capability of the security operations centre are transformed by the solution it provides against skill shortages, alert overloads, incident response delays, outdated security information and process and accelerates the response cycle (Arm security analysts with the power of cognitive security, 2018).

Cognitive computing is characterized by features like adaptive, interactive, iterative and stateful and contextual which makes it more suitable for social mining services (What is cognitive computing? Features, Scope & Limitations, n.d.). Cognitive computing, artificial intelligence and natural language processing are used in all fields of science and engineering to provide accurate solutions. It is used in a wide variety of sectors like healthcare, education, auto, banking, etc., for tapping these technologies to transform business to cut costs and overheads, to make their platform superior, intuitive and smart (The growing role of artificial intelligence in business, 2017). For example, cognitive computing has made it easier to provide services for meeting the growing requirements of customers in the digitally driven world, to analyze millions of documents across the company's server to find compliance failures, dynamic pricing applications, accurate language translations, human decision making, etc.

BASIC ELEMENTS OF COGNITIVE COMPUTING

The cognitive computing framework consists of six components like understanding, verifying, planning, evaluating, attention and perception which are interrelated (Zheng et al., 2017). Any of these components can be the starting point or an objective in a specific cognitive task. The basic framework of cognitive computing is given in Figure 1 (Zheng et al., 2017). It chooses a simple or complex interactive path to

Figure 1. Basic framework of cognitive computing
(Zheng et al., 2017)

interact with the outside world. The prior probability is evaluation based on understanding or planning and evaluation based on perception is the posterior probability. The process of cognitive computing is based on constant interaction with the external world to meet the specific objectives and to gradually start a thinking activity rather than knowledge-based processing (Zheng et al., 2017).

The Cognitive computing process requires construction of a casual model to explain and understand the world. The casual model is used to update the prior probability by the posterior probability. The association analysis is completed based on the probability analysis of given data and the time/space based imagination or prediction. It provides understanding, supplement and judgement of the environment or situation. Action sequences are planned to maximize future rewards and prior knowledge is applied to enrich the reasoning of small-scale data to achieve good generalization ability and for increasing the learning speed (Zheng et al., 2017).

FEATURES, SCOPE AND LIMITATIONS OF COGNITIVE COMPUTING

Features of Cognitive Computing

Algorithmic Computing is concerned with the execution of a predefined set of instructions. It takes input data, processes the same and produces information based on decision points. Optimization is the process of finding the most efficient algorithm for a given task. Whereas, cognitive computing is a goal-oriented context aware system that deals with uncertainty. It is not programmed, rather it is trained and acquires knowledge through experience and improves over time. It is used to process structured and unstructured, text based or sensory data by interpreting the context and classifying the data as information or knowledge at scale. It learns from the domain and exhibits adaptive behavior.

Cognitive systems use data inputs to reason and establish an understanding to form hypothesis, consider augments and prioritize the suggestions. It is capable of continuous learning, accumulate data and provide deeper insights through human interactions. Cognitive computing is a new generation of computing systems that are built to augment, accelerate and scale human expertise, enabling a new era of genuine human–machine collaboration.

Scope of Cognitive Computing

Though computers can process data a rate faster than human beings, it is difficult to understand natural language or recognize unique objects in an image unlike human beings. Cognitive computing can respond to complex ambiguous situations and produce effective results in the field of application. The scope of cognitive computing consists of the following three elements (Ahire, 2018).

- **Engagement**: The large volumes of structured and unstructured data repositories provide deep domain insights and expert assistance. The engagement model is built to have a deep interaction with human beings and includes the contextual relationship between the various entities of the system which can reconcile ambiguous and self-contradictory data. For example, AI chatbots are pre-trained with the domain expertise for quick adoption in any business specific application.

- **Decision:** The decision-making models are a step ahead of the engagement model and are modeled using the reinforcement learning. The decision-making ability of cognitive systems continuously evolves based on new information, outcomes and actions. The ability to trace back the decision-making process determines the autonomous decision-making process and changes the confidence score of a systems response. For example, the power of the IBM Watson machine for healthcare depends on its ability to interpret the meaning and analyze complex medical data and natural language which contains doctor's notes, patient records, medical annotations and clinical feedback (Ahire, 2018).
- **Discovery:** The discovery model developed based on deep learning and unsupervised machine learning is the most advanced scope of cognitive computing. It is helpful in finding meaning insights and understanding large volumes of information and developing skills compared with human beings. For example, the distributed intelligent agent of the Cognitive Information Management (CIM) shell at Louisiana State University (LSU) collects streaming data like text and video. The real time analysis of this data is used to produce interactive sensing, inspection and visualization. The importance of the model is that in addition to sending alerts, the model also isolates a critical event and fixes the failure (Ahire, 2018).

Limitations of Cognitive Computing

Like any other computing technology, cognitive computing also suffers from certain limitations which are given below.

- **Risk Analysis:** The cognitive computing model fails to identify the risk in the unstructured data. Socio economic factors, culture, political environments and people are the different risks that are not identified by the cognitive computing models. For example, the location for oil exploration identified by the predictive model will be of no use if the political scenario is about to change. Thus, human intervention is essential for complete risk analysis and for decision making finally (Ahire, 2018).
- **Meticulous Training Process:** Training large volumes of unstructured data is considered the reason for its slow adoption. For example, the IBM Watson for insurance, reviews every medical policy with IBM engineers.
- **More Intelligence Augmentation Rather Than Artificial Intelligence:** The scope of cognitive computing is limited to engagement and decision. Cognitive systems are most effective as assistants and supplements human thinking which are more like intelligence augmentation instead of artificial intelligence. It depends on the human beings for critical decisions. For example, smart assistants and chat bots are more effective than simple messaging apps.

POWER OF COGNITIVE TECHNOLOGIES

With the increase in globalization, the reliance on technology for critical business solutions has increased. The complexity of technologies and security threats in turn have increased the responsibility of the information technology managers to reduce business downtime that reduces the customer experience, reduces business productivity and leads to revenue (Burre, 2018)

Cognitive systems detect and analyze large volumes of data and automate complete IT processes or workflows while learning and adapting in the process. These systems are also powered by autonomous and seamless decision-making ability when there are aberrations in the process of implementation (Burre, 2018).

Cognitive systems understand the context and natural language and correlate security data from multiple language sources.

IBM's Watson is a cognitive technology based artificial intelligence system which understands the world in the way humans do, through senses, learning and experience but at a speed no human can match. For example, it can read 800 million pages per second as per reports (Doley, 2016). For example, IBM's Watson machine for Cyber security can interpret unstructured security and multiple language sources. Compared with Google's Search engine, if the search topic is "Don't show me a cat", unfortunately Google will list down a number of cat images while Watson's machine will not do so as it understands natural language.

It is reported that IBM security experienced more than 54million security events in 2016(Arm security analysts with the power of cognitive security, n.d). Every year around 1.3million US dollars are spent just dealing with false positive which amounts to 21,000 hours of investigation (Arm security analysts with the power of cognitive security, n.d)32]. The data analysts should be abreast of 75,000 software vulnerabilities listed in the National Vulnerability Database and more than 1 million security bulletins, threat reports and news articles published each year (Arm security analysts with the power of cognitive security, n.d).

Another challenge is in sifting through the existing data. Only 8 per cent of the unstructured data such as blogs and videos are leveraged by an average organization (Arm security analysts with the power of cognitive security,n.d). Inspite of it, the security teams are expected to move fast. Chad Holmes, Principal and Cyber-Strategy, Technology and Growth Leader (CTO) at Ernst & Young LLP has says that there is a massive amount of noise in the data which the human brain cannot process everything on a day-to-day basis. He also adds that something like AI or cognive technologies is needed to help (Arm security analysts with the power of cognitive security, n.d).

APPLICATIONS OF COGNITIVE COMPUTING

Cognitive computing is used in applications that can handle very minute routing activity to a complex set of tasks involving logical reasoning. The promising performance of cognitive computing is driving interest and investment in technology and all types of applications in all fields. Some of the applications of cognitive computing are discussed below.

- **Predictive Maintenance:** Cognitive technologies based predictive maintenance systems leverage large volumes of data sets to anticipate failures before they happen so that potential security breaches could be handled effectively (Burre, 2018).
- **Interdependency Analytics:** The lack of complete visibility of the current infrastructure and application performance suites consumes increasing amounts of time unraveling and troubleshooting complex environments. With cognitive based interdependency analytics, it is easy to map relationships between systems, predict events based on dependencies and help engineers make well informed decisions about data center optimization and planning (Burre, 2018).

- **Self-Healing and Autonomous Remediation:** There is no accepted reliable mechanism for automating recovery of critical infrastructure, applications and software after a crash due to internal or external system breach. Cognitive technologies integrated with automatic instrumentation, machine learning analytics and integrated remediation has made it easy to self-heal and auto remediate the systems (Burre, 2018).
- **Self-Learning System and Knowledge Management:** With cognitive technologies, intelligent learning systems use self regulated content, enhances performances and generates competitiveness for the enterprises. Intelligence is always ensured in such systems due to the frequent update of learning out of relevant information, resources, methods, tools, templates, techniques and examples (Burre, 2018).
- **Role of Smart Agents to Manage L0/L1:** Enterprises are becoming more efficient and use predictive and autonomous control mechanisms with smart agents. Smart agents are connected to AI based virtual assets and are capable of detecting and responding to internal and external environments which makes them more intelligent (Burre, 2018).
- **Healthcare:** New artificial intelligent systems integrated with cognitive computing technologies provides promising healthcare solutions. The cognitive era brings together individual and clinical research and social data from a wide range of healthcare sources to provide personalized health care services to redefine a patient's path towards better health. It augments the role of doctors and engage patients that will expand access, lower costs and improve outcomes ultimately making our world healthier and happier (Ahmed et al., 2017).
- **Chatbots:** Cognitive computing enables Chatbots to have a certain level of intelligence and simulate human conversation by understanding the communication in a contextual sense like understanding the user needs based on a past communication, giving suggestions, etc.
- **Sentiment Analysis:** It is the science of understanding emotions conveyed in a communication. While human beings can easily understand the underlying sentiments, it is difficult for the machines to realize the same. Training data of human conversations has to be fed to the machines and analyze the accuracy of the analysis. It is used in social media communications like tweets, comments, reviews, complaints, etc.
- **Face Detection:** A cognitive system uses the features like structure, contours, eye color etc. of the face to differentiate it from others. The facial image thus generated is used to identify the face from an image or video. With cognitive systems, greater accuracy is achieved using 3D sensors compared with the 2D images used in traditional systems. This can be used in security systems for a locker or even mobile phone.
- **Social Media Data Classification:** Cognitive computing is used in social media data classification. For example, it is used to explore social activity maps by discovering regions of cognitive interest (Wang et al., 2017).
- **Cognitive Marketing:** It plays a vital role in brand messaging by segmenting audiences in new ways. Instead of using demographics for identifying similar wants and needs, cognitive marketing transform the customer lists into a database where each member is connected to others in many different ways wherein a customer will be part of several segments based on their behaviors observed (Rajeck, 2016). Personalization is an important aspect in digital marketing. With cognitive marketing an engine could redesign the messaging so that virtually every person sees a different content in the right way at the right time for each customer. It also ensures that irrelevant messages are not delivered leading to the risk of turning out by the customers. Cognitive computing gives a

win-win situation for the marketers as well as for its customers, meaning to say that it also helps the customer make better decisions, identify customers with an unstated need and converse with customers around topics which matters to them.

IBM WATSON SERVICES

IBM Watson is an ecosystem of cognitive computing capabilities. Hence, it is essential to make a special mention of the same. It is a platform of new computing abilities, capable of processing large volumes of disparate forms of big data in natural language at unprecedented speeds to discover insights.

Unlike other computing technologies, Watson generates hypotheses based on a wide variety of potentially relevant information and connections and produces the answers as recommendations with confidence rankings. The Watson machine can learn more from more data, unlike traditional analytical tools.

The key areas of innovation in IBM Watson include Watson Explorer Platform, Watson Developer Cloud and Watson industry solutions. The Watson Explorer Platform provides services like Powerful indexing and natural language search, Hybrid cloud connectors for information access, Advanced multimedia content analytics to aggregate and visualize unstructured content to reveal hidden insights and patterns, App Builder framework for quickly creating custom cognitive applications and Integration of cognitive results into analytics applications.

The various products and services provided by IBM Watson are given in Table 1 (Products and services, n.d).

The Watson Explorer Content Analytics and Knowledge Studio are used to mine information and review hidden insights. Business users can mine large amounts of text for new business insights using the Content Analytics Miner using trends, patterns and anomalies in information. Business Analysts could create advanced rule-based annotators using Watson Knowledge Studio. To improve the decision-making process, the information processed with the cognitive framework, additional output destinations and integration with analytics applications is done. Watson Explorer unified information application is used for customer care, research, marketing, sales, etc. Providing contextually relevant insights using structured and unstructured information is the power of cognitive applications. Integrated cognitive services within business applications helps to scale human expertise. The IBM Watson explorer is depicted in Figure 2 (Underwood, 2018).

IMPORTANCE OF COGNITIVE SECURITY

With the increasing risk of threats from cyber criminals to state sponsored agencies, the global cost of cybercrime is expected to hit $2trillion by 2019 (Ash, 2016). Securing data is a potential endeavor every organization and government has to adapt. Though traditional systems are programmed to recognize viruses, malwares and exploits, new creative means for breaching the same are adapted and the vulnerability and degree of damage increases. To distinguish and eliminate the new threats, organizations should have the ability to detect the activity which is so delicate or precise as to be difficult to analyze or describe. Nearly 80% of the total generated is invisible in the form of natural language which is either spoken, visual or written. It is quite difficult for the traditional systems to make an insight into everything

Table 1. IBM Watson products and services (Products and services, n.d.)

Type of Service	Product and Services	Features
Conversation Integrate diverse conversation technology into the application	Conversation Quickly build a chatbot with easy tooling and dialog trees	Developer Friendly Enterprise Grade Robust and Secure
	Virtual Agent Create a bot for customer service	Automated Services Customized Content
Knowledge Get insights through accelerated data optimization capabilities	Discovery Unlock hidden value in data to find answers, monitor trends and surface patterns	Rapid Results Domain Intelligence AI ready for business
	Discovery News Access pre-enriched news content in real-time	Intelligence Infused News See the big picture Stay alert
	Natural Language Understanding Natural Language processing for advanced text analysis	Uncover insights from structured and unstructured data Understand sentiment and emotion Grasp multiple languages
	Knowledge Studio Teach Watson to discover meaningful insights in unstructured text	Teach by Example Engage your experts Use everywhere Accuracy Security Better and deeper Insights
Vision Identify and tag content then analyze and extract detailed information found in an image	Visual Recognition Tag and classify visual content using machine learning	Classify virtually any visual content Create your own classifiers Detect Faces
Speech Convert text and speech with the ability to customize models	Speech to Text Easily convert audio and voice into written text	Powerful real-time speech recognition Highly accurate speech engine Built to support various use-cases
	Text to Speech Convert written text into natural sounding audio	Enable your systems to "speak" like humans Customize and control pronunciation Synthesizes across languages and voices
Language Analyze text and extract meta-data from unstructured content	Language translator Translate text from one language to another	Translate Customize Protect
	Natural Language Classifier Interpret and classify natural language with confidence	Classify Text Passages Evaluate Results Build Conversational applications
Empathy Understand tone, personality and emotional state	Personality Insights Predict personality Characteristics through text	Get detailed personality portraits Understand consumption preferences Tailor the customer experience
	Tone Analyzer Understand emotions and communication style in text	Conduct social listening Enhance customer service Integrate with chatbots

Figure 2. IBM Watson explorer
(Underwood, 2018)

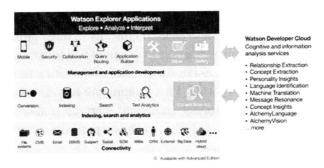

and make a clear decision about which is a true one to act on and which is a false alarm (IBM Cognitive security white paper, evolve your defenses with security that understands, reasons and learns, 2018).

According to Ponemon Institute report, "The Cost of Malware Containment", it is reported that an average organization captures over 17,000 malware alerts every day and spends about $1.3millions for responding to erroneous or inaccurate malware alerts. The risk exposure is high as 19 percent of these alerts are reliable and 4% alone is investigated. Cognitive analytics is considered the best to consume and prioritize large volumes of security data using predictive analytics. IBM's Watson for cyber security augment with the human analysts to understand, reason and learn about rapidly evolving security threats (Ash, 2016).

COGNITIVE COMPUTING AND NATIONAL AND INTERNATIONAL SECURITY

Cyber threats are increasing, and the annual cost of cybercrime is expected to rise from $3trillion today to $6trillion by 2021 (Golden & Johnson, 2017). The responsibility of the government to protect their citizens has increased. It is reported that the promising approach to combat the situation is to use cognitive technologies with cyber security professionals. Using advanced analytics, automation and artificial intelligence, it is claimed to train the technology to deliver key insights that optimize the work of cyber professionals, streamline operational processes and improve national and international security outcomes.

Figure 3. Comparison of manual and IBM Watson threat analysis
(Ash, 2016)

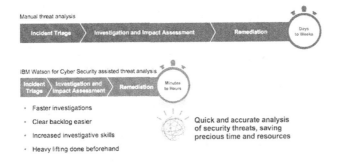

A comparison of the activities carried out by cyber security professionals in the presence and absence of cognitive technologies is given in Figure 4 (Golden & Johnson, 2017).

An integration of artificial intelligence, text and speech processing, automation and robotics and machine learning, cognitive technologies could be used typically in three primary ways: in product applications to improve customer benefits, in processing applications to improve an organization's workflow and operations and for insights that can help inform decisions. Cognitive technologies can be used to mitigate the effects of cyber threats in two ways. First by applying cognitive technologies to remedying the cyber security issues arising out of personnel strains and shortages and second using artificial intelligence and advanced techniques like data analytics which is a proactive measure for handling security challenges than taking the reactive stance.

The global average cost of a data breach for 2017 is down 10% over the previous year to $3.62 million. Similarly, the average cost for each lost or stolen record containing sensitive and confidential information has decreased from $158 to $141 in 2017. In spite of the decrease in cost, this year's study has revealed that the average size of the data breaches has increased 1.8% to more than 24,000 records (2017 Ponemon cost of data breach study, 2018).

According to the FBI Director James Comey, there are two kinds of big companies in the United States – those who have been hacked and those who don't know that they have been hacked (Hunter, 2018). The ever-increasing growth rate of the organization data is considered as the only challenge of the cyber security systems in keeping pace with the threats as it evolves more rapidly. Therefore, the organizations have to narrow down the gap between when an attacker enters the network and whey they launch a defense.

Verizon found that 80% of attackers took just days to infiltrate their targets whereas only a third of companies managed to detect the attacks within the same time frame according to the Data Breach Investigations Report (Hunter, 2018). With 12,000 security events per second (nearly one billion events per day) generated by large enterprises, according to FireEye, a security technology and services company, it is practically difficult for the human beings to process such huge volumes of data. Hence, automation of data analysis is the apt solution for the problem. Unlike the static systems that are currently used, cognitive systems evolve as threat evolve and learns from data in real time to identify hidden patterns and anomalous behavior. Hence, it can easily anticipate changes in the cyber land space to predict hidden patterns and anomalous behaviors. It can also easily identify the false positives that the data produces, flagging up deviations that could indicate that a system is compromised (Hunter, 2018).

Grady Summers, Senior Vice President of Cloud Analytics for FireEye, has reported that a number of companies have already started using cognitive systems. Cognitive systems help secure electrical grids from terrorist attacks, while IBM has developed a system on their own. It helps to predict and prevent new security threats as it emerges (Hunter, 2018).

The use of cognitive computing for autopilots was explored by the Department of Defense, United States which adapts to changing conditions. It is also reported that cognitive computing reduces the time needed to develop new smart weapons and unmanned combat aerial vehicles (Carafano, 2007). Cognitive computing is used to create instant translator which converts the spoken language in real time. A demonstration of the translation between spoken English and Spanish and between English and Mandarin Chinese was done simultaneously (Pleinis, 2006).

With the increasing number of sensor systems on the battlefield, the volume of raw information flowing to military commanders and decision makers also increases. Filtering out the essential data becomes a difficult task with the existing technologies. Cognitive computing has made this task easier. The ability

Figure 4. Comparison of the activities carried out by cyber security professionals in the presence and absence of cognitive technologies (Golden & Johnson, 2017)
Source: Deloitte analysis Deloitte University Press dupress.deloitte.com

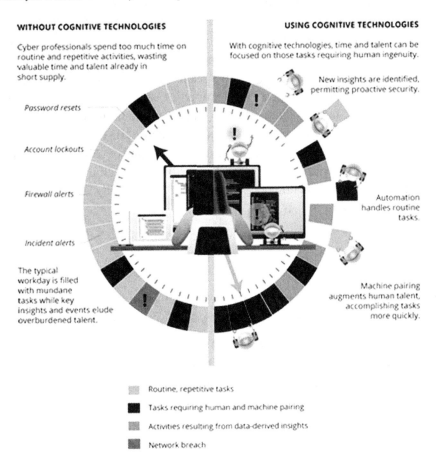

of cognitive computers to learn and re-learn has made them capable of not only working around battle damages, but also improves the speed and accuracy of the calculations which is gained out of experience (Self-Regenerative Systems: Mission, 2006).

Predictive maintenance using cognitive technologies is used for military applications. For example, the U.S Air Force Research Laboratory has conducted research on creating an advanced aircraft engine that adapts to changing flight conditions and self-identify maintenance problems and needed repairs (Lewis, 2006).

The New IDC Spending Guide has reported that the global spending on Cognitive and AI solutions will have a compounding annual growth rate of 54.4% through 2020 when revenues will be more than $46 billion and the US will be the largest market (Daquilla & Shirer, 2017). Of the many technologies like big data and wealth management cognitive intelligence demands the first priority in the technologies of the future in securing the nation. Cognitive Intelligence is concerned with building machine learning based intelligent systems which learn on an ongoing basis and the top trends are smart environments, Predictive analytics driven customer 360, Artificial intelligence driven multi structured analytics and immersive multi modal user experiences.

SUMMARY

The advances in information and communication technology have made the world a global village. Cognitive computation and intelligence as the enrichment layer on top of this digital village is very much helpful in providing much deeper and rapid global national and international security insights out of the services and massive data produced in social media. With increasing reliance on technology and software in all fields of science and engineering to streamline the everyday operations, it is crucial to have cognitive systems in place to protect the digital property. Cognitive Technologies extends the power of information technologies to tasks traditionally performed by humans and enables organizations break the trade-offs between speed, cost and quality. A research study by IBM institute of business value has reported that nearly 60% of security professionals believe that cognitive security systems can slow done cybercrimes significantly. It has also revealed that there will be a threefold increase i.e., 7% to 21% in the percentage of companies implementing cognitive security systems by 2020 (Firms look to security analytics to keep pace with cyber threats, 2017).

REFERENCES

Ahire, J. B. (2018, January 8). Cognitive computing: everything you should know. *Buzzrobot*. Retrieved from https://buzzrobot.com/cognitive-computing-everything-you-should-know-8896590bb1

Ahmed, M.N., Toor, A.S., Neil, K. & Friedland, D (2017, May 17). Cognitive Computing and the Future of Health Care, The cognitive power of IBM Watson has the potential to transform global personalized medicine. *IEEE Pulse*. Retrieved from https://pulse.embs.org/may-2017/cognitive-computing-and-the-future-of-health-care/

Alakali, T. T., Sambe, I. I., Adekole, F. E., & Tarnongo, M. O. (2013). The impact of social Media on information dissemination and challenges of national insecurity in Nigeria: An overview of BokoHaram Insurgence in Northern Nigeria. *Journal of Management and Entrepreneurial Development*, *3*(2), 1–11.

Anandakumar, H., & Umamaheswari, K. (2017). A bio-inspired swarm intelligence technique for social aware cognitive radio handovers. *Computers & Electrical Engineering*, (Sep). doi:10.1016/j.compeleceng.2017.09.016

Anandakumar, H., & Umamaheswari, K. (2018). Cooperative Spectrum Handovers in Cognitive Radio Networks. In Cognitive Radio, Mobile Communications and Wireless Networks (pp. 47–63). Springer. doi:10.1007/978-3-319-91002-4_3

Anandakumar, H., Umamaheswari, K., & Arulmurugan, R. (2019). A Study on Mobile IPv6 Handover in Cognitive Radio Networks. In *International Conference on Computer Networks and Communication Technologies* (pp. 399-408). Springer Singapore. doi:10.1007/978-981-10-8681-6_36

Ash, M. (2016, December 9). Security intelligence, augmented intelligence: making the case for cognitive security. *Security Intelligence*. Retrieved from https://securityintelligence.com/augmented-intelligence-making-the-case-for-cognitive-security/

Bannister, K. (2015, January 26). Understanding sentiment analysis: what it is & why it's used. *Brand Watch*. Retrieved from https://www.brandwatch.com/blog/understanding-sentiment-analysis/

Beig, E. F. G. M. (2015). Data Mining Techniques for Web Mining: A Review. *Applied mathematics in Engineering Management and Technology*, *3*(5), 81–90.

Burre, P. (2018, February 28). Power up IT operations with Cognitive Technologies. Retrieved from https://blog.csscorp.com/power-up-it-operations-with-cognitive-technologies

Carafano, J. (2007, July 5). Future computing and cutting edge national security. Heritage. Retrieved from https://www.heritage.org/defense/report/future-computing-and-cutting-edge-national-security

Daquilla. M & Shirer. M (2017, April 3). Worldwide spending on cognitive and artificial intelligence systems forecast to reach $12.5 billion this year, according to new idc spending guide. *IDC*. Retrieved from https://www.idc.com/getdoc.jsp?containerId=prUS42439617

Doley, K. (2016, December). Financial express. Move over artificial intelligence, 'cognitive technology' is the future. *Financial Express*. Retrieved from http://www.financialexpress.com/lifestyle/science/move-over-artificial-intelligence-cognitive-technology-is-the-future/470711/

Anandakumar, H., & Umamaheswari, K. (2014, May). Energy Efficient Network Selection Using 802.16g Based GSM Technology. *Journal of Computational Science*, *10*(5), 745–754. doi:10.3844/jcssp.2014.745.754

Fearn, N. (2017). Firms look to security analytics to keep pace with cyber threats. *Computer Weekly*. Retrieved from https://www.computerweekly.com/feature/Firms-look-to-security-analytics-to-keep-pace-with-cyber-threats

Flair, D. (2018 February 9). Datamining tutorials. Disadvantages of data mining-data mining issues. *Data Flair*. Retrieved from https://data-flair.training/blogs/disadvantages-of-data-mining/

Gharibi, W., & Shaabi, M. (2012). Cyber threats in social networking websites. *International Journal of Distributed and Parallel Systems*, *3*(1). doi:10.5121/ijdps.2012.3109

Golden, D. & Johnson, T. (2017, June 8). AI-augmented cybersecurity How cognitive technologies can address the cyber workforce shortage. *Deloitte*. Retrieved from https://www2.deloitte.com/insights/us/en/industry/public-sector/addressing-cybersecurity-talent-shortage.html

Graffigna, G., & Riva, G. (2015). Social media monitoring and understanding: An integrated mixed methods approach for the analysis of social media. *International Journal of Web Based Communities*, *11*(1), 57–72. doi:10.1504/IJWBC.2015.067083

Haldorai, A., & Ramu, A. (2018). An Intelligent-Based Wavelet Classifier for Accurate Prediction of Breast Cancer. In *Intelligent Multidimensional Data and Image Processing* (pp. 306–319). doi:10.4018/978-1-5225-5246-8.ch012

Hunter, E. (2018, January 20). Cognitive computing takes on cyber-security. *The Innovation Enterprise*. Retrieved from https://channels.theinnovationenterprise.com/articles/cognitive-computing-takes-on-cyber-security

IBM. (2017). Ponemon cost of data breach study. Retrieved from https://www.ibm.com/security/data-breach

IBM. (2017). Arm security analysts with the power of cognitive security. Retrieved from https://www-01.ibm.com/common/ssi/cgi-bin/ssialias?htmlfid=WGS03087GBEN

IBM. (n.d.). Products and services. Retrieved from https://www.ibm.com/watson/products-services/

IBM. (n.d.). Evolve your defenses with security that understands, reasons and learns [white paper]. Retrieved from https://cognitivesecuritywhitepaper.mybluemix.net/

Kemp, S. (2018, January). 11 New People Join Social Media Every Second (And Other Impressive Stats). *Hootsuite*. Retrieved from https://blog.hootsuite.com/11-people-join-social-every-second/

Kulkarni, P. (2018, May 8). Analytics. pros and cons of datamining social interactions. *The Innovation Enterprise*. Retrieved from https://channels.theinnovationenterprise.com/articles/pros-and-cons-of-datamining-social-interactions

Lewis, T. (2006, November 20). Future Aircraft Jet Engines Will Think for Themselves. *AFRL Horizons*. Retrieved from www.afrlhorizons.com/Briefs/Dec01/PR0105.html

Liu, H. (2014, April 29). Challenges in Mining Social Media Data. *Carlson School of Management, University of Minnesota*. Retrieved from http://sobaco.umn.edu/content/challenges-mining-social-media-data

Lyudmyla, K., Tamara, R., & Anders, C. (2017). Detecting cyber threats through social network analysis: Short survey. *SocioEconomic Challenges*, *1*(1), 20–34.

Marutitech. (n.d.). What is cognitive computing? Features, Scope & Limitations. Retrieved from https://www.marutitech.com/cognitive-computing-features-scope-limitations/

Mathur, K. (2016). Online social network mining. *International Journal of Computer Trends and Technology*, *35*(4), 202–206.

Mcneese, M. (2012). Perspectives on the role of cognition in cyber security. In *Proceedings of the human factors and ergonomics society 56th annual meeting*, Boston, MA. Human Factors and Ergonomics Society.

Miller, S. D. (2015). *The internet as a tool for terrorism*. Waco, TX: Baylor University.

Niekerk, B. V. (2013). Social media and information conflict. *International Journal of Communication*, *7*, 1162–1184.

Nsude, I., & Onwe, E. C. (2017). Social Media and Security Challenges in Nigeria: The Way Forward. *World Applied Sciences Journal*, *35*(6), 993–999. doi:10.5829/idosi.wasj.2017.993.999

Olowe, A., Gaber, M.M., & Stahl, F. (2013). A survey of data mining techniques for social media analysis. Retrieved from http://arxiv.org/abs/1312.4617v1

Pak, A., & Paroubek, P. (2010). *Twitter as a Corpus for Sentiment Analysis and Opinion Mining. In Proceedings of the international conference on language resources and evaluation (LREC 2010)*. Valletta, Malta: ELRA.

Pawar, S. C., & Solapur, R. S. (2016). Research Issues and Future Directions in Web Mining: A Survey. In *Proceedings on National Seminar on Recent Trends in Data Mining (RTDM 2016)*, Periye, India.

Pleinis, J. (2006, November 20). Advanced adaptive autopilot. Retrieved from www.afrlhorizons.com/Briefs/Jun03/MN0213.html

Rajeck, J. (2016, December 13). Three ways brands will use cognitive marketing. *Econsultancy*. Retrieved from https://econsultancy.com/blog/68634-three-ways-brands-will-use-cognitive-marketing/

Raju, E., & Sravanthi, K. (2012). Analysis of social networks using the techniques of web mining. *International Journal of Advanced Research in Computer Science and Software Engineering*, 2(10), 443–450.

Self-Regenerative Systems. Mission (2006, November 15). Retrieved from www.darpa.mil/ipto/programs/srs/index.htm

Sharma, A., Sharma, M. K., & Dwivedi, R. K. (2017). Literature Review and Challenges of Data Mining Techniques for Social Network Analysis. *Advances in Computational Sciences and Technology*, 10(5), 1337–1354.

Smith, M., Hansen, D. L., & Gleave, E. (2009). *Analyzing enterprise social media networks. In proceedings of the international symposium on social computing applications (SCA09)*. Vancouver, Canada: IEEE Computer Society.

Tang, L., & Liu, H. (2010) Graph mining applications to social network analysis. In C. Aggarwal & H. Wang (Eds.), *Managing and mining graph data. Springer, New York The growing role of artificial intelligence in business*. Retrieved from http://www.livemint.com/Opinion/UKCvUCD1mVgVp8CcR62uvJ/The-growing-role-of-artificial-intelligence-in-business.html

Underwood, J. (2018, March 28). IBM Watson cognitive computing. Retrieved from http://www.jenunderwood.com/2017/03/28/ibm-watson-cognitive-computing/

Vilic, V. M. (2017). Cyber terrorism on the internet and social networking: a threat to global security. In *Proceedings of international scientific conference on information technology and data related research (SINTEZA 2017)*, Belgrade, Serbia.

Wang, Y., Baciu, G., & Li, C. (2017). Cognitive exploration of regions through analyzing geo-tagged social media data. In *Proceedings of IEEE 16th International Conference on Cognitive Informatics & Cognitive Computing (ICCI*CC)*. UK: IEEE Computer Society.

Waqas. (2012, March 4). Hacking news. Six Automotive Giants: FORD, KIA, Subaru, Suzuki, Kawasaki, SsangYong Hacked and Defaced by Q8 Spy. Retrieved from https://www.hackread.com/six-automotive-giant-ford-kia-subaru-suzuki-kawasaki-ssangyong-hacked-and-defaced-by-q8-spy/

Wheaton, K. J., & Richey, M. K. (2014, January 9). The potential of Social Network Analysis in Intelligence. *E-international Relations*. Retrieved from http://www.e-ir.info/2014/01/09/the-potential-of-social-network-analysis-in-intelligence/

Wikipedia. (n.d.). Social network analysis Practical Applications. Retrieved March 17, 2018 from https://en.wikipedia.org/wiki/Social_network_analysis#Practical_applications

Wong, J. C., & Solon, O. (2017, May 12). Massive ransomware cyber-attack hits nearly 100 countries around the world. *The Guardian*. Retrieved from https://www.theguardian.com/technology/2017/may/12/global-cyber-attack-ransomware-nsa-uk-nhs

Zheng, N., Liu, Z., Ren, P., Ma, Y., Chen, S., Yu, S., ... Wang, F. (2017). Hybrid-augmented intelligence: Collaboration and cognition. *Frontiers of Information Technology & Electronic Engineering, 18*(2), 153–179. doi:10.1631/FITEE.1700053

Chapter 2
Data Mining Techniques for Social Network Analysis

Vijayaganth V.
Bannari Amman Institute of Technology, India

ABSTRACT

Social networks have increased momentously in the last decade. Individuals are depending on inter-personal organizations for data, news, and the assessment of different clients on various topics. These issues often make social network data very complex to analyze manually, resulting in the persistent use of computational means for analyzing them. Data mining gives a variety of systems for identifying helpful learning from huge datasets and a wide range of techniques for detecting useful knowledge from massive datasets like trends, patterns and rules. This chapter discusses different data mining techniques used in mining social networks.

INTRODUCTION

Interpersonal organization is a term used to portray online administrations that enable people to make an open/semi-open profile inside an area to such an extent that they can informatively associate with different clients inside the system (Chen, 2009). Interpersonal organization has enhanced the idea and innovation of Web 2.0, by empowering the arrangement and trade of User-Generated Content (Kaplan & Haenlein, 2010). Basically, informal community is a diagram comprising of hubs and connections used to speak to social relations on interpersonal organization destinations. The hubs incorporate elements and the connections between them frames the connections (Borgatti, 2009). The nodes include entities and the relationships between them forms the *links*.

Social networks are important sources of online interactions and contents sharing (Thompson, 2013; Chelmis & Prasanna, 2011), subjectivity (Asur & Huberman, 2010), assessments (Kim & Hsu, 2013), approaches (Korda & Itani, 2013), evaluation (Kaur, 2013), influences (Bakshy & Hofman, 2011), ob-servations (Chou & Hunt, 2009), feelings (Kaplan & Haenlein, 2010), opinions and sentiments expres-

DOI: 10.4018/978-1-5225-7522-1.ch002

sions (Pang & Lee, 2008) borne out in text, reviews, blogs, discussions, news, remarks, reactions, or some other documents (Liu, 2011). The exercises on social network as of late appear to have changed the World Wide Web (www) into its proposed unique creation. Social network stages empower fast data trade between clients paying little heed to the area. Numerous associations, people and even legislature of nations now take after the exercises on social network. Data mining techniques have been found to be capable of handling the three dominant disputes with social network data namely; size, noise and dynamism. The voluminous idea of social network datasets requires robotized data preparing for dissecting it inside a sensible time. Strikingly, information mining procedures likewise require immense informational collections to mine momentous examples from information; social network locales give off an impression of being ideal destinations to mine with information mining instruments (Cortizo & Carrero, 2009). This structures an empowering factor for cutting edge indexed lists in web crawlers and furthermore helps in better comprehension of social information for inquire about and hierarchical capacities (Aggarwal, 2011).

SOCIAL NETWORK BACKGROUND

Amid the most recent decade social network have turned out to be prominent as well as reasonable and all-around acclaimed correspondence implies that has flourished in making the world a global village. Social network locales are regularly known for data spread, individual exercises posting, item audits, online pictures sharing, proficient profiling, ads and supposition/conclusion articulation. News alerts, breaking news, political debates and government policy are also posted and analyzed on social network sites (Pang & Lee, 2008). It is watched that more individuals are getting to be occupied with and depending on the social network for data continuously. Clients once in a while settle on choices in light of data posted by new people on social network expanding the level of dependence on the validity of these locales. Social network has prevailing with regards to changing the way unique substances source and recover profitable data independent of their area. Social network has likewise given clients the benefit to give feelings with next to no or no limitation.

Social Network: Power to the Users

Social sites have undoubtedly bestowed unimaginable privilege on their users to access readily available never-ending uncensored information. Twitter, for example, permits its users to post events in real time way ahead the broadcast of such events on traditional news media. Also, social network allows users to express their views, be it positive or negative (Aggarwal, 2011). Organizations are now conscious of the significance of consumers' opinions posted on social network sites to the patronage of their products or services and the overall success of their organizations. On the other hand, important personalities such as celebrities and government officials are being conscious of how they are perceived on social network. These entities follow the activities on social network to keep abreast with how their audience reacts to issues that concerns them (Castellanos & Dayal, 2011; Chen & Lee, 2011; Hoffman, 2008). Considering the enormous volume of data being generated on social network, it is imperative to find a computational means of filtering, categorizing, classifying and analyzing the social network contents.

RESEARCH ISSUES ON SOCIAL NETWORK ANALYSIS

- **Linkage-Based and Structural Analysis:** This is an examination of the linkage conduct of the social network in order to learn applicable hubs, connections, groups and unavoidable territories of the network.
- **Dynamic Analysis and Static Analysis:** Static examination, for example, in bibliographic networks is attempted to be less demanding to do than those in spilling networks. In static investigation, it is assumed that social network changes progressively after some time and examination on the whole network should be possible in bunch mode. On the other hand, dynamic examination of spilling networks like Facebook and YouTube are extremely hard to do. Information on these networks is created at fast and limit. Dynamic investigations of these networks are frequently in the region of connections between elements.

GRAPH THEORETIC

Chart hypothesis is presumably the fundamental strategy in social network analysis in the early history of the social network idea. The approach is connected to social network analysis with a specific end goal to decide critical highlights of the network, for example, the nodes and links (for instance influencers and the supporters). Influencers on social network have been recognized as clients that have effect on the exercises or feeling of different clients by method for followership or impact on choice made by different clients on the network. Diagram hypothesis has turned out to be extremely compelling on substantial scale datasets, (for example, social network information). This is on the grounds that it is equipped for bye-passing the working of a genuine visual portrayal of the information to run straightforwardly on information lattices (Scott, 2011). In centrality measure was utilized to assess the portrayal of energy and impact that structures groups and cohesiveness on social network (Borgatti & Everett, 2006). The creators of utilized parameterized centrality metric ways to deal with contemplate the network structure and to rank nodes availability (Ghosh & Lerman, 2011). Their work framed an augmentation of a-centrality approach which measures the quantity of lightened ways that exist among nodes.

Community Detection Using Hierarchical Clustering

A community is a littler packed gathering inside a bigger network. Clients with comparative intrigue shape groups on social network in this manner showing solid sectional structure. Groups on social networks, similar to some other groups in reality, are extremely perplexing in nature and hard to recognize. Applying the proper devices in distinguishing and understanding the conduct of network groups is significant as this can be utilized to display the dynamism of the area they have a place (Aggarwal, 2008). Distinctive creators have connected various clustering procedures to identify groups on social network with hierarchical clustering being for the most part utilized (Fortunato, 2010; Girvan & Newman, 2002; Papadopoulos & Kompatsiaris, 2012). This strategy is a blend of numerous methods used to assemble nodes in the network to uncover quality of individual gatherings which is then used to circulate the network into groups. Vertex clustering has a place with hierarchical clustering techniques, diagram vertices can be settled by including it in a vector space so pair wise length between vertices can be estimated. Structural equivalence measures of hierarchical clustering focus on number of basic network associations shared by two nodes. Two individuals on social network with a few common companions will probably be nearer than two individuals with less shared companions on the network. Clients in a similar social network community frequently prescribe things and administrations to each other in view of the experience on the things or administrations included.

Recommender System in Social Network Community

Based on the commonality between nodes in social network gatherings, collaborative filtering (CF) procedure, which frames one of the three classes of the recommender system (RS), can be utilized to misuse the relationship among clients (Liu & Lee, 2010). Things can be prescribed to a client based on the rating of his common association. Where CF's primary drawback is that of information sparsity, content-based (another RS strategy) investigate the structures of the information to deliver proposals. In any case, the crossover approaches more often than not propose suggestions by consolidating CF and content-based proposals. The investigation in (Burke, 2002; Pham & Cao, 2011) proposed a crossover approach named EntreeC, a system that pools learning based RS and CF to suggest eateries.

Semantic Web of Social Network

The Semantic Web platform makes knowledge sharing and re-use possible over different applications and community edges. Discovering the involvement of Semantic Web (SW) enhances the knowledge of the prominence of Semantic Web Community and envisages the synthesis of the Semantic Web. The work employed Friend of a Friend (FOAF) to explore how local and global community level groups develop and evolve in large-scale social networks on the Semantic Web. The study revealed the evolution outlines of social structures and forecasts future drift (Ruan, Hu & Zhang, 2014). Likewise, application model of Semantic Web-based Social Network Analysis Model creates the ontological field library of social network analysis combined with the conventional outline of the semantic web to attain intelligent retrieval of the Web services. Furthermore, VoyeurServer (Murthy & Gross, 2013) improved on the open-source Web-Harvest framework for the collection of online social network data in order to study structures of trust enhancement and of online scientific association. Semantic Web is a relatively new area in social network analysis and research in the field is still evolving.

OPINION ANALYSIS ON SOCIAL NETWORK

User's feelings on social network locales can be alluded to as disclosure and acknowledgment of positive or negative articulation on assorted topics of intrigue (Tepper, 2012). These suppositions are regularly persuading, and their markers can be utilized as inspiration when settling on decisions and choices on support of specific items and benefits or even underwriting of political hopeful amid races (Kaschesky & Sobkowicz, 2011; Pang & Lee, 2008). Even however online assessments can be found utilizing conventional strategies, this frame is then again lacking considering the extensive volume of data created on social network destinations. This reality underscores the significance of information mining methods in mining sentiment communicated on social network site.

Different techniques have been created to break down the sentiment emerging from items, administrations, occasions or identity audit on social network (Godbole & Srinivasaiah, 2007). Information digging apparatuses effectively utilized for assessment and estimation investigation incorporate accumulations of straightforward checking strategies to machine learning. Arranging assessment-based content utilizing twofold qualification of positive against negative (Hatzivassiloglou & McKeown, 1997; Dave & Pennock, 2003; Pang & Lee, 2002; Turney, 2002), is observed to be lacking when positioning things as far as suggestion or examination of a few commentators' feelings.

Aspect-Based/Feature-Based Opinion Mining

Aspect-based otherwise called feature-based analysis is the way toward mining the territory of element clients has checked on (Hu & Liu, 2004). This is on account of not all aspects/features of a substance are frequently checked on by clients. It is then important to compress the aspects evaluated to decide the extremity of the general audit whether they are positive or negative. Suppositions communicated on a few substances are simpler to examine than others, one of the reasons being surveys can be vague.

The aspect/element (which might be a PC gadget) explored is either 'thumb up' or 'thumb down', thumb up being positive audit while thumb down means negative survey (Liu, 2011). On the other hand, in web journals and gathering talks the two aspects and substance are not perceived and there are elevated amounts of unimportant information which constitute commotion. It is consequently important to recognize conclusion sentences in each audit to decide whether in fact every sentiment sentence is positive or negative (Hu & Liu, 2004). Assessment sentences can be utilized to outline aspect-based sentiment which improves the general mining of item or administration survey. A sentiment holder communicates either positive or negative supposition (Bethard & Yu, 2004; Kim & Hovy, 2004; Wiebe & Riloff, 2005) on an element or a segment of it when giving a consistent conclusion and nothing else (Hu & Liu, 2004). Nonetheless, (Koppe & Schler, 2006) put need on separating the two assignments of discovering impartial from non-nonpartisan slant, and furthermore positive and negative notion. This is accepted to enormously build the accuracy of electronic structures.

Homophily Clustering in Opinion Formation

Opinion of influencers on social network is based to a great extent on their own perspectives and can't be hold as total certainty. Be that as it may, their opinions are equipped for influencing the choices of different clients on various topics. Opinions of persuasive clients on Social network frequently include, coming about opinion development evolvement. Grouping method of information mining can be used to demonstrate opinion arrangement by method for surveying the influenced hubs and unaffected hubs. Clients that portray a similar opinion are connected under similar hubs and those with contradicting opinion are connected in different hubs. This idea is alluded to as homophily in social network (McPherson & Smith-Lovin, 2001). Homophily can likewise be shown utilizing other criteria, for example, race and sexual orientation (Jackson, 2010).

Conduct of members in every hub is liable to changes in familiarity with the conduct of members in different hubs (Kaschesky & Sobkowicz, 2011). Opinion arrangement begins from the underlying stage where heft of members gives careful consideration to plan of action activity on noteworthy issue at this stage. This is so since they don't consider the activity practical. At the point when apt data is presented opinion is fell and members start to settle on either positive or negative choices. At this stage the choice of persuasive members who are either effective in the field or in correspondence aptitude pulls in the followership of the minority. The permeate arrange sets in when the minority can frame an alternate opinion based on other specialists' conduct and presentation of new data.

Opinion Definition and Opinion Summarization

Broad data offers meet people's high expectations of programmed summarization. Opinion definition and opinion summarization are fundamental procedures for perceiving opinion. Opinion definition can be situated in a content, sentence or subject in a record; it can likewise live in the whole report (Ku & Liang, 2006). Opinion summarization wholes up various opinions disclosed on bit of composing by investigating the assumption polarities, degree and the related events. Support Vector Machine (SVM) with direct part to take in the extremity of unbiased cases in reports. Their outcomes recommend that extremity entanglements can be sufficiently handled as three class intricacies utilizing pairwise coupling while at the same time combining results in noteworthy ways (Dave & Pennock, 2003; Morinaga & Yamanishi, 2002). Opinion extraction is imperative for summarization and resulting following. Writings, themes and records are sought to remove opinionated part. It is fundamental of compress opinion on the grounds that not all opinion communicated in a report are relied upon to be of significance to issue under thought (Wang & Lu, 2010).

Opinion Extraction

Sentiment analysis manages foundation and grouping of subjective data show in a material (Van de Camp & Van den Bosch, 2010). This may not really be certainty based as individuals have diverse sentiments toward a similar item, benefit, point, occasion or individual. Opinion extraction is vital keeping in mind the end goal to focus on the correct piece of the archive where the genuine opinion is communicated. Opinion from a person in a particular subject may not check with the exception of if the individual is an expert in the field of the topic. By the by, opinion from a few elements requires both opinion extraction and outline (Liu, 2011).

In opinion extraction, the more the quantity of individuals that give their opinion on a specific subject, the more imperative that bit may be worth removing. Opinion can go for a specific article while then again can analyze at least two articles. The formal is a consistent opinion while the last is similar (Jindal & Liu, 2003). Opinion extraction recognizes subjective sentences with sentimental arrangement of either positive or negative.

SENTIMENT ANALYSIS ON SOCIAL NETWORK

Sentiment analysis can be alluded to as disclosure and acknowledgment of positive or negative articulation of opinion by individuals on various topics of intrigue (Das & Chen, 2001; Tong, 2001). Opinions communicated by social network clients are frequently persuading and these pointers can be utilized to shape the premise of decisions and choices made by individuals on support of specific items and administrations or underwriting of political hopeful amid races (Kaschesky & Sobkowicz, 2011; Pang & Lee, 2002; Pang & Lee, 2008).

It is deserving of note that the huge opinions of a few a huge number of social network clients are overpowering, extending from essential ones to minor affirmations. Significantly it has turned out to be important to break down sentiment communicated on social network with data mining techniques keeping in mind the end goal to create significant structures that can be utilized as choice help apparatuses. Different calculations are utilized to find out sentiment that issues to a theme, content, record or identity under survey. The reason for sentiment analysis on social network is to perceive potential float in the general public as it concerns the demeanors, perceptions, and the desires of partner or the masses. This acknowledgment empowers the elements worry to take incite activities by settling on vital choices. It is imperative to make an interpretation of sentiment communicated to helpful information by method for mining and analysis.

Sentiment Orientation (SO)

Far reaching items are probably going to pull in a large number of surveys and this may make it troublesome for imminent purchasers to track usable audits that may help with settling on choice. Then again merchants make utilization of Sentiment Orientation (SO) for their rating standard in other to defend insignificant or deceiving audits present to commentators the 5-star scale rating with five meaning best appraised while one connotes poor rating. In Keshtkar and Inkpen (2009) SO was utilized to enhance the execution of mood characterization. Procedure effortlessly actualized together with SO properties and machine learning methods. The underlying consequence of grouping precision however recorded somewhat over the standard. A consolidation of adaptable hierarchy-based mood approach to mood order finds that ascribes that focuses to precise arrangement of mood articulation can be recovered from the different thick blog corpus area.

Product Ratings and Reviews

The dependence on the web (particularly social network destinations) for data when settling on decisions about items or administrations has expanded the need of investigating into the electronic-informal (Gamon & Aue, 2005; Tang & Tan, 2009). Items (administrations) appraisals and investigating frequently contains sentiment articulations a thing can be evaluated based on the mood of the commentator at the time (Bollen & Mao, 2011). Social network destinations, for example, Epinions and Ciao enable clients to build up a trust network among them demonstrating who to confide in offering item audits and evaluations. Most online stores similarly bear the cost of their clients the chance to either rate/survey item or administration they obtained. This procedure empowers planned clients to approach direct data about these items/benefits before making buy. Ineffectively appraised or checked on items/administrations have a tendency to draw in low support or no support by any means.

Reviews and Ratings (RnR) Architecture

RnR is an applied design made as an intelligent structure. It is client input situated that creates relative new reviews. The client supplies the name of item or administration whose execution has been before assessed online by clients. This framework checks through the corpus of as of now audited to see whether it is put away in the nearby reserve of the design for most recent reviews. On the off chance that the provided information is observed to be late, it is in this manner utilized. On the off chance that it is observed to be out of date, slithering is done on optional site, for example, TripAdvisor.com and Expedia.com.au. The information recovered on these destinations are then privately worked to find the required support. RnR design delivered finish comments of item and administration (under survey) inside a timetable by using transient measurement examination with diffuse plot and straight relapse. Labeling of few words was utilized for nothing open space philosophy for include recognizable proof. This is on the grounds that labeling POS of each word in entire reviews and sentiment word recognizable proof process could be tedious and computationally costly despite the fact that it creates high exactness. The utilization of neighbor word (words around the element events) likewise helps the pruning down of computational overhead.

Aspect Rating Analysis

Aspect-rating is numerical assessments in connection to the aspect indicating the level of fulfillment depicted in the remarks accumulated toward this aspect and the aspect rating. It makes utilization of minor expressions and their modifiers, for instance 'great item, incredible cost'. Every aspect is separated and examined utilizing Probabilistic latent semantic analysis (pLSA). It can be utilized as a part of place of structure of the expression. The definitely known finish present is abused on find out the aspect rating. Aspect bunch are words that commonly stands for an aspect that clients are worried in and would remark on.

Latent Aspect Rating Analysis (LARA) approach endeavors to dissect sentiment borne by various analysts by completing a content mining at the purpose of topical aspect. This empowers the determinacy of each commentator's latent score on every aspect and the applicable effect on them while touching base at a positive conclusion. The disclosure of the latent scores on various aspects can in a split second maintain aspect-base feeling synopsis. The aspect impacts are relative to examining score execution of commentators (Wang & Lu, 2010). The combination latent scores and aspect impacts is equipped for managing customized aspect-level scoring of elements utilizing only those reviews began from analysts with tantamount aspect impacts to those considered by a specific client. An aspect-based synopsis makes utilization of set of client reviews of a subject as information and makes an arrangement of imperative aspects mulling over the joined sentiment of every aspect and supporting literary indication (Titov & McDonald, 2008).

Sentiment Lexicon

Sentiment Lexicon is a word reference of sentimental words analysts frequently utilized as a part of their demeanor. Sentiment lexicon is rundown of the normal words that upgrade information mining methods when utilized mining sentiment in record. Diverse corpus of sentiment lexicon can be made for assortment of topics. For example, sentimental words utilized as a part of game are frequently not quite the same as those utilized as a part of legislative issues. Expanding the event of sentiment lexicon concentrates more on breaking down point particular event, yet with the utilization of high labor (Godbole & Srinivasaiah, 2007). Lexicon-based approaches require parsing to take a shot at basic, near, compound, contingent sentences and inquiries (Ding & Liu, 2008).

Sentiment lexicon can be expanded by utilization of equivalent words. In any case, lexicon extension using equivalent words has a disadvantage of the wording losing its essential significance after a couple of restatement. Sentiment lexicon can likewise be upgraded by 'discarding' neutral words that delineates neither positive nor negative articulation. Impartial articulation is regular particularly in items ratings and reviews.

UNSUPERVISED CLASSIFICATION OF SOCIAL NETWORK DATA

Semi-Supervised Classification

Semi-supervised learning is an objective focused on movement yet dissimilar to unsupervised; it can be particularly assessed. Creators of (Esuli & Sebastiani, 2005), dealt with a scaled down preparing set of seed in positive and negative articulations chose for preparing a term classifier. Equivalent word and antonym comparatives were added to the seed sets in an online lexicon (Santorini, 1995). The approach was intended to deliver the expanded sets P' and N' that makes up the preparation sets. Different students were utilized and a parallel classifier was constructed utilizing each sparkle in the word reference for both term in P' ∪ N' and making an interpretation of them to a vector. Their approach finds the cause of data which they announced was absent in before systems utilized for the undertaking. Semi-supervised lexical order proposed by (Sindhwani & Melville, 2008) coordinated lexical information into supervised learning and spread the approach to contain unlabelled information. Bunch supposition was locked in by gathering together two records with a similar group fundamentally supporting the positive - negative sentiment words as sentiment archives. It was noticed that the sentiment extremity of report chooses the extremity of word and the other way around.

In Rao and Ravichandran (2003) semi-supervised learning utilizes extremity location as semi-supervised name engendering issue in graphs. Every hub speaking to words whose extremity is to be found. The outcomes demonstrate name engendering advances outstandingly over the pattern and other semi-supervised methods like Mincuts and Randomized Mincuts. Crafted by Goldberg and Zhu (2004) contrasted graph-based semi-supervised learning and relapse and (Pang & Lee, 2005) proposed metric marking which runs SVM relapse as the first name inclination work tantamount to closeness quantify. Their outcome demonstrates that the graph-based semi-supervised learning (SSL) calculation according to PSP (positive-sentence-percentage) correlation (SSL+PSP) demonstrated to perform well.

Supervised Classification

While clustering techniques are utilized where premise of information is set up however information design is obscure (Aggarwal, 2011), grouping techniques are supervised learning techniques utilized where the information association is as of now distinguished. It is deserving of say that understanding the issue to be fathomed and settling on the correct information mining device is exceptionally fundamental when utilizing information mining techniques to illuminate social network issues. Pre-preparing and considering security privileges of individual (as said under research issues of this paper) ought to likewise be considered. In any case, since social media is a dynamic stage, effect of time must be sound in the issue of point acknowledgment, yet not generous on account of network broadening, amass conduct/ impact or showcasing. This is on the grounds that this credit will undoubtedly change every once in a while. Data refreshes in some Social network, for example, twitters and Facebook introduce Application Programmers Interfaces (APIs) that makes it workable for crawler, which accumulate new data in the site, to store the data for later use and refresh.

In Turney (2002) a supervised learning calculation utilized the blend of various bases of certainties to mark couple of descriptive words having comparable or unique semantic orientations. The calculation brought about a graph with hubs and connections which speaks to descriptors and closeness (or divergence) of semantic orientation individually.

SUMMARY

Different data mining techniques have been used in social network analysis as covered in this survey. The techniques range from unsupervised to semi-supervised and supervised learning methods. So far different levels of successes have being achieved either with solitary or combined techniques. The outcome of the experiments conducted on social network analysis is believed to have shed more light on the structure and activities of social network. The diverse experimental results have also confirmed the relevance of data mining techniques in retrieving valuable information and contents from huge data generated on social network. Future survey will tend to investigate novel state-of-the-art data mining techniques for social network analysis. The survey will compare similar data mining tools and recommend the most suitable tool(s) for the dataset to be analyzed.

REFERENCES

Adedoyin-Olowe, M., Gaber, M., & Stahl, F. (2013). A Methodology for Temporal Analysis of Evolving Concepts in Twitter. In *Proceedings of the 2013 ICAISC, International Conference on Artificial Intelligence and Soft Computing*. 10.1007/978-3-642-38610-7_13

Adomavicius, G., & Tuzhilin, A. (2005). Toward the next generation of recommender systems: A survey of the state-of-the-art and possible extensions. *IEEE Transactions on* Knowledge and Data Engineering, *17*(6), 734–749.

Aggarwal, C. (2011). *An introduction to social network data analytics*. Springer. doi:10.1007/978-1-4419-8462-3

Aggarwal, N., & Liu, H. (2008). Blogosphere: Research issues, tools, applications. *SIGKDD Explorations, 10*(1), 20. doi:10.1145/1412734.1412737

Aiello, L. M., Petkos, G., Martin, C., Corney, D., Papadopoulos, S., Skraba, R., ... Jaimes, A. (2013). Sensing trending topics in Twitter. *IEEE Transactions on Multimedia, 15*(6), 1268–1282.

Asur, S., & Huberman, B. (2010). Predicting the future with social network. In *2010 IEEE/WIC/ACM International Conference on Web Intelligence and Intelligent Agent Technology (WI-IAT)* (Vol. 1). IEEE.

Au Yeung, C. M., & Iwata, T. (2011). Strength of social influence in trust networks in product review sites. In *Proceedings of the fourth ACM international conference on Web search and data mining* (pp. 495-504). ACM. 10.1145/1935826.1935899

Bakshy, E., Hofman, J. M., Mason, W. A., & Watts, D. J. (2011). Identifying influencers on twitter. In *Fourth ACM International Conference on Web Search and Data Mining (WSDM)*.

Becker, H., Chen, F., Iter, D., Naaman, M., & Gravano, L. (2011). *Automatic Identification and Presentation of Twitter Content for Planned Events*.

Becker, H., Iter, D., Naaman, M., & Gravano, L. (2012). Identifying content for planned events across social media sites. In *Proceedings of the fifth ACM international conference on Web search and data mining* (pp. 533-542). ACM. 10.1145/2124295.2124360

Becker, H., Naaman, M., & Gravano, L. (2011). Beyond trending topics: Real-world event identification on Twitter. *ICWSM, 11*, 438–441.

Bekkerman, R., & McCallum, A. (2005). Disambiguating web appearances of people in a social network. In *Proceedings of the 14th international conference on World Wide Web* (pp. 463-470). ACM. 10.1145/1060745.1060813

Bethard, S., Yu, H., Thornton, A., & Hatzivassiloglou, V. Jurafsky. D. (2004). Automatic Extraction of Opinion Propositions and their Holders. In *Proceedings of the AAAI Spring Symposium on Exploring Attitude and Affect in Text*.

Boiy, E., & Moens, M. (2009). A Machine Learning Approach to Sentiment Analysis in Multilingual Web Texts. *Information Retrieval, 12*(5), 526–558. doi:10.100710791-008-9070-z

Bollen, J., Mao, H., & Pepe, A. (2011). *Modelling public mood and emotion: Twitter sentiment and socio-economic phenomena*.

Borgatti, S. P. (2009). 2-Mode concepts in social network analysis. In Encyclopedia of Complexity and System Science (pp. 8279-8291). doi:10.1007/978-0-387-30440-3_491

Borgatti, S. P., & Everett, M. G. (2006). A graph-theoretic perspective on centrality. *Social Networks, 28*, 466–484.

Burke, R. (2002). Hybrid recommender systems: Survey and experiments. *User Modeling and User-Adapted Interaction, 12*(4), 331–370. doi:10.1023/A:1021240730564

Burt, R. S. (2005). *Brokerage and closure: An introduction to social capital*. Oxford University Press.

Castellanos, M., Dayal, M., Hsu, M., Ghosh, R., & Dekhil, M. (2011). LCI: A Social Channel Analysis Platform for Live Customer Intelligence. In *Proceedings of the 2011 international Conference on Management of Data*.

Chelmis, C. Prasanna. VK. (2011). Social networking analysis: A state of the art and the effect of semantics. In *2011 IEEE third international conference on Privacy, security, risk and trust (PASSAT), and 2011 IEEE third international conference on social computing (Socialcom)*. IEEE.

Chen, Y., & Lee, K. (2011). *User-centred sentiment analysis on customer product review. World Applied Sciences Journal, 12, 32-38.*

Chen, Z. S., Kalashnikov, D. V., & Mehrotra, S. (2009). Exploiting context analysis for combining multiple entity resolution systems. In *Proceedings of the 2009 ACM International Conference on Management of Data (SIGMOD'09)*.

Chou, W. Y. S., Hunt, Y. M., Beckjord, E. B., Moser, R. P., & Hesse, B. W. (2009). Social media use in the United States: Implications for health communication. *Journal of Medical Internet Research*, *11*(4), e48. doi:10.2196/jmir.1249 PMID:19945947

Conover, M. D., Gonçalves, B., Ratkiewicz, J., Flammini, A., & Menczer, F. (2011, October). Predicting the political alignment of twitter users. In *2011 IEEE Third International Conference on Privacy, Security, Risk and Trust (PASSAT) and 2011 IEEE Third International Conference on Social Computing (SocialCom)* (pp. 192-199). IEEE.

Cordeiro, M. (2012). Twitter event detection: Combining wavelet analysis and topic inference summarization. In *Doctoral Symposium on Informatics Engineering, DSIE*.

Cortizo, J., Carrero, F., Gomez, J., Monsalve, B., & Puertas, E. (2009). Introduction to Mining SM. In *Proceedings of the 1st International Workshop on Mining SM* (pp. 1 – 3).

Das, S., & Chen, M. (2001). Yahoo! for Amazon: Extracting M arket Sentiment from Stock Message Boards. In *Proceedings of the Asia Pacific Finance Association Annual Conference (APFA)*.

Dave, K. L., & Pennock, D. (2003). Mining the peanut gallery: Opinion Extraction and Semantic Classification of Product Re views. In *Proceedings of WWW* (pp. 519-528).

Ding, X., Liu, B., & Yu, P. (2008). A Holistic Lexicon-based Approach to Opinion Mining. In *Proceedings of the Conference on Web Search and Web Data Mining (WSDM-2008)*. 10.1145/1341531.1341561

Esuli, A. Sebastiani. F. (2005). Determining the semantic orientation of terms through gloss classification. In *Proceedings of ACM International Conference on Information and Knowledge Management (CIKM-2005)*.

Fortunato, S. (2010). Community detection in graphs. *Physics Reports*, *486*(3), 75–174. doi:10.1016/j.physrep.2009.11.002

Gamon, M., Aue, A., Corston-Oliver, S., & Ringger, E. (2005). Pulse: Mining Customer Opinions from Free Text. In *International symposium on intelligent data analysis* (pp. 121-132). Springer.

Ghosh, R., & Lerman, K. (2011). Parameterized centrality metric for network analysis. *Physical Review. E*, *83*(6), 066118. doi:10.1103/PhysRevE.83.066118 PMID:21797452

Girvan, M., & Newman, M. E. (2002). Community structure in social and biological networks. *Proceedings of the National Academy of Sciences of the United States of America*, *99*(12), 7821–7826. doi:10.1073/pnas.122653799 PMID:12060727

Godbole, N., Srinivasaiah, M., & Steven, S. (2007). Large Scale Sentiment Analysis for News and Blogs. In *Proceedings of the International Conference on Weblogs and SM (ICWSM)*.

Goldberg, A., & Zhu, X. (2004). Seeing stars when there aren't many stars: Graph-based semi supervised learning for sentiment categorization. In *HLT-NAACL 2006 Workshop on Textgraphs: Graph-based Algorithms for Natural Language Processing*.

Gomes, J. B., Adedoyin-Olowe, M., Gaber, M. M., & Stahl, F. (2013). Rule type identification using TRCM for trend analysis in twitter. In *Research and Development in Intelligent Systems XXX* (pp. 273–278). Springer International Publishing. doi:10.1007/978-3-319-02621-3_20

Hatzivassiloglou, V., & McKeown, K. (1997). Predicting the Semantic Orientation of Adjectives. In *Proc. 8th Conf. on European chapter of the Association for Computational Linguistics*, Morristown, NJ (pp. 174-181). Association for Computational Linguistics.

Hoffman, T. (2008). Online Reputation Management is Hot — but is it Ethical? *Computerworld*.

Hu, M., & Liu, B. (2004). Mining and Summarizing Customer Reviews. In *Proceedings of the tenth ACM SIGKDD International Conference KDD '04*.

Jackson, M. O. (2010). *Social and economic networks*. Princeton University Press.

Jindal, N. Liu. B. (2006). Mining Comparative Sentences and Relations. In *Proceedings of National Conf. on Artificial Intelligence (AAAI-2006)*.

Kagdi, H., Collard, M. L., & Maletic, J. I. (2007). A survey and taxonomy of approaches for mining software repositories in the context of software evolution. Journal of software maintenance and evolution: Research and practice, *19*(2), 77–131. doi:10.1002mr.344

Kaji, N., & Kitsuregawa, M. (2006). Automatic construction of polarity-tagged corpus from HTML documents. In *Processing of the COLING, ACL Main Conference Poster Sessions*.

Kaplan, A.M. & Haenlein, M. (2010). Users of the world unite! The challenges and opportunities of social media. *Science direct, 53*(1), 59-68.

Kaschesky, M., Sobkowicz, P., & Bouchard, G. (2011). Opinion Mining in Social network: Modelling, Simulating, and Visualizing Political Opinion Formation in the Web. In *The Proceedings of 12th Annual International Conference on Digital Government Research*.

Kaur, G. (2013). Social network evaluation criteria and influence on consumption behaviour of the youth segment.

Keshtkar, F., & Inkpen, D. (2009). Using sentiment orientation features for mood classification in blogs. In *Proceedings of the IEEE International Conference on Natural Language Processing and Knowledge Engineering (IEEE NLP-KE 2009)*.

Kim, P. (2006). The Forrester Wave: Brand Monitoring, Q3 2006 [white paper]. Forrester.

Kim, S., & Hovy, E. (2004). Determining the Sentiment of Opinions. In *Proceedings of Intentional Conference on Computational Linguistics (COLING-2004)*.

Kim, Y., Hsu, S.-H., & de Zuniga, H. G. (2013). Influence of social network use on discussion network heterogeneity and civic engagement: The moderating role of personality traits. *Journal of Communication, 63*(3), 498–516. doi:10.1111/jcom.12034

Koppel, M., & Schler, J. (2006). The importance of neutral examples for learning sentiment computational intelligence. *Computational Intelligence, 22*(2), 100–109.

Korda, H., & Itani, Z. (2013). Harnessing social network for health promotion and behaviour change. *Health Promotion Practice, 14*(1), 15–23. doi:10.1177/1524839911405850 PMID:21558472

Ku, L.-W., Liang, Y.-T., & Chen, H.-H. (2006). Opinion extraction, summarization and tracking in news and blog corpora. In *Proc. of the AAAI-CAAW'06*.

Liu, B. (2011). Sentiment analysis and opinion Mining. In AAAI-2011, San Francisco, CA. doi:10.1007/978-3-642-19460-3_11

Liu, F., & Lee, H. J. (2010). Use of social network information to enhance collaborative filtering performance. *Expert Systems with Applications, 37*(7), 4772–4778. doi:10.1016/j.eswa.2009.12.061

Mathioudakis, M., & Koudas, N. (2010). Twittermonitor: trend detection over the twitter stream. In *Proceedings of the 2010 ACM SIGMOD International Conference on Management of data* (pp. 1155-1158). ACM. 10.1145/1807167.1807306

McPherson, M., Smith-Lovin, L., & Cook, J. M. (2001). Birds of a feather: Homophily in social networks. *Annual Review of Sociology, 27*(1), 415–444. doi:10.1146/annurev.soc.27.1.415

Morinaga, S., Yamanishi, K., Tateishi, K., & Fukushima, T. (2002). Mining product reputations on the web. In ACM SIGKDD (pp. 341–349).

Murthy, D., Gross, A., Takata, A., & Bond, S. (2013). Evaluation and Development of Data Mining Tools for Social Network Analysis. In *Mining Social Networks and Security Informatics* (pp. 183–202). Springer Netherlands. doi:10.1007/978-94-007-6359-3_10

Newman, M. (2010). *Networks: An introduction*. Oxford University Press. doi:10.1093/acprof:oso/9780199206650.001.0001

Osborne, M., Petrovic, S., McCreadie, R., Macdonald, C., & Ounis, I. (2012). Bieber no more: First story detection using twitter and wikipedia. In *Proceedings of the Workshop on Time-aware Information Access*.

Pang, B., & Lee, L. (2005). Seeing stars: Exploiting class relationships for sentiment categorization with respect to rating scales. In *Proceedings of the Association for Computational Linguistics (ACL)* (pp. 115–124).

Pang, B., & Lee, L. (2008). Opinion mining and sentiment analysis. Foundations and trends in information Retrieval, 2(1–2), 1–135.

Pang, B., & Lee, L. (2008). Using very simple statistics for review search: An exploration. In *Proceedings of the International Conference on Computational Linguistics (COLING)* [Poster paper].

Pang, B., Lee, L., & Vaithyanathan, S. (2002). Thumbs up? Sentiment classification using machine learning techniques. In *Proceedings of Conference on Empirical methods in natural Language Processing (EMNLP)*, Philadelphia, PA, July (pp. 79 – 86). Association for Computational Linguistics. 10.3115/1118693.1118704

Papadopoulos, S., Kompatsiaris, Y., Vakali, A., & Spyridonos, P. (2012). Community detection in social media. *Data Mining and Knowledge Discovery*, *24*(3), 515–554. doi:10.100710618-011-0224-z

Pham, M. C., Cao, Y., Klamma, R., & Jarke, M. (2011). A clustering approach for collaborative filtering recommendation using social network analysis. *J. UCS*, *17*(4), 583–604.

Phuvipadawat, S., & Murata, T. (2010). Breaking news detection and tracking in twitter. In *2010 IEEE/ WIC/ACM International Conference on Web Intelligence and Intelligent Agent Technology (WI-IAT)* (Vol. 3, pp. 120-123). IEEE.

Rahayu, D. A., Krishnaswamy, S., Alahakoon, O., & Labbe, C. (2010). RnR: Extracting rationale from online reviews and ratings. In *2010 IEEE International Conference on Data Mining Workshops (ICDMW)* (pp. 358-368). IEEE.

Rao, D., & Ravichandran, D. (2009). Semi-supervised polarity lexicon induction. In *Proceedings of the European Chapter of the Association for Computational Linguistics (EACL)*. 10.3115/1609067.1609142

Riloff, E., Wiebe, J., & Wilson, T. (2003). Learning subjec tive nouns using extraction pattern bootstrapping. In *Proceedings of the Conference on Natural Language Learning (CoNLL)* (pp. 25–32).

Ruan, X. H., Hu, X., & Zhang, X. (2014). Research on Application Model of Semantic Web-Based Social Network Analysis. In *Proceedings of the 9th International Symposium on Linear Drives for Industry Applications* (Vol. 2, pp. 455-460). Springer Berlin Heidelberg. 10.1007/978-3-642-40630-0_59

Santorini, B. (1995). *Part-of-speech tagging guidelines for the Penn treebank project (3rd revision, 2nd printing) [Technical Report]*. Department of Computer and Information Science, University of Pennsylvania.

Scott, J. (2011). Social network analysis: Developments, advances, and prospects. *Social Network Analysis and Mining*, *1*(1), 21–26. doi:10.100713278-010-0012-6

Sindhwani, V., & Melville, P. (2008). Document-word co-regularization for semi-supervised sentiment analysis. In *8th IEEE International Conference on Data Mining*.

Symeonidis, P., Tiakas, E., & Manolopoulos, Y. (2011). Product recommendation and rating prediction based on multi-modal social networks. In *Proceedings of the fifth ACM conference on Recommender systems* (pp. 61-68). ACM. 10.1145/2043932.2043947

Tang, H., Tan, S., & Cheng, X. (2009). A survey on sentiment detection of reviews. *Expert Systems with Applications*, *36*(7), 10760–10773. doi:10.1016/j.eswa.2009.02.063

Tepper, A. (2012). How much data is created every minute? [infographic]. *Mashable*. Retrieved from http://mashable.com/2012/06/22/data-created-every-minute/

Thompson, J. B. (2013). *Media and modernity: A social theory of the media*. John Wiley & Sons.

Titov, I., & McDonald, R. (2008). A joint model of text and aspect ratings for sentiment summarization. In *Proceedings of 46th Annual Meeting of the Association for Computational Linguistics (ACL'08)*.

Tong, R. (2001). An operational system for detecting and tracking opinions in on-line discussion. In *Proceedings of the Workshop on Operational Text Classification (OTC)*.

Turney, P. (2001). Mining the web for synonyms: PMI-IR Versus LSA on TOEFL. In *Proceedings of the Twelfth European Conference on Machine Learning (pp. 491*-502). Springer-Verlag.

Turney, P. (2002). Thumbs Up or Thumbs Down? Semantic orientation applied to unsupervised Classification of Reviews. In *Proceedings of the Association for Computational Linguistics (ACL)* (pp. 417–424).

Van De Camp, M., & van den Bosch, A. (2011, June). A link to the past: constructing historical social networks. In *Proceedings of the 2nd Workshop on Computational Approaches to Subjectivity and Sentiment Analysis* (pp. 61-69). Association for Computational Linguistics.

Wang, H., Lu, Y., & Zhai, C. (2010). Latent aspect rating analysis on review text data: A rating regression approach. In KDD '10, New York, NY (pp. 783-792).

Weng, J., & Lee, B.-S. (2011). Event detection in twitter. In *ICWSM*.

Chapter 3
Semantic–Based Indexing Approaches for Medical Document Clustering Using Cognitive Search

Logeswari Shanmugam
Bannari Amman Institute of Technology, India

Premalatha K.
Bannari Amman Institute of Technology, India

ABSTRACT

Biomedical literature is the primary repository of biomedical knowledge in which PubMed is the most absolute database for collecting, organizing and analyzing textual knowledge. The high dimensionality of the natural language text makes the text data quite noisy and sparse in the vector space. Hence, the data preprocessing and feature selection are important processes for the text processing issues. Ontologies select the meaningful terms semantically associated with the concepts from a document to reduce the dimensionality of the original text. In this chapter, semantic-based indexing approaches are proposed with cognitive search which makes use of domain ontology to extract relevant information from big and diverse data sets for users.

INTRODUCTION

The huge volume of biomedical text in the online repositories provides a rich source of knowledge for biomedical research. The rapid growth of data is a challenge for the modern society and the 80% percent of the current available data is not structured or indexed. As the cognitive computing becomes the current era, new searching techniques are evolved by combining powerful indexing technology with advanced Natural Language Processing (NLP) capabilities and machine learning algorithms in order to build an increasingly deep corpus of knowledge.

DOI: 10.4018/978-1-5225-7522-1.ch003

Text mining takes advantage of machine learning specifically in determining features, reducing dimensionality and removing irrelevant attributes. Text mining facilitates the researchers to extract information and mine knowledge from a pile of text and it is now extensively applied in biomedical research. Text mining outcomes are obtained with noisy information and false positives from natural language text. This is due to the ambiguities caused by semantics, syntax, sparsity of class specific core words and high dimensionality. In the recent researches many methods have been developed to facilitate discovering trends and patterns in medical documents. These researches proved that the new searching techniques developed are no longer based on just keyword matching; all these techniques are become cognitive with the ability to deliver the most relevant answers to search queries. It is observed from the literature that the inclusion of domain knowledge with the cognitive search during the mining process enhances the efficiency as well as the quality of the mined patterns.

The high dimensionality of the natural language makes the text data quite noisy and sparse in the vector space model. There is a possibility that mining may lead to inaccurate results in clusters if the input has noisy information. Hence the data preprocessing and feature selection are the important practices for the text mining. The transformation from unstructured text document into Bag-of-Words (BOW) representation is the compassion of document indexing. The preprocessing tasks which include tokenization, stop-word removal, Part-of-Speech (POS) tagging and weighting are incorporated during indexing.

The traditional term-based indexing suffers on semantic issues related to the synonymy and polysemy problems. Thus, the term-based methods are not appropriate for clustering the medical documents which involve with complex semantics. In order to deal with the issues, a concept-based indexing is proposed for medical document clustering using Medical Subject Headings (MeSH) ontology as the domain reference.

The MEDLINE contains a major entry point to biomedical research for biologists (Hersh 2008). The handling of biomedical domain is complex due to its ambiguous nature of terminologies. The cost of manual indexing of the biomedical documents is high; so many efforts have been prepared in order to offer automatic indexing. The MEDLINE database gives MeSH ontology for biomedical research articles. MeSH based representations cover the conceptual content of entire articles. Its representation has been shown to be consistent across different indexers (Funk & Reid 1983). Hence MeSH-based document representation gets more attraction in IR. The Mesh descriptors are not only sufficient for extracting information from the PubMed documents. Feature or term weighting is an important part in the process of IRS. Precise term weighting can greatly improve the process of finding index terms. The amount of influence of term in representing the document reflects on term weight. Hence a concept-based indexing is proposed for biomedical document clustering with concept weight which is computed using the frequency and weight of the semantic relation.

LITERATURE REVIEW

Medical document analysis is one of the innovative fields with remarkable research potential. It employs with the extraction of novel, significant information from the huge quantity of biomedical associated documents. The substantial amount of biomedical text offers a comfortable source of knowledge for biomedical research.

IR is involved with choosing from a group of documents, those that are probable to be appropriate to a user's information requirement expressed using a query. The objective of IR is to extend the users with documents that satisfy their requirements. The retrieval of documents involves with the indexing of documents, formulating queries, document representations and query representations. The documents that match the representation are collected by the IRS. The transformation from unstructured text document into BOW representation is the compassion of document indexing. The main aim of document indexing is to link a document with a descriptor characterized by a set of features manually allocated or automatically obtained from its content.

A conventional indexing approach that supports Vector Space Model (VSM) is proposed (Sebastiani, 2002). In this model, documents and queries are characterized as weighted vectors of indexed terms where the size of the vectors matches the vocabulary space. The weight of each index term within each document indicates its significance in terms of its representation and discriminative power. Documents are retrieved using the similarity based on a cosine or Euclidean distance metric and fast search algorithms can be applied to match documents to a query.

A phrase-based document similarity model is developed to compute the pair-wise similarities of documents based on the STD model (Chim, & Deng, 2008). The unique feature term in the VSM model is mapped onto each node of the STD model. The phrase-based document similarity is computed from STD which naturally inherits the *tf-idf* weighting scheme. The experimental results indicate that, the new clustering approach is very effective on clustering the documents.

A clustering method based on frequent word sequences is proposed to address the various special requirements related to the text retrieval (Li, Chung, & Holt, 2008). A generalized suffix tree is built using the frequent words within each document to facilitate the discovery of the frequent word sequences. Then, the documents are clustered using a new algorithm based on frequent word meaning sequences. The results show that the proposed method is used to measure the closeness between documents.

A hybrid distance-based document clustering method is developed with keyword and phrase indexing (Subhadra, & Shashi, 2012). It uses an improved indexing and substitution method for document phrases. It delivers a superior performance in terms of purity owing to the mechanism employed for measuring the content similarity.

The important problems related to the use of semantics in IR are discussed and a new approach is proposed for the document representation (Baziz, Boughanem, & Traboulsi 2005). The content of a document is represented as a semantic network. It involves with the concept extraction through mono and multiword terms from a document, driven by external general-purpose ontology, namely WordNet. The second step builds the best semantic network by achieving a global disambiguation of the extracted concepts regarding to the document. Thus, selected concepts senses represent the nodes of the semantic network while the similarity measure values between them represent the arcs. The resulted scored concepts senses are used for conceptual indexing in IR.

The phrases are having significant contribution in the identification of concepts involved in a document (Li, & Wu, 2006). A key phrase identification program is developed for identifying topical concepts from medical documents. It combines the noun phrase extraction and key phrase identification functions. The key phrase identification functions assign weights to extract noun phrases for a medical document based on how important they are to that document and how domain specific they are in the medical domain. The experimental results show that the noun phrase extractor is effective in identifying noun phrases from medical documents.

A hybrid clustering method based on MeSH ontology is proposed for enhancing the performance of the document clustering (Zhu, Zeng & Mamitsuka, 2009). This proposed approach integrates both the semantic information embedded in the MeSH thesaurus and the content information of texts in the integrated similarity matrix. MEDLINE documents are clustered using spectral clustering on the integrated similarity matrix. The pragmatic results demonstrate the efficiency of this proposed method.

A concept-based mining model is developed to improve the text clustering quality (Khare, & Jadhav, 2010). The relations between verbs and their arguments (Anandakumar & Umamaheswari, 2018) in the same sentence have the potential for analyzing terms within a sentence. By exploiting the semantic structure of the sentences in documents, a better text clustering result is achieved.

The recent researches on document clustering involves with concept weight computation (Tar, & Nyaunt, 2011). The concept weight calculation includes the information about frequency, length, specific area and score of the concept. The experimental results show that the clustering system could improve the accuracy and performance of text documents using the weighted concepts.

In order to extract biomedical information from MEDLINE documents, a text mining approach is developed (Imambi, & Sudha, 2013). In this approach, a global relevant weight schema based on the probability of term relevance is proposed to find the relevant index terms. The relevance of the terms is measured with Bayes classification. The performance of this text mining approach is evaluated using the documents collected from the diabetic literature of MEDLINE.

A context-sensitive semantic smoothing method is presented for agglomerative clustering to identify multiword phrases in a document automatically (Zhou, Hu, Zhang, Lin & Song, 2006). Then it maps the multiword phrases into individual terms of document using statistical methods. Kullback-Leibler (KL) divergence metric is used as the similarity measure in this approach. The incorporation of semantic smoothing and KL-divergence similarity measure considerably improves the quality of clusters generated using agglomerative hierarchical clustering is exposed by the experimental results (Haldorai & Ramu, 2018).

A context based semantic smoothing model is developed for document clustering in which documents are represented as semantic graphs (Verma, & Bhattacharyya, 2009). This approach makes use of semantically related and not-necessarily-consecutive word tuples for document smoothing. The semantically relatable sequences are tuples of words appearing in the semantic graph of the sentence as linked nodes depicting dependency relations.

A vector space model based on semantic smoothing is proposed for document clustering (Nasir, Varlamis, Karim, & Tsatsaronis, 2013). In this approach semantic relatedness between words is used to smooth the similarity and the representation of text documents. The generalized vector space model improves VSM by removing the pairwise orthogonality assumption and taking into account the term-to-term correlations, which are based either on the semantic correlations between terms or on the frequency co-occurrence statistics computed in large text corpora. The evaluation results demonstrated that the proposed method dominates VSM in performance in most of the combinations.

PROBLEM STATEMENT

Traditional lexicon-based approaches cannot effectively address the word mismatch or ambiguity problems in document clustering. The poor efficiency of the unconventional query expansion and local context detection approaches is (Anandakumar & Umamaheswari 2017) due to the noise created by the large number of expanded terms in the documents. The dissimilar factors affecting the efficiency of biomedical IR system including term weighting, query expansion, and document expansion models are discussed (Dinh, Tamine, & Boubekeur, 2013).

The major challenges faced by the term/phrase-based clustering algorithms are

- Semantic issues related to synonymy and polysemy problems in the traditional BOW
- Clustering process become too slow due to the high dimensionality of the unstructured text documents
- N-gram phrase representation suffer due to the low frequency occurrence and they can represent less statistical properties of words
- WSD is an open problem of Natural Language Processing (NLP) designed at resolving lexical ambiguities by identifying the correct meaning of a word based on its context
- Concept extraction needs domain knowledge for improving the performance of clustering
- Clustering medical document becomes too difficult because of the ambiguity and inconsistency within the field

To deal with the above-mentioned challenges, this research work applies ontology-based concept extraction method. The quality of clusters can be improved by the indexing process involved in the preprocessing stage of the clustering. It uses MeSH ontology as the domain reference for indexing the medical documents. The hidden concepts and semantic relations are extracted from the documents using cognitive search through ontology mapping.

OBJECTIVES

The main objective of this proposed chapter is to improve the performance of the clustering process by proposing semantic based indexing schemes with cognitive search. The performances of the proposed indexing techniques are evaluated using the unsupervised machine learning algorithms. The primary objectives of this research work are:

- To resolve the problems due to the semantic features of the text documents such as synonymy and polysemy by mining the indexes from recognized concepts using concept based indexing
- To devise a concept based smoothing approach to resolve the conflicts due to general words and the sparsity of class-specific core words

SEMANTIC BASED INDEXING

Preamble

Traditional machine learning algorithms performs well on numerical data and cannot easily learn semantics of natural language. In order to redefine a patient's path to better health, the epoch of cognitive healthcare will communicate together individual and clinical research and social data from a diverse range of healthcare source. Conventional clustering techniques for document clustering are mainly based on the term frequency within the documents. The keywords which are having highest frequency values are used as features for representing the documents and they are treated independently which can be easily applied to non-ontological clustering. In order to overcome the various limitations due to the sparsity of core words, a novel and an efficient solution using ontology-based computing is proposed. This system comprises of a concept weight calculation procedure based on the semantic relations between the terms as well as phrases within a document.

Methodology

The conventional VSM is used for recording the concept-document weight information. This work is proposed for clustering the PubMed documents using the MeSH ontology as the knowledge base extension for implementing cognitive search. This approach includes the following operations for indexing the documents based on the concepts in the MeSH ontology.

- Document Preprocessing
- Ontology Mapping for Concept Analysis
- Weight Assignment based on Semantic Relations
- Concept Weight Calculation

Document Preprocessing

The input for the proposed indexing method is the information about MeSH ontology and a set of documents $D = \{d_1, d2...d_n\}$ collected from PubMed journal articles. During the preprocessing, the documents are tokenized and the stop-words are removed.

Ontology Mapping for Concept Analysis

For each query term, the concept hierarchy is captured from the MeSH ontology. Table 1 shows the MeSH descriptor details for the search query "cancer" which is an entry term of Neoplasm. In the MeSH descriptor data, the entry terms represent the synonyms of the query term. Figure 1 shows the MeSH tree hierarchies for the search query "cancer". It is used to identify the hypernyms, meronyms and the concept of the search query.

Figure 1.

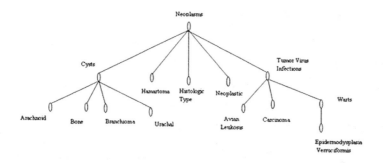

Table 1. Mesh descriptor data

National Library of Medicine – Medical Subject Headings 2015 MeSH MeSH Descriptor Data	
MeSH Heading	Neoplasms
Tree Number	C04
Annotation	general; prefer specifics; policy: see Manual Chapter 24; familial: consider also NEOPLASTIC SYNDROMES, HEREDITARY; metastatic cancer of unknown origin: index under NEOPLASM METASTASIS
Scope Note	New abnormal growth of tissue. Malignant neoplasms show a greater degree of anaplasia and have the properties of invasion and metastasis, compared to benign neoplasms.
Entry Term	Benign Neoplasms
Entry Term	Cancer
Entry Term	Neoplasia
Entry Term	Neoplasm
Entry Term	Neoplasms, Benign
Entry Term	Tumors
See Also	Antibodies, Neoplasm
See Also	Anticarcinogenic Agents
See Also	Carcinogens
Consider Also	consider also terms at CANCER, CARCINO-, ONCO-, and TUMOR
Allowable Qualifiers	BL BS CF CH CI CL CN CO DH DI DT EC EH EM EN EP ET GE HI IM ME MI MO NU PA PC PP PS PX RA RH RI RT SE SU TH UL UR US VE VI
Entry Version	NEOPL
Online Note	pre-explosion = NEOPLASMS (PX)
History Note	diagnosis was NEOPLASM DIAGNOSIS 1964-65; /etiology was NEOPLASM ETIOLOGY 1964-65; /immunology was NEOPLASM IMMUNOLOGY 1964-65; /radiotherapy was NEOPLASM RADIOTHERAPY 1964-65; /therapy was NEOPLASM THERAPY 1964-65; NEOPLASM STATISTICS was heading 1964-65; CARCINOGENESI was heading 1977
Entry Combination	Secondary Neoplasm Metastasis
Date of Entry	19990101
Unique ID	D009369

Weight Assignment Based on Semantic Relations

Each text file may consist of multiple concepts. Since the medical terms are ambiguous in nature, weight assignment is preceded in this ontology-based concept indexing. During the cognitive search, the importance of the concept in a document is derived by four types of semantic relations, namely identity, synonymy, hypernymy and meronymy (Watrous-deVersterre, Wang, & Song, 2012). Among the four semantic relations, identity and synonymy relations have equal contribution in the concept weight calculation. The hypernyms of the search query in the concept hierarchy are used to represent more general terms by means of the "Is-A" relationship. For each user query, the concept hierarchy is captured from the MeSH ontology. Each term in the concept hierarchy is designated with the initial weights as indicated in the Table 2, based on the semantic relations, namely, identity, synonymy, hypernymy and meronymy.

Table 2. Semantic relations with initial weights

Semantic Relation	Weight
Identity	1.0
Synonym	1.0
Hypernym	0.7
Meronym	0.8

The weight assignment procedure is as follows: Initially the first meronym term in the immediate lower level of the search query is assigned with a weight as 0.8. From the next level onwards, the value is decreased by 0.05 for each successive level of the hierarchy. Likewise, the hypernym at the first level is assigned with the initial weight as 0.7 which is the immediate upper level of the search query. For the ancestors, the value is decreased by 0.1 for each predecessor level of the hierarchy. The concept hierarchies have the search query are extracted from the MeSH ontology.

Concept Weight Calculation

The individual concept weight within the particular document is computed by frequency and weight information of the semantically related terms. The concept with highest weight represents that the document is semantically related to the concept. Traditional VSM is used to record the concept-document weight information. The algorithm for the proposed concept-based indexing is given in the Table 3.

In equation (1), $W\left(C_i, d\right)$ is the weight of the concept in the document, $freq_i$ is the frequency of the term i in the document, $weight_i$ is the semantic weight assigned for the term i, n is the number of unique terms in the document after stop-word removal and R is the semantic relation among identity, synonym, hypernym and meronym.

Table 3. Concept based indexing algorithm

Input: Document Corpus from PubMed
Output: Concept – Document Weight Information
Method:
Given the set of abstracts and search query
1. Tokenize the content of documents
2. Remove the stop-words from it
3. For the Concept based indexing, do:
    a. Extract the full path of the search query
    b. Assign the initial weights for the immediate hypernym as 0.7 and meronym as 0.8 of the search item.
    c. For the ancestors of hypernym, the value is decreased by 0.1 for each predecessor level of the hierarchy
    d. For the subsequent meronyms, the value is decreased by 0.05 for each successive level of the hierarchy

$$W\left(C_i, d\right) = \sum_{j \in R} \sum_{i=1}^{n} \frac{freq_i^{(j)} \times weight_i}{n} \quad (1)$$

4. Record the weight information of each concept in the traditional VSM

The performance of the proposed method is analysed by comparing the concept–document weight information with the traditional *tf-idf* weight information. The *tf-idf* values of the search query are computed as w_{ij} for all the documents using the Equation (2).

$$w_{ij} = tf_{ji} \times idf_{ji} = tf_{ji} \times \log_2 \frac{N}{df_{ji}}$$

(2)

where tf_{ji} is the number of occurrences of term i in the document j, df_{ji} is the document frequency for the term i in the collection of documents and N is the total number of documents in the collection. Ontology based Concept indexing enhances the weight of the concept because it considers not only the concept word but also all the words that are associated to the concept word by means of the semantic relations.

CONCEPT BASED SMOOTHING MODEL

Preamble

Most of the existing approaches use single term keywords as well as multiword phrases as the document features. Nevertheless, they suffer from the context insensitivity problem because of the ambiguous nature of the single term keywords. In contrast, the semantic smoothing model uses multiword phrases as topic signatures for representing document features.

The main objective behind the semantic smoothing technique is to reduce the general words and give more emphasize for core words. It is observed from the literature that the semantic smoothing models are more suitable for agglomerative clustering and not effective enough for partitional clustering (Kamaljeet, & Bhattacharyya, 2009). Prompted by the semantic smoothing model, a new ontology based semantic smoothing model is suggested in this work to address the problems associated to the sparsity of core words related to the concepts.

METHODOLOGY

This system is designed to perform semantic smoothing process based on the concept weight calculation which is supported by the ontology. This approach transforms the feature-represented documents into a concept represented one with the assistance of domain specific ontology. Therefore, the target documents will be clustered by extracting the keywords and phrases that are representing the concepts presented in the domain ontology. The phrases within the documents which contribute in the identification of the dominating concept are considered using n-gram techniques. The key idea of using a concept-based model with the semantic smoothing approach is to discount general words and assign reasonable counts to unseen core words. It is mainly based on the principle of *tf-idf* factor. So that the core words which are representing the concept are discriminated from the general words using this approach.

This proposed concept based smoothing model consists of the following modules:

- Concept Identification
  ◦ Simple language model
  ◦ Topic signature translation model
- Building the concept based smoothing model
- Clustering of documents

Concept Identification

In the medical domain, phrases are also having contributed in the identification of concepts. Thus, the proposed concept based smoothing model considers tri-gram technique to represent the phrases from the documents for the conceptual identification. Concept based model involves with the analysis of complex semantic relations for extracting the semantically related terms to the concept queries for its significance. The terms that are representing the semantic relations within the ontology can be a single term or a multiword phrase. Such multiword phrases related to the concept are taken as topic signatures. Multiword phrase translation estimates the translation probability of each topic signature (i.e.) determining the probability of translating the given phrase to concept in the vocabulary.

Simple Language Model

The first component of the semantic smoothing model is a simple language model $p_b \left(Concept \mid d \right)$. It builds the simple concept translation model of the document. This model can be obtained by using the Maximum Likelihood Estimator (MLE) document model $p_{ml} \left(Concept \mid d \right)$ together with a background smoothing model $p \left(Concept \mid Corpus \right)$ with the controlling coefficient α. The method of maximum likelihood identifies the set of values of the model parameters that maximizes the likelihood function. The effect of *tf-idf* scheme in conventional document clustering methods is roughly equivalent to the background model smoothing. The likelihood of each concept of the document can be done using the following Equations.

$$p_b \left(Concept \mid d \right) = \left(1 - \alpha\right) p_{ml} \left(Concept \mid d \right) \delta + \alpha p \left(Concept \mid Corpus \right) \tag{3}$$

$$p_{ml} \left(Concept \mid d \right) = \sum_{j \in R} \sum_{i=1}^{n} \frac{freq_i^{(j)} \times weight_i}{N_d} \tag{4}$$

$$p \left(Concept \mid Corpus \right) = \sum_{l=1}^{N} \sum_{j \in R} \sum_{i=1}^{n} \frac{freq_{l,i}^{(j)} \times weight_{l,i}}{N_c} \tag{5}$$

$$\delta = \log_2(N / n_i + 0.01) \tag{6}$$

where,

$p_{ml}\left(Concept \mid d\right)$ - Maximum likelihood probability of the document belonging to a particular concept

$p\left(Concept \mid Corpus\right)$ - Probability of the whole corpus belonging to that particular concept

$freq_i$ - Denotes the frequency of the word occurring in the document.

$weight_i$ - Weight assigned to the concept relation.

N - Total number of documents in the corpus

n_i - Number of documents which contain the particular concept

n - Number of terms in the document that belongs to the relation R

N_d - Number of unique terms in the document

N_c - Number of unique terms in the corpus

$freq_{l,i}^{(j)}$ - Frequency of the particular term i in the document l with the relation R

$weight_{l,i}$ - Weight of the particular term i in the document l with the relation R

Topic Signature Translation Model

The second component of the semantic smoothing model is the topic signature (multiword phrase) translation model. Here, the probability $p\left(Concept \mid t_k\right)$ of translating t_k to *Concept* is estimated in the training process using the following Equations.

$$p_t\left(Concept \mid d\right) = \sum_k p\left(Concept \mid t_k\right)\delta \times p_{ml}\left(t_k \mid d\right)\varphi \tag{7}$$

$$p_{ml}\left(t_k \mid d\right) - frequency\,of\,t_k\,in\,d \tag{8}$$

$$p\left(Concept \mid t_k\right) = \frac{concept\_score \text{ in } t_k}{\text{frequency of phrases in the document}} \tag{9}$$

$$\varphi = \log_2(N / n_i + 0.01) \tag{10}$$

where *concept_score* represents the product of frequency and weight of the semantic relationship.

$p_{ml}\left(t_k \mid d\right)$ - maximum likelihood of the phrase t_k, presenting in the document

$p\left(Concept \mid t_k\right)$ - probability of translating the phrase t_k into a specific concept

N - Total number of documents in the corpus

n_i - Number of documents which contain the topic signature t_i

Building the Concept Based Smoothing Model

The concept based smoothing model with ontology is a mixture model with two components, (i.e.) the simple concept translation model and the multiword phrase translation model. The influence of two components is controlled by the translation coefficient $\left(\gamma\right)$ in the mixture model. The model is organized as follows:

$$p_{bt}\left(Concept \mid d\right) = \left(1 - \gamma\right)p_b\left(Concept \mid d\right) + \gamma p_t\left(Concept \mid d\right) \tag{11}$$

The first component is the simple concept translation model, which can be obtained using the maximum likelihood estimator document model together with a background smoothing model with the controlling coefficient α. The second component of the document model is the multiword phrase translation model. Table 4 gives the algorithm for constructing the concept based smoothing model.

EVALUATION METHODOLOGY

The proposed concept based indexing method is assessed and compared with the traditional term-based approach using two biomedical datasets that are collected from the PubMed, which is a web interface of Medline documents. The abstracts of the manuscripts are collected from PubMed on ten different diseases. The dataset descriptions are given in the Table 5.

Table 4. Concept based smoothing model construction

Input: Document Corpus from PubMed
Output: Concept – Document Weight Information
Method:
Given the set of abstracts and search query
1. Tokenize the content of documents
2. Remove the stop-words from it
3. Extract keywords and topic signatures from documents using ontology mapping
4. For the weight calculation, do:
a. Extract the full path of the search query
b. Assign the initial weights for the immediate hypernym as 0.7 and meronym as 0.8 of the search item.
c. For the ancestors of hypernym, the value is decreased by 0.1 for each predecessor level of the hierarchy
d. For the subsequent meronyms, the value is decreased by 0.05 for each successive level of the hierarchy
5. Build the simple language model using the formulas (3), (4) (5) and (6)
6. Build the topic signature translation model using the formulas (7), (8), (9) and (10)
7. Build the semantic smoothing model using the formula (11)
8. Record the weight information of each concept in the traditional VSM

Table 5. Dataset descriptions

Disease	Number of Documents
Neoplasms	450
Viral Diseases	300
Cardio Vascular Diseases	350
Eye Infection	500
Respiratory Diseases	400

Similarity Measures and Distance Measures

The selection of an accurate similarity measure is also critical for cluster analysis, particularly for a specific type of clustering algorithms (Huang, 2008; Lin, Jiang, & Lee, 2013).

Euclidean Distance

The most commonly used distance measures in text clustering is the Euclidean distance. The default distance measure used with K-Means algorithm is the Euclidean distance. The Euclidean distance between the two documents x and y with m number of dimensions is defined as

$$d(x,y) = \sqrt{\sum_{i=1}^{m}(x_i - y_i)^2} \tag{12}$$

Pearson Correlation

The Pearson correlation finds the conformance of two datasets on a straight line. Correlation is always in the range -1 to 1. The value 0 indicates that there is no linear relationship between the attributes of the two data objects. Pearson correlation is defined by the following Equation (13) where x and y represents two data objects.

$$corr(x,y) = \frac{covariance(x,y)}{standard\_deviation(x) \times standard\_deviation(y)} \tag{13}$$

Clustering Algorithms and Performance Measures

The main objective of cluster analysis is to build a separation of data set into harmonized groups, called clusters. The data objects are grouped into various clusters based on the cluster hypothesis which specifies that the more similar objects are kept in a same cluster, whereas data objects assigned to different clusters should differ significantly. In the text-based approaches, the words or sometimes the phrases in the document are considered in the cluster formation. The text clustering algorithms are classified as crisp (or hard) clustering and fuzzy (or soft) clustering based on the way in which the algorithms are handling the uncertainty regarding the overlapping problem in clusters. A strict partition is followed in crisp clustering that the documents will be placed either in a cluster or not. In fuzzy clustering, the document can be placed into more than one cluster (Papageorgiou, 2016). In the agglomerative hierarchical approach, single linkage, complete linkage and centroid methods, K-means partitional clustering algorithm and Fuzzy C-Means (FCM) algorithm are used to evaluate the proposed ontology-based concept indexing approaches. The cluster quality is evaluated using the performance measures given in the Table 6.

In hard clustering algorithms, a value of S_i close to 1 indicates that the data point is assigned to a very appropriate cluster. If S_i is close to zero, it means that that data point could be assigned to another closest cluster. The higher the value of the FM index, more similar clusters. In FCM, the algorithm that produces a collection of clusters with the smallest DB index is considered as the best algorithm.

Experimental Results and Analysis

The performance of the proposed methods is experimented and analyzed with the dataset given in the Table 5 which includes the documents related to five diseases from PubMed repository and implemented in MATLAB version 7.12. The performance of the proposed approach is compared with the traditional indexing techniques such as term-based indexing and LSI indexing technique. For the experimental purpose, the number of clusters is set as 5 and the maximum number of iterations of the algorithm is 10. The high dimensionality of the input document corpus is getting reduced by the preprocessing step. The Table 7 shows the result of the preprocessing on the document corpuses.

Table 6. Performance measures

Clustering Algorithms	Performance Measures	Formula	Description
Hard Clustering	Silhouette Index	$$S_i = \frac{b_i - a_i}{max\left(a_i, b_i\right)}$$	a_i - average dissimilarity of ith data point to all other points in the same cluster; b_i - minimum of average dissimilarity of ith data point to all data points in other cluster
	Fowlkes-Mallows (FM) Index	$$FM = \sqrt{\frac{TP}{TP + FP}\frac{TP}{TP + FN}}$$	TP - number of true positives; FP - number of false positives; FN - number of false negatives
Soft Clustering	DB Index	$$DB = \frac{1}{c}\sum_{i=1, i \neq j}^{c} max\left(\frac{\sigma_i + \sigma_j}{d\left(c_i, c_j\right)}\right)$$	c - number of clusters; σ_i - average distance of all samples in cluster i to cluster center c_i; σ_j - average distance of all samples in cluster j to cluster center c_j; $d\left(c_i, c_j\right)$ - distance of cluster centers c_i and c_j

Table 7. Results of the preprocessing

Corpus	Total No. of Documents	Total No. of Terms After Tokenization	Total No. of Terms After Stop-word removal
Neoplasms	450	42077	16917
Viral Diseases	300	54967	31541
Cardio Vascular Diseases	350	49292	28228
Eye Infection	500	59943	36876
Respiratory Diseases	400	51569	27948

The performance of the proposed concept based smoothing model is evaluated for clustering the medical documents using the abstracts collected from the PubMed repository. The concept based smoothing model is developed with $\alpha = 0.5$ and $\gamma = 0.5$ (Cai, Liu, & Yin, 2007). Table 8 shows the weight information for a query term based on term; concept and smoothing from randomly selected 3 documents of the five document corpuses.

Evaluation Based on Silhouette Index

Figure 2 and Figure 3 show the performance of the silhouette index based on the Euclidean distance and Pearson Correlation Coefficient for the given dataset using the hard-clustering algorithms with the traditional term based, LSI-based and the proposed concept based indexing approaches. In Figure 2, the highest value for the silhouette index is 0.5938. In Figure 3, the maximum value for the silhouette index is 0.6874. It is observed from the experimental results that the proposed concept-based indexing performs better than the traditional term-based and LSI based indexing methods starting from the cluster size 3 onwards.

Figure 4 shows the goodness of the concept based smoothing when compared to the concept based indexing method for the given dataset. For the cluster size 5, K-Means yields maximum silhouette index, 0.7011 which reflects the good quality of clusters obtained using smoothing model. Figure 5 shows the performance comparison between the concept-based indexing and concept based smoothing approach for clustering the medical documents. It is observed from the experimental results that the concept based smoothing model comparatively produces better quality clusters than the concept based indexing method. It is also found that, regarding the proposed concept-based smoothing; both K-Means and hierarchical

Table 8. Term, concept and smoothing based weights of sample documents

Doc. Id	Query Term/Concept	Tf-idf	Concept Weight	Concept Based Smoothing Weight
C21	Cancer	0.0000	0.2816	0.3156
D19	Dengue	0.0124	0.2673	0.3021
H65	Cardiovascular	0.0427	0.4133	0.5683
E8	Conjunctivitis	0.0000	0.3728	0.4633
A48	Asthma	0.0348	0.6144	0.7863

Figure 2.

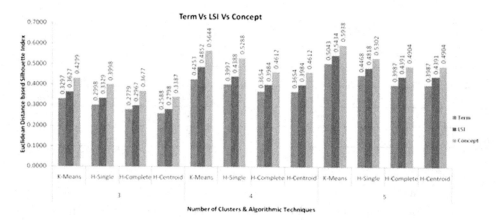

Figure 3.

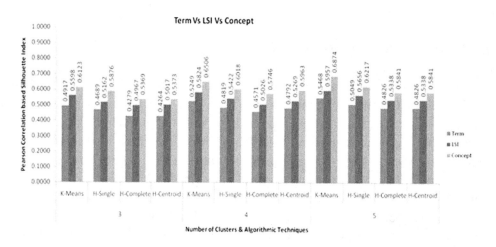

Figure 4.

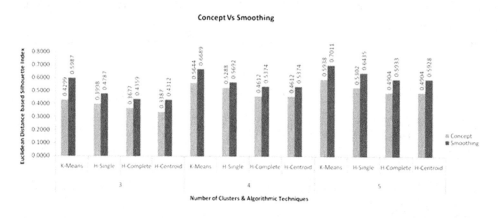

Figure 5.

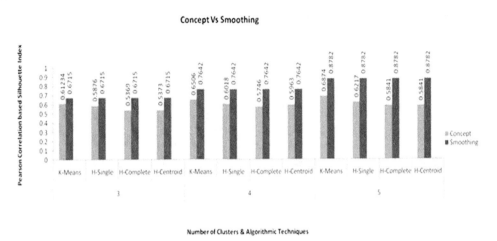

group of algorithms are producing good quality clusters starting from the cluster size 3 onwards. The maximum silhouette index is obtained for the cluster size 5 is 0.8782.

Evaluation Based on FM Index

Figure 6 and Figure 7 show the performance comparison between the proposed concepts-based indexing and the traditional BOW indexing techniques such as term based and LSI methods. In the concept-based indexing, K-Means produces better quality clusters with the maximum index value as 0.6988 for Euclidean distance and hierarchical single linkage produces better quality cluster for the index 0.6919 for Pearson coefficient.

Figure 6.

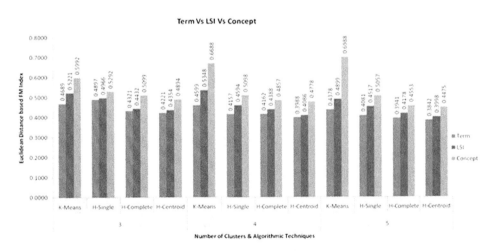

Figure 7.

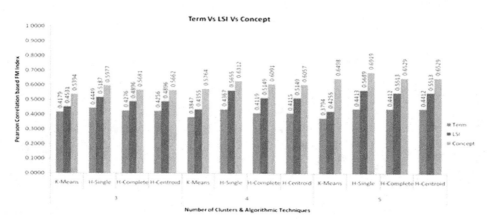

Figure 8 shows the goodness of the concept based smoothing when compared to the concept based indexing method for the given dataset. For the cluster size 5, K-Means yields maximum FM index with the value of 0.8075 which reflects the good quality of clusters obtained using smoothing model. Figure 9 shows the performance comparison between the concept-based indexing and concept based smoothing approach for clustering the medical documents in the experimental dataset. It is observed from the experimental results that the concept based smoothing model comparatively produces better quality clusters than the concept based indexing method. It is also found that, regarding the proposed concept-based smoothing, hierarchical group of algorithms are producing good quality clusters starting from the cluster size 3 onwards. The maximum FM index is obtained for the cluster size 5 is 0.8789.

Evaluation Based on DB Index

Figure 10 shows the comparison of the DB index for the proposed concept-based indexing and the traditional BOW indexing methods. It is observed from the comparisons that the DB index decreases gradually as the number of clusters increases to obtain better clustering results until it reaches its lowest value of 0.67 for the experimental dataset. These comparisons show that the values of DB Index approach

Figure 8.

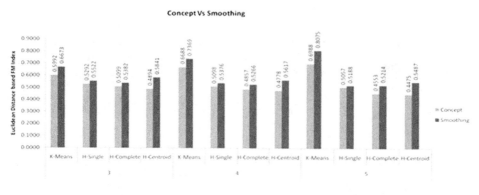

Figure 9.

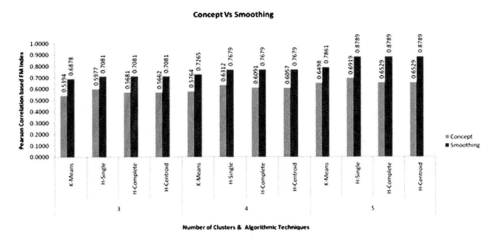

a lower value for the cluster size 5 in both of the data sets. Figure 11 shows the comparison of the DB index for the concept-based indexing with the proposed concept-based smoothing for the experimental dataset. It is observed from the comparisons that the DB index decreases gradually as the number of clusters increases to obtain better clustering results until it reaches its lowest value of 0.39.

SUMMARY

The greatest disruption resulting from the rise of cognitive computing will likely occur in the field of health care. It is observed from the existing literature that cognitive healthcare assessment support has the benefits of improving patient health and reducing the costs of missed diagnoses and optimal treatment plans. Ultimately, the purpose of cognitive computing in healthcare is about producing better, best-practice, decision-relevant information for everyone in the health system. Biomedical literature is the primary repository of biomedical knowledge in which PubMed is the most absolute database for collecting, organizing and analyzing textual knowledge. In this work concept-based indexing and concept

Figure 10.

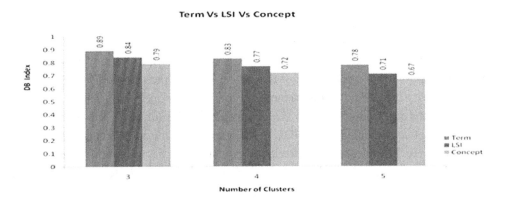

Figure 11.

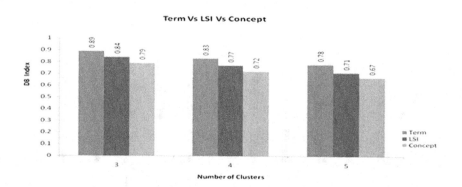

based smoothing are employed for indexing the medical documents. The concept weights are assigned based on the semantic relations that are derived from the MeSH ontology through concept mapping.

The semantic based indexing approach is developed for clustering the medical documents based on the concepts extracted from the domain ontology called MeSH using the semantic relations. The individual concept weight within the particular document is computed using frequency and weight information of the semantically related terms. A document may have multiple concepts. The concept with highest weight represents the document is semantically belongs to that concept.

The phrases also have significant contribution in the identification of the concepts in medical documents. It is observed from the literature. In the biomedical literature, more disease names are available in the form of compound words. The smoothing approach finds the concept weight using keywords and phrases in the document. The simple concept translation model is obtained using the maximum likelihood estimator document model with the background smoothing model. The phrases within the documents are considered using n-gram techniques. It resolves the limitations related to the sparsity of the core medical terms within the documents.

The proposed concept based smoothing model is implemented as the mixture models of two components namely the simple concept translation model and the multiword phrase translation model. The simple concept translation model is obtained using the maximum likelihood estimator document model with the background smoothing model. The phrases within the documents are considered using tri-gram techniques. Both the terms and the phrases are given equal importance in this smoothing process.

Table 9 shows the fuzzy validity measure for the traditional indexing methods and the proposed methods. Concept based smoothing improves the DB index for 71.79 percentage from the concept based indexing approach. Table 10 shows the silhouette index and FM index for the given dataset for the traditional indexing methods and the proposed methods using the K-Means and hierarchical clustering algorithms which use Euclidean distance measure and Pearson correlation coefficient for the cluster size 5.

Regarding the proposed concept-based smoothing; K-Means performs well in comparison to the other hierarchical group of algorithms irrespective of the cluster size for the silhouette index with Euclidean distance as the similarity measure. Both K-Means and hierarchical group of algorithms are producing good quality clusters starting from the cluster size 3 onwards for the silhouette index with respect to the Pearson correlation coefficient. For the FM index, K-means outperforms all other algorithms with respect to the Euclidean distance. For the Pearson correlation coefficient, it is observed from the experimental results that hierarchical group of algorithms are producing good quality clusters starting from the clus-

Table 9. Fuzzy validity measures for the various indexing methods

Indexing Method	DB Index
Term	0.78
LSI	0.71
Concept Based indexing	0.67
Concept Based Smoothing	0.39

Table 10. Euclidean distance-based performance measures for hard clustering

Indexing Method	Technique	Euclidean Distance		Pearson	
		Silhouette Index	FM Index	Silhouette Index	FM Index
Term	K-means	0.5043	0.4378	0.5468	0.3794
	Hierarchical Single	0.4468	0.4081	0.5049	0.4413
	Hierarchical Complete	0.3987	0.3941	0.4826	0.4412
	Hierarchical Centroid	0.3987	0.3842	0.4826	0.4412
LSI	K-means	0.5434	0.4899	0.5957	0.4255
	Hierarchical Single	0.4818	0.4517	0.5656	0.5689
	Hierarchical Complete	0.4391	0.4178	0.5338	0.5513
	Hierarchical Centroid	0.4391	0.3998	0.5338	0.5513
Concept Based Indexing	K-means	0.5938	0.6988	0.6874	0.6498
	Hierarchical Single	0.5302	0.5057	0.6217	0.6919
	Hierarchical Complete	0.4904	0.4553	0.5841	0.6529
	Hierarchical Centroid	0.4904	0.4475	0.5841	0.6529
Concept Based Smoothing	K-means	0.7011	0.8075	0.8782	0.7861
	Hierarchical Single	0.6435	0.5188	0.8782	0.8789
	Hierarchical Complete	0.5933	0.5214	0.8782	0.8789
	Hierarchical Centroid	0.5928	0.5487	0.8782	0.8789

Table 11. Percentage of improvement in silhouette index and FM index for concept vs. smoothing

Index	Clustering Algorithms							
	Euclidean Distance				Pearson Correlation			
Silhouette Index	K-Means	Hierarchical Single	Hierarchical Complete	Hierarchical Centroid	K-Means	Hierarchical Single	Hierarchical Complete	Hierarchical Centroid
	15.30	17.61	17.34	17.27	21.73	29.21	33.49	33.49
FM Index	13.46	2.53	12.68	18.44	17.34	21.28	25.71	25.71

ter size 3 onwards with maximum FM index values. Table 11 shows the percentage of improvement in silhouette index and FM index using the concept-based indexing and concept-based smoothing for the given dataset for the cluster size 5.

The experimental results confirm that concept based smoothing method via a combination of knowledge and corpus-based semantics improves clustering performance over previously proposed concept-based indexing for semantic enhancements. The indexing of documents based on the terms and topic signatures improves the significance of the core words.

REFERENCES

Anandakumar, H., & Umamaheswari, K. (2018). Cooperative Spectrum Handovers in Cognitive Radio Networks. In Cognitive Radio, Mobile Communications and Wireless Networks (pp. 47–63). Springer. doi:10.1007/978-3-319-91002-4_3

Anandakumar, H., Umamaheswari, K., & Arulmurugan, R. (2019). A Study on Mobile IPv6 Handover in Cognitive Radio Networks. In *International Conference on Computer Networks and Communication Technologies* (pp. 399-408). Springer Singapore. doi:10.1007/978-981-10-8681-6_36

Baziz, M., Boughanem, M., & Traboulsi, S. (2005). A concept-based approach for indexing documents in IR. In INFORSID (pp. 489-504).

Cai, J., Liu, Y., & Yin, J. (2007). An improved semantic smoothing model for model-based document clustering. In *Proceedings of the Eighth ACIS International Conference on Software Engineering, Artificial Intelligence, Networking, and Parallel Distributed Computing* (Vol. 3, pp. 670–675).

Chim, H., & Deng, X. (2008). Efficient phrase-based document similarity for clustering. *IEEE Transactions on Knowledge and Data Engineering*, 20(9), 1217–1229. doi:10.1109/TKDE.2008.50

Dinh, D., Tamine, L., & Boubekeur, F. (2013). Factors affecting the effectiveness of biomedical document indexing and retrieval based on terminologies. *Artificial Intelligence in Medicine*, 57(2), 155–167. doi:10.1016/j.artmed.2012.08.006 PMID:23092678

Fang, R., Pouyanfar, S., Yang, Y., Chen, S. C., & Iyengar, S. S. (2016). Computational health informatics in the big data age: A survey. *ACM Computing Surveys*, 49(1), 12. doi:10.1145/2932707

Funk, M. E., & Reid, C. A. (1983). Indexing consistency in MEDLINE. *Bulletin of the Medical Library Association*, 71(2), 176–183. PMID:6344946

Haldorai, A., & Ramu, A. (2018). An Intelligent-Based Wavelet Classifier for Accurate Prediction of Breast Cancer. In *Intelligent Multidimensional Data and Image Processing* (pp. 306–319). doi:10.4018/978-1-5225-5246-8.ch012

Hersh, W. (2008). *Information Retrieval: A Health and Biomedical Perspective: A Health and Biomedical Perspective*. Springer Science & Business Media.

Huang, A. (2008). Similarity measures for text document clustering. In *Proceedings of the sixth New Zealand computer science research student conference (NZCSRSC2008),* Christchurch, New Zealand (pp. 49-56).

Imambi, S. S., & Sudha, T. (2013). Extraction of biomedical information from MEDLINE documents – A text mining approach. *International journal of Science Environmental Technology, 2*(2), 267–274.

Kamaljeet, S. V., & Bhattacharyya, P. (2009). Context-Sensitive Semantic Smoothing using Semantically Relatable Sequences. In *Proceedings of International Joint conference on Artificial Intelligence (IJCAI'09)* (pp. 1580-1585).

Khare, A., & Jadhav, A. N. (2010). An efficient concept-based mining model for enhancing text clustering. *International Journal of Advances in Engineering and Technology, 2*(4), 196–201.

Li, Q., & Wu, Y. F. B. (2006). Identifying important concepts from medical documents. *Journal of Biomedical Informatics, 39*(6), 668–679. doi:10.1016/j.jbi.2006.02.001 PMID:16545986

Li, Y., Chung, S. M., & Holt, J. D. (2008). Text document clustering based on frequent word meaning sequences. *Data & Knowledge Engineering, 64*(1), 381–404. doi:10.1016/j.datak.2007.08.001

Lin, Y. S., Jiang, J. Y., & Lee, S. J. (2013). A similarity measure for text classification and clustering. *IEEE Transactions on Knowledge and Data Engineering, 26*(7), 1–15.

Nasir, J. A., Varlamis, I., Karim, A., & Tsatsaronis, G. (2013). Semantic smoothing for text clustering. *Knowledge-Based Systems, 54*, 216–229. doi:10.1016/j.knosys.2013.09.012

Papageorgiou, E. I. (2011). A new methodology for decisions in medical informatics using fuzzy cognitive maps based on fuzzy rule-extraction techniques. *Applied Soft Computing, 11*(1), 500–513. doi:10.1016/j.asoc.2009.12.010

Sebastiani, F. (2002). Machine learning in automated text categorization. *ACM Computing Surveys, 34*(1), 1–47. doi:10.1145/505282.505283

Subhadra, K., Shashi, M., & Ap, V. (2012). Hybrid distance based document clustering with keyword and phrase indexing. *International Journal of Computer Science Issues, 9*(2), 345–350.

Tar, H. H., & Nyaunt, T. T. S. (2011). Enhancing traditional text documents clustering based on Ontology. *International Journal of Computers and Applications, 33*(10), 38–42.

Verma, K. S., & Bhattacharyya, P. (2009). Context-Sensitive Semantic Smoothing using Semantically Relatable Sequences. In IJCAI (pp. 1580–1585).

Watrous-deVersterre, L., Wang, C., & Song, M. (2012). Concept chaining utilizing meronyms in text characterization. In *Proceedings of the twelfth ACM/IEEE-CS joint conference on Digital Libraries* (pp. 241-248). ACM.

West, V. L., Borland, D., West, D., & Hammond, W. E. (2015). An evaluation of machine learning methods and visualization of results to characterize large healthcare document collections.

Zhou, X., Hu, X., Zhang, X., Lin, X., & Song, I. Y. (2006). Context-sensitive semantic smoothing for the language modeling approach to genomic IR. In *Proceedings of the 29th annual international ACM SIGIR conference on Research and development in information retrieval* (pp. 170-177).

Zhu, S., Zeng, J., & Mamitsuka, H. (2009). Enhancing MEDLINE document clustering by incorporating MeSH semantic similarity. *Bioinformatics*, *25*(15), 1944–1951. doi:10.1093/bioinformatics/btp338 PMID:19497938

Chapter 4

Efficient Space Communication and Management (SCOaM) Using Cognitive Radio Networks Based on Deep Learning Techniques:
Cognitive Radio in Space Communication

Suriya Murugan
Bannari Amman Institute of Technology, India

Sumithra M. G.
Bannari Amman Institute of Technology, India

ABSTRACT

The future of space communications has evolved towards being cognitive in order to improve energy and spectrum efficiency. Nowadays, near-Earth space satellites for weather, civil defense, and public commercial sectors are rapidly increasing, thereby resulting in congestion. Cognitive digital radio is a form of dynamic wireless communication in which a transceiver can intelligently detect the parts of communication channels that are currently not in use and instantly move into vacant channels while avoiding occupied ones. A challenge for communication between satellites and ground terminals involves calibrating both the time and frequency channels during rapid relative movement. A more dynamic and highly-precise algorithm for enhancing communication between satellites and base station terminals such as deep learning in cognitive radios is proposed that enables significant degree of automation in the space communication networks where spectrum interference is a key issue.

DOI: 10.4018/978-1-5225-7522-1.ch004

INTRODUCTION

Communication is vitally important to astronauts while they are in space. Not only does it allow them to talk to their friends and family back home, it also allows them to communicate with the team of experts on the ground that helps them carry out their mission safely. Communication in low Earth orbit, where the International Space Station (ISS) orbits, is almost instant. When travelling further into space, communication becomes a bit tricky. The further out you travel in space, the more issues you have with communication. For example, it could take 20 minutes to send or receive a message between Earth and Mars. The majority of space missions never return to Earth. Thus, after launch, a spacecraft's tracking and communications systems is the only means with which to interact with it. In addition, any issues with the spacecraft can only be diagnosed, repaired, or mitigated via the communications system. Without a consistently effective and efficient communications system, a successful mission would be impossible.

Space missions are designed several years before deployment, using technology that is state of the art at the time of design. Once deployed, the equipment cannot be reconfigured easily without risking the loss of communication. Suppose that a future mission uses a new modulation scheme. Without cognitive capabilities, all in-orbit hardware will need to be updated with information about this scheme to co-exist. Similarly, future traffic patterns, regulatory policies or spectrum sharing guidelines are not available several years in advance. Therefore, cognition-based autonomy is especially necessary in space networks.

A cognitive radio has the potential to learn and adapt to its operating environment without intervention from human operators. Current space networks are manually configured. The Cognitive networks and cognitive radios have received a lot of attention due to their promised feature of autonomy, cost, and scalability. Adaptive radio software could circumvent the harmful effects of space weather, increasing science and exploration data returns (Chenji, Stewart, Wu, Javaid, Devabhaktuni & Bhasin, 2016). A cognitive radio network could also suggest alternate data paths to the ground. These processes could prioritise and route data through multiple paths simultaneously to avoid interference. The cognitive radio's artificial intelligence could also allocate ground station downlinks just hours in advance, as opposed to weeks, leading to more efficient scheduling. Cognitive radio may make communications network operations more efficient by decreasing the need for human intervention. An intelligent radio could adapt to new electromagnetic landscapes without human help and predict common operational settings for different environments, automating time-consuming processes previously handled by humans.

SPACE COMMUNICATION CHALLENGES

Demands placed on space communications systems are continuously increasing. NASA estimates that the space communications capability will need to increase nearly by a factor of 10 each for the next three decades. This trend is in step with our increasing knowledge of the cosmos -- as more detailed scientific questions arise, the ability to answer them requires ever more sophisticated instruments that generate even more data. New high-resolution hyperspectral imagers put further demands on their communications system, requiring even higher data rates.

An important challenge for deep space communications systems is to maintain their extreme reliability and versatility, in order to accommodate the long system lifetimes of most planetary missions. These challenges must be met with a communications system that requires maximum utilization of minimal available spectrum. The Space Network consists of antenna placed at three locations around the world and forms the ground segment of the communications system for space missions. These facilities are approximately 120 longitude degrees apart on Earth and provide continuous coverage and tracking for deep space missions. A large portion of deep space communications research addresses communications system engineering, radios, antennas, transmitters, signal detectors, modulation techniques, channel coding theory, data compression, and simulation.

As the data needs of users grow exponentially ach minute, wireless networks such as terrestrial, aerial, underground, underwater, and deep space are suffering from lack of spectrum. As indicated by the FCC Spectrum Policy Task Force, much of the billion-dollar spectrum bands sit idle most of the time. This scarcity affects both the commercial and military satellite communications sectors. Recent research has proved the efficiency of methods such as dynamic spectrum access in addressing spectrum shortfall and increasing network performance. A unique aspect of satellite networks is the cost of deployment: the cost (per kg.) to launch a satellite into LEO/GEO costs anywhere from $1000 to $20,000. Therefore, apart from minimal changes, it is cost prohibitive to modify the software or hardware of a satellite once it is in orbit. Given the risk of loss of communication due to misconfiguration because of buggy software, existing technology has relied on manual operation of satellite networks.

Deep space communications naturally causes several networking challenges including disconnection orbital, scheduling, buffering management, priorities, latency seconds to minutes and beyond, security, link management, routing, handling the uplink/downlink asymmetry, and optical and RF ground station handoffs.

However, recent successes of deep learning and machine learning in areas facilitate towards improving the cognitive ability of space communication based on available challenges (Abbas, Nasser & El Ahmad, 2015). It is now possible for not only autonomy due to the programmed operation, but also cognitive autonomy where a satellite can sense, learn and adapt to its environment without explicit programming. Almost all of the spectrum stakeholders have an ongoing interest in cognitive approaches to dynamic spectrum access in contested and denied electromagnetic environments due to intentional or unintentional spectrum interference as well as sensor resource management. Various predefined objectives of intelligent channel sensing include ensuring (i) spectrum interference and availability (ii) minimize communication delay between inter- satellite and satellite – terrestrial system to provide data delivery (iii) increase network speed and coverage to reduce transmit delay and (iv) optimize battery consumption while reducing resource consumption and operational costs.

BACKGROUND

The concept of cognitive communications defines communications proceeded by cognitive radios, which are software-defined radios that are capable of learning from and exchanging information with the environment. While space communications have witnessed rapid development in recent years, being cognitive is important to future space communications for improved energy and spectrum efficiency. Unlike in ground communications where signal propagation delays can usually be ignored, cases are much more complicated in space communication between satellites and ground based user terminals. A satellite moves at a speed near the first cosmic velocity will introduce fast varying propagation delays and doppler shifts, so a first challenge in the road to cognitive space communications is to achieve space-ground timing and frequency synchronization.

Down Time is defined as the time at a spatial location, when radio transmissions (using the electromagnetic waves) by the licensed users are totally stopped. Up Time is defined as the time at a spatial location, when radio transmissions by licensed users are totally utilizing the spectrum to the maximum potential. These Up Time and Down Time can occur over various diametrically opposite spatial locations on the earth. So, the opportunistic spectrum access can be implemented on global scale. In addition, the Downtimes at various locations on planet keep shifting from one place to another.

The cognitive and remote networks are connected to Common Gateway Interface (CGI). This is a crucial design block, which handles the complex responsibility of interfacing the network with the long-distance links. The long-distance links can be terrestrial or satellite links. The Coordinator is the heart of the architecture (Mansour, Mesleh & Abaza, 2016). During the busy time at "Cognitive Network" region, meaning, all its bands are full of primary users, the cognitive network would send a request to coordinator for enquiring about the availability of any vacant bands.

Terrestrial Satellite System

The concepts the coexistence between satellite and terrestrial communications is possible with minimal interference (Suriya, Sugandhanaa, Vaishnavi & Bharathy, 2016). Satellite systems suffer from many drawbacks such as technological complexity, high costs, and deep fading at high frequencies. Most successful satellite systems such as television broadcast and back-hauling of data in remote areas have up to now extensively exploit these advantages in a competitive way with respect to classical terrestrial networks. Other satellite systems providing for instance mobile telephony or aircraft telecommunications services have suffered from severe concurrence or insufficient market and have not enjoyed the expected success.

Telecommunication networks are making its progress and showing lights on systems that will work on different technologies such as Wi-Fi, WiMAX, 2G/3G, LTE, and satellite. In order to proficiently synchronize the working of the different technologies, the idea of hybrid networks is being sincerely taken into account. Hybrid networks have the ability to efficiently provide cost - effective solution to employ satellite communications for not only broadcast and multicast services but also for mobile services. The principal driving factor is to facilitate and then utilize different wireless communication systems to provide varied range of services to users in most efficient and seamless way, by considering signal quality (coverage), handover, traffic congestion conditions, and cost issues. The fundamental capabilities of satellite networks, for instance very large coverage areas, speed of implementation and inherent multicasting and broadcasting capabilities make them the prime choice to serve niche areas like coverage in planes, navy ships, hostile environments etc. Despite all this, satellite systems suffer from many drawbacks such as technological complexity, high costs, and deep fading at high frequencies. Therefore, the idea of jointly benefiting from the advantages and capabilities of both terrestrial and satellite telecommunication systems are gaining much impetus

TYPES OF SERVICES

Broadcasting Services

One of the main, traditional roles of the satellite systems is broadcasting or multicasting of the same content to the users over a wide geographical area. In this case, requirement is to combine a satellite and a terrestrial component to broadcast media content including TV programs and radio, to vehicular or even handheld devices. Broadcast services generally provide unidirectional satellite link between the network components and the satellite segments, mainly because of the higher bandwidth consumption in such an implementation is on the downlink (i.e. from network to user equipment) whereas the bandwidth requirement on the uplink is very less and hence, can be managed by the terrestrial component of the hybrid architecture.

The above Figure 1 explains the satellite broadcasting communication. Here the satellite broadcasts its signals and information to the antennas. The satellite gains information from the base station that has to be distributed to the end-users. The antennas pass its signals to its nearest base station. The base station provides a Wi-MAX transmission over that particular cellular network. Then the signal is passed as radio signals or for TV broadcast or for the purpose of Mobile communication.

Multicast Services

In computing network, multicast (one-to-many or many-to-many distribution) is a group communication where information is addressed to a group of destination users simultaneously. Group communication may either be as application layer multicast or network assisted multicast, where the latter makes it possible for the source to efficiently transfer to the group in one transmission. Copies are automatically generated in other network elements, such as routers, switches and cellular network base stations, but it is only limited to the network segments that currently contain the members of the group. Network assisted multicast may be used at the internet layer using IP multicast, which is often employed in Internet Protocol (IP) applications of streaming media, such as television, internet, telecommunications scheduled content (but not media-on-demand) and multipoint videoconferencing, but also for ghost distribution

Figure 1. Broadcasting signals from one terminal to other

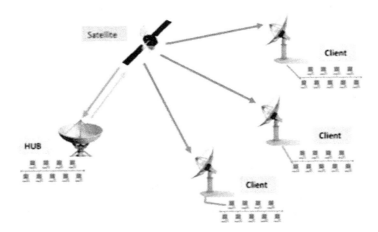

of backup disk images to multiple computers simultaneously. In IP multicast the implementation of the multicast concept occurs at the IP routing level, where routers create optimal distribution paths for datagram's forwarded to a multicast destination address. Implementation of the Network assisted multicast may also be done at the Data Link Layer using one-to-many addressing and switching such as Ethernet multicast addressing, Asynchronous Transfer Mode (ATM) point-to-multipoint virtual circuits (P2MP) or Infiniband multicast. In the below given Figure 2 multicasting is done were the data is sent to a group from source to destination.

IP Multicast

IP multicast is one of the techniques for one-to-many communication over an IP infrastructure in a computing network is indicated in Figure 2. The destination nodes leave messages, for example in the case of Internet television when the user changes from one Television channel to another.

IP multicast scales to a larger receiver population by not requiring the predictable knowledge of whom or how many receivers are available. Multicast uses network infrastructure efficiently by seeking the source to send a packet at an instance, even if it needs to be delivered to a large number of receivers. The node in the network takes care of multiplication of the packet to reach multiple receivers only when it is necessary.

Application Layer Multicast

Application layer multicast-over-unicast overlay services for application level group communication are widely used. Noticeably the Internet Relay Chat (IRC), which is busier and scales better for large numbers of small groups. IRC implements a single spanning tree between its overlay networks for all conference groups. However, this leads to suboptimal routing for some of the conference groups. Additionally, IRC keeps a large amount of distributed states that limit growth of an IRC network, leading to fractioning into many distributed non-interconnected networks. The lesser known PSYC technology uses custom multicast strategies for every conference. Also, some peer-to-peer technologies include the multicast concept while distributing contents to multiple recipients, known as peer-casting.

Figure 2. Multicasting of the information from source to destination

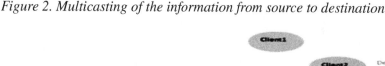
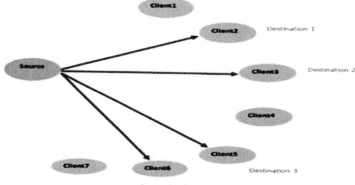

Multicast Over Wireless Networks and Cable-TV

Wireless communications as well as cable TV bus networks are widely broadcasting media, i.e. multipoint channels, especially if the antennas are omni-directional and radio/TV transmitters covering a region from a broadcasting network that sends the same content. However, the communication service provided may be unicast, multicast as well as broadcast, depending whether the data that has to be sent to some specific address or a specific group or to all receivers in that specific network.

COGNITIVE RADIOS IN SCOaM (SPACE COMMUNICATION AND MANAGEMENT)

Cognitive Handover

Cognitive radio (CR) is a formation of wireless communication in which a transceiver can intelligently detect Primary and secondary communication channels are in use and which are not, and instantaneously move into available channels while avoiding unavailable ones. Cognitive Approach is followed were when the primary users are not using their space of channel and it is available as free chambers, these free chambers can be allotted for the secondary users in order to use these unused spaces. This mechanism is called as handover mechanism. It happens dynamically and referred as Cognitive Handover. This optimizes the use of accessible radio-frequency (RF) spectrum while minimizing nosiness to other users. There are two control models for opportunistic spectrum access or flexible spectrum usage namely the centralized control model and the distributed control model. For each of the control scenarios, spectrum sensing is a critical aspect of the control of cognitive radios and policy-based adaptive radios which employ software defined radio technology. In Figure 3 the load balancing concept is explained with the help of Cognitive handover.

Centralized Method

The centralized control model is one in which the management of spectrum opportunities are controlled by a single entity or a node which has been inferred to as the spectrum broker. The spectrum broker is responsible for deciding which spectrum opportunities can be reutilized and by which radios in a net-

Figure 3. Working of cognitive radio

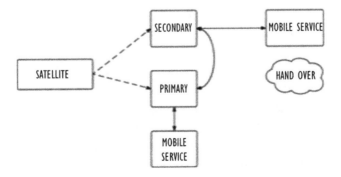

work. A central broker may use sensors from the distributed nodes or may use other means for sensing the network and spectrum awareness. Centralized control is real-time spectrum markets is one of the application.

Distributed Method

The second exploited spectrum access or flexible spectrum usage control model is the distributed control model. For some real-time scenarios, the distributed control may be between co-operative radio access networks. In this model the interaction that takes place is "peer-to-peer." In other words, the cognitive radio or policy-based adaptive radio nodes in the network are collectively responsible for identifying and negotiating use of underutilized spectrum.

IEEE 802.16 PROTOCOL

The IEEE 802.16 standards defines how wireless traffic move between subscribe equipment and core networks (Suriya, Swathi & Veeralakshmi, 2018). The IEEE Standard 802.16 is a new standard when compared to existing standards. The 802.16 standard is commonly referred to as Wireless MAN because its goal is to implement a set of broadband wireless access standards for wireless metropolitan area networks. The features of IEEE 802.16 are it uses microwave for the wireless transfer of data and specifies a frequency band in range between 2gHZ to 66gHZ.it also has the high-speed wireless networking and effective in cost. It is easy for installing purpose but leads to low installation cost, when compared to fiber, cable or DSL deployments.

The IEEE 802(16G) is effectively used in remote sensing with protocol management Techniques. This technique is used to increase the frequency band range when compared with the 802.16. It is defined in the original mobile specification; the handover process defines a "backbone" method for requesting mobile subscriber information. When the specification states that the base station may request MS information from a serving BS, this does not mean that a servings BS should provide it. A base station needs the ability to determine when it should refuse to provide MS information to a requesting BS. The handover description in 802.16 is high level and the 802.16g specifies what this request and response.

IEEE 802.16g: Terrestrial Satellite

The IEEE 802.16g appears as the good candidate for handover management in future integrated satellite/terrestrial system. The advantages of satellite communication over terrestrial communication are, the coverage area of a satellite greatly exceeds that of a terrestrial system. Transmission cost of a satellite is independent of the distance from the center of the coverage area. Satellite to satellite communication is very precise, higher bandwidths are available for use. Service types of satellite are, FSS (Fixed Service Satellite) the example of FSS is Point to Point communication. BSS (Broadcast Service Satellite) Example for BSS is Satellite Television/Radio. It is also called as Direct broadcast service (DBS). MSS (Mobile Service Satellite) example for MSS is Satellite phones. Satellite is becoming increasingly uneconomic for most trunk telephony route, but there are still good reasons to use satellite for telephony such as, thin routes, diversity, very long distance, traffic and remote locations. Land mobile /personal communications in urban areas of developed countries new terrestrial infrastructure is likely to dominate example GSM

(Anandakumar, Umamaheswari & Arulmurugan, 2018) but, satellites can provide fill-in as terrestrial networks are implemented, also provide similar services in rural areas and underdeveloped countries. The IEEE802.16g is used to provide the efficient mobile service in terrestrial areas. It has the higher bandwidth when compared to the 802.16. Despite all these, satellite system suffers from many drawbacks such as technological complexity, high cost, and deep fading at high frequencies.

Applications of Terrestrial Satellite

The applications of terrestrial satellite are online mapping, GIS applications, remote sensing, land management, observation of natural disasters, probability modeling, damage management and also used in military communication, transportation, civil engineering, agriculture, car navigation. It provides efficient handover. Wang, Chen & Gao (2015) report that IEEE 802.16g has the ability to provide the efficient mobile service in the terrestrial areas using the 802.16g module.

DEEP LEARNING TECHNIQUES

Need for Intelligent CR

NASA spacecrafts, which typically rely on human-controlled radio systems to communicate with Earth, are now looking at cognitive radios. The infusion of artificial intelligence into space communications networks to meet demand and increase efficiency. Specific portions of the electromagnetic spectrum used for communications to various users (Haldorai & Ramu, 2018). However, such channels are limited in number and can cause a bottleneck in the era of increasing communications. Software-defined radios such as cognitive radio use artificial intelligence to employ underutilised portions of the electromagnetic spectrum without human intervention. These "white spaces" are currently unused (but already licensed) segments of the spectrum. The US Federal Communications Commission (FCC) permits a cognitive radio to use the frequency while unused by its primary user until the user becomes active again. In order to understand how to actually analyze signals in intelligent way we need a cognitive engine powered by a machine or Deep learning algorithm to observe, analyze, predict and make decision (Suriya, Anandakumar & Arulmurugan, 2016). But the main difference between machine learning and deep learning is features engineering where in machine learning, the learning model decides to classify the situation based on fixed set of features (observed/measured parameters) but in deep learning, the algorithm has to decide which features fit into this situation in order to classify so learning process is based on features selection and classification. This learning process takes place always in Radios to create a radio which is brain empowered (cognitive radio) so we can think of it as a way to optimize resources and use the radio resources with the full capacity and in optimum way (Jhajj & Saluja, 2017).

Classification of Deep Learning Techniques

Figure 4 illustrates the classification various classification of deep learning techniques based on supervised and unsupervised learning mechanism for cognitive radios (Feng, 2012; Girimonte & Izzo, 2007). These intelligent techniques can form the basis of building an optimization algorithm. Artificial intelligence aims at making machines perform tasks in a manner similar to an expert. The intelligent machine will perceive its environment and take actions to maximize its own utility. The central problems in artificial intelligence include (Anandakumar & Umamaheswari, 2018) deduction, reasoning, problem solving, knowledge representation, and learning. The major steps in machine learning in cognitive radios are: (1) sensing the radio frequency (RF) parameters such as channel quality, (2) observing the environment and analyzing its feedback as responses, (3) learning, (4) keeping the decisions and observations for updating the model and obtaining better accuracy in future decision-making, and finally (5) deciding on issues of resource management and adjusting the transmission errors accordingly (Anandakumar & Umamaheswari, 2017).

SUMMARY

With the satellite communication in increase, Earth Observation Satellite-based (EOS) sensors have emerged into a rapid source of multi-sensor, multi-resolution and multispectral geospatial information for decision making in varying application domains. Space communication networks thus requires spectrum sensing, dynamic spectrum allocation, and use of spectrum databases in-order to alleviate issues like (i) spectrum interference (ii) minimize communication delay between inter- satellite and satellite – terrestrial system (iii) increase network speed and coverage and (iv) optimize battery consumption. All these factors can be improved for the single link connectivity and cognitive networking techniques for the multiple link connectivity by adapting Cognitive radio communication for space satellites. A new wide range of deep learning algorithms is analysed and proposed in this chapter which have emerged from evolutionary algorithms and CR based natural phenomenon is a good candidate for cognitive space communication applications such as satellite mobile Communication.

Figure 4. Deep learning techniques for cognitive radio

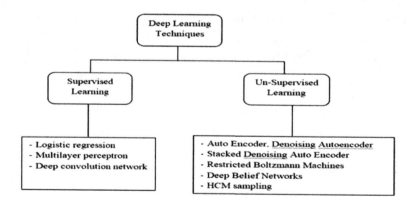

REFERENCES

Abbas, N., Nasser, Y., & El Ahmad, K. (2015). Recent advances on artificial intelligence and learning techniques in cognitive radio networks. *EURASIP Journal on Wireless Communications and Networking*, *174*(1). doi:10.118613638-015-0381-7

Anandakumar,, H.,, & Umamaheswari,, K. (2014). Energy efficient network selection using 802.16g based GSM technology. *Journal of Computational Science*, *10*(5), 745–754. doi:10.3844/jcssp.2014.745.754

Anandakumar, H., & Umamaheswari, K. (2017). A bio-inspired swarm intelligence technique for social aware cognitive radio handovers. *Computers & Electrical Engineering*, (Sep). doi:10.1016/j.compeleceng.2017.09.016

Anandakumar, H., & Umamaheswari, K. (2018). Cooperative Spectrum Handovers in Cognitive Radio Networks. In Cognitive Radio, Mobile Communications and Wireless Networks (pp. 47–63). Springer. doi:10.1007/978-3-319-91002-4_3

Anandakumar, H., Umamaheswari, K., & Arulmurugan, R. (2019). A Study on Mobile IPv6 Handover in Cognitive Radio Networks. In *International Conference on Computer Networks and Communication Technologies* (pp. 399-408). Springer Singapore. doi:10.1007/978-981-10-8681-6_36

Bhatia, N., & Rana, M. C. (2015). Deep Learning Techniques and its Various Algorithms and Techniques. *International Journal of Engineering Innovation & Research*, *4*(5).

Chenji, H., Stewart, G., Wu, Z., Javaid, A., Devabhaktuni, V., Bhasin, K., & Wang, B. (2016). An architecture concept for cognitive space communication networks. In *34th AIAA International Communications Satellite Systems Conference* (p. 5728).

Girimonte, D., & Izzo, D. (2007). Artificial Intelligence for Space Applications. In A. J. Schuster (Ed.), *Intelligent Computing Everywhere*. London: Springer. doi:10.1007/978-1-84628-943-9_12

Haldorai, A., & Ramu, A. (2018). An Intelligent-Based Wavelet Classifier for Accurate Prediction of Breast Cancer. In *Intelligent Multidimensional Data and Image Processing* (pp. 306–319). Hershey, PA: IGI Global; doi:10.4018/978-1-5225-5246-8.ch012

Jhajj, H. K., Garg, R., & Saluja, N. (2018). Aspects of Machine Learning in Cognitive Radio Networks. In *Progress in Advanced Computing and Intelligent Engineering* (pp. 553–559). Springer Singapore.

Kandeepan, S., De Nardis, L., Di Benedetto, M., Guidotti, A., & Corazza, G. E. (2010). Cognitive Satellite Terrestrial Radios. In *Global Telecommunications Conference*.

Mansour, A., Mesleh, R., & Abaza, M. (2016). New challenges in wireless and free space optical communications. *Optics and Lasers in Engineering, 89, 95-108*. doi:10.1016/j.optlaseng.2016.03.027

Qi, F., Zhihui, Y., & Keqin, S. (2012). Spectrum Environment Machine Learning in Cognitive Radio. *Procedia Engineering*, *29*, 4181–4185. doi:10.1016/j.proeng.2012.01.640

Suriya, M., Anandakumar, H., & Arulmurugan, R. (2016). Social Aware Cognitive Radio Networks: Effectiveness of Social Networks as a Strategic Tool for Organizational Business Management. In *Social Network Analytics for Contemporary Business Organizations*. Hershey, PA: IGI Global.

Suriya, M., Sugandhanaa, M., Vaishnavi, J. & Bharathy, P.D. (2016). A survey on cognitive handover between the terrestrial and satellite segments.

Suriya, M., Vaishnavi, J., Sugandhanaa, M., & Bharathy, P. D. (2016), A Survey on IEEE 802.16g Protocol Convergence between Terrestrial and Satellite Segments. In *International Conference on Explorations and Innovations in Engineering & Technology*.

Suriya, M. M., Swathi, M. R., Scholar, R. U., Surya, M. P., Scholar, U. G., & Veeralakshmi, M. R. (2018). Enhancing energy in WBAN through cognitive radio networks. *International Journal of Advanced Information and Communication Technology*, *4*(11).

Wang, M, Chen, X. & Gao, W. (2015), High Precision Uplink Time and Frequency Calibration in Cognitive Space Communications. In *IEEE 14th Int Conf. on Cognitive Informatics & Cognitive Computing*.

Chapter 5
Side Channel Attacks in Cloud Computing

Ramanujam Elangovan
Thiagarajar College of Engineering, India

Prianga M.
Thiagarajar College of Engineering, India

ABSTRACT

Cloud computing is used for storing and managing information using the remote servers, which is hosted on the internet instead of storing it in a normal server or personal computer. The main purpose of why most of the companies use the cloud for storing and managing data is to not have to pay money for storing data. The main aim is to allow users to benefit from all technologies. Virtualization is considered to be the main technology of cloud computing. Several privacy concerns are caused by the cloud because the service provider can access the data at any time. Cloud providers can also share the information for the purpose of law and order. The information gathered from the physical implementation is called a side channel attack. Some technical knowledge is required for side channel attacks and these attacks are based on statistical methods. It works by monitoring the security critical operations. The side channel attack is based on the information which is leaking and the information which is kept secret.

INTRODUCTION

Cloud computing is an open, widespread version, that's net-centric and gives various offerings both software or hardware. It offers new cost powerful offerings on-demand together with Software program as a Service (SaaS), Infrastructure as a Service (IaaS) and Platform as a Service (PaaS). A massive interest in each enterprise and academia has been generated to discover and beautify cloud computing. It has 5 critical traits: on-call for self-provisioning, measured provider, speedy elasticity, extensive community get entry to and useful resource pooling. It's far aiming at giving abilities to apply effective computing structures to reduce value, boom efficiency and performance (Manikandakumar, 2018). It consolidates the monetary application version with the evolutionary enhancement of many utilized computing methods and technology, which consist of computing infrastructure along with networks of

DOI: 10.4018/978-1-5225-7522-1.ch005

computing and storage assets, applications and distributed services. Furthermore, there is an ongoing debate in Information Technology (IT) groups approximately that how cloud computing paradigm differs from existing models and how these variations have an effect on its adoption. One view remembers it as a current or a fashionable way to supply services over the net, even as others see it as a novel technical revolution (Younis, 2015).

However, with all of these promising centers and blessings, there are still some of technical barriers which could prevent cloud computing from becoming a genuinely ubiquitous provider (Haldorai, 2018). Mainly a consumer has strict and complex requirements over the safety of an infrastructure. Security is the primary inhibitor to cloud adaptation. Cloud computing may additionally inherit some security risks and vulnerabilities from the internet, such as malicious code like Viruses, Trojan Horses. Further, cloud computing suffers from facts privateness problems and conventional disbursed structures attacks, i.e. Disbursed Denial of provider attacks (DDoS), which can have a massive effect in its offerings. Moreover, cloud computing has added new issues together with shifting resources and storing information inside the cloud with a probability to be living in a foreign country with unique policies. Computing sources can be inaccessible because of many motives which includes natural disaster or denial of carrier.

Cloud computing is a shared surroundings in which stocks massive-scale of computing sources among big purchasers (organizations and organizations) comprising a huge quantity of users. Therefore, cloud computing tenants will equally share the physical sources and are in all likelihood to face co-residence vulnerabilities. Virtual Machine (VM) physical co-residency enables attackers to intrude with other digital machines going for walks at the equal physical machine by using hardware aspect-channels. In the worst state of affairs, attackers can exfiltrate victims' sensitive and personal data. There are numerous styles of aspect-channels attacks, which might be labeled consistent with a hardware medium they target and take advantage of, for example, cache side-channel assaults. Cache side-channel assaults are forms of Micro Architectural attacks (MA), which is a huge group of cryptanalysis techniques within the aspect-channel evaluation attacks.

This chapter have a look at side-channel attacks and also have a look at how the effect on the multi-tenancy and virtualization in cloud computing. It defines aspect-channel attacks offerings, The organization of this paper is structured as follows. Session 2 illustrates side-channel attacks and its effect on virtualization. Phase three describes extraordinary sorts of cache side-channel attacks and the way they can extract records from CPU caches. Indicates gaps within the current researches and some of proposed countermeasures to cache aspect- channel attacks in cloud computing.

In computing, the multi-tendency has the biggest advantage because the physical resource is shared among multiple client with the aid of the hypervisor, virtualization assists multitendency. Using the hypervisor, cloud provider utilizes the resource like CPU, network interfaces, memory and hard disk. Virtual machines are running on the same core machine which leads to the malicious or abnormal attacks like side channel attacks. The various types of side channel attacks are: Fault attacks, Power Analysis attacks, electromagnetic (EM) attacks, cache-based attacks. But in cloud, the cache-based side channel attacks are creating the major issues. The different VMs on the same core use the cache resources.

The cache is the similar to the CPU cache memory which contain various level of cache. In processor, there are various levels of cache are presented. The user request the date to cache and if the data are not in the cache memory, cache misses will occur due to the cause of main memory reference. Whenever main memory reference occurs, it takes more time to identify the content. In that situation, the attacker performs the cache based attack during that time to read the content in the memory. CPU cache is one of the major threat in the cloud computing (Anandakumar & Umamaheswari, 2018).

In Cache-based side channel attacks, the attackers steal the user sensitive information from the victim via shared CPU among multiple users. In Infrastructure-as-a-Service (IaaS) cloud systems actually adopt with the multi-tendentious character to utilize the resources effectively and efficiently. Virtual machines (VMs) are better technology used to give the strong isolation between the multiple users, so each VMs memory content are not readable to others co-tenant. Moreover, confidentiality breaks due to the cross-VM side channel attacks.

Mitigating the side-channel attacks is one of the great challenges in the cloud. There are many drawbacks in existing defending mechanism. They are: changes in hardware, hypervisor or guest operating system (OS), etc. This chapter have proposes techniques to detect the side-channel attack and provide the mechanism to prevent information leakage by triggering VM migration upon attack detection. It is a non-trivial attack detection method. Several traditional techniques are used they are: signature based detection and anomaly based detection of side-channel attacks.

To overcome these challenges, this chapter propose a real time detection method as a Cloud Radar. The two key ideas behind that, 1) The victim has own micro-architectural behavior that need protection from side channel attacks 2) anomalous cache are created by the attackers VM. Cloud radar as a light-weight extension to the virtual machine. It utilizes the existing host system to collect the available hardware and monitor the virtual machine activities. The advantages of the Cloud Radar are mainly focused on the root cause of cache-based side channel attack and it is hard to evade. Two cache manipulation techniques are: Prime probe attacks and Flush-Reload attacks. First, it allocates an array for cacheline-sized and cacheline-aligned memory blocks. Second, identical memory pages can be shared among different VMs.

Three Different methods to defend against the cache-based side channel attacks are (Zhao, 2013).

1. **Partitioning Caches:** To prevent the cache sharing with different VMs
2. **Randomization:** This includes random memory to cache mappings.
3. **Avoiding Co-Location:** New VM placement policies were designed to reduce the co-location probability between victim and attacker VMs.

There are various side-channel attacks and according to hardware medium, they target and exploit for instance cache side-channel attacks. Cloud computing is also an open standard model which is information-centric and also provides various services like hardware and software. A significant interest in both industry and academy has been generated to explore and enhance cloud computing (Anandakumar, Umamaheswari & Arulmurugan, 2018).

VIRTUALIZATION

Virtual machine introduces the major vulnerability in cloud computing and the servers are similar to physical one because clouds are hosted in data centers. There are a number of vulnerabilities in the cloud and they are hypervisor vulnerability, vulnerable hypervisor, denial of service attack. VM is hoping and data leakage. In this the attacker can able to execute a code and gain the privileges of the hypervisor, which would help him to control all the virtual machines running on the host itself.

The threat of denial service attack is also a major concern in this virtual machine because multiple machines run on a single host. While sharing the information if one machine is affected by a denial of service attack means, then all other machines also affected by this because multiple machine runs on a

Figure 1. CPU and their cache levels
(Younis, 2015)

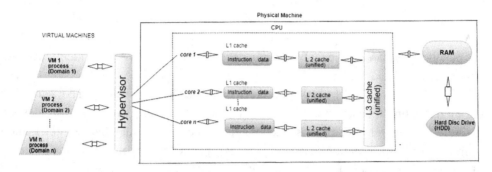

single host. Data leakage is also possible in cloud because the information which is stored in the cloud is not protected and the attacker can easily retrieve and access the data. VM hopping is also vulnerable in cloud computing, because if the attacker gains the access to one virtual machine, then the attacker can able to gain access to all other virtual machines. Physical enclosures can reduce the risk of superstitious installation of microphones, micro-monitoring devices. This makes timing attacks impossible.

SIDE CHANNEL ATTACK

Cryptographic systems rely on security mechanisms to authenticate communicating entities and make sure the confidentiality and integrity of data. The security mechanisms have to be implemented according to cryptographic algorithms and to fulfill the security dreams of the security systems. Despite the fact that the security mechanisms can control and specify what functions may be carried out, they can't specify how their capabilities are applied. For example, a security protocol specification is generally free of whether the encryption algorithms are implemented in custom hardware units or using software walking on a general processor. Moreover, cryptographic algorithms are constantly applied in the hardware or the software of physical devices that have interaction with, and are stimulated by their environments. These interactions may be monitored and instigated by means of attackers. The gap between how security features are specific and how they're carried out, has led to a brand new elegance of assault, which is an aspect-channel assault (Agosta, 2015).

Side-channel attacks are an implementation stage attack on cryptographic systems. It exploits a correlation among high-stage functionalities of the software and the underlying hardware phenomena. As an example, it appears at the correlation among the inner kingdom of the computation processing device and the bodily measurements taken at different points for the duration of the computation. They accumulate records about sure operations taking vicinity on computation processing activities i.e. power consumption of a custom hardware unit.

There are various types of side-channels attacks, which are categorized according to the hardware medium they goal and make the most, for example, cache side-channel attacks. furthermore, attackers are always seeking out hardware functions that provide high-price of computing interactions, which can facilitate attackers with distinctive information about the state of computing operations taking location. for example, CPU cache side-channels are one of the most inclined hardware gadgets focused through adversaries because of its excessive-rate of interactions and sharing between processes .

Figure 2. The cryptographic model, including side-channel (Younis, 2015)

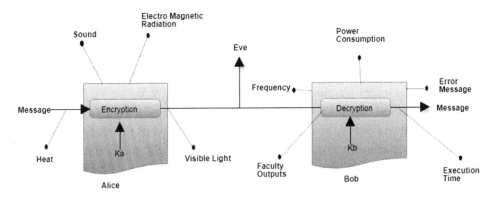

Classifications Depending at the Technique Used in the Analysis Process

This kind is classified according to the tools or techniques used to examine the sampled information gathered from attacks. It has different methods to perform analysis:

- **Easy Aspect-Channel Attack (SSCA):** This kind exploits the connection between side-channel outputs and carried out instructions. A single trace is utilized in an SSCA evaluation to extract the name of the game key. however, the side-channel information related to the attacked instructions (the sign) needs to be larger than the side-channel statistics of the unrelated instructions (the noise) to deduce the name of the game key (Kumari, 2015).
- **Differential Aspect-Channel Assault (DSCA):** It exploits the correlation between side-channel outputs and processed data. in this type, many lines are used within the evaluation, and then statistical techniques are used to infer the viable mystery keys.

Classifications Relying at the Manipulate Over the Computation System

In this type, the side-channel attacks are classified in line with the control over a computation method by means of attackers. it is divided into two primary classes:

- **Passive Attacks:** Wherein the attacked device works as there is no attack took place and the attacker has not been observed interfering with the centered operation.
- **Energetic Attacks:** It has a few interfering with the targeted operation, and a few influence might be detected.

Classifications Depending on the Manner of Accessing the Module

This type relies on the form of interfaces, which the attackers use to take advantage of the security system. These interfaces can be a set of logical, physical or electric interfaces. Anderson et al. (2006) has categorized those assaults in three different types:

- **Invasive Attacks:** De-packaging is used in an invasive assault to get direct access to the internal components of a cryptographic tool or module. For instance, an attacker would possibly open a hole in the passivation layer of a cryptographic module and place a probing needle on a record-bus to peer the information transfer.

- **Semi-Invasive Attacks:** In such attacks, an attacker gains get entry to to the tool, yet without detrimental the passivation layer consisting of the usage of a laser beam to ionize a device to adjust a number of its memories with a view to change its output.

- **Non-Invasive Attacks:** on this assault, an attacker calls for near statement or manipulation of the tool's operation and does now not want to get direct access to the inner components of cryptographic devices or modules. Accordingly become absolutely undetectable. in this technique, the attacker simply examines records that by accident leaked, along with timing analysis. Timely evaluation correlates an operation carried out by a tool by the time fed on to execute the operation as a way to deduce the cost of the name of the game keys (Haldorai & Ramu, 2018).

CACHE-BASED SIDE CHANNEL ATTACKS

Cache is a small high speed phase of memory built in and outside the CPU. It is also a Static RAM (SRAM) that any requested data must go through. It contains the maximum recently accessed information and common accessed memory addresses. Moreover, the cache can result in massive speed increases by way of maintaining frequently accessed data and decreasing time taken to evict and fetch statistics from the principle memory. It's far utilized to increase the speed of memory access because the time to execute an instruction is through far lower than the time to carry an instruction (or piece of data) into the processor (Kowarschik & Weiß, 2003). For example, a 100 MHz processor can execute maximum instructions in 1 Clock (CLK) or 10 nanoseconds (ns); while a normal access time for DRAM is 60 ns and the SRAM is 15 ns, that's 3 to 4 times faster than DRA (Sadique, 2016)

A core can have three specific tiers of cache. Level 1 (L1) is the smallest among them, but it is the fastest. If the requested data is not kept at L1, it will yield a cache miss. otherwise, it'll return a cache hit that means the data are located on the L1. Because L1 is small, therefore, Level 2 (L2) has been introduced. It is lots larger than L1, yet slower than it. whilst the core stories a cache miss from L1, it'll have a look at the L2 for the wanted facts or address of statistics. If the center receives every other cache miss, it will jump to look for the asked data at level 3 (L3). L3 is the largest cache in terms of the size, but it is the slowest among them. The L3 is shared among the processor cores, and others (L1and L2) are shared among methods and threads.

Cache side-channel attacks are a type of micro architectural attack (MA), that's a huge group of cryptanalysis techniques inside side-channel analysis attacks. CPU caches are one of the most targeted hardware devices by adversaries due to the high-free interactions between process. Cache side-channel attacks in cloud computing environments take an advantage of running multiple virtual machines simultaneously on the same infrastructure to leak secret information about a running encryption algorithm. Moreover, full encryption keys of algorithms and schemes inclusive of Data Encryption Standard (DES), Advanced Encryption Standard (AES) and RSA, have been broken using spying processes to acquire information about cache lines, which have been accessed. The records is analysed and linked to the current virtual system that occupies the processor.

In the side-channel attacks, attackers are constantly looking for high-charge hardware capabilities to discover modern running cryptographic operations and the state of the operation in execution. The high-free hardware features can speak facts more quick and deduce the needed records to yield the secret key. Thus, CPU caches are continually an thrilling goal to adversaries because of the following motives:

- It is shared among VMs or cores. Therefore, an attacker can easily use clients' co-residence or VM physical co-residency to intrude and exfiltrate touchy information of victims.
- There is a high-free of computing interactions between tactics.
- There is a maximum quality-grained and detailed records approximately the state of computing operations running on a system.
- There are 3 principal types of side-channel attacks, which facilitate adversaries with various capabilities to attack CPU caches

Access-Driven Side-Channel Attack

In order to get the information about cache units accessed by the victim. The attacker runs a spy program on the physical machine that hosts it in an access driven attacks. There are numerous types of CPU caches' architectural components can be focused. Adversaries can monitor using instruction statistics cache, branch-prediction cache or floating-point multiplier to get information approximately the executing cryptographic operation so as to get the secret key. The most attack in this category are called the high and Probe attack. It measures the time needed to examine data from memory random access memory (RAM) associated with character cache units. In this attack, an attacker uses a manner to fill cache strains with its own data called prime. Then, the process will wait for a prespecified time to permit the victim accessed the cache. Having waited for the predefined time, the process starts offevolved the probe stage, which refills the equal cache units with attacker's statistics and observes the victim's hobby on cache units. If the victim accesses a primed line, data on the line might be evicted and cause a cache miss. This will yield a better time to read this line than if it is nevertheless untouched. There is another kind of the high and probe attack, that's Flush+Reload (Yarom & Falkner, 2013). The spy process shares memory pages with the sufferer and measures the time to get admission to sure strains. The attack works as follows:

Figure 3. The monitored line in the Flush+Reload attack
(Younis, 2015)

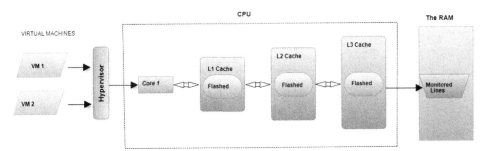

- The spy process flushes the monitored memory lines form the cache hierarchy (L1, L2 and L3 if observed) discern three: the monitored line in the Flush+Reload attack
- The spy technique waits for a predefined time to allow the victim to access the primary memory and cache hierarchy.
- The spy technique will reload the focused memory strains and measure the time. If the accessed time is much less than a predefined threshold, then it is successful and the reminiscence traces are accessed by means of the sufferer as shown in parent 4. In any other case, it's miles miss parent four: The sufferer accesses the monitored traces

Time-Driven Side-Channel Attack

In this type of attack, an attacker aims to measure the total execution times of cryptographic operations with a fixed key. The complete execution instances are influenced by the cost of the key. thus, the attacker will introduce some interference to the victim to learn indirectly whether a positive cache-set is accessed by means of the victim manner or not called Evict and Time. An attacker will execute a spherical of encryption; evict one decided on cache-set by writing its own data on it and measure the time it takes to a spherical of encryption by the victim. The time to carry out the encryption relies on values in the cache when the encryption starts. subsequently, if the victim accesses the evicted set, the round of encryption time tends to be higher.

Trace-Pushed Side-Channel Attack

The 1/3 class is trace-driven, which looks at getting information related to the whole range of cache misses or hits for a focused method or machine. An attacker can capture the profile of cache activities all through a round of encryption in phrases of the victim's misses and hits accesses. furthermore, these attacks want to display a few thing of CPU caches constantly throughout a spherical of encryption which includes electronic emanation. The capability to monitor CPU caches constantly makes these attacks quite powerful. Cloud computing has brought new concerns such as moving the resource (Saraswathi,

Figure 4. The victim accesses the monitored lines
(Younis, 2015)

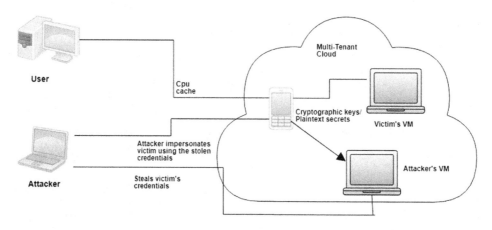

2015) and storing the data in the cloud with the probability to reside in another country with different regulations. Computing resources could be inaccessible due to many reasons such as natural disaster and denial of service attack. In cloud computing, a side channel attack is an attack on computer security which is based on information gained from the physical information of the computer system rather than the information implemented in the algorithm itself. These attacks are easy to implement against cryptographic implementations.

These attacks ensure a serious threat to the security of cryptographic module and then cryptographic implementations have to be evaluated for the resistivity against such attacks. The major concern in computing and communication is security. There are some of the cryptographic algorithms are there which includes symmetric ciphers, public key ciphers and hash functions which forms a set of primitives that can be used as a building block to construct security mechanisms that target on specific objectives. The attack which is based on side channel information is known as side channel attack. Side channel information can be retrieved through encryption. Through this it provides the plaintext or else cipher text which results in encryption process. How the encryption process works means it will receive the plaintext as input and produce the cipher text as output.

These attacks were therefore based on both plain text and cipher text. Many cryptographic systems were assumed to be mathematically secured when the key is sufficiently large. Brute force attacks were assumed to be computationally infeasible, while other approaches don't do this. Then it is good to have a system which is mathematically secured, but this alone does not tell the whole story. There are theattacks that aims not at the mathematical secure properties of the cryptographic system, but also an implementation, hardware, electromagnetic radiation, timing and even with sound. The generic name for such a method of attack is known as side-channel attack. The name stems from the notion that these attacks does not target the primary channel (the input and output of the cryptographic system, knowledge about the system itself, protocols used, etc.), but any other channel of information may reveal secret data. For example, in network the security protocols, such as Secure Shell Protocol (SSH) and Transport Layer Security (TLS), combine these primitive protocols to provide authentication between communicating entities, and ensure the confidentiality and integrity of the which is communicated, In practice, the security mechanisms only specify what functions are to be performed, irrespective of how these functions are implemented.

For example, the specification of an security protocol is usually independent of the encryption algorithms whether they are implemented in software running on a general processor, or using custom hardware units, and check whether the memory used to store intermediate data during these computations is on the same chip as the computing unit or else on a separate chip. This kind of "separation of concerns" between security mechanisms and the implementation has enabled rigorous theoretical analysis and design of cryptosystem and security protocols. However, in these process, various assumptions were made about the implementation of security mechanisms. another example is that it is typically assumed that the implementations of cryptographic computations were ideal to "black-boxes" whose internals can neither be observed nor interfered with a malicious entity. Aided by these assumptions, the level of security is widely quantified in terms of a mathematical properties of the cryptographic algorithms and their key sizes. In practice, however, the security mechanisms alone are far from complete security solution. It is unrealistic to assume that the attackers will attempt to directly take on the computational complexity of breaking the cryptographic primitives employed in a security mechanism. An interesting analogy can be drawn in this between strong cryptographic algorithms and a highly secure algorithm which locks on the front door of a house.

Burglars are attempting to break into a house which will rarely try all the combinations necessary to pick such a lock; they may break in through the windows, break a door at its hinges, or rob owners of a key as they were trying to enter the house. Similarly, almost all known security attacks on cryptographic systems target weakness in animplementation and thedeployment of mechanisms and their cryptographic algorithms. These weaknessescan allow attackers to completely attack, or significantly weaken, the theoretical strength of the security solutions. For a cryptographic system to remain secure it is necessary that the secret keys, in which it uses to perform the required security services, are not revealed in any way. Since cryptographic algorithms have been studied for a long time by the large number of experts,attackers or hackers are more likely tried to attack the hardware and systems within which the cryptographic algorithm is said to be partitioned. A new attacks were developed in the last few years and these attacks work because it seems that there is a correlation between the physical measurements taken at different points during a computation and the internal state of the processing device, which is itself related to the secret key.

Actually, in reality, cryptographic algorithms are always implemented in software or hardware on physical devices which interact with and are influenced by their environments. These physical interactions can be instigated and monitored by adversaries, like Eve, and may result in information which may useful for cryptanalysis. This type of information issaid to be side-channel information, and the attacks exploiting side-channel information is called side-channel attacks . The idea which is underlined in side channel attacks is to look at the way we're cryptographic algorithms are implemented, rather than at the algorithm itself. It is not difficult to see that conventional cryptanalysis treats cryptographic algorithms as purely asmathematical objects, whilst side-channel cryptanalysis also takes the implementations of the algorithms into account.

Hence, side channel attacks were also called as implementation attacks. Even any cryptographic algorithm must be encoded in order to function properly, such encoded algorithms must not reveal the private key information used, despite the adversary's ability to observe and manipulate the running algorithm. The British intelligence agency, is trying to break the cipher which is used by the Egyptian Embassy in London, but their efforts were stymied by a limits of their computational power. By listening to these clicks of the rotors as cipher clerks restored them each morning, Messier 15 MI5 successfully deduced that the core position of 2 or 3 of the machine's rotors.

The main principles of this side channel attacks are very easy to catch. Side channel attacks work on the principle because there is a correlation between the physical measurements taken during computations like power consumption,consuming time and also the internal state of the processing device, which is itself related to the secret key. It is the correlation between the side channel information and the operation which is related to the secret key that the side channel attack tries to analyze. Side channel attacks have proven to be several orders of magnitude which is more effective than the conventional mathematical analysis based attacks and are much more practical to mount. In the area of protocol design or software construction, one can apply a major range of formal techniques to model a device in question, and also to model the range of adversarial actions, and then to reason about the correctness properties these device is supposed to provide none of these. One can thus obtain at least some of the assurance that, within the abstraction of a model, the device may resist such adversarial attacks.

However, when you are moving from an abstract notion of security to its instantiation as a real process in the physical world,and also the things may become harder. All the real-world problems that the abstraction, hide become significant. What is the boundary of these cryptographic devices, in the real world? And what are the outputs that an adversary may observe, and the inputs an adversary may manipulate in order to act on a device? These answers are hard to find, but designing an architecture to defend against arbitrary attacks requires necessarily an attempt to find them. Moreover, the physical action of computation can often result in physical effects where an adversary can observe; these observations can sometimes affect sensitive internal data the cryptographic module architecture is supposed to protect. This style of attack is also called side-channel analysis, since the module or device leaks information through channels other than its main intended interfaces. By physically attacking the cryptographic device, the adversary hopes to subvert its security correctness properties, usually by extracting some secrets the device is not supposed to reveal.

At first step, the natural way to achieve this goal is the direct approach, somehow bye pass the cryptographic module protections and reads the data. To be fortunate, in design practice, this direct attack can be easily threatened by so called as tamper-resistant techniques. Even though this direct approach can often prove rather successful, a rather sophisticated family of indirect approaches which is emerging, where the adversary instead tries to induce an error in a modules which operation via some physical failure; if the module continues to operate despite the error, it may ends up revealing enough information for the adversary to reconstruct the secret. Researchers at Bellcore originally described this attack, in the theoretical context of inducing errors incryptographic hardware that carried out the CRT implementation of RSA. This result generated the flurry of follow-on results, some of which became known as differential fault analysis.

These theoretical attacks, then eventually became practical and demonstrable, and eventually earned the name Bellcore attacks after the authors of their original paper. One of the most popular jargons of system security today might be the trusted platform module (TPM) in the sequel. Trusted platform modules usually take the form of a cryptographically secure module and is the core of the trusted computing platform. A key component of such cryptographic modules is that they use the secrets, despites attempt by an adversary — perhaps with direct physical access — to extract them. Single-chip devices — like smart cards — have received much attention in the attacker community, perhaps due to the ubiquity of smart (Matthews, 2016) cards in the low-end commerce applications, and the low cost . Anderson and Kuhn's work provide an enlightening and also anentertaining survey of the various techniques they found effective in practice. Recently, two advents related to side channel research in Europe should better catch the eyes of the cryptography community over the world, especially those who are interested in the research of side channel attacks. (Side Channel Analysis Resistant Design Flow) SCARD project and (European Network of Excellence for Cryptology) ENCRYPT project. Both of these two projects are international joint project plans among European research members from both the cryptography research institutes and the relevant industries. In SCARD, it is proposed to enhance the typical micro-chip design flow—from a high level system description over register transfer layer description down to gate level net lists, and finally the placement and routing of the micro-chip—in order to provide a means for designing side-channel analysis resistant circuits and systems. Moreover, it is intended to study a whole phenomenon of side-channel analysis in the consistent manner, and also it is used to provide appropriate analysis tools and to design tools for the designer of secure systems. In fact, these additional ingredients of the traditional design flow of microchips are considered to be in order to enable the design of the next generation of secure and dependable devices. ENCRYPT is a 4-year network of excellence which is funded within the Information Societies Technology Program of the European Commission. It falls under an action line towards the global dependability and security framework and its main objective is to intensify the collaboration of European researchers in information security, and more particularly in cryptology and digital watermarking.

One of the four working groups of VAMPIRE which is a class of denial of service attack is consider to be a research group in the side channel analysis. From these two advents alone, it is roughly estimated that the Europe, in our own opinion, was likely one step further over the other continents in an international collaborative research on such attacks. It is an interesting story that the side channel attacks evaluation was already explicitly suggested manyyears ago to be encompassed in an cryptographic algorithm evaluation and in many internationalstandards bodies, such as the 3rd Generation Partnership Project (3GPP) security architecture. However, due to lack of testable methods and practical tools, this insightful suggestion virtually is like a vacant shapes in sight. So it is very easy to understand the final evaluation report of this standard bodies draw the conclusion ontime "…in the design process it was concluded not to be feasible to design a general algorithm framework that by itself it would not be vulnerable to side channel attacks." Recently, Tiri presented a digital Very Large Scale Integration (VLSI) design flow inorder to create secure, side-channel attack resistant integrated circuits (IC in the sequel). Even though this is the first significant attempt in a secure design of IC, they only considered the power analysis attack in the comprehensive top-down automated synchronous VLSI design flow which pursues a constantpower dissipation. The threat of side channel attacks also caught the attention from NoC research community. Then a framework for security of NoCs by providing them a network level symmetric key cryptography for key distribution and at the core level by illustrating modification of software with extremely low overheads for added security against power based attacks(Cilio 2013). Clearly, a cryptographic algorithm which is strong with respect to conventional cryptanalytic attacks is useless if it cannot be implemented securely on a broad range of platforms. Already during the Advanced Encryption Standard (AES) algorithm and NESSIE (European Research Project) processes, the cryptographic community has come to this conclusion. To evaluate the impacts of Side Channel attacks on a security testing of cryptographic modules; to identify the possible research trends in this area and so on.

CROSS GUEST VM BREACHES

Attacker compromises the cloud by placing a malicious virtual machine in close proximity to a target cloud server and then launch side channel attack. During an inside channel attack, attacker runs a virtual machine on the same physical host of the victim's virtual machine and takes advantage of shared physical resources (processor cache) to steal data (cryptographic key) from the victim (Anwar, 2017). Side channel attack can be implemented by any co-resistent user and are mainly due to the vulnerabilities in shared technology resources.

There are various attacks involved here they are:

- Timing attack
- Data remanence
- Acoustic cryptanalysis
- Power monitoring attack
- Differential fault analysis
- Electromagnetic attack

Figure 5. Side channel attacks [cloud computing module]

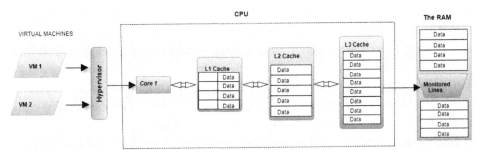

TIMING ATTACK

A timing attack is a security exploit which allows an attacker or hacker to discover the number of vulnerabilities in the security of a computer or a network system by knowing how long it takes the system to respond to different inputs (Cilio, 2013).

DATA REMANENCE

There are many number of critical data and it must not only be protected against unauthorized access and distribution, but also kept secured and deleted at the end of the life cycle. Considering an organization storing information, related to health (Balachander et al., 2017), finance is more important and it is mandatory to ensure that no data is stealed on disk from where it is exposed to a risk of being recovered by malicious users. If you have full control of your server then you can use some tools that overwrite the corresponding sector on the risk to destry any physical trace of a file. The cloud provider must collaborate to make the techniques work. You are given access only to higher level abstraction like file systems or key value based API's not to physical device. The cloud providers must start paying attention to these issues and should offer secure deletion of these services. Among this only one solution that works atleast today on information as a service platforms. This will encrypt your data and keep it in a safer place that is wherever you store your data in cloud it encrypts it and provide security.

ACOUSTIC CRYPTANALYSIS

Acoustic cryptanalysis is also a type of side channel attack that exploits sounds which is emitted by computers or any other devices. Nowadays most of the modern acoustic cryptanalysis focuses on the sounds produced by the computer keyboards and internal computer components, but historically it has also been applied to impact printers, and to electromechanical deciphering machines.

POWER MONITORING ATTACK

In cryptography, power analysis is consider as a form of side channel attack in which the attacker or hacker study about the power consumption of a cryptographic hardware device which includes smart card,tamper-resistant,integrated circuit etc. The attack can non-invasively extract cryptographic keys and also other secret information from the device. There are two types of power analysis one is simple power analysis and differential power analysis. Simple power analysis (SPA) involves visually interpreting power traces, and graphs of electrical activity over time. Differential power analysis (DPA) is said to be the more advanced form of power analysis, which allows an attacker to compute the intermediate values within cryptographic computations or algorithms through statistical analysis of a data collected from multiple cryptographic operations.

DIFFERENTIAL FAULT ANALYSIS

Differential fault analysis (DFA) is also a type of side channel attack in which the field of cryptographic implemetation,specifically cryptanalysis (Ruedinger, 2006). The main aim of this is to induce faults—unexpected environmental conditions—into cryptographic implementations, and this is to reveal their internal states. Consider an example, a smartcard containing an embedded processor might be subjected to a high temperature, unsupported supply current, excessively high overclocking, strong electric and magnetic fields, or even ionizing radiation to influence the operation of a processor. Due to physical data corruption the processor may begin to result incorrectly, which may help a cryptanalyst deduce the instructions that the processor is running. For DES and Triple DES, about 200 single-flipped bits, where necessary to obtain the secret key. Differential Fault Analysis was also applied successfully to the advanced encryption standard (AES) cryptographic algorithm. Many countermeasures were proposed to defend from such kind of attacks. Most of them are based on error detection methods.

ELECTROMAGNETIC ATTACK

Electromagnetic attacks are attacks based on electromagnetic radiation, which is leaked, which can directly provide plaintexts and other information. Such measurements can be further used to infer cryptographic implementation keys using techniques which are equivalent to those in power analysis or can be used in non-cryptographic implementation attacks (Anandakumar, 2014). In the cloud environment, it is accepted that among the various types of side channel attack only timing attack and differential fault analysis need to paid attention. In fact, there have been some research works were done based on these two types of attacks in the past few years.

CO-RESIDENCE RELATED ATTACKS

In this author used the Amazon EC2 as an example to demonstrate possible side channel attacks in the cloud computing environment. In this study, the network probing technique uses some of the popular networking tools like nmap, hping, and get to gather networking information which is employed to collect the host interconnect information associated with the cloud. using this the collected data, the infrastructure of the cloud can be mapped. Given a target instance (virtual machine), the map can offer lots of knowledge of how to select launching parameters to launch attacking instances (virtual machines) with co-residence property. If attacking SMs can be co-resided with a target on the same physical machine, cross-VM information leakage could happen. After establishing a coincidence relationship with a target SM, attacking SMs can use side channels attacks to attack information from the target.

CROSS VM SIDE CHANNEL ATTACKS

In these virtual machines share their physicalmemory, CPU cycles, network buffers. These attacks take place in two types they are placing the virtual machine on the same physical machine and exploiting the shared resources.

SECURITY ISSUES IN A CLOUD

There are various security issues in cloud and they are as follows:

- Privileged access
- Regulatory compliance
- Data location
- Data segregation
- Recovery
- Investigative support
- Long term viability
- Data availability

PRIVILEGED ACCESS

The sensitive data which are processed outside the enterprise brings an inherent level of risk because physical,logical and personnel controls are byepassed by outsourced services. So better get as much information about people who manage your data. Then ask cloud providers to supply specific information on the hiring and oversight of privileged domains and also their controls over their access.

REGULATORY COMPLIANCE

Customers should take the responsibility for the security and integrity of their own data, even when it is held by a service or cloud provider. Service providers who are providing traditional services were subjected to external audits and security certifications. Cloud computing providers who indicate to undergo this security are signalling that customers can only use them for the most of the trivial functions.

DATA LOCATION

Cloud storage or data location is a model of data storage in which a digital data is stored in logical pools and the physical storage spans multiple servers. Here the physical environment is typically owned and managed by hosting a company. These cloud storage providers are the only responsibility for keeping the data available and accessible at any time, and the physical environment is protected and running. Some People and Some organizations buy or contract storage capacity of the providers to store a user, organization, or application data. Cloud storage services may access through the co-located cloud computing service, a web service application programming interface which is the API or by applications that utilize the application programming interface, such as cloud desktop storage, a cloud storage gateway or a web-based content management systems (Chen, 2017). Using cloud you could not exactly know where our data is hosted. In general, they may not know at what place it will be stored usually and they may ask cloud providers, whether they will commit to store and process data in specific jurisdictions and also check whether they will make a contractual commitment to obey the local privacy requirements based on the customers.

DATA SEGREGATION

Data which is stored in the cloud is typically stored in a shared environment. Encryption is considered as an effective method, all the cloud provider has responsibility to provide evidence that these encryption schemes were designed and tested by experienced specialists. To maximize the business more effective cloud providers use multi-tenant infrastructures, so that business should address data separation and Geo-location within an increased complex international and political landscape. Business people need to consider two major factors for separating data in the public cloud tenancy. Basically cloud computing is based on the virtualization technology that shares computing resources. Also cloud environments are always multi tenantand it isn't a concern for private theusers who use cloud privately. And also for the users who share memory space,disk, space and processor cycles which runs on the same physical infrastructure.

RECOVERY

According to disaster recovery cloud computing based on visualization takes a very different approach. Within a single software bundle or virtual server virtualization, the entire server including the operating system and applications, patches the data is encapsulated. Then the entire data or virtual servers copied or backed up into an off-site data center. Without the burden of reloading each data or component of the server the data can be safely and accurately transferred from one data center to another data center because the virtual server is hardware independent. The cloud will then shift the disaster recovery tradeoff to the left and hence cloud computing disaster recovery becomes more and more cost effective with significantly faster recovery times.

INVESTIGATIVE SUPPORT

In cloud computing investigating inappropriate or illegal activity is impossible. Because cloud services are specially difficult to investigate. Data's for multiple customers might be co-located and may also spread across an ever changing set of data centers.

LONG-TERM VIABILITY

Usually cloud provider will never get broke or get acquired by a larger company, but the cloud provider must give assurance that if such event happens the data's should remain available.

DATA AVAILABILTY

In cloud, customer data is often stored in chunk on different servers in different locations in different areas or in different clouds. In such case data availability becomes a major issue and the provision becomes relatively difficult. Data availability is defined as a term which is used by some computers, storage manufacturers and storage providers which describes products and services that ensure data continues to be available at any time in a required level of performance in situations ranging from normal condition through disastrous. Generally data availability is achieved through redundancy which involves a number of data which is stored and also it involves how the data can be reached. The need for a data center and a storage centric rather than a server centric philosophy and the environment can be described by some vendors (Park, 2014).

To run multiple virtual machines, monitors are created which is used to host operating systems and applications which resides within a single host computer to provide isolation between the VMs. Virtual machine monitor has the potential maintain a strong separation between the virtual machine and the operating system. When compared to operating system hypercisor is very large and complex too which ignore the isolation advantage. It integrates an adjusted linux kernel to carry out the privileged partition for an input and output operations. Here the attacker choose the target virtual machine to attack. To attack the particular machine, you should first get all the information and location of the targeted machine. There is an open source software called Nmap which is used to measure the location of the targeted machine. Get which tracks the website information through the network probing. Then places the malicious code which is the neighbor to the targeted virtual machine. To target the virtual machine in the same region the attackers find a close Domo IP address. When the malicious code or a malicious virtual machine is placed successfully, then the attacker can easily extract the data from the targeted virtual machine observing different processing operation. Performing different data analytics on the network the attackers find any location of the targeted virtual machine and analysis of the processing method, timing and power analysis of the system.

In cloud data security many researchers were already working. They already know side channel attack is the most common attack in cloud computing. There has been many possible solutions implemented for security against side channel attack. A proposal also made to change the encryption key periodically. Cloud user is only providing the encryption key, but it is beneficial for both the cloud users and cloud providers. Once the keys changed the cloud providers must inform about the update to the users because the user should also update regularly accumulate, serve on process, proportional Time Division Multiple Access (TDMA) and shared memory access were used to avoid the attack. To serve a process, they accumulate increases of the execution time of the process in the real execution process. A virtual firewall is also used to protect data from the side channel attack using a malicious virtual machine. The data can be encrypted and decrypted randomly. The main work of virtual firewall is to protect the user data from unexpected users. Virtual machines also plays a role to retrieve the user data from the targeted virtual machine. Random key generation is introduced to encrypt the data and also used to decrypt the same data. And this process is processed only when the users want to see an execution. It also provides security to the users.

COUNTER MEASURES FOR CACHE-BASED ATTACKS

Although side-channel attacks in general and cache based side-channel attack in particular are known for a quite long time, it seems there is a lack of remedies and countermeasures that may be carried out in cloud computing (Kim, 2011). Multi-tenancy and co-residency in cloud computing have received the researchers' attention to explore and look at the level of damage side-channel attacks can do with cloud computing. Furthermore, it's also tested that side-channel attacks can extract cryptographic non-public keys from unwary digital machines. This attacks may be focusing on some of the proposed solutions to tackle cache based side-channel attacks in cloud computing. The proposed mitigation tactics may be classified in different types of techniques: software-based mitigation strategies or hardware-based solutions (Page, 2003).

HARDWARE-BASED SOLUTIONS

A significant number of hardware answers have been proposed to address and save your side-channel attacks in general. Most of these solutions attention on decreasing or casting off interfereing in cache accesses including cache randomization and cache partitioning. In the randomization technique, the cache interferences are randomized through randomizing the cache eviction and permutation of the memory-cache mapping. But, the cache partitioning approach is focusing on partitioning the cache into distinctive zones for different processes. Therefore, the cache interfering might be eliminated because of each technique can best get entry to its partition that has reserved cache traces. Although hardware-based defense techniques seem to be more secure to be carried out as they more efficient and thwart the basic cause of these attacks, they cannot be nearly implemented till CPU makers put in force them into CPUs and that does not to be feasible in the recent time.

SOFTWARE-BASED MITIGATION TECHNIQUES

Software-based mitigation techniques are attacked-unique solutions, which can best tackle attacks that they're proposed for. Therefore, those solutions might not have the capability to mitigate new side- channel attacks.

- **Assigning Predefined Cache Pages to CPU Cores:** This solution is predicated on assigning one or many prespecified personal pages of the CPU cache, especially the closing level of cache (L3) to the CPU cores. So, every middle will have a confined quantity of reminiscence, in order to no longer be accessed by or shared with different cores. However, it suffers from inadequate makes use of of CPU cache as operations executed by CPU cores demand one of a kind sizes of cache pages. They require various sizes of the pages consistent with the operations they may be performing. Accordingly, cores will be assigned with extra or less than they need of cache pages. Moreover, when numbers of virtual machines are improved, this approach will suffer from scalability and protection issues, as virtual machines can overlap the usage of a CPU core that assigns one of a kind bags. Therefore, assigning personal pages to a CPU center utilized by diverse virtual machines will not prevent cache side-channel attack. Finally, the proposed solution handiest objectives the closing level of cache (L3) with extra cost and ambitions to mitigate energetic time-driven and hint-driven side-channel attacks. subsequently, it cannot save you different varieties of facet-channel attacks together with access-pushed facet-channel attacks or cope with different CPU cache ranges (L1 and L2).
- **Flushing the CPU Cache:** This solution focuses on the high and Probe attack, that's presented in section 3. It flushes the CPU cache to prevent an adversary from gaining any information about timing to examine information from memory related to man or woman cache units. When machines overlap and use the same CPU cache, the CPU cache could be flushed at once after converting from one VM to every other. Therefore, while a digital gadget primes the CPU cache and waits for every other virtual system to access the CPU cache, the cache can be flushed immediately after the second digital device takes control of the CPU cache, and with a purpose to break the probe step. Although this answer can prevent access-driven cache side- channel attacks by stopping interfering among virtual machines, it affects the cache usefulness by flushing the CPU cache whilst virtual machines overlapping occurs. It also introduces overhead, particularly when the numbers of virtual machines are elevated.
- **Inject Noise to Cache Timing:** The noise to cache timing aims to inject extra noise into the timing that an adversary may additionally have a look at from the CPU cache. It is also concentrated in the prime and probe assaults. When an attacker periodically primes the CPU cache with its own facts, a periodic cache cleansing process may be called to cleanse the CPU cache. So, the attacker can't observe any timing information about the victim while it launches the probe step. The periodic cache cleaning process primes the CPU cache in random order till all the cache entries have been evicted. However, this approach actually flushes all of the CPU cache entries, which will reduce the cache usefulness and introduce unacceptable overhead to the CPU.

- **Partition Catches:** A cache is consider as a small area in which it contains fast RAM and also contain associated control logic which is placed between a processor and the main memory. The number of cache lines is typically organized by the are of RAM which is used to comprise the sub words that is used to store contiguous address from the main memory. The cache is smaller than the main memory and it stores the subset of the memory content. As a result of incoming address stream by holding the current working set of data and instructions the cache reduce the load on the rest of the memory hierarchy accesses that are serviced by a cache is termed as cache-hits and are finished very quickly and access which are not helpd by the cache is termed as cache misses and it takes much longer time to complete since the main memory is accessed. Because of guarantee they should get more cache hits than cache misses and the performance of the average case application is also improved. The address in the main memory can map to the same location in the cache. The data items in the cache can compete for each other and evict space which is termed as cache interference or contention.

SUMMARY

Side-channel attacks are micro architectural attacks (MA), which forms the correlation between the higher level functionalities of the software and the underlying hardware phenomena. Their effect gets worse with cloud computing, multi-tenancy specific vulnerabilities, which include clients co-residence and virtual system physical co-residency. They allow adversaries to interfere with sufferers on the equal physical system and exfiltrate sensitive information. In this paper, they have surveyed cache side-channel attacks and the way they gain from multi-tenancy and virtualization in cloud computing. We've defined them and gift their sets with ways to penetrate the safety of cryptographic algorithms. We also presented gaps in current research and a variety of viable countermeasures. In this chapter, a generic method to cache side-channel attack was proposed. It will focus on preventing these attacks without affecting the cache and CPU efficiencies.

REFERENCES

Agosta, G., Barenghi, A., Pelosi, G., & Scandale, M. (2015). Trace-based schedulability analysis to enhance passive side-channel attack resilience of embedded software. *Information Processing Letters*, *115*(2), 292–297. doi:10.1016/j.ipl.2014.09.030

Anandakumar, H., & Umamaheswari, K. (2018). Cooperative Spectrum Handovers in Cognitive Radio Networks. In Cognitive Radio, Mobile Communications and Wireless Networks (pp. 47–63). Springer. doi:10.1007/978-3-319-91002-4_3

Anandakumar, H., Umamaheswari, K., & Arulmurugan, R. (2019). A Study on Mobile IPv6 Handover in Cognitive Radio Networks. In *International Conference on Computer Networks and Communication Technologies* (pp. 399-408). Springer Singapore. doi:10.1007/978-981-10-8681-6_36

Anwar, S., Inayat, Z., Zolkipli, M. F., Zain, J. M., Gani, A., Anuar, N. B., ... Chang, V. (2017). Cross-VM cache-based side channel attacks and proposed prevention mechanisms: A survey. *Journal of Network and Computer Applications*, *93*, 259–279. doi:10.1016/j.jnca.2017.06.001

Balachander, J., & Ramanujam, E. (2017). Rule based Medical Content Classification for Secure Remote Health Monitoring. *International Journal of Computers and Applications*, *165*(4).

Chen, S., Wang, R., Wang, X., & Zhang, K. (2010, May). Side-channel leaks in web applications: A reality today, a challenge tomorrow. In *2010 IEEE Symposium on Security and Privacy (SP)* (pp. 191-206). IEEE.

Cilio, W., Linder, M., Porter, C., Di, J., Thompson, D. R., & Smith, S. C. (2013). Mitigating power-and timing-based side-channel attacks using dual-spacer dual-rail delay-insensitive asynchronous logic. *Microelectronics Journal*, *44*(3), 258–269. doi:10.1016/j.mejo.2012.12.001

Anandakumar, H., & Umamaheswari, K. (2014). Energy Efficient Network Selection Using 802.16g Based GSM Technology. *Journal of Computational Science*, *10*(5), 745–754. doi:10.3844/jcssp.2014.745.754

Haldorai, A., & Ramu, A. (2018). An Intelligent-Based Wavelet Classifier for Accurate Prediction of Breast Cancer. In *Intelligent Multidimensional Data and Image Processing* (pp. 306–319). Hershey, PA: IGI Global; doi:10.4018/978-1-5225-5246-8.ch012

Haldorai, A., & Ramu, A. (2018). The Impact of Big Data Analytics and Challenges to Cyber Security. In Handbook of Research on Network Forensics and Analysis Techniques (pp. 300–314). Hershey, PA: IGI Global. doi:10.4018/978-1-5225-4100-4.ch016

Kim, H., Han, D. G., & Hong, S. (2011). First-order side channel attacks on Zhang's countermeasures. *Information Sciences*, *181*(18), 4051–4060. doi:10.1016/j.ins.2011.04.049

Kim, T. H., Kim, C., & Park, I. (2012). Side channel analysis attacks using AM demodulation on commercial smart cards with SEED. *Journal of Systems and Software*, *85*(12), 2899–2908. doi:10.1016/j.jss.2012.06.063

Kowarschik, M., & Weiß, C. (2003). An overview of cache optimization techniques and cache-aware numerical algorithms. In *Algorithms for Memory Hierarchies* (pp. 213–232). Springer. doi:10.1007/3-540-36574-5_10

Kumari, N., & Chugh, S. (2015). Reduction Of Noise From Audio Signals Using Wavelets. *International Journal For Advance Research In Engineering And Technology, 3*.

Manikandakumar, M., & Ramanujam, E. (2018). Security and Privacy Challenges in Big Data Environment. In Handbook of Research on Network Forensics and Analysis Techniques (pp. 315–325). Hershey, PA: IGI Global. doi:10.4018/978-1-5225-4100-4.ch017

Matthews, A. (2006). Side-channel attacks on smartcards. *Network Security*, (12), 18–20. doi:10.1016/S1353-4858(06)70465-2

Page, D. (2003). Defending against cache-based side-channel attacks. *Information Security Technical Report, 8*(1), 30–44. doi:10.1016/S1363-4127(03)00104-3

Park, J. Y., Han, D. G., Yi, O., & Kim, J. (2014). An improved side channel attack using event information of subtraction. *Journal of Network and Computer Applications, 38,* 99–105. doi:10.1016/j.jnca.2013.05.001

Ruedinger, J. (2006). The complexity of DPA type side channel attacks and their dependency on the algorithm design. *Information security technical report, 11*(3), 154-158.

Sadique, U. M., & James, D. (2016). A Novel Approach to Prevent Cache-Based Side-Channel Attack in the Cloud. *Procedia Technology, 25,* 232–239. doi:10.1016/j.protcy.2016.08.102

Saraswathi, A. T., Kalaashri, Y. R. A., & Padmavathi, S. (2015). Dynamic resource allocation scheme in cloud computing. *Procedia Computer Science, 47,* 30–36. doi:10.1016/j.procs.2015.03.180

Younis, Y. A., Kifayat, K., Shi, Q., & Askwith, B. (2015, October). A new prime and probe cache side-channel attack for cloud computing. In *2015 IEEE International Conference on Computer and Information Technology; Ubiquitous Computing and Communications; Dependable, Autonomic and Secure Computing; Pervasive Intelligence and Computing (CIT/IUCC/DASC/PICOM)* (pp. 1718-1724). IEEE.

Zhao, X., Guo, S., Zhang, F., Wang, T., Shi, Z., Liu, H., & Huang, J. (2013). Efficient Hamming weight-based side-channel cube attacks on PRESENT. *Journal of Systems and Software, 86*(3), 728–743. doi:10.1016/j.jss.2012.11.007

Chapter 6
Cognitive Social Mining Analysis Using Data Mining Techniques

Dharmpal Singh
JIS College of Engineering, India

ABSTRACT

Social media are based on computer-mediated technologies that smooth the progress of the creation and distribution of information, thoughts, idea, career benefits and other forms of expression via implicit communities and networks. The social network analysis (SNA) has emerged with the increasing popularity of social networking services like Facebook, Twitter, etc. Therefore, information about group cohesion, contribution in activities, and associations among subjects can be obtained from the analysis of the blogs. The analysis of the blogs required well-known knowledge discovery tools to help the administrator to discover participant collaborative activities or patterns with inferences to improve the learning and sharing process. Therefore, the goal of this chapter is to provide the data mining tools for information retrieval, statistical modelling and machine learning to employ data pre-processing, data analysis, and data interpretation processes to support the use of social network analysis (SNA) to improve the collaborative activities for better performance.

INTRODUCTION

Socials media are based on computer mediated technologies to enable the user to converse with each other by their videos, post, comments, sharing etc. It allows individuals to create public profile in their domain to be in touch with other users within that network. The concept of Social network has also improved the technology of Web 2.0 by formation and exchange of User-Generated Content. Social network is the graph which comprises the nodes and links to form the social relations among social network websites to interact with each other for the online sources and contents.

Social network platforms permit rapid information exchange between users, organizations, individuals and even government of countries to pursue the activities of social network. The set of connections network permits the effective compilation of large-scale data which gives climb to major computational challenges. Most of the challenges have been solved by the data mining techniques to discover valuable,

DOI: 10.4018/978-1-5225-7522-1.ch006

accurate and social useful knowledge from social network data. These techniques are also competent for handling network data viz., size, noise and dynamism. The information processing of social network datasets required enormous nature of automatically analyzing within a reasonable time.

Data mining techniques discover the useful knowledge from huge data sets to mine the noteworthy patterns, inference from data of social networking sites. This helps advanced results searches in search engines to understanding the social data for research and organizational functions.

Social sites provide privilege for the users to access the uncensored information post by them in real time for the broadcast. It also provides the platform to the use to express their views, opinions on products and services of the organizations to know their interest. This will generate the enormous volume of data which need to find a computational means to filter, categories, organize and scan the social network contents.

Data mining techniques are also capable to handle the social network anomalies like size, noise and dynamism to perform the automated information processing to analyzing the data within a reasonable time. Data mining techniques also enable the advanced search results in search engines to help in better understanding of social data for research and organizational functions.

This chapter provides the survey of data mining techniques range from supervised to unsupervised learning to analyze the data of social network to generate the meaningful knowledge and inference on the data. This chapter also includes the survey and anomalies of the social network site used by the data mining tools for the analysis.

BACKGROUND

Now a day, social networks became very popular due to increasing propagation and affordability of internet enabled devices such as personal computers, mobile devices and internet tablets. This is also a vital source of online interactions and contents sharing, assessments, subjectivity, influences, approaches, evaluation, feelings, observations. opinions and sentiments expressions in form of text, reviews, blogs, discussions, news, remarks, reactions, or some other document.

The authors used the data mining tools to mine patterns from social network data sites with advanced search results to understand the social data for research and organizational betterment.

User also takes the decisions, give opinions in a different form with very little or no restriction on information posted on social network. These view and opinion used by the organization for the betterment of their service.

There has been a lot of work done on as friend of a friend (FOAF) to look into how nearby and worldwide group level gatherings create and develop in substantial scale of social media platforms on the Semantic Web, Web administrations and online investigative affiliation.

It has been observed from the literature survey that most of authors described the data mining usage in the analysis of the social network sites data but what are techniques actual used to generate the meaningful information is not sated by most of the authors.

The main objective this paper is to show the data mining techniques used to generate the analyzed pattern from the social network data along with the implication and future scope of data mining in social network.

Social Network Analysis

Social Network Analysis used as research approach to allows researchers to enumerate the pattern of relations among people, animals, organizations or nations. This has been applied on substantive problems to cut across many subjects and disciplines into a possible of a measurable effect among the people.

There "sociocentric" or "whole" are two types of networks consist to form the group of a classroom of children, members of a club, a village or the executive board of a Fortune 500 company. The concept of sociocentric network studies the structure within the group. Whereas, "egocentric" or "personal" networks use the people known by individuals. The concept of research methods and theoretical approaches can be also used in used in for social network analysis. This will provide the idea where you will collect social network data and how learn, how to analyze it after input, into the appropriate software. At the end of the it will provide a good idea about how to apply social network analysis into many domains.

Introduction of Social Network Analysis

Socials media are based on computer mediated technologies to enable the user to converse with each other by their videos, post, comments, sharing etc. It allows individuals to create public profile in their domain to be in touch with other users within that network. The concept of Social network has also improved the technology of Web 2.0 by formation and exchange of User-Generated Content. Social network is the graph which comprises the nodes and links to form the social relations among social network websites (Kaur & Singh, 2016) to interact with each other for the online sources and contents.

Social network platforms permit rapid information exchange between users, organizations, individuals and even government of countries to pursue the activities of social network. The set of connections network permits the effective compilation of large-scale data which gives climb to major computational challenges. Most of the challenges have been solved by the data mining techniques to discover valuable, accurate and social useful knowledge from social network data. These techniques are also competent for handling network data viz., size, noise and dynamism. The information processing of social network datasets required enormous nature of automatically analyzing within a reasonable time (Olowe et al., 2013).

Data mining techniques discover the useful knowledge from huge data sets to mine the noteworthy patterns, inference from data of social networking sites. This help for advanced results searches in searching engines to understanding the social data for research and organizational functions (Zatari, 2015).

Social sites provide privilege for the users to access the uncensored information post by them in real time for the broadcast. It also provides the platform to the use to express their views, opinions on products and services of the organizations to know their interest. This will generate the enormous volume of data which need to find a computational means to filter, categories, organize and scan the social network contents.

Data mining techniques are also capable to handle the social network anomalies like size, noise and dynamism to perform the automated information processing to analyzing the data within a reasonable time. Data mining techniques also enable the advanced search results in search engines to help in better understanding of social data for research and organizational functions.

This chapter provides the survey of data mining techniques range from supervised to unsupervised learning to analyze the data of social network to generate the meaningful knowledge and inference on the data. This chapter also includes the survey and anomalies of the social network site used by the data mining tools for the analysis.

PROBLEM IN SOCIAL NETWORK ANALYSIS

Social network was created by organizations with combination nodes to relate one or more community, like relationships of beliefs, friendship, knowledge common interest and many more. In easy ways a social network is the map of all of the all the nodes exist in studied.

Many association or persons are likely to spend important time, attempt and money only to shelve in time another user's account because Social Network Analysis surge the popularity. Social networking has three big problems like make trust, dispelling the illusion of accuracy, and taming the expert mindset.

Make Trust

Social Network data is very sensitive which flesh out user's names and relationships with other vital information which may create powerful emotions when discourse in a group.

Therefore, it required the trust, expressed effort in building trust or avoiding distrust is require in grouping with a strong set of right values to ensure systems network architecture (SNA) results are not tainted.

The Illusion of Accuracy

Social network analysis utilizes a host of metrics and measures and measures degree of closeness among peoples with believe that the underlying data sets are accurate. It may be possible that some missing data create illusion in accuracy.

The Expert Mindset

SNA has prompt from a research tool to a management technique where expert move from 'expert' towards 'facilitator'. This move generates social networks artificially that look much like the real thing.

RESEARCH ISSUES ON SOCIAL NETWORK ANALYSIS

Graph Theoretic Tools for SNA

Visual representation used numerous methods of visualization of data of SNN to understand the network data and express the result of the analysis. This method is the powerful method for conveying complex information with care in interpreting node and graph properties from visual displays which captured through quantitative analyses

Signed graphs can be used to demonstrate good and bad relationships between humans where positive edge represent positive relationship between two nodes (friendship, alliance, dating) and a negative edge represent negative relationship (hatred, anger) between two nodes.

Signed social network graphs used the nodes sign to predict the future evolution of the graph.

Signed social networks, also used the concept of "balanced" and "unbalanced" cycles to represent a group of people who are unlikely to change their opinions of the other people in the group and likely to change their opinions of the people in their group. For example, a group of 3 people (A, B, and C) where A and B have a positive relationship, B and C have a positive relationship, but C and A have a negative relationship is an unbalanced cycle. This group is very likely to morph into a balanced cycle, such as one where B only has a good relationship with A, and both A and B have a negative relationship with C. By using the concept of balanced and unbalanced cycles, the evolution of signed social network graphs can be predicted.

Social networking potential (SNP) has a numeric coefficient, derived through algorithms to represent both the size of an individual's social network and their ability to influence that network. SNP coefficients have two primary functions: 1: the classification of individuals based on their social networking potential, and the weighting of respondents in quantitative marketing research studies.

By calculating the SNP of respondents and by targeting High SNP respondents, the strength and relevance of quantitative marketing research used to drive viral marketing strategies is enhanced. Variables used to calculate an individual's SNP are limited to participation in Social Networking activities, group memberships, leadership roles, recognition, publication/editing/contributing to non-electronic media, publication/editing/contributing to electronic media (websites, blogs), and frequency of past distribution of information within their network.

Recommender System in Social Network Community

Online data explosion compels recommender systems that will range from manually redefined un-personalized recommendations to fully automatic general-purpose recommendation engines, Collaborative Filtering and Content Based recommendations are two dominating approaches have emerged in this regard.

Collaborative Filtering

Collaborative filtering start looking for recommendations based on people views who often ask for the advice of friends. On the Internet, population can supply the advises that Shifts into identifying which part of this population is relevant for the current user.

CF methods identify similarity between users based on their rated items and recommend new items that similar users have liked. Nearest-Neighbor approaches with Pearson Correlation, computing and similarity between users may be directly used over the database to find the user item ratings. But modern systems also used some statistical model on the database and use it for recommending previously rated items for a new audience. It has been observed that Model-based approaches may produce some error in favor of a rapid recommendation generation process, better scaling up to modern applications.

CF works in independent ways to the specification of the item and provides recommendations for complex items which often used together in different ways. Create the good recommendations for new users are the major drawback of this approach and were not rated by many users.

Content-Based Recommendation

Content-Based recommendations system created in the field of information filtering, where some analysis of their text of document done and items are defined by a set of features or attributes. The user using preference over this set of features and obtain recommendations by matching item profiles.

Separate methods that can learn preferred attribute based on the user rated items that ask the user to specify his preferences over item attributes, but researcher preferred the item attribute preferences by CB recommendation. CB approaches used statistical models match user profiles and item profiles directly from it. This can also result in very expected items of user which he is unaware of but may like. However, CB systems can easily provide valid recommendations to new users based on their profile which has gathered from questionnaire or some other method for preferences elicitation, which they never used the system before.

CB engines can provide recommendations for new items that were never rated before based on the item description and are therefore very useful in environments. Many researchers opined hybrid approaches of CF and CB to reduce the disadvantages of the methods.

Communities and Social Networks

The main idea of a Social Network (SN) is to use some relations that users sharing between them. Social networks can be divided into several groups in terms of different criteria:

- **Dedicated:** Dating or business networks, networks of friends, graduates, fun clubs, etc.
- **Indirect:** Online communicators, address books, e-mails, etc.
- **Common Activities:** Co-authors of scientific papers, co-organizers of events, etc.
- **Local Networks:** People living in the neighborhood, families, and employee networks, etc.
- **Hyperlink Networks:** Links between home pages, etc.

Good systems take all the value of the above criteria and forms the inference in such a way that each user can invite other users and make friend and invitation can be approve or decline the invitation based on those direct relations the users.

Tools Used to Analyze Opinions Conveyed on Social Network

It has been observed that every day about 1.2 million new posts, 75,000 new blogs and giving opinion on services and products. These opinions also vary diverse subject ranging from personal to global issues which will be used to generate and recognition the positive or negative expression of users on various topics.

These opinions may further use to convincing the customers to make choices and decisions to support of political candidate during elections and motivate to investment of certain products and services. Moreover, aforesaid opinion can further discovered by traditional methods from the big volume of information generated by customer on social network sites. This generated information can further used to mine the meaningful information/inference using the techniques of data mining techniques to articulate the view on social network site.

Many researchers have developed the tools to analyze the opinion of customer, people on products, services, events or personality review of social network using data mining tools. Furthermore, researcher also used binary distinction of positive against negative to categorize the opinion-based text to find and rank the items in terms of recommendation or comparison of several reviewers.

Aspect-Based/Feature-Based Opinion Mining

Aspect-based /Feature-Based Opinion Mining used to mine area of entity of customers which they have reviewed from known feature-based analysis. It is then necessary to summaries the aspects reviewed to determine the polarity of the overall review whether they are positive or negative. Sentiments expressed of some customers are easier to analyze due to less ambiguity of others.

According to researcher aspect-based opinion problem based upon more in blogs and forum discussions of product or service reviews by either 'thumb up' or 'thumb down', to show the positive review negative review respectively. Conversely, in forum, blogs and discussions, it is not possible to recognized both aspects and entity due to high levels of insignificant data constitutes noise. Therefore, it is necessary to identify opinion sentences in each review by positive or negative thumb. Opinion sentences can be further used to sum up aspect-based opinion to enhance the overall mining of product or service review. It depends on holder to express either positive or negative opinion product or service.

DATA MINING

Introduction

The past two decades have seen a dramatic increase in the amount of information or data being stored in electronic format. This accumulation of data has taken place at an explosive rate. It has been estimated that the amount of information in the world doubles every 20 months and the size and number of databases are increasing even faster. The search for patterns in data is a human endeavor that is as old as it is ubiquitous, and has witnessed a dramatic transformation in strategy throughout the years. Whether refer to hunters seeking to understand the animals' migration patterns, or farmers attempting to model harvest evolution, or turn to more current concerns, like sales trend analysis, assisted medical diagnosis, or building models of the surrounding world from scientific data, the same conclusion can be reached as hidden within raw data to find important new pieces of information and knowledge.

Traditional approaches for deriving knowledge from data rely strongly on manual analysis and interpretation. For any domain – scientific, marketing, finance, health, business, etc. the success of a traditional analysis depends on the capabilities of one/more specialists to read into the data: scientists go through remote images of planets and asteroids to mark interest objects, such as impact craters; bank analysts go through credit applications to determine which are prone to end in defaults. Such an approach is slow, expensive and with limited results, relying strongly on experience, state of mind and specialist know-how.

Moreover, the volume of generated data is increasing dramatically, which makes traditional approaches impractical in most domains. Besides the possibility to collect and store large volumes of data, the information era has also provided us with an increased computational power. The natural attitude is to employ this power to automate the process of discovering interesting models and patterns in the raw data. Thus, the purpose of the knowledge discovery methods is to provide solutions to one of the problems triggered by the information era, "data overload". Knowledge Discovery in Databases (KDD) is the non-trivial process of identifying valid, novel, potentially useful, and ultimately understandable patterns in data.

By data the definition refers to a set of facts (e.g. records in a database), whereas pattern represents an expression which describes a subset of the data, i.e. any structured representation or higher-level description of a subset of the data. The term process designates a complex activity, comprised of several steps, while non-trivial implies that some search or inference is necessary, the straightforward derivation of the patterns is not possible. The resulting models or patterns should be valid on new data, with a certain level of confidence. The patterns have to be novel for the system and that have to be potentially useful, i.e. bring some kind of benefit to the analyst or the task. Ultimately, these should be interpretable, even if this requires some kind of result transformation.

An important concept is that of interestingness, which normally quantifies the added value of a pattern which combines validity, novelty, utility and simplicity. This can be expressed either explicitly, or implicitly, through the ranking performed by the data mining (DM) system on the returned patterns. Initially DM has represented a component in the knowledge discovery in databases (KDD) process which is responsible for finding the patterns in data.

Application of Data Mining in Different Domain

Data Mining is primarily used by companies in financial, retail, communication, and marketing organizations, to "drill down" into their transactional data and determine, customer preferences, pricing and product positioning to create impact on sales, customer satisfaction and corporate profits. Data mining can be also used in the following furnished areas:

Future Healthcare

Data mining holds used data and analytics to identify best practices to improve care and reduce costs with the help of data mining approaches of soft computing, multi-dimensional databases, machine learning, data visualization and statistics. It is used to foretell the volume of patients in every category to developed a system that make sure that the patients obtain suitable care at the exact place and at the exact time.

Market Basket Analysis

Market basket analyses based upon a theory to buy a certain group of items you are more probable to buy from group of items. This will help to the retailer to recognize the purchase nature of a buyer and henceforth retailer change the store's layout accordingly to differential analysis comparison of results, between customers in different demographic groups and between different stores.

Education

Data mining can also be used to discover knowledge from data originating from educational Environments to identify the students' future learning behavior, advancing scientific knowledge about learning and studying the effects of educational support. It is used by the institution to take precise decisions and also to inference the results of the student which can helpful for teacher to know what to teach and how to teach.

MANUFACTURING ENGINEERING

Fraud Detection

Traditional methods to detect are time consuming and complex which is used to stop the loss of billions of dollars frauds. With the help of Data mining, it is very easy to find the meaningful patterns to detect the fraud information of all the users. Using the supervised model built by data mining techniques and the algorithm of the records of user to classified as fraudulent or non-fraudulent among the users.

Customer Segmentation

Traditional market research only helps to segment customers, but data mining techniques use its techniques to enhance the market effectiveness. Data mining techniques categorized the customers into a separate segment and can adapt their needs according to the customers. Business always support to retaining the customers and data mining used to the customers details to offer them a special offers and incentive to make them happy.

Data Mining Preprocessing Techniques

A reduced/idealist view of the DM process presents it as the development of computer programs which automatically examine raw data, in the search for models and regularities. In reality, execution of data mining implies the application of required techniques from a series of domains, such as, statistics, machine learning, artificial intelligence, visualization. Essentially, the DM process is iterative and semi-automated, and it may require human intervention in several instances.

Data filtering is responsible with the selection of relevant data for the intended analysis, according to the problem formulation. Data cleaning is responsible for handling missing values, smoothing noisy data, identifying or removing outliers, and resolving inconsistencies, in order to compensate for the learning algorithms' inability to deal with such data irregularities. Data transformation activities include aggregation, normalization and solving syntactic incompatibilities, such as unit conversions or data format synchronization (according to the requirements of the algorithms used in the processing steps). Data projection translates the input space into an alternative space, (generally) of lower dimensionality. The benefits of such an activity include processing speed-up, increased performance and/or reduced complexity for the resulting models.

During the processing steps, learning models/patterns are inferred, by applying the appropriate learning scheme on the pre-processed data. The processing activities are included in an iterative process, during which the most appropriate algorithm and associated parameter values are established (model generation and tuning). The correct choice of the learning algorithm for the given established goals using various data characteristics is essential. There are situations in which it is required to adapt existing algorithms, or to develop new methods in order to satisfy all requirements. Subsequently, the output model is built using the results after the application of the selected model, and its expected performance is assessed.

Knowledge presentation employs visualization methods to display the extracted knowledge in an intuitive, accessible and easy way to understand its behavior. Decisions on how to proceed with future iterations are made based on the conclusions reached at this point.

DM process modeling represents an active challenge, through their diversity and uniqueness for a certain application. All process models contain activities which can be grouped into three types: pre-processing, processing and post-processing.

Data Preprocessing

Data preprocessing is an important step in the data mining process. The phrase "garbage in, garbage out" is particularly applicable to data mining. Data gathering methods handle out-of-range values (e.g., Income: 100), impossible data combinations (e.g., gender: male, pregnant: yes), missing values, etc. Analyzing data that has not been carefully screened for such problems can produce misleading results. Thus, the representation and quality of data is first reviewed before running an analysis.

If there exists irrelevant and redundant information or noisy and unreliable data, knowledge discovery during the training phase becomes more difficult. Data preparation and filtering steps can take considerable amount of processing time. Data cleaning (or data cleansing) routines attempt to fill in missing values, smooth out noise while identifying outliers, and correct inconsistencies in the data. The method of data preprocessing is shown in figure 2.3. The data processing and data post processing depends on user to form and represent the knowledge of data mining. Therefore, it has been not discussed in details.

Data preprocessing includes the following techniques:

- **Data Cleaning:** This technique includes fill in missing values, smooth noisy data, identify or remove outliers and resolve inconsistencies.
- **Data Transformation:** This technique includes normalization and aggregation.
- **Data Integration:** This technique includes integration of multiple databases, data cubes, or files.
- **Data Reduction:** This technique is used to obtain reduced representation in volume but to produce the same or similar analytical results.
- **Data Discretization:** This is the part of data reduction, but it is important especially for numerical data.

Data Cleansing

Data cleansing, data cleaning or data scrubbing is the process of detecting and correcting (or removing) corrupt or inaccurate records from a record set, table, or database. The term refers in identifying incomplete, incorrect, inaccurate, irrelevant, etc. parts of the data and then replacing, modifying, or deleting this dirty data.

After cleansing, a data set will become consistent with other similar data sets in the system. The inconsistencies may have been originally caused by wrong user entry or by corruption in transmission or storage, or by using different data dictionary definitions of similar entities in different sources.

Data cleaning tasks include

- Fill in missing values
- Correct inconsistent data
- Identify outliers and smooth out noisy data

Data Transformation

Through the application of the following techniques, data have been consolidated into forms suitable for data mining:

- Smoothing (remove noise)
- Aggregation (summarization, data cube construction)
- Generalization (replaces data with higher level concepts, e.g. address details of city)
- Normalization (scale to within a specific range)
  - min-max normalization
  - Z-score normalization
  - Normalization by decimal scaling
- Attribute/feature construction: New attributes constructed from the given ones

Data Integration

Data integration has the following techniques to handle the data.

1. Combines data from multiple sources into a coherent store, i.e.
   a. Schema integration: e.g., A.cust-id ≡ B.cust-id#
   b. Integrate metadata from different sources
2. **Entity Identification Problem:** It identifies real world entities from multiple data sources, e.g., Bill Clinton = William Clinton.
3. **Detecting and Resolving Data Value Conflicts:** The attribute from different sources is taken and converted into same format. Different representations, different scales, e.g., metric vs. British units can also be converted into same representation.

Handling Redundancy in Data Integration Redundant data occur often when integration of multiple databases have occurred viz. the same attribute or object may have different names in different databases and one attribute may be a "derived" attribute in another table. Redundant attributes may be able to be detected by correlation analysis.

Data Reduction

Databases or data warehouses often contain Terabytes of data, which result in very long run times for the execution of data mining algorithms. This high-dimensionality often creates problems through the use of algorithms on the original data (curse of dimensionality). This has necessitated the use of following data reduction techniques:

- Data cube aggregation
- Dimensionality reduction, e.g., remove unimportant attributes
- Data compression
- Numerosity reduction, e.g., fit data into models
- Discretization and concept hierarchy generation.

Discretisation

The discretisation technique includes the following steps:

- Reduce the number of values for a continuous attribute by dividing the range into intervals.
- Construct hierarchies for numerical attributes.
- Apply binning (smoothing, distributing values into bins, then replace each value with mean, median or boundaries of the bin).
- Perform histogram analysis (equi-width, equi-depth, etc.).
- Execute clustering.
- Apply entropy based discretisation.
- Perform segmentation by natural partitioning (partition into uniform intervals

DATA MINING TECHNIQUES AND THEIR ROLE IN SOCIAL MEDIA

Unsupervised Classification

Unsupervised learning algorithm used to do the classification on available data in different field of semantic orientation and Opinion summarization without training set. Few authors used the used Support Vector Machine (SVM) with linear kernel to study the polarity of neutral examples in documents.

Sentiment Lexicon

Sentiment Lexicon is used as dictionary of sentimental words to reviewers the customer review used in their expression. This list of the common words further used to enhance the data mining techniques in document to inference the variety of subject matters. But the sentimental words used in politics are often different sport. However, growing the occurrence of sentiment lexicon may help to center of attention to analyzing the topic-specific occurrence, t with the use of high manpower. Lexicon-based approaches may also be used in parsing work on comparative, simple, compound, conditional sentences and query. It has been observed that lexicon expansion has the drawback of wording losing after a few recapitulations which will be enhanced by 'throwing away' neutral words that depicts neither positive nor negative expression.

Opinion Extraction

It has been observed that every day about 1.2 million new posts, 75,000 new blogs and giving opinion on services and products. These opinions also vary diverse subject ranging from personal to global issues which will be used to generate and recognition the positive or negative expression of users on various topics (Anandakumar, Umamaheswari & Arulmurugan, 2018).

These opinions may further use to convincing the customers to make choices and decisions to support of political candidate during elections and motivate to investment of certain products and services. Moreover, aforesaid opinion can be further discovered by traditional methods from the big volume of information generated by customer on social network sites. This generated information can further be used to mine the meaningful information/inference using the techniques of data mining techniques to articulate the view on social network site

Semi-Supervised Classification

Semi-supervised learning worked on a mini training set of seed for positive and negative expressions to build the goal targeting activity to add the inference in online dictionary. This approach may produce the extended sets P' and N' for the training sets while binary classifier was built to dictionary for both P'∪ N' and translating them to a vector also.

Semi-supervised lexical classification was proposed to integrate lexical knowledge into supervised learning for comprise unlabeled data.

It uses the polarity detection as semi-supervised label propagation problem in graphs where node representing words polarity to be discovered using semi supervised techniques like Mincuts and Randomized Mincuts. The Semi supervised also used compared graph-based semi-supervised learning with regression and proposed metric labeling. Ii has been observed that the graph-based semi-supervised learning (SSL) algorithm as per PSP (positive-sentence-percentage) comparison (SSL+PSP) proved have to be perform

Supervised Classification

Clustering techniques are used to establish the data pattern from unknown data set in supervised and unsupervised manner, but classification techniques used supervised learning techniques to identify the date from available training set. It is extremely important to understanding the problem to be solved and used of appropriate data mining tool to solve social network issues. Social media is not only a dynamic platform to be a rational in the issue of topic but also enlargement the group behavior/influence or marketing.

Social network site such as Twitter and Facebook provides application programmers interfaces (APIs) to people and gather new information in the site and store for later usage and update using the crawler. But supervised learning algorithm works on multiple adjectives with similar or dissimilar Semantic orientations to represents similarity (or dissimilarity) of semantic orientation.

Support Vector Machine

Its task involved to select the best separating hyperplane from among several of them to move toward the maximum marginal hyperplane (MMH). It is also used as classification measure to detect the anomalies in various applications otherwise being a two class copy approach, which used as a one class algorithm H, A., & K, U. (2018) with fact that only a positive data set is taken as a class and the ''anomalies'' treated as the other class. Support vector machine model used to inference anomalous behavior detected by Cortes and Vapnik, Manevitz and Yousef for classification of various documents represented in different formats Multiple Classifier Payload-based Anomaly Detector (McPAD) to constituting one-class classier, detect the anomalies by the use of trajectory analysis used in traffic monitoring and video surveillance and deployed method makes use of one-class SVM clustering to detect anomalous (Kaur & Singh, 2016) trajectories respectively.

Naïve Bayers

Naïve Bayes classifiers making use of the prediction probabilities of any data object belonging to a particular class of Bayesian classification which involves the use of data mining techniques for supervised and unsupervised learning. Its shows two properties which makes use of the Bayes' theorem of posterior probability and class conditional independence (Haldorai & Ramu, 2018).

Theoretically, Bayesian classifiers are more accurate than other classifiers with minimum error rate due to inferences drawn from it and threshold-based systems. There are a number of models which assess dissimilar set of features and return dissimilar probabilistic values as irregular scores which are aggregated into a single value using a Bayesian classifier.

Neural Network

Neural network also used backpropagation method or connectionist learning in classification methods to learn consist of weighted connected components at the initial phase of learning the associated weights to make a correct prediction of the classes. These methods are highly used in classification and other prediction tasks despite to its difficulty for interpretation by human beings and long training times for both to the single class and multiclass environment. In multiclass problem it is used to detect the normal or the attack pattern with inference of type of the attack. NNID examined using MultiLayer Perceptron (MLP) neural network with important commands to know the user's behavior. Furthermore, this process carried out by identifying each user's profile and detection of intrusions for every user based upon the evaluation of their commands.

In common, the classification process can be summed up as a sequence of following 4 steps

- begin by discovering a set of class attributes and from training classes of data.
- Suitable Attribute for classification.
- A model has the capability to learn.
- The model used for the classification of unknown data value of data objects.

K-Nearest Neighbor

K-Nearest Neighbors algorithm used supervised learning in pattern recognition for classification, but it can also be used for prediction and estimation. A k-NN classifier used memory-based (instance-based) training procedure to classify the set of observations from collecting vectors. It used the intensive computations for classification involving two steps for each test observation. First one to: finding k nearest neighbors from observations and performing a training to retrieve a majority voting among (Anandakumar, 2014) the retrieved k neighbors to allocate the most frequent class label. Researcher used k-NN to formulate the problem of predicting of customer's buying the product from a Web store predict the fact of purchase transaction in session. S-KNN is instance-based learning which not used the construction of a model but delayed approach for lazy learner. The training set further used to classifying a new unclassified object by comparing it with the most similar object in the training set

Decision Tree

A decision tree (Wikipedia, n.d.) is a flowchart-like structure in which each internal node represents a "test" on an attribute (e.g. whether a coin flip comes up heads or tails), each branch represents the outcome of the test, and each leaf node represents a class label (decision taken after computing all attributes). The paths from root to leaf represent classification rules.

In decision analysis, a decision tree and the closely related influence diagram are used as a visual and analytical decision support tool, where the expected values (or expected utility) of competing alternatives are calculated.

- A decision tree consists of three types of nodes:
  - **Decision Nodes:** Typically represented by squares
  - **Chance Nodes:** Typically represented by circles
  - **End Nodes:** Typically represented by triangles
- Decision trees are commonly used in operations research and operations management but nowadays it is used to do the prediction base on the already stored training data.
- Decision trees, influence diagrams, utility functions, and other decision analysis tools and methods are taught to undergraduate students in schools of business, health economics, and public health, and are examples of operations research or management science methods.

CHAID (Chi-Square Automatic Interaction Selection)

In today's era, market research plays a vital activity for every business to identify and analyses the market trends, market demand, market size and the strength of others company which further assess the viability of a possible (Anandakumar & Umamaheswari, 2017) product or service before coming to the market. This one becomes the interesting field that use to identify the importance of data to make decisions to become popular in worldwide market.

Chi-square Automatic Interaction Detector (CHAID) analysis is the algorithm used to discover relationships between a categorical predictor variables and categorical response variable to find the relationships of the variable that can be easily visualized. It is used in direct marketing to show how different groups of customers have given their view on the campaign. Initially, CHAID builds a "tree" of different customer characteristics on the likelihood of response then progress down the tree to find the first "branch", which have the greatest impact on the likelihood of response from overall population and broken down into groups ("leaves") upon their differing values of this characteristic like urban/rural.

The process repeats to on each leaf to find the predictor variable which have significantly response and go on branch by branch find the significant effect on the response (e.g., likelihood of responding to the marketing campaign) of variable.

Text Mining

Text mining is the automated process apply to unstructured textual data resources to detect and reveal new, exposed knowledge with inter-relationships patterns whereas, information retrieval (IR) and search engine systems have specific search target of query keywords and return the result to related documents. In this research, data mining algorithms, such as clustering, classification, association rules, and many more are used to discover new information and relationships in textual sources. At the outset, text mining takes a set of un-structured text documents and pre-processing the to remove noise and commonly used words, stop words, stemming to produces a structured representation of the documents known as Term document matrix, where, every column represents a document and every row represents a term incidence throughout the document. Thereafter, data mining techniques such as classification, clustering etc. will apply to find the relevant information. With the high rate of online content, it is increasing the challenge to monitor sentiment and reactions to a new product, service or event.

With Linguamatics I2E text mining people can automate the extraction of anything information people viz. reviewer comments, customer complaints or praise, even competitor claims from online media.

DIFFERENT TECHNIQUES IN SOCIAL NETWORK ANALYSIS

Expert Discovery in Networks

Social media data is richest, largest and most dynamic system based on human behavior, bringing new opportunities to understand individuals, groups and society to motivate industry professionals and innovative scientists to find the novel ways to collect, combine and analyzing the data.

Expert discovery in the SNN typically done by companies in retail and finance to harness their product/customer service improvement, brand awareness, advertising/marketing strategies, network structure analysis, news propagation and for fraud detection. Furthermore, researcher has stated that Twitter data use Dow Jones Industrial Average (DJIA) prices to correlate with the Twitter sentiment 2–3 days earlier with 87.6 percent accuracy. They also used the Twitter train Support Vector Regression (SVR) model to predict prices of individual NASDAQ stocks to finding the 'significant advantage' for forecasting prices for15 min in the future (Anandakumar & Umamaheswari, 2017).

Few researcher and innovator have developed a systems and techniques to track the spread of infectious diseases, from the web sites new, blogs and social media to perfume the necessary action on time. They have also used the computational social science applications and computational linguistics to automatically inference the effect of news on the public based on the public responses on announcement, speeches and political comments and initiatives, insights into community behavior, social media polling of (hard to contact) groups. Researcher also use the various approaches to extract text features using four machine learning methods: Maximum Entropy, K-Means clustering, Naive Bayes and Bio inspired algorithm like BAT (Singh, 2018), ACO (Singh, 2017); find the useful pattern.

Text Mining in Social Networks

People tweets 80 million tweets in a day, 29 billion tweets in a year large with of unrelated 'noise' and corrupted spammers. Therefore, the keyword searches across this information often results in too much irrelevant information, which may take long time to analyze by sophisticated NLP approach used by I2E.

I2E can used in the SNN to inference that what people are say about 'Product X' with like and dislike opinion and cluster together the different people way of talking on the same sentence, e.g. "I like the object." Therefore, text mining used to categorize the populations tweeters according to behaviors and opinions on the product with elimination of irrelevant or unwanted tweets.

Integrating Sensors and Social Networks

A number of technical advances of software and hardware, enable the integration of sensors and social networks to collect a diversity of user-specific data in audio or video format. Many researchers used the of the applications software to compute the location of people using GPS enabled devices to collect large amounts of data, for continuously stored and processed for analysis. But the due to large number of users in a social network can be leads to natural scalability challenges for the storage and processing for underlying streams for data. Therefore, many naive solutions and hardware and software advances technology will require performing the task.

In this area, IBM has developed an IBM System S platform Development for Fast Stream Processing Platforms which can processed a number of fast stream processing platforms in real time and capable for storing and processing. Researcher also developed a Stream Synopsis Algorithms and Software to collected data explicitly and design an algorithms and methods to stream synopsis construction and analysis on its to make fruitful inference. Increased Bandwidth often required for to send the large (Anandakumar & Umamaheswari, 2017) wireless data in audio or video streams in real time. Therefore, bandwidth and storage capacity is the real challenge for the today world to processed the real time stream of data, has encouraged Integrating Sensors and Social Networks to developed an ever-increasing number of social-centered applications to collecting a large number of such interactive behaviors and model interactions among users to processed in efficient ways.

Multimedia Information Network Analysis in Social Media

Web 2.0 applications, such as Flickr, YouTube and Facebook are developing recommendation systems for community media to attract people to see their own comments and ratings on multimedia items, such as images, amateur videos and movies. It has been observed that a small piece of the multimedia rated and available databased user ratings required an automatic recommendation system to predict users' ratings on multimedia items, so that other people can easily find the interesting videos, images and movies from shared multimedia contents.

E-commerce web sites such as Amazon, eBay, Netflix, TiVo and Yahoo used the recommendation systems measure to provide personalized recommendations based on user review about the product. This will provide many advantages to new buyer to purchase the product based on the used given review. Now a day's, existing recommendation systems categorized into content-based approach which creates a profile of each user or product based on their personal information and historical rating records on movies whereas collaborative filtering (CF) recommendation systems used past user ratings about the products without explicit profiles of user. The CF method also used the neighborhood approach and latent factor models to compute the relationships between users or items or combination thereof to predict the preference of a user to a product whereas latent factor models with singular value decomposition (SVD) transform both users and items into the same latent factor space and measure their interactions in this space directly.

Social Tagging

Social networks used online communities to contribute and collect knowledge by their online tagging e resources. It has been observed that tagging behavior increased dramatically between 2005 and 2007 based on the data gathered from Delicious, Flickr and YouTube for the years 2005, 2006 and 2007 respectively. Delicious used the tagging data of Flickr or YouTube to create more representative venue for analyzing the social tagging behavior of users.

Amazon.com also permit to users to tag most of the products available on its website with the tags of "thriller," "mystery" and "quick read." Social tagging now a day's is popular social bookmarking for the users to share bookmarks to websites which they have collected from Digg, Del.icio.us and Reddit. Social tags from time to time grouped together into tag clouds, to create the visual representations of the popularity of different social tags associated with the object with larger the font size for popular tag. The tags are often rotated and arranged to resemble a cloud in the sky. For an example Last.fm – the digital music community site displays tag clouds of British artist Adele to describe tagged as soul and singer-songwriter.

SUMMARY

Social sites provide privilege for the users to access the uncensored information post by them in real time for the broadcast. It also provides the platform to the use to express their views, opinions on products and services of the organizations to know their interest. This will generate the enormous volume of data which need to find a computational means to filter, categories, organize and scan the social network contents. Data mining techniques are also capable to handle the social network anomalies like size, noise and dynamism to perform the automated information processing to analyzing the data within a reasonable time. Data mining techniques also enable the advanced search results in search engines to help in better understanding of social data for research and organizational functions

REFERENCES

Adedoyin-Olowe, M., Gaber, M., & Stahl, F. (2013). A Survey of Data Mining Techniques for Social Media Analysis. *Journal of Data Mining and Digital Humanities*, 9(2).

Anandakumar, H., & Umamaheswari, K. (2014). Energy Efficient Network Selection Using 802.16g Based GSM Technology. *Journal of Computational Science*, 10(5), 745–754. doi:10.3844/jcssp.2014.745.754

Anandakumar, H., & Umamaheswari, K. (2017). A bio-inspired swarm intelligence technique for social aware cognitive radio handovers. *Computers & Electrical Engineering*. doi:10.1016/j.compeleceng.2017.09.016

Anandakumar, H., & Umamaheswari, K. (2017). An Efficient Optimized Handover in Cognitive Radio Networks using Cooperative Spectrum Sensing. *Intelligent Automation & Soft Computing*, 1–8. doi:10.1080/10798587.2017.1364931

Anandakumar, H., & Umamaheswari, K. (2017). Supervised machine learning techniques in cognitive radio networks during cooperative spectrum handovers. *Cluster Computing*, 20(2), 1505–1515. doi:10.100710586-017-0798-3

Anandakumar, H., & Umamaheswari, K. (2018). Cooperative Spectrum Handovers in Cognitive Radio Networks. In Cognitive Radio, Mobile Communications and Wireless Networks (pp. 47–63). Springer. doi:10.1007/978-3-319-91002-4_3

Anandakumar, H., Umamaheswari, K., & Arulmurugan, R. (2019). A Study on Mobile IPv6 Handover in Cognitive Radio Networks. In *International Conference on Computer Networks and Communication Technologies* (pp. 399-408). Springer Singapore. doi:10.1007/978-981-10-8681-6_36

Haldorai, A., & Ramu, A. (2018). An Intelligent-Based Wavelet Classifier for Accurate Prediction of Breast Cancer. In Intelligent Multidimensional Data and Image Processing (pp. 306–319). doi:10.4018/978-1-5225-5246-8.ch012

Kaur, R., & Singh, S. (2016). A survey of data mining and social network analysis based anomaly detection techniques. *Egyptian Informatics Journal, 17*(2), 199-216. doi:10.1016/j.eij.2015.11.004

Kaur, R., & Singh, S. (2016). A survey of data mining and social network analysis based anomaly detection techniques. *Egyptian Informatics Journal, 17*(2), 199–216.

Singh, D. (2017). An Effort to Design an Integrated System to Extract Information Under the Domain of Metaheuristics. *International Journal of Applied Evolutionary Computation, 8*(3), 13–52. doi:10.4018/IJAEC.2017070102

Singh, D. (2018). A Modified Bio Inspired: BAT Algorithm. *International Journal of Applied Metaheuristic Computing, 9*(1), 60–77. doi:10.4018/IJAMC.2018010105

Zatari, T. (2015). Data Mining in Social Media. *International Journal of Scientific & Engineering Research, 6*(7), 152–154.

Chapter 7

Cognitive Mining for Exploratory Data Analytics Using Clustering Based on Particle Swarm Optimization:
Cognitive Mining for Exploratory Data Analytics

Suriya Murugan
Bannari Amman Institute of Technology, India

Sumithra M. G.
Bannari Amman Institute of Technology, India

Logeswari Shanmugam
Bannari Amman Institute of Technology, India

ABSTRACT

This chapter examines the exploratory data analytics that require statistical techniques on data sets which are in the form of object-attribute-time format and referred to as three-dimensional data sets. It is very difficult to cluster and hence a subspace clustering method is used. Existing algorithms like CATSeeker are not actionable and its 3D structure complicates the clustering process, hence they are inadequate to solve this clustering problem. To cluster these three-dimensional data sets, a new centroid-based concept is introduced in the proposed system called clustering using particle swarm optimization (CPSO). This CPSO framework can be applied to financial and stock domain datasets through the unique combination of (1) singular value decomposition (SVD), (2) particle swarm optimization (PSO), and (3) 3D frequent item set mining which results in efficient performance. CPSO framework prunes the entire search space to identify the significant subspaces and clusters the datasets based on optimal centroid value.

DOI: 10.4018/978-1-5225-7522-1.ch007

INTRODUCTION

Data Mining

Data mining is the process of discovering new patterns from large data sources. Knowledge discovery from databases (KDD) is an interdisciplinary subfield of computer science which is used for discovering patterns in large data sets involving methods at the intersection of artificial intelligence, machine learning, statistics, and database systems. The overall goal of the data mining process is to extract information from a data set and transform it into an understandable structure for further use.

The analysis step involves database and data management aspects, data pre-processing, model and inference considerations, interestingness metrics, complexity considerations, post-processing of discovered structures, visualization and online updating. Data mining is not only for the analysis of large-scale data or information processing but is also generalized to any kind of computer decision support system, including artificial intelligence, machine learning, and business intelligence.

Data mining uses information from past data to analyze the outcome of a particular problem or situation that may arise. Data mining works to analyze data stored in data warehouses that are used to store that data that is being analyzed.

Managers also use data mining to decide upon marketing strategies for their product. They can use data to compare and contrast among competitors.

Data mining interprets its data into real time analysis that can be used to increase sales, promote new product, or delete product that is not value-added to the company. Data mining interprets its data into real time analysis that can be used to increase sales and promote new product. Data mining mostly is used in decision making process which is also called business intelligence. Business-related decision-making is made using data mining techniques. Data mining is the entire process of applying computer methodology for knowledge discovery.

Steps in data mining:

- **Data Cleaning:** It is a phase in which noise and irrelevant data are removed from the collection.
- **Data Integration:** In this stage, multiple data sources, often heterogeneous may be combined in a common source.
- **Data Selection:** At this stage, the data relevant to the analysis is decided on and retrieved from the data collection.
- **Data Transformation:** It is also known as data consolidation. It is a phase in which the selected data is transformed into forms appropriate for mining procedure.
- **Data Mining:** It is the crucial step in which clever techniques are applied to extract patterns potentially useful.
- **Pattern Evaluation:** In this step, strictly interesting patterns representing knowledge are identified based on given measures.
- **Knowledge Representation:** It is the final phase in which the discovered knowledge is visually represented to the user. This essential step uses visualization techniques to help users understand and interpret the data mining results. Finally, the output will be represented in some human readable format which will be easy to understand.

Applications of Data Mining

- **Medical and Personal Data:** From government census to personnel and customer files, very large collections of information are continuously gathered about individuals and groups. Governments, companies and organizations such as hospitals, are stockpiling very important quantities of personal data to help them manage human resources, better understand a market, or simply assist clientele. Regardless of the privacy issues this type of data often reveals, this information is collected, used and even shared. By referring the old history of patients, the treatment method will be chosen.

- **Business Transactions:** Every transaction in the business industry is (often) "memorized" for perpetuity. Such transactions are usually time related and can be inter-business deals such as purchases, exchanges, banking, stock, etc., or intra-business operations such as management of in-house wares and assets. Large department stores, for example, thanks to the widespread use of bar codes, store millions of transactions daily representing often terabytes of data. Storage space is not the major problem, as the price of hard disks is continuously dropping, but the effective use of the data in a reasonable time frame for competitive decision-making is definitely the most important problem to solve for businesses that struggle to survive in a highly competitive world.

- **Scientific Data:** The data like protein data and gene data is referred as scientific data. Data mining task also used to deal with these scientific data. The society is amassing colossal amounts of scientific data that need to be analyzed. Unfortunately, the more new data captured and stored faster than the analysis the old data already accumulated. This will lead to wrong decision. But availing effective data mining task avoids this drawback.

CLUSTERING

Campbell and Shiller (2005) speak of the goal of clustering is to organize data by finding some 'sensible' grouping of the data items. Clustering is unsupervised learning because it doesn't use predefined category labels associated with data items and is shown in Figure 1. Clustering algorithms are engineered to find structure in the current data, not to categorize future data. Clustering applications are,

- Data mining (DNA analysis, marketing studies, insurance studies)
- Text mining (text type clustering)
- Information retrieval (document clustering)
- Image mining
- Statistical computational linguistics (cluster-based n-gram models)

Clustering Methods

There are so many well-known clustering algorithms. The main reason for having many clustering methods is the fact that the notion of "cluster" is not precisely defined. Consequently, many clustering methods have been developed, each of which uses a different induction principle. The clustering methods can be into two main groups: hierarchical and partitioning methods.

Figure 1. Clustering process

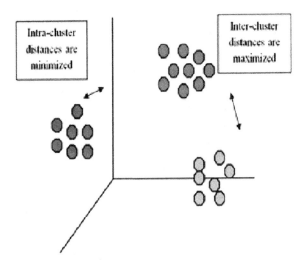

- **Hierarchical Methods:** These methods construct the clusters by recursively partitioning the instances in either a top-down or bottom-up fashion. These methods can be subdivided as following: Agglomerative hierarchical clustering and Divisive hierarchical clustering which is explained as follows.
- **Agglomerative Hierarchical Clustering:** Each object initially represents a cluster of its own. Then clusters are successively merged until the desired cluster structure is obtained.
- **Divisive Hierarchical Clustering:** All objects initially belong to one cluster. Then the cluster is divided into sub-clusters, which are successively divided into their own sub-clusters.
- **Partitioning Methods:** Partitioning methods relocate instances by moving them from one cluster to another, starting from an initial partitioning. Such methods typically require that the number of clusters will be pre-set by the user. To achieve global optimality in partitioned-based clustering, an exhaustive enumeration process of all possible partitions is required. Because this is not feasible, certain greedy heuristics are used in the form of iterative optimization.

CENTROID

A cluster is a set of objects such that an object in a cluster is closer (more similar) to the "center" of a cluster, than to the center of any other cluster. The center of a cluster is often called a centroid. The average of all the points in the cluster, or a medoid is the most "representative" point of a cluster. Centroid methods calculate the proximity between two clusters by calculating the distance between the centroids of clusters. The centroid based techniques may seem similar to K means, but as, Ward's method is the correct hierarchical analogue.

Initial Centroid Selection

Choosing the proper initial centroids is the key step of the centroid based clustering procedure. It is easy and efficient to choose initial centroids randomly, but the results are often poor. It is possible to perform multiple runs, each with a different set of randomly chosen initial centroids. Because random sampling may not cover all clusters, other techniques are often used for finding the initial centroids. For example, initial centroids are often chosen from dense regions, and so that they are well separated, i.e., so that no two centroids are chosen from the same cluster. In Figure 2, as long as two initial centroids fall anywhere in a pair of clusters, since the centroids will redistribute themselves, one to each cluster, and so achieve a globally minimal error.

Centroid Updation

Instead of updating the centroid of a cluster after all points have been assigned to clusters, the centroids can be updated as each point is assigned to a cluster. In addition, the relative weight of the point being added may be adjusted. The goal of these modifications is to achieve better accuracy and faster convergence. However, it may be difficult to make a good choice for the relative weight.

Incremental update also has another advantage that empty clusters are not produced. In Figure 3, all clusters start with a single point and if a cluster ever gets down to one point, then that point will always be reassigned to that cluster. Empty clusters are often observed when centroid updates are performed only after all points have been assigned to clusters. This imposes the need for a technique to choose a new centroid for an empty cluster, for otherwise the squared error will certainly be larger than it would need to be.

Figure 2. Centroid based clustering

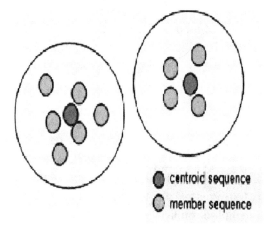

Figure 3. Centroid updation

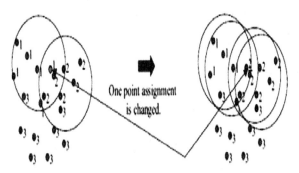

SUBSPACE CLUSTERING

Subspace clustering overcomes the curse of dimensionality that traditional clustering suffered, by finding groups of objects that are homogeneous in subspaces of the data, instead of the full space. Subspace clustering is the task of detecting all clusters in all subspaces. The new algorithms also was proposed which exploit the anti-monotone property of the clusters to efficiently mine the complete and stable set of results. For mining significant subspace clusters, an information theory concept known as correlation information, to measure the significance of the subspace clusters was introduced.

2D Subspace Clustering

The dataset which is in the form of object-attribute is referred as 2D datasets and is shown in Figure 4. The figure represents a mere two-dimensional space where a number of clusters can be identified. In the one-dimensional subspaces, the clusters c_a (in subspace $\{x\}$) and c_b, c_c c_d (in subspace $\{y\}$) can be found. C_c cannot be considered a cluster in a two-dimensional (sub)space, since it is too sparsely distributed in the x axis. In two dimensions, the two clusters c_{ab} and c_{ad} can be identified.

If the subspaces are not axis-parallel, an infinite number of subspaces are possible. Hence, subspace clustering algorithm utilizes some kind of heuristic to remain computationally feasible, at the risk of producing inferior results. For example, the downward-closure property can be used to build higher-

Figure 4. 2D Spaces with subspace clusters

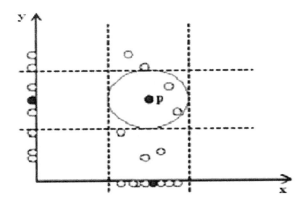

dimensional subspaces only by combining lower-dimensional ones, as any subspace T containing a cluster will result in a full space S also to contain that cluster (i.e. S ⊆ T), an approach taken by most of the traditional algorithms such as CLIQUE and SUBCLU.

3D Subspace Clustering

The dataset which is in the form of object-attribute-time is referred as 3D datasets and is shown in Figure 5. Subspace clusters represent useful information in high-dimensional data. However, mining significant subspace clusters in continuous-valued 3D data such as stock-financial-ratio-year data, is difficult. Besides, typical 3D subspace clustering approaches abound with parameters, which are usually set under biased assumptions, making the mining process a 'guessing game'. So an information theoretic measure was introduced, which allows us to identify 3D subspace clusters that stand out from the data.

ACTIONABLE CLUSTERS

The framework is the first of its kind that provides an approach to mine actionable clusters using an extrinsic measure. A cluster is actionable if the user can act upon it to his advantage. The extrinsic measure defines the value of the pattern with respect to an externally defined task. In order to mine these actionable clusters, the algorithm must be able to change the clustering process so as to obtain clusters based on which an optimal strategy can be provided. This approach is called "utility-driven clustering". Since the mined clusters are used to make important decisions these clusters are called "actionable clusters".

Figure 5. 3D subspace clustering

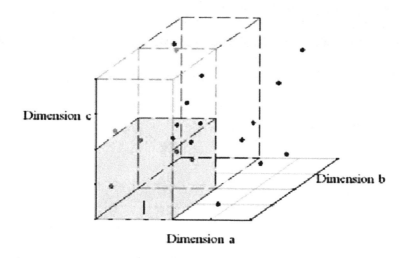

FEASIBILITY ANALYSIS

3D subspace clustering plays an important role in every field like stock market data analysis, protein structural analysis and gene data analysis. This clustering is used to identify the user preferred data which is important to make decisions.

G. Moise and J. Sander (2008) proposed a novel problem formulation that aims at extracting axis-parallel regions that stand out in the data in a statistical sense. The set of axis-parallel, statistically significant regions that exist in a given data set is typically highly redundant. Therefore, the highly redundant dataset should be reduced. So, this chapter deals with the concept of non-redundant set of axis-parallel, statistically significant regions as an optimization problem.

Exhaustive search is not a viable solution due to computational infeasibility, and the approximation algorithm STATSC is proposed. STATSC significantly outperforms existing projected and subspace clustering algorithms in terms of accuracy (Haldorai & Ramu, 2018). Reminal research has shown that increasing data dimensionality results in the loss of contrast in distances between data points. Thus, clustering algorithms measuring the similarity between points based on all features/attributes of the data tend to break down in high dimensional spaces.

It is hypothesized that data points may form clusters only when a subset of attributes, i.e., when a subspace, is considered. Global dimensionality reduction techniques cluster data only in a particular subspace in which it may not be possible to recover all clusters, and information concerning points clustered differently in different subspaces is lost. Therefore, several algorithms for discovering clusters of points in subsets of attributes have been proposed. They can be classified into two categories:

- Subspace clustering algorithms
- Projected clustering algorithms

Subspace clustering algorithms search for all clusters of points in all subspaces of a data set according to their respective cluster definition. A large number of overlapping clusters is typically reported. To avoid an exhaustive search through all possible subspaces, the cluster definition is typically based on a global density threshold that ensures anti- monotonic properties necessary for an Apriori style search. However, the cluster definition ignores that density decreases with dimensionality (Anandakumar & Umamaheswari, 2018).

Projected and subspace clustering algorithms search for clusters of points in subsets of attributes. Projected clustering computes several disjoint clusters, plus outliers, so that each cluster exists in its own subset of attributes. Subspace clustering enumerates clusters of points in all subsets of attributes, typically producing many overlapping clusters. One problem of existing approaches is that their objectives are stated in a way that is not independent of the particular algorithm proposed to detect such clusters.

Advantages

- Propose a novel problem formulation that aims at extracting from the data axis-parallel regions that "stand out" in a statistical sense.
- Intuitively, a statistically significant region is a region that contains significantly more points than expected.

Disadvantages

- Global dimensionality reduction techniques cluster data only in a particular subspace in which it may not be possible to recover all clusters.
- Information concerning points clustered differently in different subspaces is lost.

Kroger, Kriegel and Kailing (2004) introduced SUBCLU (density-connected Subspace Clustering), an effective and efficient approach to the subspace clustering problem. Using the concept of density-connectivity underlying the algorithm DBSCAN, SUBCLU is based on a formal clustering notion. In contrast to existing grid-based approaches, SUBCLU is able to detect arbitrarily shaped and positioned clusters in subspaces.

The monotonicity of density-connectivity is used to efficiently prune subspaces in the process of generating all clusters in a bottom up way. And then all small clusters are Automated analysis tools is used because there is an ever-increasing need for ancient and elective data mining methods to make use of the information contained implicitly in that data. One of the primary data mining tasks is clustering which is intended to help a user discovering and understanding the natural structure or grouping in a data set (Anandakumar, Umamaheswari & Arulmurugan, 2018).

Nevertheless, the data sets often contain interesting clusters which are hidden in various subspaces of the original feature space. Therefore, the concept of subspace clustering has recently been addressed, which aims at automatically identifying subspaces of the feature space in which clusters exist. In general, dimensionality reduction methods map the whole feature space onto a lower-dimensional subspace of relevant attributes in which clusters can be found. The attribute selection is usually based on attribute transformations by creating functions of attributes. Only important attributes have been chosen.

Advantages

- This algorithm automatically identifying subspaces of the feature space in which clusters exist very efficiently.
- SUBCLU is able to detect arbitrarily shaped and positioned clusters in subspaces.
- In contrast to CLIQUE and its successors, in SUBCLU the underlying cluster notion is well defined more points than expected.

Disadvantages

- The transformed attributes often have no intuitive meaning anymore and thus the resulting clusters are hard to interpret. In some cases, dimensionality reduction does not yield the desired results
- Using dimensionality reduction techniques, the data is clustered only in a particular subspace. The information of objects clustered differently in varying subspaces is lost.
- Clustering is based on use of grids. In this the clustering depends on the positioning of the grids.

Liu, Sim, Li, and Wong (2009) introduced subspace clustering which has been proposed to find clusters embedded in subspaces of high dimensional datasets. Many existing algorithms use a grid-based approach to partition the data space into non overlapping rectangle cells, and then identify connected dense cells as clusters.

A deterministic algorithm was developed, called Maxn-Cluster, to mine nClusters efficiently. Maxn-Cluster uses several techniques to speed up the mining, and it produces only maximal nClusters to reduce result size. Non-maximal nClusters are pruned without the need of storing the discovered nClusters in the memory, which is key to the efficiency of MaxnCluster. The results show that MaxnCluster can produce maximal nClusters efficiently and accurately.

The concept of maximal δ-nClusters is used to remove redundant δ-nClusters, and it is similar to the frequent closed itemset concept, which is used to remove redundant itemsets. An itemset is closed if it is maximal in the set of transactions containing it. If a δ-nCluster is maximal, then its corresponding attribute symbol set is a closed itemset in the attribute lists. The frequent closed itemset mining algorithms to mine maximal δ-nClusters. The concept of fascicles is introduced to create clusters which is similar to δ-nClusters. The objective is to use fascicles to compress data instead of enumerating all fascicles. Based on minimal and maximal value the clustering process is done.

Advantages

- New subspace clustering model called 'nClusters' to find clusters embedded in subspaces of high dimensional datasets.
- Compared with the traditional grid-based approach, the 'nCluster' model uses a more flexible method to partition dimensions.

Disadvantages

- The sliding window approach generates more bins than the grid-based approach, thus it incurs higher mining cost.
- Frequent itemset mining produces only itemsets (attribute sets), the corresponding object sets have to be generated in a post-processing step, which can be time-consuming when the number of objects and the number of generated attribute sets are very large.

Fromont, Prado and Robardet (2009) proposed an approach to deal with the high dimensional data. In high dimensional data, the general performance of traditional clustering algorithms decreases. This is partly because the similarity criterion used by these algorithms becomes inadequate in high dimensional space. Another reason is that some dimensions are likely to be irrelevant or contain noisy data, thus hiding a possible clustering. To overcome these problems, subspace clustering techniques, which can automatically find clusters in relevant subsets of dimensions, have been developed. However, due to the huge number of subspaces to consider, these techniques often lack efficiency.

The framework of bottom up subspace clustering algorithm was introduced by integrating background knowledge and, in particular, instance-level constraints to speed up the enumeration of subspaces. This new framework can be applied to both density and distance-based bottom-up subspace clustering techniques.

The algorithm called SC-MINER was introduced which is a data mining algorithm that mines subspace clusters under instance-level constraints and can be integrated into the common framework which includes preprocessing, data mining post processing.

Motivated by this need, the new approach is to extend the common framework for bottom-up subspace clustering techniques, by integrating IL constraints such as Must-link and Cannot-link constraints into the data mining step was introduced, so as to obtain not only more efficient algorithms but also more accurate results. These two constraints enable the end-user to guide the unsupervised subspace clustering task by adding some expert knowledge.

Advantages

- Clustering algorithms by integrating instance-level constraints into the mining process can increase the efficiency.
- The extended framework is able to consider several evaluation criteria (e.g. density, distance) in order to identify meaningful clusters in the data.

Disadvantages

- Must-link (two objects must be in the same cluster) and cannot-link (two objects must be in different clusters), concept is used. So, there is no possibility to get updated result.
- It becomes difficult to handle high dimensional data like 3D.

Sim, Aung, and Gopakrishnan (2010) stated that the subspace clusters represent useful information in high-dimensional data. However, mining significant subspace clusters in continuous-valued 3D data such as stock-financial ratio-year data, is difficult. Firstly, typical metrics either find subspaces with very few objects, or they find too many insignificant subspaces those which exist by chance.

Besides, typical 3D subspace clustering approaches abound with parameters, which are usually set under biased assumptions, making the mining process a 'guessing game'. Information theoretic measure is introduced to group the datasets, which allows us to identify 3D subspace clusters that stand out from the data. And a highly effective, efficient and parameter-robust algorithm, which is a hybrid of information theoretical and statistical techniques, to mine these clusters is introduced here.

Three-dimensional (3D) data, in the general form of object-attribute-time/location has become increasingly popular in data analysis. Many real-world applications, such as stock analysis based on stock-financial ratio-year data, basically cluster the continuous 3D data to perform the task. However, because these data are essentially high dimensional, traditional clustering approaches operating on the full data space become ineffective and traditional algorithms could not find the subspaces.

The problem to cluster subspaces in the 3D data is solved easily. The objects are grouped based upon their similarity in some subset of attributes and time. In such formulations, a 3D subspace cluster can be considered as a cuboid spanned by a group of objects, a group of attributes and a group of timestamps. The MASC algorithm used which consist of two modules.

- **Projection Into Standard Relational Database***: The actionable and sequential database is projected into a standard relational database, based on a chosen cluster center c.
- **Subspace Clustering:** After projecting into a standard relational database, the subspace clusters are mined from that projected database.

Advantages

- Cuboid is inherently axis-parallel, which is important for the user to easily interpret and understand the cluster.
- The notion of rarity to measure significance is used in which a high correlation information is significant when its occurrence is extremely rare.
- It can handle 3D dataset.

Disadvantages

- It is hard to find clusters in dataset that has larger number of time stamps. Clustering result produces the biased result.

Fu and Banerjee (2009) proposed a data matrix approach which deals with the problem of finding dense/uniform sub-blocks in the matrix is becoming important in several applications. The problem is inherently combinatorial since the uniform sub-blocks may involve arbitrary subsets of rows and columns and may even be overlapping. While there are a few existing methods based on co-clustering or subspace clustering, they typically rely on local search heuristics and in general do not have a systematic model for such data.

A Bayesian Overlapping Subspace Clustering (BOSC) model which is a Hierarchical generative model for matrices with potentially overlapping uniform sub-block structures is introduced. The BOSC model can also handle matrices with missing entries. So, an EM-style algorithm based on approximate inference using Gibbs sampling and parameter estimation using coordinate descent used with the BOSC model.

Advantages

- Matrix concept is used to cluster the data in which the pruning process is easy. Dividing entire search space into sub-blocks is the easy task.

Disadvantages

- The sub-blocks may overlap so that some entries may belong to more than one sub block.
- The matrix may have missing entries.
- Not all rows and columns may be a part of a sub-block.
- Mean squared residue scores do not have the anti-monotone property, which poses difficulties on developing efficient mining algorithms.

Ji, Tan, and Tung (2006) introduced the concept of frequent closed cube (FCC), which generalizes the notion of 2D frequent closed pattern to 3D context. Two novel algorithms to mine FCCs from 3D datasets is introduced. The first scheme is a representative slice mining (RSM) framework that can be used to extend existing 2D FCP mining algorithms for FCC mining. The second technique, called CubeMiner, is a novel algorithm that operates on the 3D space directly. In 3D context the frequent closed pattern is referred as frequent closed cube (FCC). Even in the traditional 'market-basket' analysis, it is not uncommon to have consumer information on a number of dimensions.

The problem of mining FCC from 3D datasets is solved by RSM. First, the notion of FCC is introduced and formally it is defined. Second, two approaches to mine FCCs is proposed. The first approach is a three-phase framework, called Representative Slice Mining algorithm (RSM) that exploits 2D FCP mining algorithms to mine FCCs.

The basic idea is to transform a 3D dataset into a set of 2D datasets, mine the 2D datasets using an existing 2D FCP mining algorithm, and then prune away any frequent cubes that are not closed. The second method is a novel scheme, called CubeMiner, which operates directly on the 3D dataset to mine FCCs. Third, RSM and CubeMiner can be easily extended to exploit parallelism. Parallelism is mainly used to reduce the time and space complexities during clustering process.

Advantages

- It can handle binary attributes.
- The parallel versions of both schemes can further reduce the computation time significantly.

Disadvantages

- Even though it handles both 2D and 3D datasets it is not efficient for 3D datasets.

RSM performs best when one of the dimensions is small.

Sequeira and Zaki (2004), says high-dimensional data pose challenges to traditional clustering algorithms due to their inherent sparsity and data tend to cluster in different and possibly overlapping subspaces of the entire feature space. Finding such subspaces is called subspace mining. The SCHISM, a new algorithm is proposed for mining interesting subspaces, using the notions of support and Chernoff-Hoeffding bounds.

The vertical representation of the dataset is used, and depth-first search with backtracking to find maximal interesting subspaces also used here to extract the clusters. The problem of finding statistically 'interesting' subspaces in a high dimensional dataset using an algorithm called SCHISM (Support and Chernoff-Hoeffding bound-based Interesting Subspace Miner) is used here. The Chernoff-Hoeffding bound is used to prune the search for interesting subspaces, as a nonlinear function of the number of dimensions in which the subspace is constrained.

- **SCHISM Algorithm:** A number of the subspace mining algorithms use a bottom-up, breadth-first search. In contrast, SCHISM, which is based on the GenMax algorithm that mines maximal item sets, uses a depth-first search with backtracking to mine the maximal interesting subspaces. First the dataset is discretized and converted it to a vertical format. Then at last the maximal interesting subspaces are mined. Finally, each point is assigned to its cluster, or labeled it as an outlier.
- **Mining Interesting Subspaces:** In SCHISM, interesting subspaces are mined using a depth-first search with backtracking, allowing us to prune a considerable portion of the search space. The method first finds all interesting subspaces in one dimensions (IS1) and two dimensions (IS2). And then the recursive MIS-backtrack procedure is called recursively to mine the set of maximal interesting subspaces (MIS).

Advantages

- Firstly, better memory utilization results from having only the relevant subspaces in memory at a time, as opposed to the horizontal format in which the entire dataset is scanned.
- Secondly, computing support of subspaces to be merged via item set intersections is very fast.

Disadvantages

- Vertical representation of the dataset only mines maximal interesting subspaces.
- Chernoff-Hoeffding bound is used to prune the search space in which the calculation is difficult.

Kailing, Kriegel, Kroger, and Wanka (2004) propose a method to handle the application domains such as life sciences, e.g. molecular biology produce a tremendous amount of data which can no longer be managed without the help of efficient and effective data mining methods. A common approach to cope with the curse of dimensionality for data mining tasks is dimensionality reduction methods. In general, these methods map the whole feature space onto a lower-dimensional subspace of relevant attributes, using e.g. principal component analysis (PCA). However, the transformed attributes often have no intuitive meaning anymore and thus the resulting clusters are hard to interpret.

The dimensionality reduction.even does not yield the desired results in some cases. In addition, using dimensionality reduction techniques, the data is clustered only in a particular subspace. The information of objects clustered differently in varying subspaces is lost. This is also the case for most common feature selection methods.

- **RIS Algorithm:** RIS finds all interesting subspaces and presents them to the user ordered by relevance. For each object, RIS computes a set of relevant subspaces. All these sets are then merged. A pruning and sorting procedure are applied to the resulting set of subspaces. For each detected subspace, statistical data is accumulated. The detected subspaces are pruned according to certain criteria.

Advantages

- RIS finds all interesting subspaces and presents them to the user in an ordered way.
- The whole feature space mapped onto a lower-dimensional subspace to produce the efficient results.

Disadvantages

- A PCA technique uses the ranking concept to identify the subspaces which is a time-consuming task.

CLUSTERING USING PARTICLE SWARM OPTIMIZATION (CPSO)

The CPSO framework has been chosen based on Arigela and Bansal (2014) as the parallelization technique in order to tackle the computational and space complexities since the large datasets causes an efficiency degradation of the clustering. The proposed CSPO is an algorithm in which the optimal centroids have been chosen to cluster the data during clustering process, rather than choosing fixed centroids. Choosing the best optimal centroid values improves the clustering results in 3D attributes. The proposed algorithm (CPSO) makes use of the CPSO framework that has been proven successful as a parallelization methodology for data-intensive applications. CPSO, two main operations need to be adapted and implemented to apply the clustering task on large scale data: the fitness evaluation, and particle centroids updating.

Particle centroids updating is based on PSO movement and the new centroids is calculated in each iteration for the individual particles. The particle centroids update takes a long time, especially when the particle swarm size is large. The CPSO algorithm the clustering task is considered as an optimization technique to obtain the best and optimal clustering result based on the optimal centroid value.

The optimal solution is obtained by calculating the distance between the data points and the centroid. The CPSO is similar to the K-means clustering algorithm. In k-means algorithm the centroid value depends on the weighted average value of all the points within the cluster. But in CPSO particle's velocity used to update the centroid value. In CPSO the particles contain the information which is used to accelerate the clustering task.

The CPSO algorithm uses the following important terms.

- **Centroids Vector (CV):** Current cluster centroid vector
- **Velocities Vector (VV):** Current velocity vector
- **Fitness Value (FV):** Current fitness value for the particle at iteration t
- **Best Personal Centroids (BPC):** Best personal centroid seen so far for Pi
- **Best Personal Fitness Value (BPCFV):** Best personal fitness value seen so far for Pi
- **Best Global Centroid (BGC):** Best global centroid seen so far for whole swarm
- **Best Global Fitness Value (BGCFV):** Best global fitness value seen so far for whole swarm

Particle swarm optimization algorithm is introduced to cluster the large set of data. This algorithm produces the efficient clusters based on the set of centroids. PSO is the swarm intelligence technique. The of particle swarm optimization is explained by the groups of birds that are looking for the optimal food origins. To get the optimal food sources the birds should move in one direction. This movement of birds referred to as current movement. If any of the birds in the group get the optimal food sources, then the other birds in the group go in the same direction to get the optimal food sources.

While moving the particle resides in two locations. They are personal finest location, and the global finest location. A particle resides in the swarm and the swarm comprises of many particles. The particles reside in the swarm owns a fitness value. This fitness value is described by the objective function which is based on the particle's placement. And the particle may have additional information like fitness value and velocity (position) which is useful in the motion of the particle.

Figure 6 indicates the overall system architecture, where the 3D value dataset is taken as input and fed into the Singular Value Decomposition (SVD) phase in which attribute pruning process is done by calculating the singular value for all attributes. After calculating SVD, using CPSO algorithm the optimal centroid value has been chosen. To calculate optimal centroid value the fitness value will be found. Then based on the fitness value the centroid will be updated. By using Bound Contrained Lagrangian Multiplier the probability value is calculated. Finally, the probability value is binarized to "0" or "1" then the actionable clusters is mined in which the output data is extracted from large collection of data.

CENTROID CALCULATION

Parallel particle swarm optimization clustering (CPSO) algorithm makes use of the parallelization methodology for data-intensive applications. Clustering has recently received a significant amount of attention in many computing fields but especially in the data mining area. Clustering has numerous applications and is becoming more challenging as the amount of data rises. To tackle space and time constraints, there is a need for parallel data clustering algorithms which can reduce the time and space complexities very effectively. Clustering task is expressed as an optimization problem to obtain the best solution based on the minimum distances between the data points and the cluster centroids.

For this task, the Particle Swarm Optimization (PSO) is introduced which is like a globalized search to find the best solution for the clustering task problem (this solves the selection of the initial cluster centroids and avoids the local optima convergence problem). PSO is one of the common optimization

Figure 6. System architecture

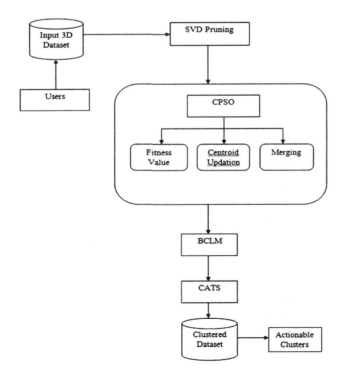

techniques that iteratively proceeds to find the best solution based on a specific measure. PSO acts as parallelization technique to avoid time and space complexities.

Updating Centroids

The first task in the CPSO is to update the particle centroids. There are two functions in this technique. They are map function and reduce function. First the map function is used to get the particles which have the identification numbers. The particle ID called as the Map key whereas the particle indicates the value. All the particle information like CV, VV, FV, BPC and BGC is associated with the map value. Using PSO the centroids are updated in the map function. Entropy values also used while updating the particle centroids. The entropy values are inactivity weight (W), PSO coefficients. These entropy values are applied to get the updated centroid value. Finally, the map function finds the updated centroid value.

And this value will be given to the Reduce function for further processing. The reduce function also called as identity reduce function. This reduce function is used to sort out the results which are made by the Map function. And also, the reduce function used to aggregate the results in a single file which is made by the Map function. Thus, the centroid value created in the Map function will be preserved for future operation. The particle may have additional information like fitness value and velocity (position) which is useful in the motion of the particle and to cluster the datasets which have more timestamps.

$$\text{Distance}\left(\text{Ri}, \text{Cj}\right) = \sum_{v=1}^{D} \left| R_{iv} - C_{jv} \right| \tag{1}$$

where,

Distance (Ri, Cj) – Distance between data and centroid
D – Dimension
V – Value
R_{iv} – Value of Dimension in data i
C_{jv} – Value of Dimension in Centroid C_j

Fitness Evaluation

The fitness value is calculated during the Reduce function. The map function is used to get the records which have the identification numbers (record ID). The record ID called as the Map key whereas the data record indicates the value. The distributed cache is used to store the particles. The map function collects the particles from this cache. The CPSO technique uses the cache concept to increase the clustering speed.

For every particle the centroid vector is extracted from the Map function and now the distance between the centroid and the record is calculated. This minimum distance is represented by the centroidID. Thus, using the ParticleID and centroidID which has the small and minimum distance, the composite key is formulated. Now, the new value is found by the minimum distance. And for each iteration the Map function produces the new key and the new value. Finally, these new values and new keys handed over to the reduce function.

The reduce function aggregates all the values and keys to obtain the average distance. This average distance is referred as fitness value. Now this fitness value acts as the centroids until the reduce function emits the key with new average distances. And after the reduce function emitting the key with new average distance, this new average distance considered as centroids. And this process repeats until get the good quality clusters.

$$\text{Fitness} = \sum_{i=j}^{k} \sum_{i=1}^{n_j} \left(\text{Distance}\left(R_i C_j\right) / n_j \right) / k \tag{2}$$

where,

Distance (Ri, Cj) – Distance between data and centroid
n_j – Number of records that belong to cluster j
k – Number of clusters

Merging

The third task is to merge the results from the first two tasks. The final fitness value is calculated by taking the summation of all the centroids' which is generated in the updating fitness value (second) task. Then BPCFV is calculated for each particle. The calculated BPCFV compared with the fitness value. If the new particle fitness value is less than the BPCFV, the centroid and BPCFV are updated. And also, the BGCFV is calculated for each particle. The calculated BGCFV compared with the fitness value. If the new particle fitness value is less than the BGCFV, the centroid and BGCFV are updated. At last in the distributed file system the new swarm with new information is saved which is the input to the next iteration. Merging will be done to identify the updated centroid value for each iteration.

SUMMARY

Mining actionable 3D subspace clusters from continuous valued 3D (object-attribute-time) data is useful for various domains ranging from finance to biology. The proposed method called CPSO is applied to large amount of datasets and it is the optimization and parallel methodology which is used to obtain the best clustering results. In CPSO (1) clustering is done based on centroid value and (2) CPSO is used to find optimal centroids based on the velocity of particle. The clustering task using CPSO is used to obtain the best solution based on minimum distances between data points and cluster centroids. This CPSO framework can be applied to data with increasing sizes and achieves high cluster quality with minimal time and space requirements.

REFERENCES

Anandakumar, H., & Umamaheswari, K. (2018). Cooperative Spectrum Handovers in Cognitive Radio Networks. In Cognitive Radio, Mobile Communications and Wireless Networks (pp. 47–63). Springer. doi:10.1007/978-3-319-91002-4_3

Anandakumar, H., & Umamaheswari, K. (2018). Cooperative Spectrum Handovers in Cognitive Radio Networks. In Cognitive Radio, Mobile Communications and Wireless Networks (pp. 47–63). Springer. doi:10.1007/978-3-319-91002-4_3

Arigela, A. K., & Bansal, V. (2014). *Value decomposition and dimension selection in multi-dimensional datasets using map-reduce operation.* Paper presented at the International Conference on Recent Trends in Computer Science Engineering (ICRTCSE'14).

Campbell, J. Y., & Shiller, R. J. (2005). *Valuation Ratios and the Long Run Stock Market Outlook: An Update.*

De Lathauwer, L., De Moor, B., & Vandewalle, J. (2000). A Multilinear Singular Value Decomposition. *SIAM Journal on Matrix Analysis and Applications, 21*(4), 1253–1278. doi:10.1137/S0895479896305696

Fromont, E., Prado, A., & Robardet, C. (2009). Constraint-Based Subspace Clustering. In *Proc. SIAM Int'l Conf. Data Mining (SDM)* (pp. 26-37).

Fu, Q., & Banerjee, A. (2009). Bayesian Overlapping Subspace Clustering. In *Proc. IEEE Ninth Int'l Conf. Data Mining (ICDM)* (pp. 776-781).

Haldorai, A., & Ramu, A. (2018). An Intelligent-Based Wavelet Classifier for Accurate Prediction of Breast Cancer. In Intelligent Multidimensional Data and Image Processing (pp. 306–319). doi:10.4018/978-1-5225-5246-8.ch012

Ji, L., Tan, K. L., & Tung, A. K. H. (2006). Mining Frequent Closed Cubes in 3D Data Sets. In *Proc. 32nd Int'l Conf. Very Large Databases (VLDB)* (pp. 811-822).

Kailing, K., Kriegel, H. P., Kroger, P., & Wanka, S. (2003). *Ranking Interesting Subspaces for Clustering High Dimensional Data. In Proc. Practice of Knowledge Discovery in Databases* (pp. 241–252). PKDD.

Kriegel, H. P., Borgwardt, K. M., Kröger, P., Pryakhin, A., Schubert, M., & Zimek, A. (2007). Future Trends in Data Mining. *Data Mining and Knowledge Discovery, 15*(1), 87–97. doi:10.100710618-007-0067-9

Kroger, P., Kriegel, H. P., & Kailing, K. (2004). Density-Connected Subspace Clustering for High-Dimensional Data. In *Proc. SIAM Int'l Conf. Data Mining (SDM)* (pp. 246-257).

Liu, D., & Nocedal, J. (1989). On the Limited Memory BFGS Method for Large Scale Optimization. *Mathematical Programming, 45*(1), 503–528. doi:10.1007/BF01589116

Liu, G., Sim, K., Li, J., & Wong, L. (2009). Efficient Mining of Distance-Based Subspace Clusters. *Statistical Analysis and Data Mining*, 2(5/6), 427–444. doi:10.1002am.10062

Moise, G., & Sander, J. (2008). Finding non-redundant, statistically significant regions in high dimensional data: A novel approach to projected and subspace clustering. In *Proc. 14th ACM SIGKDD Int'l Conf. Knowledge Discovery and Data Mining (KDD)* (pp. 533-541).

Preethi, V., & Suriya, M. (2013). A survey on mining actionable clusters from high dimensional datasets. *International Journal of Advanced Research in Computer Science and Software Engineering*, 3(11).

Sequeira, K., & Zaki, M. J. (2004). SCHISM: A new approach for interesting subspace mining. In *Proc. IEEE Fourth Int'l Conf. Data Mining (ICDM)* (pp. 186-193). 10.1109/ICDM.2004.10099

Sim, K., Aung, Z., & Gopakrishnan, V. (2010). Discovering correlated subspace clusters in 3D continuous-valued data. In *Proc. IEEE Int'l Conf. Data Mining (ICDM)* (pp. 471-480).

Sim, K., Poernomo, A. K., & Gopalkrishnan, V. (2010). Mining actionable subspace clusters in sequential data. In *Proc. SIAM Int'l Conf. Data Mining (SDM)* (pp. 442-453).

Sun, J., Tao, D., & Faloutsos, C. (2006). Beyond streams and graphs: Dynamic tensor analysis. In *Proc. 12th ACM SIGKDD Int'l Conf. Knowledge Discovery and Data Mining (KDD)* (pp. 374-383). 10.1145/1150402.1150445

Suriya, M., Anandakumar, H., & Arulmurugan, R. (2016). Social Aware Cognitive Radio Networks: Effectiveness of Social Networks as a Strategic Tool for Organizational Business Management. In *Social Network Analytics for Contemporary Business Organizations*. Hershey, PA: IGI Global.

Wang, K., Zhou, S., & Han, J. (2002). Profit mining: From patterns to actions. In *Proc. Eighth Int'l Conf. Extending Database Technology: Advances in Database Technology (EDBT)* (pp. 70-87).

Chapter 8

A Review of Artificial Intelligence Technologies to Achieve Machining Objectives

Deivanathan R.
VIT Chennai, India

ABSTRACT

Bridging the design, planning and manufacturing departments of a production enterprise is not a conclusive effort for the implementation of computer integrated manufacturing. Continuous interaction and seamless exchange of information among these functions is needed and requires the maintenance of a large database and user-friendly search and optimization techniques. Among several artificial intelligence techniques capable of the above task, four important and popular ones are, expert systems, artificial neural networks, fuzzy logic and genetic algorithms. In this chapter, these four techniques have been conceptually studied in detail and exemplified by reviewing an application in the manufacturing domain. Successful implementations of artificial intelligence that are recently reported in machining domain are also reviewed, suggesting potential applications in the future.

INTRODUCTION

Decision support systems are in use in the technical domain for quite a long time. Their value would be greatly improved if they could perform a decision-making step even in the absence of a human expert, given the fact that the human thought processes can be modeled by computers. By tracking human expertise and learning their preference strategies in a competitive or tie-breaking situation, decision making could be imitated. But this exercise need not be scientific, rather it is humanistic. "The scientific approach analyzes a phenomenon in quantitative terms, and has a tendency to analyze the behavior of humanistic systems as if they were mechanistic systems..." (Zadeh, 1973). Therefore, a modern problem-solving paradigm, known as Artificial Intelligence (AI) is being practiced when working out heuristic and experiential solutions to industrial problems.

DOI: 10.4018/978-1-5225-7522-1.ch008

The scope of this article is to assess the basic nature of problems faced in the production engineering domain which are sought to be solved by an intelligent manufacturing approach. This is followed by a discussion on the various AI techniques in vogue to implement intelligent manufacturing systems. Further, successful applications of AI recently reported in machining domain are reviewed.

BACKGROUND

The global research firm, Forrester says that 58% of business and technology professionals are researching AI systems and 12% are actively using them ("Power of AI," 2018). Accenture research on the impact of AI in twelve developed economies extrapolated a significant boost in labour productivity of up to 38% in 2035 (Purdey, 2016). Using AI, manufacturers could make informed decisions at each stage in the production process. There are several methods by which the human problem-solving abilities are imitated; of which Expert System, Neural Network, Fuzzy Logic and Genetic Algorithm are popular. Figure 1 displays the total number of published works, noted annually, featuring different AI techniques, as observed from Microsoft Academic Search website. It is seen that over the last two decades, neural network and genetic algorithm are used by researchers in large numbers, compared to knowledge-based system and fuzzy logic technique.

Technologies based on AI are helping to ease and uplift the living standards of human life, in many cases even we not being aware of it. Nowadays in the medical field, devices are produced with embedded software incorporating expert systems or neural networks for the automatic interpretation of clinical electrocardiograms (Celler, 1997). Banks and insurance firms could detect fraud and misappropriation through image processing and neural networks that can analyse data pattern and its day to day deviations. Genetic algorithms serve logistics planning functions in airports and factories, where they are used to help solve the resource-allocation problems. Fuzzy logic schemes are inbuilt into television sets to automatically adjust screen parameters based on ambient lighting and the time of the day.

Figure 1. Graphical presentation of total number of publications (annual) worldwide falling under the keywords 'knowledge-based system', 'artificial neural network', 'fuzzy logic', and 'genetic algorithm'
Source: Microsoft Academic Search website

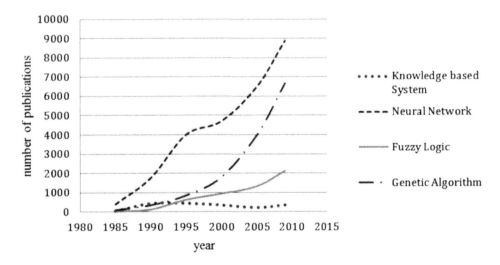

THE MANUFACTURING DOMAIN

Manufacturing is defined broadly as the process by which, material, labour, energy and equipment are brought together to produce a product having a greater value than the sum of materials put in. In fact, manufacturing aims at production of goods from raw materials and also it aims to improve productivity and quality of production. Several approaches have been taken in the industry to realize these objectives and the implementation of intelligent manufacturing system is an epitome of the industrial efforts. Intelligent Manufacturing Systems are said to have the ability to self-regulate a manufacturing process within design specifications.

Knowledge Based Decision Support

Business persons may seek expert advice to make a best choice from alternative options, for example, a product search, i.e., the search for a best product in a market, which is flooded with competing options. A systematic approach would be to converge from vast pool, by need based pruning of alternatives while matching user needs to available features of a product. The desirable process or product characteristics should be listed by the customer to match with the product features of available options. This situation can be automated by a program to first seek/collect the list of features desirable of the product and then searching the database for a product, whose feature best meets the demand. Products may then be ranked based on their suitability for intended usage. Product search is therefore a classical area of research for intelligent decision support.

Another popular domain where intelligent systems are in demand is the production environment involving machines, whose downtime due to repair could defer their production schedule. Hence, they are unproductive until the domain expert corrects the irregularities that caused the breakdown. Fault identification and correction at the shopfloor, in the absence of expert, is enticing. The remedy to a fault could be as many as their causative factors. Intelligent systems mimicking human experts are known to be helpful in drawing conclusions from a 'situation: action' or 'stimuli: response' paradigm. Expert knowledge about a 'system' corresponding to various 'subsystems' and levels of functioning can be captured and stored in a retractable database. Then, a fault observed by the operator can be traced back to its root cause using the interactive database and finally one can arrive at a remedy. The input could be abstract, but the advisory system would guide the respondent (customer) through, to search a stable and safe condition. So, developing the Human-Machine Interface is an essential component of intelligent system. Apart from this, safety monitoring is a special case of fault identification where intelligent decision making is needed when hazardous condition of a machine is detected through sensors.

Classification and Modeling

Engineering research is quite often dominated by data analysis involving classification or clustering of data to extract information about the process represented by the data. The information extracted could help in decision making about the state of the process. On a simple instance, data within known boundaries may be categorized; a data point under consideration may be above / below, larger or smaller, within or beyond a dividing criterion. Also, there can be more than one factor (criterion) influencing the state of a process and so the values of all such factors are to be considered into a formula, in attempting ascribe a data point to one group or other. Hence the criterion for dividing data into groups could be a function of several factors; and may need to be repeatedly computed for the data to be classified. Quite often, the parametric relationship is not explicit and not easily described by formulae. Learning and representing the obscure relation among a set of data is major task for intelligent machines.

An extension of this concept, of learning the relation between variables in a set of data and relating it to a state of a process, would supplement the efforts to develop mathematical models of a process. The usefulness of a process model (mathematical or AI) are manifold, such as, describing relationship between input and output, predicting the output for any change in input or other process variables. Further, as the process model relates the control variable with the dependent variable, it helps to simulate alternate trial runs of the process by adjusting the control variables in order to set an optimum output.

INTELLIGENT SYSTEMS

Human intelligence is known to be learnt, assimilated and practiced over years. The fundamental hypothesis of Artificial Intelligence (AI) is that intelligent behavior is constituted by symbolic inference and computers are capable of doing symbolic processing (Engelmore, 1993). Learning and assimilation of knowledge by computers requires the representation of human knowledge and expertise in the form of symbolic patterns. Therefore, knowledge representation and symbolic inference are the central research issues for modelling intelligent systems. Knowledge can be factual, i.e., worldly truth or it can be heuristic, i.e., experiential; both need to be stored in memory for knowledge processing by a computer (Honavar, 1995).

Knowledge Based Systems

Knowledge Based systems, also known as Expert Systems, are computer programs that can partially perform the role of an expert in his absence. An expert system has a user interface, a knowledge storage subsystem, and an inferencing or reasoning subsystem to work over a problem at hand, as shown in Figure 2. These components are comparable to user interface, database and algorithm in the sense of conventional programming.

The representation of factual and heuristic knowledge of a domain in the form of structured database (knowledge base) is an important stage in developing expert systems. One common method of knowledge representation is the 'production system' – a rule-based system in the form of IF-THEN rules (IF 'condition' THEN 'action'). Here, the IF part has a list of conditions, proclaiming a combination of information available initially, to deduce a preliminary solution. Given a set of rules covering the entire problem domain, a piece of knowledge in a rule is relevant during a user interaction, if the line of reasoning being developed (after user interaction) matches with 'IF' part of the rule. The 'THEN' part yields the deduced information, thus taking the user closer to the solution or conclusion.

In cases where knowledge regarding the problem domain is hierarchical in nature, a pure rule based system can result in an unnecessarily large number of rules and it is suggested to use an alternative knowledge representation method along with rules (Sudhir,1992). Another form of knowledge representation, invented by Minsky (1975), is the 'frame', also termed as the 'unit' or 'list' or 'scheme'. A frame is an assemblage of the properties of an entity being represented, synonymous to 'facts' in a rule-based system. Each property defines a characteristic of an entity and may have a value assigned to it. Sometimes, relations between entities may need to be represented. In a frame structure, the properties contain the relations possessed by an entity; its value refers to other entity related by this property.

The 'knowledge engineer' is a person who compiles the real-world knowledge of a problem domain constituting the knowledge base. He also develops a program module that can search through the knowledge base by chaining the 'IF_THEN' rules, manipulating the symbolic phrases and thereby yielding a logical conclusion. The search program can either start with a set of known conditions and narrow down the search for a conclusion (forward chaining) or it can refer to a fixed conclusion and backtrack the knowledge base to suggest possible conditions that are causative (backward chaining). LISP and PROLOG are the earliest programming tools (languages) available for the 'knowledge engineer' to build this inferencing mechanism and hence the Expert System. 'Backtracking', 'recursion' and 'inheritance' are the special capabilities of such programming languages. Working with uncertain knowledge and explanation of the line of reasoning for a conclusion are other commendable features.

Neural Networks

An artificial neural network (ANN) is a network of neurons interconnected by weight vectors (synapse), analogical to biological nervous system (brain cell) of neurons and the synapse. ANN topology consists of an input layer of neurons used to present data to the network, Anandakumar and Umamaheswari (2018) has an output layer of neurons to produce ANN's response, and one or more hidden layer of neurons in between them, as shown in Figure 3(a). The number of neurons in the input and output layer is decided by the number of input and output variables respectively, with reference to the problem that is modelled.

In addition to their topology, ANNs are characterized by weight vectors (synapse), and activation function used in the neurons of the network, as shown in Figure 3(b). The weight of a synapse, multiplied by the strength of the data on that synapse, defines the contribution of that synapse to the activation of a neuron for which it is an input. The total activation of a neuron is the sum of the activations of all its inputs. That is, activation $= \Sigma w_i x_i$, for i $= 1$ to n, where, 'i' is the number of synaptic inputs to a neuron. This activation determines the value of the output from that neuron, according to its transfer function. Transfer functions are S-shaped curve with the output confined between limits of 0 to 1 at $-\infty$ to ∞. Depending on the type of transfer function the limits may be -1 to 1, or 1/2, to -1/2 (Mishra, 2010). The

Figure 2. Structure of rule based expert system

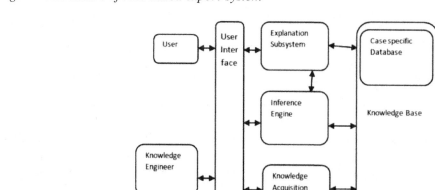

Figure 3. (a) Neural network topology (b) Inputs and outputs at a neuron

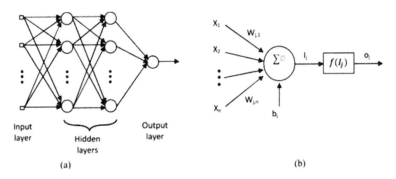

S-curve or sigmoid curve is a special case of logistics function defined by $S(t) = 1/(1+e^{-t})$. Hyperbolic functions are also used to define the sigmoid, given by $S(t) = \tanh(t) = (1-e^{-2t})/(1+e^{-2t}) = (e^{t}-e^{-t})/(e^{t}+e^{-t})$.

Neural networks can be designed to function in a feed forward mode or as a feedforward with back propagation (FFBP) of errors. A multilayer perceptron (MLP) is a feedforward neural network with one or more hidden layers. A feedforward neural network has sequence of layers consisting of a number of neurons in each layer. The output of one layer becomes input to neurons in the succeeding layer (Chandrasekaran, 2010).

ANN learns the relation between a set of input and output variables corresponding to an experimental data presented. A neural network is trained with a sample data of input-output relations and tested with another set of data to assess the effectiveness of learning and arrive at an optimum topology and weights. Actually, the topology and weights are the ANN parameters by which the given input is mapped on to a given output, in the training phase. Once trained, the neural networks can be used for prediction of output for a set of input variables. During the training process, the network adjusts its weights to minimize the errors between the output of the network and actual output (Anandakumar, Umamaheswari & Arulmurugan, 2018).

The Back Propagation algorithm is based on a steepest-descent approach for adjusting the weight values to minimize the error, in an iterative fashion. An iteration of the training process consists of two passes of computation: a forward pass and a backward pass through different layers of the network. To start with, the synaptic weights are initialized at random between 0 and 1. In the forward pass, the input data are applied to the neurons of the input layer. The activation function of each neuron is computed and its weighted value (according to the synaptic weight) propagates through the network, layer by layer. During the forward pass, synaptic weights are all fixed. The error which is the difference between the output value from the network and the corresponding true value is propagated back during the backward pass, to adapt the synaptic weights. The neural network is trained in an iterative manner until a stopping criterion is reached in the form of allowable training error. After each iteration the synaptic weights are updated in accordance with the learning rate constant (μ) and the momentum coefficient (η), initially defined in the neural network (Hou, 1995).

Fuzzy Logic

When mathematical information available about a problem is highly complex or incomplete, the fuzzy logic approach is useful instead of the classical approach to formalize information and systematically trace the cause-effect relation. It is used when subjective knowledge and suggestion by the expert are significant in defining objective function and decision variables. It differs from conventional computing in that, it is tolerant of imprecision, uncertainty, partial truth and approximation.

Lofti Zadeh (1965) put forward the idea of fuzzy set theory, in which the elements i.e., classes of objects can have partial membership and so the transition from membership to non-membership is gradual rather than abrupt. Indeed, the logic behind human reasoning is (based on) fuzzy truths, fuzzy connectives and fuzzy rules of inference. "The fuzzy logic approach has the ability to summarize the information and extract from the collection of data impinging on the human brain, only those subcollections which are relevant to the performance of the task at hand" (Zadeh, 1973).

Problem resolution by fuzzy logic involves three important stages, viz., fuzzification of inputs, fuzzy inferencing with fuzzy rules and defuzzification of processed information into outputs, as shown in figure 4. A fuzzy set-based prediction system takes the crisp input data and carries out "fuzzification". In the fuzzification process, the real-world input data (input parameters like, feed, speed, depth of cut, cutting force, etc.) undergo some translation in the form of linguistic terms such as "small feed", "medium cutting speed", "large depth of cut", "very large cutting force", etc.

To affect this, the fuzzy set concept is used. The linguistic terms thus obtained are converted into a fuzzy set with the help of subject knowledge of domain experts. For example, the "low feed" can be represented by a fuzzy set in which the feed values more than an upper threshold value can be assigned a membership grade 1 and those lower than a lower threshold value can be assigned a membership grade

Figure 4. Three important stages in fuzzy logic approach

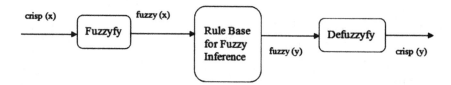

Figure 5. Fuzzification and Defuzzification process in a fuzzy logic solution

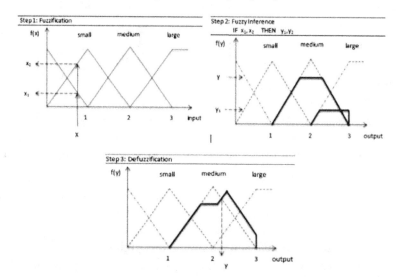

0. Between lower and upper threshold, the feed values can have a gradual variation of membership grades from 0 to 1. Thus, each input parameter is associated with a linguistic variable and a membership grade, forming the fuzzified input.

The fuzzy inference system applies the fuzzy rules to the set of fuzzy input to produce an output. The fuzzy rules is a set of predefined 'IF: Condition-THEN: Action' rules and a combination of which leads to a solution, in the context of the problem. In the fuzzy inferencing process, the membership value of the consequent of a rule is made equal to the minimum membership value of the antecedents. The defuzzification process uses the weighted value of the memberships of the consequents of all the relevant rules. The fuzzy output is defuzzified into crisp numeric data considering the output linguistic variables and the membership grades.

Membership to a fuzzy set can be decided by a triangular or trapezoidal membership function, as shown in figure, and conversion from fuzzy to crisp values could be established by well-known techniques like the centroid theorem. Once the linguistic variables have been converted into fuzzy sets, set theoretic operations on them can be carried out (Zadeh, 1973).

Genetic Algorithm

A Genetic Algorithm (GA) is a paradigm that tries to mimic the genetic evolution of a species over generations in a population. GA can be construed as a population-based search methodology, where a population is formed of innumerable feasible solutions, which are filtered by a fitness test in order to yield a new population of feasible solutions, called the 'next generation'. The optimality of a solution is tested over generations by introducing 'modified feasible solutions' into each generation. Thus, a feasible solution adapts itself to a fitness function. The adaptation process resembles the natural process of genetic inheritance from parents to children and survival of the fittest.

In GA, a feasible solution is represented by binary or decimal numbers, known as a string or 'chromosome' and the total population of feasible solutions forms the 'search space'. The string of numbers, forming the genes of a chromosome, encodes the various input/output variables corresponding to an optimization problem. The feasible solution is evaluated against an objective or fitness function. Each chromosome is then assigned a fitness value that indicates how closely it satisfies the desired objective and its chances of survival into the next generation. Whenever a feasible solution violates the constraints of the problem, a penalty is assigned to its fitness value.

The evolution of a feasible solution is ensured by three fundamental operations, viz., reproduction, crossover and mutation of the set of chromosomes forming the population. Reproduction operation replaces the population with large number of good strings having high fitness values, crossover operation produces new chromosomes by combining the various pairs of chromosomes in the population, and mutation operation produces slight random modification of chromosomes. Crossover and mutation are not applied to the entire population, but are taken as probabilistic events. A sequence of these three operations constitute one generation. The process repeats till the system converges to a solution, decided by a predefined number of iterations (generations). The finally obtained optimum solution combines the best elements of previous generation of chromosomes (Chandrasekaran, 2010; Man, 1996). It is to be noted that while the crossover enables the algorithm to extract the best genes from different individuals and recombine them into potentially superior children, the mutation adds to the diversity of a population and thereby increases the likelihood that the algorithm will generate individuals with better fitness values. Both processes are essential to the GA.

To further illustrate the operational procedure, a one-point crossover mechanism is depicted on Figure 6. A crossover point can be randomly fixed, as shown by a dividing line across the parent strings. The portion of the two chromosomes beyond this cut-off point to the right is to be exchanged to form the offspring. An operation rate with a typical value of between 0.6-1.0 is normally used as the probability of crossover. However, in mutation, the operation is applied to each offspring individually after the crossover exercise and it alters each bit randomly with a small probability of less than 0.1 (Namdari, 2014).

Manufacturing Applications of Artificial Intelligence

Manufacturing automation has evolved over ages. Initially hard automation was implemented followed by programmed automation and flexible automation. Based on our assessment of the manufacturing problems, we find that they are not purely logical or methodical to automate by a writing simple code and executing. At several stages in the implementation of computer aided manufacturing, the skill and knowledge of an expert are quintessential. Therefore, a new research topic named as 'Soft Automation' has arisen, that is utilizing computational resources and exhibiting intelligent behavior to fulfill the goals of manufacturing automation.

Application of Knowledge Based System

The designing, process planning and manufacturing functions have been traditionally managed in separate departments due to their colossal and unique functions. After computerization, several proponents have attempted to integrate these functions. This section describes briefly, a case study by Prabhakar et al. (2004) on the development of Knowledge Based System for integration of Computer Aided Design and Manufacturing (CAD & CAM) for machining process using feature technology.

Process planning is the function that bridges CAD and CAM to implement computer integrated manufacturing. It involves determination of appropriate machines, tools for machining the parts, cutting fluid and machining parameters under cutting conditions for each operation on a given part. There are two different methods of preparing the process plan. A variant system uses 'group technology' technique to create process plans from a set of standard plans prepared earlier. A generative system creates process plan automatically, based on logical procedures similar to that of a human planner.

While the user creates a feature-based model, the features and their attributes are stored in a database in the same order. Using this data, process plan for its manufacture can be generated based on the sequence in which features on the model were created. The base features of the component (for example, circular or square section) are used to select the workpiece. The inner features are used to identify the

Figure 6. Crossover and mutation phenomena in GA
(Namdari, 2014)

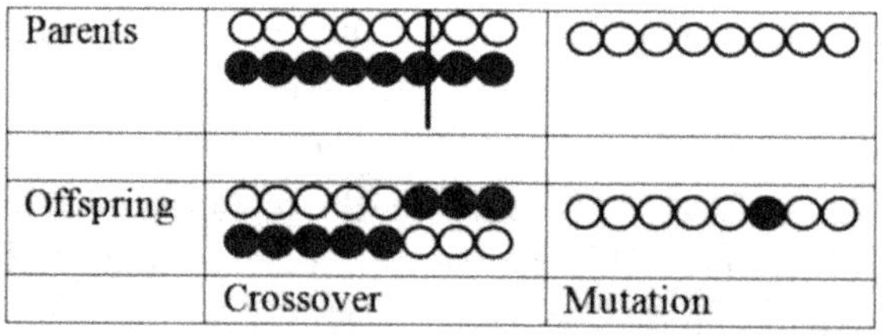

operations, machines and cutting tools and the sequence of operations. The parameters required in the process plan can also be derived from the design features or from the knowledge base. The technical knowledge of process planners are captured and coded into a computer program. In this work around fifty process rules (of the IF-THEN-ELSE type) were used for converting the design features of a CAD model into manufacturing features.

Strength of the work: The authors proposed a hybrid of variant and generative approach for process planning. Feature recognition is the strength of this work. Features are considered as information carriers between CAD, CAPP and CAM. A feature library is maintained consisting of templates of all elements of a part drawing with geometric and other parameters. The software was designed for generating process plans by interacting with CATIA (part modeller) and a virtual factory environment offering the database of available machines, cutting tools, workpieces, time and cost data. Their database was created and updated using query-based user inputs.

Application of Artificial Neural Network

This section describes an intelligent system developed using ANN, to monitor and estimate the tool wear in face milling, using Acoustic Emission (AE) and cutting force signals (Raimond, 2008; Kumudha, 1998). The ANN was trained using Back Propagation Algorithm (BPA) as it has the capability to solve nonlinear problems, given the fact that tool wear is a nonlinear phenomenon. In order to relate the sensor values to the actual wear, axial flank wear was measured off-line at regular intervals of machining.

Selecting the representative patterns of data to model the process is an important step. An AE monitoring system was used to sense and analyze the acoustic emission resulting from the machining process and was translated into the AE parameters like, Ring down Count, Rise Time, Event, Event Duration, and Energy. Machining force was measured using a three component (Fx, Fy, Fz) piezoelectric dynamometer in-process. Data acquired through sensors during machining (5 AE parameters and 3 force components) are normally highly variant due to the stochastic nature of the tool wear process. So, for proper training

Figure 7. (a) CAD model of a sample mechanical component (b) Representative design features and manufacturing features of CAD model (Prabhakar, 2004)

Design feature	Size X	Size Y	Size Z	diameter	Manufacturing feature
Block_Extrude	60	60	15	0	Milling(step)
Block_Extrude	40	40	15	0	Milling(step)
Block_Extrude	20	20	15	0	Milling(step)
Cylinder_cut	0	0	20	14	Drilling(hole)
Block_cut	20	10	15	0	Milling(step)
Cylinder_cut	0	0	15	10	Drilling(hole)
Cylinder_cut	0	0	15	10	Drilling(hole)
Cylinder_cut	0	0	15	10	Drillng(hole)

(b)

of MLP and to achieve the desired performance, it is necessary to input the normalized data with higher order variance from among those acquired. Usually, 50- 70% of the acquired data is used for training the ANN. The internal process of updating the weights in the network is mostly dependent on η and μ parameters and hence they were optimized to 0.1 and 0.7 respectively. In the present work, the number of input nodes equals eight, with single output node (to estimate the flank wear). The network was trained until its output converged to the point defined by the stopping criterion of a small error threshold of value 6.6×10^{-5} along with minimum validation error.

Strength of the work: It is difficult to obtain analytical models based on cutting parameters to estimate the tool wear since complex phenomena occurs during the machining process. Typical flank wear characteristics of coated carbide when machining the steel workpiece indicates that the coated carbide experienced rapid tool wear initially, followed by a slow propagating wear region and then there is a further rise in the propagation rate. But, TiN coated carbide inserts undergo certain dynamic changes such as deformation of coating material, formation of ledge over the rake face and continuously changing wedge geometry, which influence the nature of machining. Hence a simple mathematical model of the wear curve falls short of accurate predictions under dynamic environment.

Sensor based data can be fused along with cutting parameters using ANN for the purpose of identification of tool status (Madhava Reddy, 2012; Nathan, 2001). But, a single sensor information often remains unreliable and tool condition monitoring may fail to achieve the objectives. So, when more number of input features are to be considered for modelling the machining process, ANN is the most suitable technique. Also, we can include features measured in-process such as force and AE signals.

Application of Fuzzy Logic

This section describes certain aspects of a fuzzy logic-based model to predict the roughness after milling a rectangular piece of soda lime glass plate (Sarhan, 2012). Soda-lime glass has been used as a mould material with good dimensional accuracy even at elevated temperatures. The machining performance characteristic of glass material is of great concern for silicone mould manufacturers in order to produce good quality.

In glass milling operation, the lubricant pressure, spindle speed, feed rate and depth of cut are the significant parameters affecting surface roughness. The conventional method to achieve low surface roughness and cutting forces at different machining parameters is the "trial and error" approach. A reliable systematic approach to predict the surface roughness after milling is to capture the input-output relation of a limited set of experimental data, followed by a fuzzy logic approach for learning of the said relationship and subsequent tests. Based on L13 experimental array of operating parameters (lubrication pressure, spindle speed, feed rate and depth of cut) experimental data on the glass milling process was collected in a random sequence.

First, the input and output parameters in the numeric form were mapped to the linguistic variables. While generating the fuzzy rules, the authors used the term 'A' for lubrication pressure, 'B' for cutting speed, 'C' for feed rate and 'D' for depth of cut. For each input variable, four membership functions were used which are Low, Medium, High, and Very High. The entire range of input variables would fall into these four sets. Gauss shape of membership function was employed to map the fuzzy sets for the four input variables. The output variable (roughness) also used four membership functions; Best, Good, Average and Bad. In output fuzzy set, and triangular shape of membership function was used with its single peak and linear variation. A set of 13 rules were constructed (based on the experimental array of parameters and the surface roughness of a machined glass surface), to support the fuzzy inferencing process of roughness prediction. Typical fuzzy rules are listed here.

1. IF (A is L) and (B is L) and (C is L) and (D is L) then (Roughness is Best)
2. IF (A is L) and (B is M) and (C is M) and (D is M) then (Roughness is Best)
3. IF (A is L) and (B is H) and (C is H) and (D is H) then (Roughness is Average)

Fuzzy logic modelling was carried out in the Matlab software on the basis of Mamdani Fuzzy Logic concept. The centroid of area defuzzification method was used. In this method, the resultant membership functions are developed by considering the union of the output of each rule. Results from the fuzzy logic model indicate that, for better surface roughness, the recommended settings are the lowest values of the depth of cut and feed rate and the highest values of the lubrication pressure and spindle speed.

Strength of the work: The fuzzy logic model could predict roughness values within 8.75% error. The Gaussian membership function at the input side, well differentiates a nonlinear range of different input data into fuzzy sets. Even a novice user gets benefited as he can work on the model using linguistic terms for control. Moreover, the errors of numeric computation and optimization are avoided. However, profitable fuzzy applications are frequently noted in process control and optimization applications. Further, Mamdani systems are intuitive and well suited to human input compared to Sugeno systems which are well suited to mathematical analysis.

Application of Genetic Algorithm

A typical application of GA to machining parameter optimization is next described. The machining economics problem concerns the determination of the right process parameters, usually cutting speed, feed rate and depth of cut, in order to achieve the machining objectives. To find optimal cutting parameters during a turning process, D'addona and Teti (2013) used the genetic algorithm as an optimal solution finder.

The main objective is to determine the optimal machining parameters that minimize the production time without violating any imposed cutting parameter and quality constraints.

Usually, the production time, T_p, is the time necessary for the fabrication of a product and is estimated as,

$$T_p = T_s + V(1 + T_c/T)/MRR + T_i$$

where, T_s, T_c, T_i, V and MRR are the tool set-up time, the tool change time, the tool idle time, the volume of the removed material and the material removal rate. In some operations, the T_s, T_c, T_i and V are constants so that T_p is the function of MRR and the tool life, T, given by Taylor's formula.

The most important criterion for the assessment of the surface quality constraint is roughness, R_a, calculated empirically from the machining parameters using exponents relevant to a specific tool-workpiece combination. Another constraint related to machine is the maximum permissible value for cutting power. Due to the limitations on the machine and cutting tool and due to the safety of machining, the cutting parameters have a limited range. So, the cutting force, must be limited to a maximum value determined by the strength and stability of the machine as well as the cutting tool.

It was desired to arrive at the optimal cutting parameters satisfying an objective function of minimum production time, subject to constraints of roughness and power. This was performed using Matlab's GA toolbox. Priorly, machining data was collected from NC lathe while machining a cast steel blank by an HSS tool. The basic GA program was setup with a population size = 20 -100 individuals; number of generation = 10; probability for crossover = 0.8 and mutation rate = 0.1.

First, an initial population of 100 individuals, each comprising of cutting conditions (the combination of speed, feed, depth of cut), were generated at random within the specified limits and encoded into a string of numbers. Thus, each string (i.e) chromosome represents a set of cutting parameters, which is a likely solution to the optimization problem. For each one of the initial population of chromosomes, the constraints of power, force and roughness were calculated using formulae and checked for non-violation of appropriate limits. Thus, a set of feasible solutions was obtained. The best among the feasible solutions, in terms of fulfilling the objective function, will be the optimal solution.

The individuals that survive this selection step, undergo alteration by two genetic operators, crossover and mutation, to produce the next generation of chromosomes. The crossover and mutation operations were performed with a probability factor of 0.8, and 0.1 respectively. Subsequently, the new chromosomes will be evaluated by the objective function. The cycle of activities were carried out up to ten generations. Production time was found to be minimum in the 6th generation.

Strength/Justification of the work: GA is an optimization algorithm that does not require a strong mathematical background, rather it is a bio inspired method. Compared to traditional optimization paradigms, a GA is robust and may be applied exhaustively without recourse to domain-specific heuristics. So, GAs are widely used for machine learning, function optimizing and system modeling. Since the genetic algorithm-based approach can obtain a near optimal solution, it is preferable for machining parameter selection for parts with complicated detailing and bound by several machining constraints. GA is capable of multi objective optimization and its integration into an intelligent manufacturing system will lead to unimaginable improvement in quality and economic production.

RECENT RESEARCH IN AI APPLICATIONS

Knowledge Based Systems

An integrated manufacturing system needs automated conversion of design information into its manufacturing information. The information required at the manufacturing stage such as, the dimensional tolerance specifications, operation sequence, part fixturing and orientation data, cutting tool and material data, etc., are preferably extracted from CAD database in a CIM environment. Explicit programs are developed to perform this task by a feature-based approach considering manufacturing features as the common link between various design and manufacturing functions (Manafi, 2017; Elaakil, 2017). Moreover, a multi agent system can be used for the capture of domain specific knowledge (Djapic, 2017). The collective manufacturing information was also used by Ji et al. (2018), to assess both machinability and machining cost.

Further, KBS has been extended to perform economic analysis of production process through machining parameter selection and operations scheduling (Agrawal, 2017). Deng, et al. (2018) constructed an expert system for green cutting process using a knowledge base of part models and process models of typical components.

Successful implementation of process monitoring and control has been reported through hybrid AI techniques involving expert systems like the fuzzy expert system (Cica, 2017). Bio-inspired algorithms, such as genetic algorithm (GA) and particle swarm optimization (PSO) are used for tool wear prediction in hard turning of bearing steel. Zhu et al. (2018) proposed a smart monitoring system for CNC machining based on Cyber Physical Production System framework, which involves the physical and virtual modelling of the machine tool, process monitoring and big data analytics.

Artificial Neural Network

ANN has found widespread use for prediction of roughness, cutting force, tool wear and also for optimization of machining parameters in various machining processes like turning, milling, drilling. ANN models have been developed for predicting surface roughness due to milling of various novel materials, using the machining parameters as the input factors in addition to humidity, vibration, white noise, etc. (Bozdemir, 2018; Khorasani, 2017; Alharthi, 2017; Kilickap, 2017; Cirak, 2017; Ighravwe, 2015). Similarly, tool wear in milling has been predicted through ANN models by several authors (Kilickap, 2017; Ighravwe, 2015; Pohokar, 2014), and cutting force was predicted by Kilickap, et al. (2017) and Malghan et al. (2018). ANN process models have also been reported for roughness prediction in drilling by Roy and Bhagat (2015), roughness prediction in turning by Fang, et al. (2016) and for cutting force prediction in turning by Abbas, et al. (2018) and Makfi, et al. (2018).

By a better design of the ANN model, it has been shown that the machined surface roughness characteristics such as Ra, Rz, Rt, Rq could also be predicted. For this purpose, a FFBP neural network with 20 hidden layers was used by Al Hazza et al. (2013) while Fang, et al. (2016) applied both MLP and Radial Basis Function. Lipinski, et al. (2017) argued that while developing the ANN for process modeling, the determination of proper network architecture is a significant issue. The presented a neural network with generalization ability, to predict the surface roughness, tangential force and normal force in grinding of three different materials (Ti6Al4V, 100Cr6, Inconel) with a selected set of wheels under various operating parameters. After extensive analysis the 11-8-9-3 ANN structure was found to produce the lowest modeling error. Saric et al. (2016) used back propagation ANN to investigate the dependency of plane parallelism error while CNC grinding of multilayered ceramics. They considered the machine, operator, ceramic foil and the production line as the factors influencing the pane parallelism and tested diverse network architectures with different learning rules (delta, delta bar delta) and transfer functions (sigmoid, hyperbolic tangent) for getting the best performing network.

For roughness prediction in CNC milling, Cirak et al. (2017) showed after trials with MLFFBP neural networks, that a 4-7-1 architecture trained with LM algorithm gives the best performance. Makfi et al. (2018) proposed an improved design of ANN model with eleven hidden layer neurons, trained with Bayesian regularisation in combination with LM algorithm. Roy and Bhagat (2015) reported an improved performance of BP algorithm by allowing the learning rate to change during the training process. Ighravwe et al. (2015) used a two hidden ANN layer model for prediction of tool wear and surface roughness in milling and further optimization using fuzzy goal programming, big-bang big-crunch and PSO as modelling tools. A novel Edgeworth–Pareto optimization of ANN was presented by Abbas et al. (2018) and they suggested a 4-12-3 network for surface roughness prediction. Zhang et al. (2016) developed a neuro fuzzy network for tool condition monitoring in milling using the vibration signals.

Kannan, et al. (2014) applied ANN model for parameter optimization in drilling after evaluating the machining time, thrust and ovality. ANN technique was applied for machining parameter optimization in milling by Harinath et al. (2014), Chaskar et al. (2017) and by Pohokar (2014) in turning. Machining time, tool wear and cost factors were considered for optimization by Abbas et al. (2018).

Fuzzy Logic

Fuzzy logic model has been developed to aid in the selection of cutting parameters in drilling based on material hardness, hole dia and federate (Pendokhare, 2012). Mahesh and Rajesh (2014), Al Sahib (2014) used fuzzy logic for cutting parameter selection in end milling considering the roughness and material removal rate.

Fuzzy logic-based machining parameter optimization to produce desirable surface roughness characteristics, such as Ra, Rz, etc., has been studied by Das et al. (2014, 2016) when machining copper alloys and composites.

Hu et al. describe the implementation of real-time machining process control in a new STEP-NC controller, involving the transfer of information between CAPP and CNC, wherein a fuzzy control algorithm for cutting force control is designed and embedded in the software kernel of the STEP-NC controller (Hu, 2016).

Kalaichelvi et al. (2012) used fuzzy classification method to classify the tool wear states so as to facilitate defective tool replacement at the proper time. Salimi et al. (2015) implemented a fuzzy logic-model to predict the tool wear in turning operation using cutting parameters and forces as the input. They suggested tool replacement based on ISO 3685 standard.

Different techniques have been employed to relate the input/output data to fuzzy sets such as the use of Triangular membership function or Gaussian function (Barzani, 2015; Tanikic, 2017). Fuzzy logic model was developed for predicting surface roughness while machining different engineering materials (Rajasekhar, 2014; Naresh, 2014; Barzani, 2015; Babu, 2015).

Iqbal, et al. (2017) puts forward the application of fuzzy modeling for optimizing the machining process in respect of various combinations of minimizing specific energy consumption and maximizing productivity as well as tool life. Jogendra et al. (2018) applied grey-fuzzy hybrid analysis to optimize milling parameters and to improve the quality. Machining parameter optimization of turning process has been carried out using grey fuzzy logic approach by Senthilkumar et al. (2015) to obtain optimum MRR, surface roughness and tool wear.

Genetic Algorithm

Tool path optimization in CNC milling has been successfully implemented by Barclay et al. (2015) using evolutionary algorithm for optimizing the machining time and straightness achieved. GA approach is also reported for achieving energy efficient work table movements (Raja, 2018). Guiotoko et al. (2018) carried out GA based optimization of hole tolerance in 5 axis machining, in order to get low machining time and high accuracy.

Response Surface Methodology (RSM) as a statistical technique, has been collectively used with GA, to overcome the limitations of RSM and reach the global optimization process conditions. GA was applied to obtain the proper choice of machining parameters to maximize MRR and minimize cutting force and roughness, after an initial assessment of the parametric influence by RSM (Rishi, 2014; Vijayakumar, 2014). Similarly, Shaik and Srinivas (2017) proposed a multi-objective optimization approach based on genetic algorithms to simultaneously minimize the tool vibration amplitudes and work-piece surface roughness. The optimum combination of process variable thus obtained was further verified by the radial basis neural network model.

A hybrid genetic algorithm combines the exploration of GA with the exact convergence of a deterministic algorithm. The hybrid GA has all of the steps of a regular GA (e.g., selection, mating, mutating, elitism), however, after the mutation routine, each candidate is optimized locally (Tummuluru, 2016). Nafeez et al. (2014) presented a hybrid approach to machining parameter optimization using ANN and GA concepts. They considered cutting force, surface finish, machine power and speed to search for optimum machining parameters. Agrawal, et al. (2017) developed a hybrid genetic algorithm and expert system for machining parameter selection and operations scheduling based on a precedence cost matrix for features of cylindrical components.

SUMMARY

Problems in manufacturing engineering are knowledge intensive and unavoidably involve decision making by experts at various levels. Considering the scarcity of expertise and the push for unattended manufacturing, development and implementation of knowledge-based systems or intelligent systems for process modeling and optimization is important. Further expert advisory systems are well suited in planning and maintenance.

Soft computing techniques are preferred to physics-based methods for modeling and optimizing manufacturing systems which are characterized by complexity, uncertainty and lack of accuracy and precision.

Intelligent manufacturing can be achieved by utilizing the proven technologies of AI (fuzzy logic, neural networks, etc.) to monitor and control the manufacturing functions such as production planning, scheduling and shop floor operations. Four key technologies of AI domain, viz., expert system, neural network, fuzzy logic and genetic algorithm, have been studied and are seen to be taking semantic and evolutionary approach to model the machining process. Successful implementation examples stand proof to the benefits of the intelligent systems.

Knowledge based systems, like those intended for cutting tool selection, tend to be a peripheral unused system if they do not form part of regular information exchange activities of a manufacturing system. Therefore, KBS should be preferably integrated with the manufacturing system to increase their usage. ANN and fuzzy logic techniques have found widespread use for prediction of roughness, cutting force, tool wear and also for optimization of machining parameters in various machining processes like turning, milling, drilling. GA has found widespread application in machining process optimization under multiple constraints. Successful implementation of process monitoring and control has been reported through hybrid AI techniques like fuzzy expert system, neuro fuzzy system and hybrid genetic algorithm.

REFERENCES

Abbas, A. T., Pimenov, D. Y., Erdakov, I. N., Taha, M. A., Soliman, M. S., & El Rayes, M. M. (2018). ANN surface roughness optimization of AZ61 magnesium alloy finish turning: Minimum machining times at prime machining costs. *Materials (Basel)*, *11*(5), 808. doi:10.3390/ma11050808 PMID:29772670

Agrawal, A., Rajput, R. S., & Shrivastava, N. (2017). Operation sequencing and machining parameter selection in CAPP for cylindrical part using hybrid feature based genetic algorithm and expert system. *International Research Journal of Engineering and Technology*, *4*(6), 858–863.

Al Hazza, M. H., & Adesta, E. Y. (2013). Investigation of the effect of cutting speed on the surface roughness parameters in CNC end milling using artificial neural network. *IOP Conference Series. Materials Science and Engineering, 53*(1), 012089. doi:10.1088/1757-899X/53/1/012089

Al-Sahib, N. K. A., & Abdulrazzaq, H. F. (2014). Selection of optimum cutting speed in end milling process using fuzzy logic. *Innovative Systems Design and Engineering, 5*(2), 14–30.

Alharthi, N. H., Bingol, S., Abbas, A. T., Ragab, A. E., El-Danaf, E. A., & Alharbi, H. F. (2017). Optimizing Cutting Conditions and Prediction of Surface Roughness in Face Milling of AZ61 Using Regression Analysis and Artificial Neural Network. *Advances in Materials Science and Engineering.*

Anandakumar, H., & Umamaheswari, K. (2018). Cooperative Spectrum Handovers in Cognitive Radio Networks. In M. H. Rehmani & R. Dhaou, (Eds.), Cognitive Radio, Mobile Communications and Wireless Networks, pp. 47-64. Springer. doi:10.1007/978-3-319-91002-4_3

Anandakumar, H., Umamaheswari, K., & Arulmurugan, R. (2019). A Study on Mobile IPv6 Handover in Cognitive Radio Networks. In *International Conference on Computer Networks and Communication Technologies* (pp. 399-408). Springer Singapore. doi:10.1007/978-981-10-8681-6_36

Babu, K. A., Kumar, G. V., & Venkataramaiah, P. (2015). Prediction of surface roughness in drilling of Al 7075/10%-SiCp composite under MQL condition using fuzzy logic. *Indian Journal of Science and Technology, 8*(12).

Barzani, M. M., Zalnezhad, E., Sarhan, A. A., Farahany, S., & Ramesh, S. (2015). Fuzzy logic based model for predicting surface roughness of machined Al–Si–Cu–Fe die casting alloy using different additives-turning. *Measurement, 61*, 150–161. doi:10.1016/j.measurement.2014.10.003

Bozdemir, M. (2018). Prediction of surface roughness considering cutting parameters and humidity condition in end milling of polyamide materials. *Computational Intelligence and Neuroscience*, 1–7. doi:10.1155/2018/5850432 PMID:30050565

Celler, B., De Chazal, P., & Lovell, N. (1997). A comparison of expert systems for the automated interpretation of the ECG: regulatory implications of the use of neural networks. In *APAMI-HIC 1997: Managing Information for Better Health Outcomes in Australia and the Asia Pacific Region: 11 to 13 August 1997, Asia Pacific Association of Medical Informatics, HISA: Conference Proceedings* (p. 492). Health Informatics Society of Australia.

Chandrasekaran, M., Muralidhar, M., Krishna, C. M., & Dixit, U. S. (2010). Application of soft computing techniques in machining performance prediction and optimization: A literature review. *International Journal of Advanced Manufacturing Technology, 46*(5-8), 445–464. doi:10.100700170-009-2104-x

Chaskar, P. R., Lad, A. S., Mane, J. K., Sangre, A., & Kirkire, M. S. (2017). Optimization of CNC Milling Parameters Using "Artificial Neural Network." *Imperial Journal of Interdisciplinary Research, 3*(2).

Cica, D., Sredanovic, B., Borojevic, S., & Kramar, D. (2017). An Integration of Bio-inspired Algorithms and Fuzzy Logic for Tool Wear Estimation in Hard Turning. In *International Conference on Advanced Manufacturing Engineering and Technologies* (pp. 1-12). Cham: Springer.

Cirak, B. (2017). Mathematically Modeling and Optimization by Artificial Neural Network of Surface Roughness in CNC Milling–A Case Study. *World Wide Journal of Multidisciplinary Research and Development, 3*(8), 299–307.

D'addona, D. M., & Teti, R. (2013). Genetic algorithm-based optimization of cutting parameters in turning processes. *Procedia CIRP, 7,* 323–328. doi:10.1016/j.procir.2013.05.055

Das, B., Roy, S., Rai, R. N., & Saha, S. C. (2014). Surface Roughness of Al-5Cu Alloy using a Taguchi-Fuzzy Based Approach. *Journal of Engineering Science & Technology Review, 7*(2).

Das, B., Roy, S., Rai, R. N., & Saha, S. C. (2016). Application of grey fuzzy logic for the optimization of CNC milling parameters for Al–4.5% Cu–TiC MMCs with multi-performance characteristics. *Engineering Science and Technology, an International Journal, 19*(2), 857-865.

Deng, Z., Zhang, H., Fu, Y., Wan, L., & Lv, L. (2018). Research on intelligent expert system of green cutting process and its application. *Journal of Cleaner Production, 185,* 904–911. doi:10.1016/j.jclepro.2018.02.246

Djapic, M., Lukic, L., Fragassa, C., Pavlovic, A., & Petrovic, A. (2017). Multi-agent team for engineering: A machining plan in intelligent manufacturing systems. *International Journal of Machining and Machinability of Materials, 19*(6), 505–521. doi:10.1504/IJMMM.2017.088893

Elaakil, R., Ahmed, R., El Mesbahi, A., & Jaider, O. (2017). Technical Data Extraction and Representation in Expert CAPP System. *Transactions on Machine Learning and Artificial Intelligence, 5*(4).

Engelmore, R. S., & Feigenbaum, E. (1993). Expert systems and artificial intelligence. *Expert Systems: International Journal of Knowledge Engineering and Neural Networks, 100,* 2.

Fang, N., Fang, N., Pai, P. S., & Edwards, N. (2016). Neural Network Modeling and Prediction of Surface Roughness in Machining Aluminum Alloys. *Journal of Computer and Communications, 4*(5), 1–9. doi:10.4236/jcc.2016.45001

Guiotoko, E. H., Aoyama, H., & Sano, N. (2017). Optimization of hole making processes considering machining time and machining accuracy. *Journal of Advanced Mechanical Design, Systems, and Manufacturing, 11*(4).

Harinath Gowd, G., Theja, K. D., Rayudu, P., Goud, M. V., & Roa, M. S. (2014). Modeling & Analysis of End Milling Process Parameters Using Artificial Neural Networks. *Applied Mechanics and Materials, 592,* 2733–2737. doi:10.4028/www.scientific.net/AMM.592-594.2733

Honavar, V. (1995). Symbolic artificial intelligence and numeric artificial neural networks: towards a resolution of the dichotomy. In *Computational Architectures integrating Neural and Symbolic Processes* (pp. 351–388). Boston, MA: Springer.

Hou, T. H., & Lin, L. (1995). Using neural networks for the automatic monitoring and recognition of signals in manufacturing processes. In *Design and implementation of intelligent manufacturing systems* (pp. 141–160). Prentice-Hall, Inc.

Hu, P., Han, Z., Fu, Y., & Fu, H. (2016). Implementation of Real-Time Machining Process Control Based on Fuzzy Logic in a New STEP-NC Compatible System. *Mathematical Problems in Engineering,* 2016.

Ighravwe, D. E., & Oke, S. A. (2015). Machining performance analysis in end milling: Predicting using ANN and a comparative optimisation study of ANN/BB-BC and ANN/PSO. *Engineering Journal (New York)*, *19*(5), 121–137.

Iqbal, A., & Al-Ghamdi, K. A. (2017). Incorporating Energy Efficiency in Performance Measures of Machining: Experimental Investigation and Optimization. In *Sustainable Machining* (pp. 47–65). Cham: Springer. doi:10.1007/978-3-319-51961-6_3

Ji, W., Wang, L., Haghighi, A., Givehchi, M., & Liu, X. (2018). An enriched machining feature based approach to cutting tool selection. *International Journal of Computer Integrated Manufacturing*, *31*(1), 1–10.

Jogendra, J., Amit, K. V., & Sanjay, V. (2018). Experimental Investigation of Machining Parameters on Milling Machine using Grey-Fuzzy Logic Method. *International Journal of Mechanical and Production Engineering*, *6*(2).

Kalaichelvi, V., Karthikeyan, R., Sivakumar, D., & Srinivasan, V. (2012). Tool wear classification using fuzzy logic for machining of al/sic composite material. *Modeling and Numerical Simulation of Material Science*, *2*(02), 28–36. doi:10.4236/mnsms.2012.22003

Kannan, T. D. B., Kumar, B. S., & Baskar, N. (2014). Application of artificial neural network modeling for machining parameters optimization in drilling operation. *Procedia Materials Science*, *5*, 2242–2249. doi:10.1016/j.mspro.2014.07.433

Khorasani, A., & Yazdi, M. R. S. (2017). Development of a dynamic surface roughness monitoring system based on artificial neural networks (ANN) in milling operation. *International Journal of Advanced Manufacturing Technology*, *93*(1-4), 141–151. doi:10.100700170-015-7922-4

Kilickap, E., Yardimeden, A., & Celik, Y. H. (2017). Mathematical modelling and optimization of cutting force, tool wear and surface roughness by using artificial neural network and response surface methodology in milling of Ti-6242S. *Applied Sciences*, *7*(10), 1064. doi:10.3390/app7101064

Kumudha, S., Srinivasa, Y. G., & Krishnamurthy, R. (1998). Estimation of Tool Status Using Artificial Neural Network in Face Milling Operation. *Journal for Manufacturing Science and Production*, *1*(3), 189–198. doi:10.1515/IJMSP.1998.1.3.189

Lipiński, D., Bałasz, B., & Rypina, Ł. (2018). Modelling of surface roughness and grinding forces using artificial neural networks with assessment of the ability to data generalisation. *International Journal of Advanced Manufacturing Technology*, *94*(1-4), 1335–1347. doi:10.100700170-017-0949-y

Madhava Reddy, S., Chennakesava Reddy, A., & Sudhakar Reddy, K. (2012). Latest Developments in Condition Monitoring of Machining Operations. *Journal of Applied Sciences (Faisalabad)*, *12*(10), 938–946. doi:10.3923/jas.2012.938.946

Mahesh, T. P., & Rajesh, R. (2014). Optimal selection of process parameters in CNC end milling of Al 7075-T6 aluminium alloy using a Taguchi-fuzzy approach. *Procedia Materials Science*, *5*, 2493–2502. doi:10.1016/j.mspro.2014.07.501

Makhfi, S., Haddouche, K., Bourdim, A., & Habak, M. (2018). Modeling of machining force in hard turning process. *Mechanics, 24*(3), 367–375. doi:10.5755/j01.mech.24.3.19146

Malghan, R. L., Rao, K., Shettigar, A. K., Rao, S. S., & D'Souza, R. J. (2018). Forward and reverse mapping for milling process using artificial neural networks. *Data in Brief, 16*, 114–121. doi:10.1016/j.dib.2017.10.069 PMID:29188231

Man, K. F., Tang, K. S., & Kwong, S. (1996). Genetic algorithms: Concepts and applications. *IEEE Transactions on Industrial Electronics, 43*(5), 519–534. doi:10.1109/41.538609

Manafi, D., Nategh, M. J., & Parvaz, H. (2017). Extracting the manufacturing information of machining features for computer-aided process planning systems. *Proceedings of the Institution of Mechanical Engineers. Part B, Journal of Engineering Manufacture, 231*(12), 2072–2083. doi:10.1177/0954405415623487

Minsky, M. (1974). *A framework for representing knowledge.*

Mishra, R., Malik, J., Singh, I., & Davim, J. P. (2010). Neural network approach for estimating the residual tensile strength after drilling in uni-directional glass fiber reinforced plastic laminates. *Materials & Design, 31*(6), 2790–2795. doi:10.1016/j.matdes.2010.01.011

Nafeez, A., Tomohisha, T., & Yoshio, S. (2014). Machining parameter optimisation by genetic algorithm and artificial neural network. *International Journal of Data Analysis Techniques and Strategies, 6*(3), 261–274. doi:10.1504/IJDATS.2014.063061

Namdari, M., Jazayeri-Rad, H., & Hashemi, S. J. (2014). Process fault diagnosis using support vector machines with a genetic algorithm based parameter tuning. *Journal of Automation and Control, 2*(1), 1–7.

Naresh, N., (2014). Modeling and Analysis of Machining GFRP Composites Using Fuzzy Logic and ANOVA. *IUP Journal of Mechanical Engineering, 7*(4).

Nassehi, A., Essink, W., & Barclay, J. (2015). Evolutionary algorithms for generation and optimization of tool paths. *CIRP Annals, 64*(1), 455–458. doi:10.1016/j.cirp.2015.04.125

Nathan, R. D., Vijayaraghavan, L., & Krishnamurthy, R. (2001). Intelligent estimation of burning limits to aid in cylindrical grinding cycle planning. *International Journal of Heavy Vehicle Systems, 8*(1), 48–59. doi:10.1504/IJHVS.2001.001154

Pendokhare, D. G., & Quazi, T. Z. (2012). Fuzzy Logic Based Drilling Control Process. *Int. J. Scientific and Engg. Research, 5*(12), 61–65.

Pohokar, N., & Bhuyar, L. (2014). Neural Networks Based Approach for Machining and Geometric Parameters optimization of a CNC End Milling. *Neural Networks, 3*(2).

Prabhakar, A., Kingsley, D., Singh, J., & Jebaraj, C. (2004). Creating process plan sheet from a feature based model. In *Proceedings of the National Conference on Advanced Manufacturing and Robotics* (pp. 247-254).

Purdy, M., & Daugherty, P. (2016). Why Artificial Intelligence is the Future of Growth.

Raimond, K. (2008). Effective tool wear estimation through multisensory information fusion using Artificial Neural Network. *Journal of EEA, 25*, 33–42.

Raja, C., & Saravanan, M. (2018). Tool path optimization by genetic algorithm for energy efficient machining. *TAGA Journal of Graphic Technology*, *14*, 1670–1679.

Rajasekhar, K., & Naresh, N. (2014). Modeling and analysis of process parameters in machining Aisi 304 stainless steel using fuzzy logic. *i-Manager's Journal on Mechanical Engineering, 4*(2), 18.

Rishi, K., Pradhan, M. K., & Rajesh, K. 2014. Modeling and optimization of milling parameters on Al-6061 alloy using multi- objective genetic algorithm. In *Proc. of 26th AIMTDR Conference*, IIT Guwahati, India, December 12-14.

Roy, A., & Bhagat, K. (2015). An application of Artificial Neural Network to predict surface roughness during drilling of AISI1020 steel. *International Journal of Scientific Research Engineering and Technology*, *4*(8).

Salimi, A., Özdemir, A., & Erdem, A. (2015). Simulation and monitoring of the machining process via fuzzy logic and cutting forces. *Iranian Journal of Materials Science and Engineering*, *12*(3), 14–26.

Sarhan, A. A., Sayuti, M., & Hamdi, M. (2012). A Fuzzy Logic Based Model to Predict Surface roughness of a machined surface in glass milling operation using CBN grinding tool. *World Academy of Science, Engineering and Technology*, *6*, 564–570.

Šarić, T., Šimunović, G., Lujić, R., Šimunović, K., & Antić, A. (2016). Use of soft computing technique for modelling and prediction of CNC grinding process. *Technical Gazette*, *23*(4), 1123–1130.

Senthilkumar, N., Sudha, J., & Muthukumar, V. (2015). A grey-fuzzy approach for optimizing machining parameters and the approach angle in turning AISI 1045 steel. *Advances in Production Engineering & Management*, *10*(4), 195–208. doi:10.14743/apem2015.4.202

Shaik, J. H., & Srinivas, J. (2017). Optimal selection of operating parameters in end milling of Al-6061 work materials using multi-objective approach. *Mechanics of Advanced Materials and Modern Processes*, *3*(1), 5. doi:10.118640759-017-0020-6

Sudhir, K., & Rajagopalan, R. (1992). An artificial intelligence approach to precedence network generation for assembly line balancing. *Computers in Industry*, *18*(2), 177–191. doi:10.1016/0166-3615(92)90112-Z

Tanikić, D., Marinković, V., Manić, M., Devedžić, G., & Ranđelović, S. (2016). Application of response surface methodology and fuzzy logic based system for determining metal cutting temperature. *Bulletin of the Polish Academy of Sciences. Technical Sciences*, *64*(2), 435–445. doi:10.1515/bpasts-2016-0049

The Manufacturer. (2018, February 26). *Power of artificial intelligence*. Retrieved from https://www.themanufacturer.com/articles/power-artificial-intelligence-manufacturing/

Tumuluru, J. S., & McCulloch, R. (2016). Application of hybrid genetic algorithm routine in optimizing food and bioengineering processes. *Foods*, *5*(4), 76. doi:10.3390/foods5040076 PMID:28231171

Vijaykumar, K., Panneerselvam, K., & Sait, A. N. (2014). Machining Parameter Optimization of Bidirectional CFRP Composite Pipe by Genetic Algorithm. *Materials Testing*, *56*(9), 728–736. doi:10.3139/120.110623

Zadeh, L. (1965). Fuzzy sets. *Information and Control, 8*(3), 338–353. doi:10.1016/S0019-9958(65)90241-X

Zadeh, L. A. (1973). Outline of a new approach to the analysis of complex systems and decision processes. *IEEE Transactions on Systems, Man, and Cybernetics, SMC-3*(1), 28–44. doi:10.1109/TSMC.1973.5408575

Zhang, C., Yao, X., Zhang, J., & Jin, H. (2016). Tool condition monitoring and remaining useful life prognostic based on a wireless sensor in dry milling operations. *Sensors (Basel), 16*(6), 795. doi:10.339016060795 PMID:27258277

Zhu, K., & Zhang, Y. (2018). A Cyber-Physical Production System Framework of Smart CNC Machining Monitoring System. *IEEE/ASME Transactions on Mechatronics*, 1. doi:10.1109/TMECH.2018.2834622

Chapter 9
Data Mining for Social Network Analysis Using a CLIQUE Algorithm

Phu Ngoc Vo
Duy Tan University, Vietnam

Tran Vo Thi Ngoc
Ho Chi Minh City University of Technology, Vietnam & Vietnam National University – Ho Chi Minh City, Vietnam

ABSTRACT

Many different areas of computer science have been developed for many years in the world. Data mining is one of the fields which many algorithms, methods, and models have been built and applied to many commercial applications and research successfully. Many social networks have been invested and developed in the strongest way for the recent years in the world because they have had many big benefits as follows: they have been used by lots of users in the world and they have been applied to many business fields successfully. Thus, a lot of different techniques for the social networks have been generated. Unsurprisingly, the social network analysis is crucial at the present time in the world. To support this process, in this book chapter we have presented many simple concepts about data mining and social networking. In addition, we have also displayed a novel model of the data mining for the social network analysis using a CLIQUE algorithm successfully.

INTRODUCTION

Technology science in the world has had many accomplishments for the recent years in the world. Many science fields have successfully been created. Artificial intelligence and data mining have already been developed more and more for many years. They have successfully been applied to many different fields in everyone's life. Lots of algorithms, methods and models of the data mining (DM) have already been built and developed fully, and they have been very helpful. They have also been applied to many commercial applications, surveys, successfully. Many economies of the countries in the world have had many

DOI: 10.4018/978-1-5225-7522-1.ch009

breakthroughs certainly. Therefore, social networks have been generated fully and successfully for everyone's life. The social network (SN) has already had many sub-fields which have been very important for everyone's life, industry and economy. However, to get many positive benefits of the social network in the recent years in the world, it has also been many negative problems which have been solved for the years. People have spent lots of cost and time for these disadvantage problems to be solved fully and successfully for themselves in the world. Thus, social network analysis has been very crucial for developing the social networks in the world certainly. Semantic analysis has been a crucial sub-field of the SN. Many hard problems and challenges have been generated and grown from which a lot because there have been billions of sentences and documents in many different languages of billions of reviews, comments, and billions of users on billions of websites of the social networks. These sentences and documents should have been processed in more details or not. How the sentences and documents have been processed in more details.

Based on our opinion, the data mining is a process which patterns and relationships of these patterns have been discovered fully, certainly, and successfully in massive data sets to solve many complex problems through data analysis of these big data sets in more details. We can predict future trends according to the tools and algorithms of data mining.

The social network according to our opinion is a structure of society which has been made up of a set of social actors (individuals, organizations, users, etc.), sets of dyadic ties, and other social interactions between actors. Many sets of methods for analyzing the structure of whole social entities and a variety of theories have been provided for explaining the patterns observed in the structures certainly.

The social networking (SNG) based on our opinion is defined that connections between friends, family, classmates, customers, and clients are made by using of internet-based social media programs. It can happen for social purposes, business purposes or both through sites: Facebook, Twitter, LinkedIn, etc., it is also a significant target area for marketers seeking to engage users.

The social network analysis (SNA) according to our opinion has been used for the study of these above structures to identify local and global patterns, locate influential entities, and It has also been used for examining network dynamics.

We have known why these above problems and challenges have been crucial as follows:

1. The SNs have been many big advantages certainly.
2. They have been applied to many benefit areas successfully such as ecommerce and advertising
3. To maximize the positives of the social networks, lots of algorithms, methods, models and tools have been developed for a long time.
4. Billions of the sentences and documents of the reviews and comments of the users have certainly been a lot of potential benefits for many years.

In this chapter, we have presented a novel model of the DM for the SNA a CLIQUE algorithm (CLA). Especially, this novel model has been built for sentiment analysis (SA) which is a crucial sub-field of the SNA. The SNA (also known as opinion mining (OM) or emotion classification (EC)) uses natural language processing (NLP), text analysis (TA), computational linguistics (CL), etc., to identify, extract, quantify, study systematically affective states, and study subjective information. The SNA means that a sentence is identified semantics such as positive, negative, or neutral. If a valence of a sentence is less than 0, this sentence is identified as the positive polarity. If a valence of a sentence is greater than 0, this sentence is identified as the negative polarity. If a valence of a sentence is as equal as 0, this sentence is identified as the neutral polarity.

The problem has been performed so far by others as follows:

1. Many algorithms, methods and models have been researched for the OM, but there is not enough.
2. There have not been enough algorithms, methods and models of the DM for the SNA yet to be applied to many different fields for the economies, countries, societies, corporations, organizations
3. There have not been many algorithms, methods and models of the DM for the SNA which have been performed in sequential environments (SEs) – sequential systems (SSs)
4. Those algorithms, methods and models of the DM for the SNA in the SSs have already been built with small samples.
5. There have also been not a lot of the algorithms, methods, and models of the DM for the SNA which have been implemented in distributed network systems (DNSs) – parallel network environments (PNEs)
6. The algorithms, methods, and models of the DM for the SNA in the DNS have also been implemented with small samples

The main contributions of this chapter to the problem from many studies related to lots of new models for the OM have been as follows:

1. This chapter helps the readers have information and knowledge about the DM, the SNA, and SA
2. The chapter also helps the reader understand most of all novel computational models of the EC certainly.
3. Most of those computational models of the OM in many different fields are shown in both the SEs and the DNSs in more details in the below sections.
4. From lots of the information and knowledge above, the readers (comprising scientists, researchers, CEO, managers, etc.) can build, develop and deploy many commercial applications, studies, etc.
5. Many different technologies of those models have already been displayed carefully.
6. We also show that a novel computational model (NCM) of us for the SA have successfully been built

The contribution original of this chapter has been as follows:

1. This chapter helps the readers understand many simple concepts of the DM, the SN, the SNG, the SNA, clearly.
2. This chapter also helps the readers know many NCMs of the SA fully in the SEs and the DNSs
3. A novel model, which we have built and developed in the SE and the DNS successfully, is presented in this chapter.
4. Many techniques, algorithms, methods, and models to handle the OM in the SE and the DNS are fully shown in this chapter.
5. Based on all the things displayed in this chapter, many commercial applications and research can be developed and deployed successfully.

The contribution non-trivial has been as follows: We have built and developed a novel model which has been presented in the below sub-sections of this chapter in more details. This model has used the CLA of the DM field with the multi-dimensional vectors (MULTDIMVECTs) based on the sentiment lexicons (SENTLEXs) and 2,000,000 documents of a training data set (TrDS) for English document-level sentiment classification (SENTCLASS) in English. A Sorgenfrei coefficient (SC) through a Google search engine (GSE) with AND operator and OR operator (AndOr) has been used for creating the opinion lexicons. This proposed approach has been tested on a testing data set (TeDS) – 1,000,000 reviews in English and we have achieved 87.96% accuracy.

We have shown a variety of models for processing the OM in both the SEs and the PNEs.

BACKGROUND

We have displayed the studies related to our novel model briefly in this part.

We have used the results of the surveys related to PMI, Jaccard measure (JMEAS), Cosine coefficient (COSC), Ochiai measure (OCHM), Tanimoto coefficient (TCOEFF), and Sorensen measure (SORM). So, we have proved that the Sorgenfrei coefficient (SC) has also been used for identifying valence and polarity of one word (or one phrase) in English for the basis English semantic lexicons of the basis English emotional dictionary (bESD).

The authors have used the PMI in the works in (Bai, & Hammer, 2014; Turney, & Littman, 2002; Malouf, & Mullen, 2017; Scheible, 2010; Jovanoski et al., 2015; Htait et al., 2016; Wan, 2009; Brooke et al., 2009; Jiang et al., 2015; Tan & Zhang, 2007; Du et al., 2010; Zhang et al., 2010; Wang, & Araki, 2007).

In addition, there have been the two studies related to the PMI and the JMEAS in (Shi Feng, & et al., 2013) and (Nguyen Thi Thu An, & Masafumi Hagiwara, 2014).

We have been the surveys of the JMEAS in (Shikalgar, & Dixit, 2014; Ji et al., 2015; Omar et al., 2013; Mao et al., 2014; Ren et al., 2014; Netzer et al., 2012; Ren et al., 2011).

The surveys related to the similarity coefficients to calculate the valences of words have been presented in (Vo Ngoc Phu et al., 2017d; Vo Ngoc Phu et al., 2017e; Vo Ngoc Phu et al., 2017f; Vo Ngoc Phu et al., 2017g; Vo Ngoc Phu et al., 2017h).

The English dictionaries are (English Dictionary of Lingoes, 2017; Oxford English Dictionary, 2017; Cambridge English Dictionary, 2017) and there are more than 55,000 English words (including English nouns, English adjectives, English verbs, etc.) from them.

The authors have used the SC in the works (Seung-Seok Choi et al., 2010; Lefki, & Dormans, 1998; Hansen et al., 2000).

The vector space modeling (VECTSM) has been displayed in (Singh, & Singh, 2015; Carrera-Trejo et al., 2015; Soucy, & Mineau, 2015).

The surveys (Hadoop, 2017; Apache, 2017; Cloudera, 2017) have allowed many algorithms, applications, approaches and models to be performed in a parallel way easily and successfully. The Hadoop has been the two main tasks: Hadoop Map (M) and Hadoop Reduce (R). Cloudera in (Cloudera, 2017) has been a DNS which can process many big data sets (BIGDSs) successfully in the distributed way.

There have been the studies of the CLA in (Segundo et al., 2013; McCreesh, & Prosser, 2013; Depolli et al., 2013; Scozzari, & Tardella, 2008; Shih, & Hsu, 1989).

All the documents of the TrDS and TeDS have automatically been extracted from Facebook, websites and social networks in English. Then, we have labeled positive and negative for them.

In Figure 1, the TrDS has included the 2,000,000 documents in the movie field having the 1,000,000 positives and the 1,000,000 negatives in English.

In Figure 2, the TeDS has comprised the 1,000,000 documents in the movie field containing the 500,000 positive documents and the 500,000 negative documents in English.

MAIN FOCUS OF THE CHAPTER

Issues, Controversies, Problems

In this section, we have displayed all the possible NCMs for the SA in the different areas such as: (Phu et al., 2017, 2017a, 2017b, 2017c, 2018a, 2018b, 2018c, 2018d, 2018e, 2018f, 2018g, 2018h, 2018i, 2018j, 2018k, 2018l).

The NCMs in this chapter have been divided into the two environments: a SE and a DNS.

A Fuzzy C-Means (FCM) algorithm in (Phu, 2017a) has been used for sentiment mining with the M and the R in English in a CPNE. This work could classify the semantics of millions of documents in the PNE in English. This novel model was tested on the 25,000 documents of a TeDS and the 60,000

Figure 1. Our English training data set

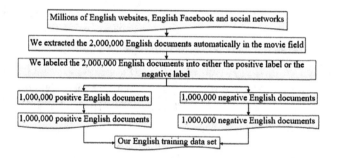

Figure 2. Our English testing data set

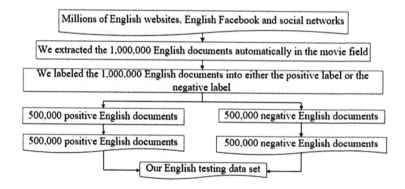

sentences of a TrDS comprising the 30,000 positive English sentences and 30,000 negative English sentences. This survey was implemented in both the SE and the DNS.

A new model in Nguyen Duy Dat (2017) has been used for big data opinion classification in the PNE. The authors used STING Algorithm (STA) for English document-level semantic classification with the M and the R according to the 90,000 sentences of a TrDS in English in the CPNE. This model could classify sentiments of millions of documents with the shortest execution time in the distributed environment. The authors tested the model on the 25,000 documents of a TeDS and the 90,000 sentences of a TrDS including the 45,000 positive English sentences and 45,000 negative English sentences. This work was performed in both the SE and the DNS successfully.

In Vo Ngoc Phu et al. (2017b), a novel approach using a SVM algorithm has been proposed with the M and the R for emotional classification of English documents in the CPNE. A TrDS of this model comprised the 90,000 sentences in English which was divided into the 45,000 positive sentences and 45,000 negative sentences in English. This survey was tested in both the SE and the DNS successfully.

A novel model for massive data sentiment analysis in the CPNE has been built with the M and the R in (Phu et al., 2017c). A Statistical Information Grid Algorithm (STING) was used with multi-dimensional vectors and the 2,000,000 documents of a TrDS for document-level opinion classification in English. The 2,000,000 documents of the TrDS comprised the 1,000,000 positives and 1,000,000 negatives. Millions of documents in English could be classified semantics according to the documents of the TrDS in the DNS. This research was implemented in both the SE and the DNS successfully.

A new approach has been proposed using a Gower-2 Coefficient (GW2CO) and a Genetic algorithm (GENAL) with a Fitness proportionate Selection (FITPS) for the OM in Vo Ngoc Phu et al. (2018a). This study could be applied to many large-scale data sets (LARDSs). The authors used the 7,000,000 sentences of a TrDS for this model comprising the 3,500,000 positives and 3,500,000 negatives. This model was performed in both the SE and the DNS successfully.

A new survey has been proposed using a Fager and MacGowan Coefficient (FMCO) and a GENAL with a Rank Selection (RNKS) for the EC in (Phu et al., 2018b). This work could be applied to many massive data sets (MASDSs). The authors also used the 7,000,000 sentences of a TrDS for this model comprising the 3,500,000 positives and 3,500,000 negatives. This approach was tested in both the SE and the DNS successfully.

In the below sub-section "Solutions and Recommendations," we have displayed many technologies and many algorithms for a novel proposed model which has used the CLA with the MULTDIMVECTs based on the SENTLEXs by using the SC through the GSE with the and or in the SS and the CPNE.

SOLUTIONS AND RECOMMENDATIONS

The CLA has certainly been an algorithm of the clustering field of the DM.

To implement our new model, we have proposed the following basic principles:

1. Each sentence has been m words (or phrases) in English.
2. The maximum number of one sentence has been m_max. It has meant that m has been less than m_max or m has been as equal as m_max.
3. Each document has been n sentences in English.

4. The maximum number of one document has been n_max. It meant that n has been less than n_max or n has been equal to n_max.

5. Each sentence has been transferred into one ONEDIMVECT. Thus, the length of the vector has been m. When m has been less than m_max, each element of the vector from m to m_max-1 has been 0 (zero).

6. Each document has been transferred into one MULTDIMVECT. Therefore, the MULTDIMVECT has been rows and m columns. When n has been less than n_max, each element of the MULTDIMVECT from n to n_max-1 has been 0 (zero vector).

In this study, we have developed a new model by using the CLA with the SENTLEXs-based MULT-DIMVECTs to classify the emotions (positive, negative, neutral) of English documents in the SS and the CPNE

First of all, we have calculated the valences of the SENTLEXs by using a SC through a GSE with AndOr. Based on the COSC, OCHM, SORM, TCOEFF, PMI, and JMEAS, we have built many equations related to the SC to calculate the valence of English terms. Methods based on the SENTLEXs related to extraction and emotional score collection of terms, which are offered by lexicons to perform a prediction of emotions. This identifying sentiment scores of the SENTLEXs was implemented in both a SE and a DNS

Next, we have transferred all the document of both the TeDS and the TrDS into the MULTDIMVECTs based on the above SENTLEXs. This was implemented in both a SE and a DNS.

Then, the positive documents of the TrDS have been transformed into the positive MULTDIMVECTs, called the positive MULTDIMVECT group (POSMULTDIMVECTG). The negative documents of the TrDS have been transferred into the negative MULTDIMVECTs, called the negative MULTDIMVECT group (NEGMULTDIMVECTG).

Finally, we have used the CLA to cluster one MULTDIMVECT (corresponding one document of the TeDS) into either the NEGMULTDIMVECTG or the POSMULTDIMVECTG. This was implemented in both the SE and the DNS.

The most significant contributions of our proposed model have been displayed briefly as follows:

1. Many surveys and commercial applications can use the results of this work in a significant way.
2. The SC has been used in identifying opinion scores of the English verb phrases and words through the GSE on the internet.
3. The formulas have been proposed in the chapter.
4. The algorithms have been built in the proposed model.
5. This survey can certainly be applied to other languages easily.
6. The results of this study can significantly be applied to the types of other words in English.
7. Many crucial contributions have been listed in the Future Research Directions section.
8. The algorithm of data mining has been applicable to the OM of the NLP.
9. This study has also proved that many different fields of the scientific research can be related in many ways.
10. Millions of English documents have successfully been processed for the EC.
11. The EC has been implemented in the DNS
12. The principles have been proposed in the research.
13. The CPNE has been used in this study.

14. The proposed work can be applied to other distributed systems.
15. This survey has used the M and the R.
16. Our proposed model can be applied to many different parallel network environments such as a Cloudera system
17. This study can be applied to many different distributed functions such as the M and the R.
18. The CLIQUE – related algorithms are proposed in this research.

This section has two parts: "Transferring the Documents Into the MULTDIMVECTs Based on the SENTLEXs" and "Implementing the CLA in the SS and the DNS."

Transferring the Documents Into the MULTDIMVECTs Based on the SENTLEXs

This section has three parts.

Calculating the Valences of the SENTLEXs

According to English Dictionary of Lingoes (2017), Oxford English Dictionary (2017), and Cambridge English Dictionary (2017), we have been at least the 55,000 English terms, including nouns, verbs, adjectives, etc. In this part, we have calculated the valence and the polarity of the English words or phrases for our basic sentiment dictionary in English (bESD) by using the SC in Figure 3.

According to the works in Bai and Hammer (2014), Turney and Littman (2002), and Malouf and Mullen (2017), the equation of the PMI of the two words wi and wj has been as follows:

Figure 3. Overview of English sentiment dictionary using the SC

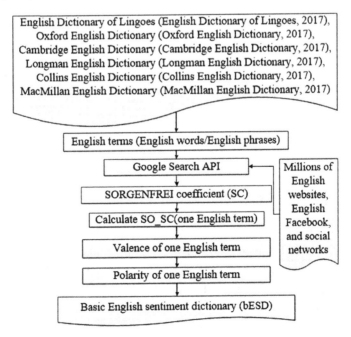

$$PMI\left(wi, wj\right) = \log_2\left(\frac{P\left(wi, wj\right)}{P\left(wi\right)xP\left(wj\right)}\right) \tag{1}$$

and the SO (sentiment orientation) of the word wi has been the equation

$$SO\left(wi\right) = PMI\left(wi, positive\right) - PMI\left(wi, negative\right) \tag{2}$$

In Bai and Hammer (2014), Turney and Littman (2002), Malouf and Mullen (2017), and Scheible (2010), the positive and the negative of Eq. (2) in English have been as follows: positive = {good, nice, excellent, positive, fortunate, correct, superior} and negative = {bad, nasty, poor, negative, unfortunate, wrong, inferior}.

With the surveys (Jiang et al., 2015; Tan & Zhang, 2007; Du et al., 2010; Zhang et al., 2010), the PMI equations have been used in Chinese, not English, and Tibetan has also been added in Jiang et al (2015). About the search engine, the AVSE has been used in (Du et al., 2010) and (Zhang et al., 2010) and the studies have used three search engines, such as the GSE, the Yahoo search engine and the Baidu search engine. The PMI equations have also been used in Japanese with the GSE in (Wang & Araki, 2007). Feng et al. (2013) and An and Hagiwara (2014) have also used the PMI equations and JMEAS equations with the GSE in English.

According to Feng et al. (2013), An and Hagiwara (2014), and Shikalgar and Dixit (2014), the JMEAS of the two words wi and wj has been the equations

$$Jaccard\left(wi, wj\right) = J\left(wi, wj\right) = \frac{\left|wi \cap wj\right|}{\left|wi \cup wj\right|} \tag{3}$$

and other type of the JMEAS of the two words wi and wj has been the equation

$$Jaccard\left(wi, wj\right) = J\left(wi, wj\right) = sim\left(wi, wj\right) = \frac{F\left(wi, wj\right)}{F\left(wi\right) + F\left(wj\right) - F\left(wi, wj\right)} \tag{4}$$

and the SO of the word wi has been the equation

$$SO\left(wi\right) = \sum Sim\left(wi, positive\right) - \sum Sim\left(wi, positive\right) \tag{5}$$

In Feng et al. (2013), An and Hagiwara (2014), and Shikalgar and Dixit (2014), Ji et al. (2015), Omar et al. (2013), Mao et al. (2014), Ren et al. (2014), and Netzer et al. (2012), the positive and the negative of Equation (5) in English have been: positive = {good, nice, excellent, positive, fortunate, correct, superior} and negative = {bad, nasty, poor, negative, unfortunate, wrong, inferior}.

The JMEAS equations with the GSE in English have been used Feng et al. (2013), An and Hagiwara (2014), and Ji et al. (2015). Shikalgar and Dixit (2014) and Netzer et al. (2012) have used the JMEAS equations in English. Ren et al. (2014) and Ren et al. (2011) have used the JMEAS equations in Chinese. Omar et al. (2013) has used the JMEAS equations in Arabic. The JMEAS equations with the Chinese search engine in Chinese have been used in Mao et al. (2014).

The GSE with the AndOr has been used with the OCHM, COSC, SORM, JMEAS, and TCOEFF in Vietnamese, English to calculate the sentiment values of the words in the studies (Phu et al., 2017d, 2017e, 2017f, 2017g, 2017h).

With the above proofs, we have been the information: The PMI has been used with the AVSE in English, Chinese, and Japanese with the GSE in English. The JMEAS has been used with the GSE in English, Chinese, and Vietnamese. The OCHM has been used with the GSE in Vietnamese. The COSC and SORM have been used with the Google in English.

According to the above surveys, the PMI, JMEAS, COSC, OCHM, SORM, TCOEFF and SC have been the similarity measures of the two words, and they can perform the same functions and the same characteristics; so the SC has been used in calculating the valence of the words. In addition, we have proved that the SC can be used in identifying the valence of the English word through the GSE with the AndOr

With the SC in Choi et al (2010), Lefki and Dormans (1998), and Hansen et al (2000), we have been the equation of the SC:

$$
\begin{aligned}
\text{SORGENFREI Coefficient}\,(a,\ b) &= \text{SORGENFREI Measure}\,(a,b) \\
&= \text{SC}\,(a,b) \\
&= \frac{(a \cap b)*(a \cap b)}{\left[(a \cap b) + (\neg a \cap b)\right]*\left[(a \cap b) + (a \cap \neg b)\right]}
\end{aligned}
\tag{6}
$$

when a and b are the vectors.

Based on Equations (1), (2), (3), (4), (5), (6), we have proposed the new equations of the SC to calculate the valence and the polarity of the words (or the phrases) in English through the GSE.

In Eq. (6), when a has been only one element, a has been one word. When b has been only one element, b has been one word. In Eq. (6), a has been replaced by w1 and b has been replaced by w2.

$$
\begin{aligned}
\text{SORGENFREI Measure}\,(w1,\ w2) &= \text{SORGENFREI Coefficient}\,(w1,\ w2) = \\
\text{SC}\,(w1,\ w2) &= \frac{P\,(w1,w2)*P\,(w1,w2)}{\left[P\,(w1,w2) + P(\neg w1,\ w2)\right]*\left[P\,(w1,\ w2) + P\,(w1,\neg\ w2)\right]}
\end{aligned}
\tag{7}
$$

Equation (7) has been similar to Equation (1). In Equation (2), Equation (1) has been replaced by Equation (7). We have been Equation (8)

$$
\text{Valence}\,(w) = \text{SO\_SC}\,(w) = \text{SC}\,(w, \text{positive\_query}) - \text{SC}\,(w, \text{negative\_query})
\tag{8}
$$

In Equation (7), w1 has been replaced by w, and w2 has been replaced by position_query. We have been Equation (9):

$$SC\left(w, positive\_query\right) = \frac{P\left(w, positive\_query\right) * P\left(w, positive\_query\right)}{A9} \tag{9}$$

with

$$A9 = \begin{aligned}&\left[P\left(w, positive\_query\right) + P(\neg w, positive\_query)\right]\\ &* \left[P\left(w, positive\_query\right) + P\left(w, \neg positive\_query\right)\right]\end{aligned}$$

In Equation (7), w1 has been replaced by w, and w2 has been replaced by negative_query. We have been Equation (10):

$$SC\left(w, negative\_query\right) = \frac{P\left(w, negative\_query\right) * P\left(w, negative\_query\right)}{A10} \tag{10}$$

with

$$A10 = \begin{aligned}&\left[P\left(w, negative\_query\right) + P(\neg w, negative\_query)\right]\\ &* \left[P\left(w, negative\_query\right) + P\left(w, \neg negative\_query\right)\right]\end{aligned}$$

We have been the information of w, w1, w2, P(w1, w2), as follows:

1. w, w1, and w2 have been the words (or the phrases) in English.
2. P(w1, w2) has been the number of the returned results in the GSE by the keyword (w1 and w2). We have used the API of the GSE to get the number of the returned results in the GSE online by the keyword (w1 and w2).
3. P(w1) has been the number of the returned results in the GSE by the keyword w1. We have used the API of the GSE to get the number of the returned results in the GSE online by the keyword w1.
4. P(w2) has been the number of the returned results in the GSE by the keyword w2. We have used the API of the GSE to get the number of the returned results in the GSE online by the keyword w2.
5. Valence(W) = SO_NLC(w) has been the valence of the word/the phrase w in English, and it has been the SO of word (or phrase) by using the SC
6. positive_query has been {active or good or positive or beautiful or strong or nice or excellent or fortunate or correct or superior} with the positive_query has been a group of the positive words in English.
7. negative_query has been {passive or bad or negative or ugly or week or nasty or poor or unfortunate or wrong or inferior} with the negative_query has been a group of the negative words in English

8.   P(w, positive_query) has been the number of the returned results in the GSE by the keyword (positive_query and w). We have used the API of the GSE to get the number of the returned results in the GSE online by the keyword (positive_query and w)

9.   P(w, negative_query) has been the number of the returned results in the GSE by the keyword (negative_query and w). We have used the API of the GSE to get the number of the returned results in the GSE online by the keyword (negative_query and w)

10. P(w) has been the number of the returned results in the GSE by keyword w. We have used the API of the GSE to get the number of the returned results in the GSE online by the keyword w

11. P(¬w,positive_query) has been the number of the returned results in the GSE by the keyword ((not w) and positive_query). We have used the API of the GSE to get the number of the returned results in the GSE online by the keyword ((not w) and positive_query).

12. P(w, ¬positive_query) has been the number of the returned results in the GSE by the keyword (w and (not (positive_query))). We have used the API of the GSE to get the number of the returned results in the GSE online by the keyword (w and [not (positive_query)]).

13. P(¬w,negative_query) has been the number of the returned results in the GSE by the keyword ((notw) and negative_query). We have used the API of the GSE to get the number of the returned results in the GSE online by the keyword ((not w) and negative_query).

14. P(w,¬negative_query) has been the number of the returned results in the GSE by the keyword (w and (not (negative_query))). We have used the API of the GSE to get the number of the returned results in the GSE online by the keyword (w and (not (negative_query))).

According to the above proofs, we have identified the opinion value of the word w in English based on the proximity of positive_query with w, the remote of positive_query with w, the proximity of negative_query with w, and the remote of negative_query with w

- When the value SC(w, positive_query) has been as equal as 1, the word w in English has been the nearest of positive_query.
- When the value SC(w, positive_query) has been as equal as 0, the word w in English has been the farthest of positive_query.
- When the value SC(w, positive_query) > 0 and SC(w, positive_query) ≤ 1, the word w has belonged to positive_query of the positive group of the words in English.
- When the value SC(w, negative_query) has been as equal as 1, the word w has been the nearest of negative_query.
- When the value SC(w, negative_query) has been as equal as 0, the word w has been the farthest of negative_query.
- When the value SC(w, negative_query) > 0 and SC(w, negative_query) ≤ 1, the word w has belonged to negative_query of the negative group of the words in English.
- Therefore, the semantic value of the word w in English has been the value (SC(w, positive_query)-SC(w, negative_query)), and Eq. (8) has been the formula of identifying the opinion score of the word w.

We have been the value SC:

1. $SC(w, positive\_query) \geq 0$ and $SC(w, positive\_query) \leq 1$.
2. $SC(w, negative\_query) \geq 0$ and $SC(w, negative\_query) \leq 1$.
3. When the value $SO\_SC(w) = 0$, the value $SC(w, positive\_query) = 0$ and $SC(w, negative\_query) = 0$
4. When the value $SO\_SC(w) = 0$, the value $SC(w, positive\_query) = 1$ and $SC(w, negative\_query) = 0$.
5. When the value $SO\_SC(w) = -1$, the value $SC(w, positive\_query) = 0$ and $SC(w, negative\_query) = 1$
6. When the value $SO\_SC(w) = 0$, the value $SC(w, positive\_query) = 1$ and $SC(w, negative\_query) = 1$

Thus, the value $SO\_SC(w) \geq -1$ and $SO\_SC(w) \leq 1$.

When the value $SO\_SC(w) > 0$, the polarity of the w has been the positive. When the value $SO\_SC(w) < 0$, the polarity of the w has been the negative. When the value $SO\_SC(w) = 0$, the polarity of the w has been the neutral. Furthermore, the sentiment score of the w has been the value $SO\_SC(w)$

We have calculated the valence and the polarity of the word/the phrase w using a training corpus of approximately one hundred billion of the words of the websites and social networks in English that have been indexed by the GSE on the internet.

The AVSE has been chosen because it has been a NEAR operator. However, it has been no longer. We have used the GSE which has not been a NEAR operator. The GSE has used the AndOr.

The results of calculating the opinion value of the w using the GSE has been similar to the results of identifying the valence the w using the AVSE.

The bESD has been at least 55,000 word/phrase in English, and it has been stored in Microsoft SQL Server 2008 R2.

Transferring the Documents Into the MULTDIMVECTs in the SS

In this part, we have transferred the documents of both the TeDS and the TrDS into the MULTDIM-VECTs in the SS.

In Figure 4, we have presented how to transfer one English document into one MULTDIMVECT based on the SENTLEXs in the SS.

Then, we have applied this to transfer all the documents of both the TeDS and the TrDS into the SS.

We have proposed the algorithm 1 to transfer one English document into one MULTDIMVECT based on the SENTLEXs in the SS.

Input: one English document

Output one MULTDIMVECT based on the SENTLEXs

1. Set MULTDIMVECT:= { };
2. Set ONEDIMVECT:= { };
3. Split this document into the n sentences
4. Each sentence in the n sentences, do repeat:
5. Split this sentence into the n_n meaningful words (or meaningful phrases);
6. Each term in the n_n terms, do repeat:
7. Get the valence of this term based on the bESD;

Figure 4. Transferring the documents into the MULTDIMVECTs in the SS

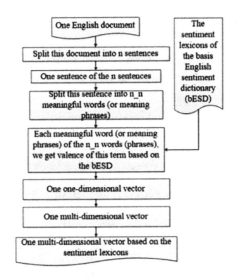

8.   Add this term (term, valence) into ONEDIMVECT;
9.   End Repeat-End (6);
10. Add the ONEDIMVECT(corresponding to this sentence) into the MULTDIMVECT;
11. End Repeat–End (4);
12. Return the MULTDIMVECT;

Transferring the Documents Into the MULTDIMVECTs in the DNS

We have transformed the documents of both the TeDS and the TrDS into the MULTDIMVECTs in the DNS

In Figure 5, we have displayed how to transfer one English document into one MULTDIMVECT based on the SENTLEXs in the CPNE. The input of the M in the CPNE has been one English document, the SENTLEXs of the bESD. The output of the M has been one ONEDIMVECT (corresponding to one sentence of this document). The input of the R in the CPNE has been the output of the M. The output of the R has been one MULTDIMVECT (corresponding to this document).

Then, we have applied this to transfer all the documents of both the TeDS and the TrDS into the CPNE

```
In the M:
Input:       One English document;
       The SENTLEXs of the bESD.
Output: one o ONEDIMVECT;
Input: One English document;
```

The SENTLEXs of the bESD into the M in the CPNE.

1.   Set ONEDIMVECT:= {};
2.   Set MULTDIMVECT:= {};

Figure 5. Transferring the documents into the MULTDIMVECTs in the DNS

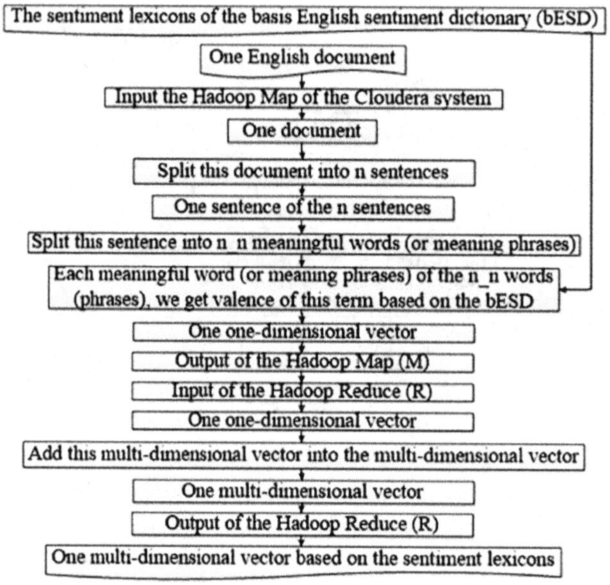

3. Split this document into the n sentences;
4. Each sentence in the n sentences, do repeat:
5. Split this sentence into the n_n meaningful words (or meaningful phrases)
6. Each term in the n_n terms, do repeat:
7. Get valence of this term based on the bESD;
8. Add this term into ONEDIMVECT;
9. End Repeat-End (6);
10. Return ONEDIMVECT;
11. The output of the M has been ONEDIMVECT;

In the R:
Input: one ONEDIMVECT of the M (the input of the R has been the output of the M)
Output: one MULTDIMVECT (corresponding to one English document)

1. Receive one one-dimensional vector of the M
2. Add ONEDIMVECT into MULTDIMVECT;
3. Return MULTDIMVECT;

Implementing the CLA in the SS and the DNS

This section has been divided into two main parts: "The CLA in the SS" and "The CLA in the DNS."

We have been the two groups of the TrDS: All the positive documents of the TrDS have been transformed into the positive MULTDIMVECTs, called the positive MULTDIMVECT group (POS-MULTDIMVECTG). All the negative documents of the TrDS have been transferred into the negative MULTDIMVECTs, called the negative MULTDIMVECT group (NEGMULTDIMVECTG)

The CLA in the SS

In Figure 6, in the SE, the documents of the TeDS have been transferred to the MULTDIMVECTs: each document of the TeDS has been transferred to each MULTDIMVECT according to (a.2).

Based on Figure 6, the positive documents of the TrDS have been transferred into the positive MULT-DIMVECTs – POSMULTDIMVECTG, and the positive documents of the TrDS have been transferred into the negative MULTDIMVECTs – NEGMULTDIMVECTG in the SE.

We have launched this part in Figure 7: In the SE, the CLA has been implemented to cluster one MULTDIMVECT (called A) of the TeDS into either the NEGMULTDIMVECTG or the POSMULT-DIMVECTG. When A has been clustered into the POSMULTDIMVECTG, the document corresponding to A has been the positive polarity. When A has been clustered into the NEGMULTDIMVECTG, the document corresponding to A has been the negative polarity. When A has been clustered into neither the NEGMULTDIMVECTG nor the POSMULTDIMVECTG, the document corresponding to A has been the neutral polarity.

We have built the algorithm 2 to create the POSMULTDIMVECTG in the SE: Each document in the positive documents in the TrDS has been transformed into one MULTDIMVECT based on (a.2). Then, the positive documents in the TrDS have been transferred to the positive MULTDIMVECTs.

Figure 6. Transferring all English documents into the MULTDIMVECTs

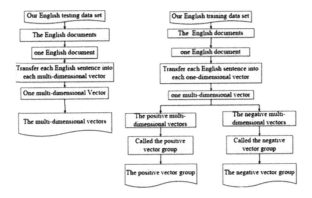

Figure 7. A CLIQUE Algorithm in SS

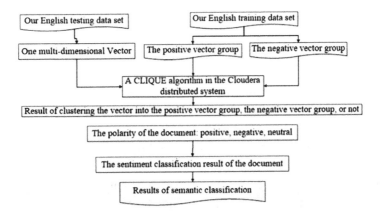

Input: the positive English documents of the TrDS

Output: the positive vector group - POSMULTDIMVECTG

1. Each document in the positive documents of the TrDS, do repeat:
2. OneMultiDimensionalVector:= Call the algorithm 1 to transfer one English document into one MULTDIMVECT based on the SENTLEXs in the SS in (a.2) with the input has been this document.
3. Add OneMultiDimensionalVector into POSMULTDIMVECTG;
4. End Repeat-End (1);
5. Return POSMULTDIMVECTG;

We have proposed the algorithm 3 to create the NEGMULTDIMVECTG in the SS: Each document in the negative documents in the TrDS has been transferred into one MULTDIMVECT according to (a.2). Then, the negative documents in the TrDS have been transferred to the negative MULTDIMVECTs.

Input: the negative English documents of the TrDS.

Output: the negative vector group - NEGMULTDIMVECTG

1. Each document in the negative documents of the TrDS, do repeat:
2. OneMultiDimensionalVector:= Call the algorithm 1 to transfer one English document into one MULTDIMVECT based on the SENTLEXs in the SS in (a.2) with the input has been this document.
3. Add OneMultiDimensionalVector into NEGMULTDIMVECTG;
4. End Repeat-End (1);
5. Return NEGMULTDIMVECTG;

We have developed the algorithm 4 to cluster one MULTDIMVECT (corresponding to one document of the TeDS) into either the POSMULTDIMVECTG or the NEGMULTDIMVECTG in the SS.

Input: one MULTDIMVECT A (corresponding to one English document of the TeDS), the POSMULTDIMVECTG and the NEGMULTDIMVECTG;

Output: positive, negative, neutral;

1. Implement the CLIQUE Algortihm based on the CLA in Segundo et al (2013), McCreesh & Prosser (2013), Depolli et al (2013), Scozzari and Tardella (2008), and Shih and Hsu (1989) with the input has been A, the POSMULTDIMVECTG, the NEGMULTDIMVECTG
2. With the results of (1), If the vector is clustered into the POSMULTDIMVECTG Then Return positive
3. Else If the vector is clustered into the NEGMULTDIMVECTG Then Return negative; End If-End (2)
4. Return neutral

The CLA in the DNS

In Figure 8, all the documents of both the TeDS and the TrDS have been transferred into all the MULTDIMVECTs in the CPNE.

With the documents of the TrDS, we have transferred them into the MULTDIMVECTs by using the M and the R in the CPNE with the purpose of shortening the execution time of this task.

Figure 8. Transferring all English documents into the MULTDIMVECTs in the CPNE

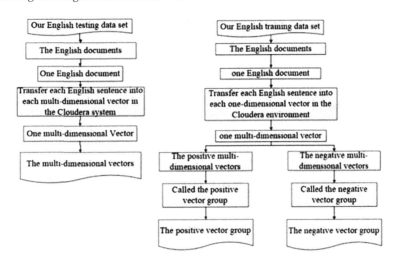

The positive documents of the TrDS have been transferred into the positive MULTDIMVECTs in the CPNE, called the POSMULTDIMVECTG.

The negative documents of the TrDS have been transferred into the negative MULTDIMVECTs in the CPNE, called the NEGMULTDIMVECTG.

Besides, the documents of the TeDS have been transferred to the MULTDIMVECTs by using the M and the R in the CPNE with the purpose of shortening the execution time of this task.

We have performed this part in Figure 9: In the CPNE, by using the CLA, one MULTDIMVECT (called A) of one document in the TeDS has been clustered into either the POSMULTDIMVECTG or the NEGMULTDIMVECTG.

When A has been clustered into the POSMULTDIMVECTG, the document corresponding to A has been the positive. When A has been clustered into the NEGMULTDIMVECTG, the document corresponding to A has been the negative. When A has been clustered into neither the NEGMULTDIMVECTG nor POSMULTDIMVECTG, the document corresponding to A has been the neutral.

An overview of transferring each English sentence into one ONEDIMVECT in the CPNE has been displayed in Figure 10.

Figure 9. A CLIQUE Algorithm in the DNS

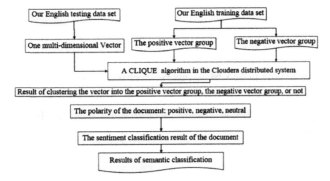

Figure 10. Transforming each English sentence into one vector in the CPNE

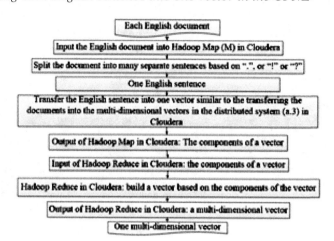

In Figure 10, transferring each English document into one MULTDIMVECT in the CPNE has included two phases: The M phase and the R phase. The input of the M phase has been one document, and the output of the M phase has been many components of a MULTDIMVECT corresponding to the document. One document, the input into the M, has been separated into the sentences. Each sentence in the English document has been transferred into one ONEDIMVECT based on (a.3). This has been repeated for all the sentences of the document until all the sentences have been transferred into all the ONEDIMVECTs of the document. After finishing to transfer each sentence of the document into one ONEDIMVECT, the M phase of the CPNE has automatically transferred the ONEDIMVECT into the R phase.

In Figure 10, the input of the R phase has been the output of the M phase, and this input has comprised the components (the ONEDIMVECTs) of a MULTDIMVECT. The output of the R phase has been a MULTDIMVECT corresponding to the document. In the R phase of the CPNE, those components of the vector have been built into one MULTDIMVECT.

The documents of the TeDS have been transferred into the MULTDIMVECTs based on Figure 10.

The CLA in the CPNE has been the two main phases: the first main phase has been the M phase in the CPNE, and the second main phase has been the R phase in the CPNE.

In the M phase of the CPNE, the input of the phase has been the MULTDIMVECT of one English document, the POSMULTDIMVECTG, the NEGMULTDIMVECTG. The output of the phase has been the clustering results of the MULTDIMVECT of the document into either the POSMULTDIMVECTG or the NEGMULTDIMVECTG.

With the R phase of the CPNE, the input of the phase has been the output of the M phase of the CPNE, and this input has been the clustering results of the MULTDIMVECT of the document into either the MULTDIMVECTG or the NEGMULTDIMVECTG. The output of the phase has been the EC result of the document into either the positive, the negative, or the neutral.

In the R phase, when the MULTDIMVECT has been clustered into the POSMULTDIMVECTG, the document has been classified into the positive emotion. When the MULTDIMVECT has been clustered into the NEGMULTDIMVECTG, the document has been classified into the negative sentiment. When the MULTDIMVECT has been clustered into neither the NEGMULTDIMVECTG nor the POSMULT-DIMVECTG, the document has been classified into the neutral opinion.

Hadoop Map (M)

This phase has been implemented in Figure 11.

The CLA in the CPNE has been based on the CLIQUE algorithm in (Segundo et al., 2013; McCreesh & Prosser, 2013; Depolli et al., 2013; Scozzari & Tardella, 2008; Shih & Hsu, 1989). The input has been one MULTDIMVECT in the TeDS, the POSMULTDIMVECTG and the NEGMULTDIMVECTG of the TrDS. The output of the CLA has been the clustering results of the MULTDIMVECT into either POSMULTDIMVECTG or the NEGMULTDIMVECTG.

The main ideas of the CLA have been as follows:

1. Enter values for the two parameters: c (1 <c <N), m and initializing the sample matrix
2. Repeat:
3. j=j+1;
4. Calculating fuzzy partition matrix Uj following formula (1)
5. Updating centers V(j) = [v1(j), v2(j), ..., vc(j)] basing on (2) và Uj matrix;
6. Until ($\parallel$ U(j+1) – U (j) $\parallel$F $\leq$ ϵ);
7. End Repeat – End Step 2;
8. Performing results of the clusters

After finishing to cluster the MULTDIMVECT into either the POSMULTDIMVECTG or the NEG-MULTDIMVECTG, the M phase has transferred these results into the R in the CLA.

Hadoop Map (M)

This phase has been performed in Figure 12. After receiving the clustering result of the M, the R has labeled the semantic polarity for the MULTDIMVECT which has been classified. Then, the output of the R has returned the semantic polarity of one document (corresponding to the MULTDIMVECT) in the TeDS.

When the MULTDIMVECT has been clustered into the POSMULTDIMVECTG, the document has been the positive. When the MULTDIMVECT has been clustered into the NEGMULTDIMVECTG, the document has been the negative. When the MULTDIMVECT has been clustered into neither the NEGMULTDIMVECTG nor the POSMULTDIMVECTG, the document has been the neutral.

We have used an Accuracy (A) to calculate the accuracy of the results of the emotion classification of this proposed model.

Figure 11. The CLA in the M in the CPNE

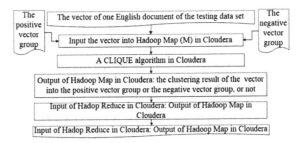

179

Figure 12. The R in the CPNE

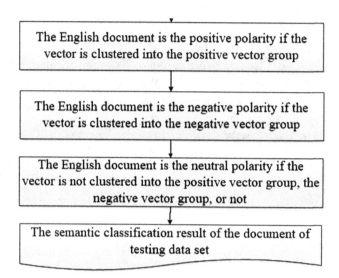

Java programming language (JPL) has been used for programming to save data sets, implementing our proposed model to classify the opinions (positive, negative, or neutral) of the documents of the TeDS. To implement the proposed model, we have already used the JPL to save the TrDS, the TeDS, and to save the results of the EC.

The configuration of the server in the SE and the Cloudera system has been: Intel® Server Board S1200V3RPS, Intel® Pentium® Processor G3220 (3M Cache, 3.00 GHz), 2GB PC3-10600 ECC 1333 MHz LP Unbuffered DIMMs.

The SS in this research includes 1 node (1 server). The JPL has also been used in programming the CLA. The operating system of the server is: Cloudera.

We have performed the CLA in the CPNE; this Cloudera system includes 9 nodes (9 servers). The JPL has been used in programming the application of the CLA in the Cloudera. The operating system of each server in the 9 servers is: Cloudera. All 9 nodes have the same configuration information.

The results of the documents of the TeDS to test are presented in Table 1.

The accuracy of the emotional classification of the documents in the TeDS is shown in Table 2.

In Table 3, the average time of the classification of our new model for the English documents in TeDS are displayed

Although our new model has been tested on our TeDS, it can be applied to other languages. In this chapter, our model has been tested on the 1,000,000 English documents of the TeDS in which the data

Table 1. The results of the documents in the testing data set

	Testing Dataset	Correct Classification	Incorrect Classification
Negative	500,000	440,846	59,154
Positive	500,000	438,754	61,246
Summary	1,000,000	879,600	120,400

Table 2. The accuracy of our new model for the documents in the testing data set

Proposed Model	Class	Accuracy
Our new model	Negative	87.96%
	Positive	

Table 3. The average times of the classification of our new model for the documents in testing data set

	Average Time of the Classification /1,000,000 Documents.
The novel model in the SS	5,057,194 seconds
The novel model in the CPNE with 3 nodes	1,542,535 seconds
The novel model in the CPNE with 6 nodes	851,528 seconds
The novel model in the CPNE with 9 nodes	548,932seconds

sets are small. However, our model can be applied to larger data sets with millions of English documents in the shortest time.

In this work, we have proposed a new model to classify the sentiments of the documents using the CLA with the M and the R in the CPNE. With our proposed new model, we have achieved 87.96% accuracy of the TeDS.

In Table 3, the average time of the semantic classification of the CLA in the SE is 5,057,194 seconds /1,000,000 English documents and it is greater than the average time of the emotion classification of the CLA in the CPNE – 3 nodes which is 1,542,535 seconds/1,000,000 English documents. The average time of the emotion classification of the CLA in the CPNE – 9 nodes, which is 548,932 seconds /1,000,000 English documents, is the shortest time. Besides, the average time of the emotion classification of the CLA in the CPNE – 6 nodes is 851,528 seconds /1,000,000 English documents

The execution time of the CLA in the CPNE is dependent on the performance of the CPNE and also dependent on the performance of each server on the CPNE.

The proposed model has many advantages and disadvantages. Its positives are as follows: It uses the CLA to classify semantics of English documents based on the documents. The proposed model can process millions of documents in the shortest time. This study can be performed in distributed systems. It can be applied to other languages. Its negatives are as follows: It has a low rate of accuracy. It costs too much and takes too much time to implement this proposed model.

FUTURE RESEARCH DIRECTIONS

From those results of this novel model and according to the above proofs, we are going to study this model for applying to billions of English documents in both the SE and the PNE. In addition, we are also going to research this approach for being performed in the PNE with over 50 nodes. Furthermore, the accuracy of this new computational model can be studied to improve certainly.

From the results of this chapter, many algorithms, methods, and models are going to be developed more and more for handling the massive data sets fully in the near future.

CONCLUSION

In this chapter, we have shown the simple concepts of the DM, the SN, the SNG, and the SNA. We have also displayed the importance of the DM and the SNA in the world. The problems and challenges of the DM and the SNA have been presented.

We have already given an example of the DM for the SNA in this chapter: a novel model using the CLA of the DM with the MULTDIMVECTs according to the OPL of the SC through the GSE and or in the SS and the CPNE.

From the results of the proposed model, based on our opinion, the DM is very crucial for the SNA certainly. We believe that there are going to have many important contributions of the DM for the SNA fully and successfully.

In addition, this novel model can process billions of the documents in English of the semantic mining in a big data.

Many algorithms, methods, and models are going to be developed for the DM to be applied to the SNA from the results of the proposed approach. This is very significant for many organizations, economies, governments, countries, companies, and research in the world.

ACKNOWLEDGMENT

This book chapter has been funded by Institute of Research and Development, Duy Tan University-DTU, Da Nang, Vietnam.

REFERENCES

An, N. T. T., & Hagiwara, M. (2014). Adjective-Based Estimation of Short Sentence's Impression. In *Proceedings of the 5th Kanesi Engineering and Emotion Research International Conference (KEER2014)*, Sweden.

Andréia da Silva, M., Antonio, A. F. G., Pereira de Souza, A., & Lopes de Souza, C. Jr. (2004). Comparison of similarity coefficients used for cluster analysis with dominant markers in maize (Zea maysL). *Genetics and Molecular Biology*, 27(1), 83–91. doi:10.1590/S1415-47572004000100014

Apache. (2017). Retrieved from http://apache.org

Bai, A., & Hammer, H. (2014). Constructing sentiment lexicons in Norwegian from a large text corpus. *2014 IEEE 17th International Conference on Computational Science and Engineering.*

Brooke, J., Tofiloski, M., & Taboada, M. (2009). Cross-Linguistic Sentiment Analysis: From English to Spanish. In *International Conference RANLP 2009*, Borovets, Bulgaria (pp. 50-54).

Cambridge English Dictionary. (2017). Retrieved from http://dictionary.cambridge.org/

Carrera-Trejo, V., Sidorov, G., Miranda-Jiménez, S., Ibarra, M. M., & Cadena Martínez, R. (2015). Latent Dirichlet Allocation complement in the vector space model for Multi-Label Text Classification. *International Journal of Combinatorial Optimization Problems and Informatics*, 6(1), 7–19.

Choi, S.S., Cha, S-H & Tappert, C.C. (2010). A Survey Of Binary Similarity And Distance Measures. *Systemics, Cybernetics And Informatics, 8*(1).

Cloudera. (2017). Retrieved from http://www.cloudera.com

Dat, N. D., Phu, V. N., Tran, V. T. N., Chau, V. T. N., & Nguyen, T. A. (2017). STING Algorithm used English Sentiment Classification in A Parallel Environment. *International Journal of Pattern Recognition and Artificial Intelligence, 31*(7). doi:10.11420218001417500215

Depolli, M., Konc, J., Rozman, K., Trobec, R., & Janežič, D. (2013). Exact parallel maximum clique algorithm for general and protein graphs. *Journal of Chemical Information and Modeling, 53*(9), 2217–2228. doi:10.1021/ci4002525

Drinić, S. M., Nikolić, A., & Perić, V. (2008). Cluster analysis of soybean genotypes based on RAPD markers. In *Proceedings. 43rd Croatian And 3rd International Symposium On Agriculture*, Opatija. Croatia (pp. 367-370).

Du, W., Tan, S., Cheng, X., & Yun, X. (2010). Adapting Information Bottleneck Method for Automatic Construction of Domain-oriented Sentiment Lexicon. In WSDM'10, New York, USA.

English Dictionary of Lingoes. (2017). Retrieved from http://www.lingoes.net/

Feng, S., Zhang, L., Li Daling Wang, B., Yu, G., & Wong, K.-F. (2013). Is Twitter A Better Corpus for Measuring Sentiment Similarity? In *Proceedings of the 2013 Conference on Empirical Methods in Natural Language Processing* (pp. 897–902).

Hadoop. (2017). Retrieved from http://hadoop.apache.org

Hansen, D. L., Nielsen, S. B., & Lykke-Andersen, H. (2000). The post-Triassic evolution of the Sorgenfrei–Tornquist Zone — results from thermo-mechanical modelling. *Tectonophysics, 328*(3–4), 245–267. doi:10.1016/S0040-1951(00)00216-X

Hernández-Ugalde, J. A., Mora-Urpí, J., & Rocha, O. J. (2011). Genetic relationships among wild and cultivated populations of peach palm (Bactris gasipaes Kunth, Palmae): Evidence for multiple independent domestication events. *Genetic Resources and Crop Evolution, 58*(4), 571–583. doi:10.100710722-010-9600-6

Htait, A., Fournier, S., & Bellot, P. (2016). LSIS at SemEval-2016 Task 7: Using Web Search Engines for English and Arabic Unsupervised Sentiment Intensity Prediction. In *Proceedings of SemEval-2016* (pp. 481–485).

Ji, X., Chun, S. A., Wei, Z., & Geller, J. (2015). Twitter sentiment classification for measuring public health concerns. *Social Network Analysis and Mining, 5*(1), 13. doi:10.100713278-015-0253-5

Jiang, T., Jiang, J., Dai, Y., & Li, A. (2015). Micro–blog Emotion Orientation Analysis Algorithm Based on Tibetan and Chinese Mixed Text. In *International Symposium on Social Science (ISSS 2015)*. 10.2991/isss-15.2015.39

Jovanoski, D., Pachovski, V., & Nakov, P. (2015). Sentiment Analysis in Twitter for Macedonian. Proceedings of Recent Advances in Natural Language Processing, Bulgaria (pp. 249-257).

Lefki, K., & Dormans, J. G. M. (1998). Measurement of piezoelectric coefficients of ferroelectric thin films. *Journal of Applied Physics, 76*(3), 1764–1767. doi:10.1063/1.357693

Malouf, R., & Mullen, T. (2017). Graph-based user classification for informal online political discourse. In *Proceedings of the 1st Workshop on Information Credibility on the Web.*

Mao, H., Gao, P., Wang, Y., & Bollen, J. (2014). Automatic Construction of Financial Semantic Orientation Lexicon from Large-Scale Chinese News Corpus. In *7th Financial Risks International Forum*, Institut Louis Bachelier.

McCreesh, C., & Prosser, P. (2013). Multi-Threading a State-of-the-Art Maximum Clique Algorithm. *Algorithms, 6*(4), 618–635. doi:10.3390/a6040618

Netzer, O., Feldman, R., Goldenberg, J., & Fresko, M. (2012). Mine Your Own Business: Market-Structure Surveillance Through Text Mining. *Marketing Science, 31*(3), 521–543. doi:10.1287/mksc.1120.0713

Omar, N., Albared, M., Al-Shabi, A. Q., & Al-Moslmi, T. (2013). Ensemble of classification algorithms for subjectivity and sentiment analysis of Arabic customers' reviews. *International Journal of Advancements in Computing Technology, 5.*

Oxford English Dictionary. (2017). Retrieved from http://www.oxforddictionaries.com/

Phu, V. N., Dat, N. D., Vo, T. N. T., Vo, T. N. C., & Nguyen, T. A. (2017a). Fuzzy C-means for English sentiment classification in a distributed system. *International Journal of Applied Intelligence, 46*(3), 717–738. doi:10.100710489-016-0858-z

Phu, V. N., Vo, T. N. C., Dat, N. D., Vo, T. N. T., & Nguyen, T. A. (2017e). *A Valences-Totaling Model for English Sentiment Classification. International Journal of Knowledge and Information Systems.* doi:10.1007/S13115-017-1054-0

Phu, V. N., Vo, T. N. C., & Vo, T. N. T. (2017b). SVM for English Semantic Classification in Parallel Environment. *International Journal of Speech Technology.* doi:10.100710772-017-9421-5

Phu, V. N., Vo, T. N. C., & Vo, T. N. T. (2017f). *Shifting Semantic Values of English Phrases for Classification. International Journal of Speech Technology.* doi:10.1007/S13772-017-9420-6

Phu, V. N., Vo, T. N. C., Vo, T. N. T., & Dat, N. D. (2017d). *A Vietnamese adjective emotion dictionary based on exploitation of Vietnamese language characteristics. International Journal of Artificial Intelligence Review.* doi:10.1007/S13462-017-9538-6

Phu, V. N., Vo, T. N. C., Vo, T. N. T., Dat, N. D., & Khanh, L. D. D. (2017g). *A Valence-Totaling Model for Vietnamese Sentiment Classification. International Journal of Evolving Systems.* doi:10.100712530-017-9187-7

Phu, V. N., Vo, T. N. C., Vo, T. N. T., Dat, N. D., & Khanh, L. D. D. (2017h). *Semantic Lexicons of English Nouns for Classification. International Journal of Evolving Systems.* doi:10.100712530-017-9188-6

Phu, V. N., & Vo, T. N. T. (2017c). A STING Algorithm and Multi-dimensional Vectors Used for English Sentiment Classification in a Distributed System. *American Journal of Engineering and Applied Sciences.* doi:10.3844/ajeassp.2017

Phu, V. N., & Vo, T. N. T. (2017j). English Sentiment Classification using Only the Sentiment Lexicons with a JOHNSON Coefficient in a Parallel Network Environment. *American Journal of Engineering and Applied Sciences*. doi:10.3844/ajeassp.2017

Phu, V. N., & Vo, T. N. T. (2018a). English sentiment classification using a Gower-2 coefficient and a genetic algorithm with a fitness-proportionate selection in a parallel network environment. *Journal of Theoretical and Applied Information Technology, 96*(4), 1–50.

Phu, V. N., & Vo, T. N. T. (2018b). English sentiment classification using a Fager & MacGowan coefficient and a genetic algorithm with a rank selection in a parallel network environment. *International Journal of Computer Modelling and New Technologies, 22*(1), 57–112.

Phu, V. N., & Vo, T. N. T. (2018c). Latent Semantic Analysis using A Dennis Coefficient for English Sentiment Classification in A Parallel System. *International Journal of Computers, Communications & Control, 13*(3), 390–410.

Phu, V. N., & Vo, T. N. T. (2018e). English Sentiment Classification using A BIRCH Algorithm and The Sentiment Lexicons-Based One-dimentional Vectors in a Parallel Network Environment. *International Journal of Computer Modelling and New Technologies, 22*(1).

Phu, V. N., & Vo, T. N. T. (2018f). A Fuzzy C-Means Algorithm and Sentiment-Lexicons-based Multi-dimensional Vectors Of A SOKAL & SNEATH-IV Coefficient Used For English Sentiment Classification. *International Journal of Theoretical and Applied Information Technology, 96*(10).

Phu, V. N., & Vo, T. N. T. (2018g). A Self-Training - Based Model using A K-NN Algorithm and The Sentiment Lexicons - Based Multi-dimensional Vectors of A S6 coefficient for Sentiment Classification. *International Journal of Theoretical and Applied Information Technology, 96*(10).

Phu, V. N., & Vo, T. N. T. (2018h). The Multi-dimensional Vectors and An Yule-II Measure Used for A Self-Organizing Map Algorithm of English Sentiment Classification in A Distributed Environment. *Journal of Theoretical and Applied Information Technology, 96*(10).

Phu, V. N., & Vo, T. N. T. (2018i). Sentiment Classification using The Sentiment Scores Of Lexicons Based on A Kuhns-II Coefficient in English. *International Journal of Tomography & Simulation, 31*(3).

Phu, V. N., & Vo, T. N. T. (2018j). K-Medoids algorithm used for english sentiment classification in a distributed system. *Computer Modelling and New Technologies, 22*(1), 20–39.

Phu, V. N., & Vo, T. N. T. (2018k). A Reformed K-Nearest Neighbors Algorithm for Big Data Sets. *Journal of Computational Science*. doi:10.3844/jcssp.2018

Phu, V. N., Vo, T. N. T., & Max, J. (2018d). A CURE Algorithm for Vietnamese Sentiment Classification in a Parallel Environment. *International Journal of Computational Science*. doi:10.3844/jcssp.2018

Ponomarenko, J. V., Bourne, P. E., & Shindyalov, I. N. (2002). Building an automated classification of DNA-binding protein domains. *Bioinformatics (Oxford, England), 18*(Suppl. 2), S192–S201. doi:10.1093/bioinformatics/18.suppl_2.S192 PMID:12386003

Ren, Y., Kaji, N., Yoshinaga, N., & Kitsuregaw, M. (2014). Sentiment classification in under-resourced languages using graph-based semi-supervised learning methods. *IEICE Transactions on Information and Systems, E97–D*(4), 790–797. doi:10.1587/transinf.E97.D.790

Ren, Y., Kaji, N., Yoshinaga, N., Toyoda, M., & Kitsuregawa, M. (2011). Sentiment Classification in Resource-Scarce Languages by using Label Propagation. In *Proceedings of the 25th Pacific Asia Conference on Language, Information and Computation* (pp. 420-429). Institute of Digital Enhancement of Cognitive Processing, Waseda University.

Scheible, C. (2010). Sentiment Translation through Lexicon Induction. In *Proceedings of the ACL 2010 Student Research Workshop*, Sweden (pp. 25–30).

Scozzari, A., & Tardella, F. (2008). A clique algorithm for standard quadratic programming. *Discrete Applied Mathematics, 156*(13), 2439–2448. doi:10.1016/j.dam.2007.09.020

Segundo, P. S., Matia, F., Rodriguez-Losada, D., & Hernando, M. (2013). An improved bit parallel exact maximum clique algorithm. *Optimization Letters, 7*(3), 467–479. doi:10.100711590-011-0431-y

Shih, W.-K., & Hsu, W.-L. (1989). An O(n log n + m log log n) maximum weight clique algorithm for circular-arc graphs. *Information Processing Letters, 31*(3), 129–134. doi:10.1016/0020-0190(89)90220-2

Shikalgar, N. R., & Dixit, A. M. (2014). JIBCA: Jaccard Index based Clustering Algorithm for Mining Online Review. *International Journal of Computers and Applications, 105*(15).

Singh, V. K., & Singh, V. K. (2015). Vector Space Model: An Information Retrieval System. *Int. J. Adv. Engg. Res., 141*, 143.

Soucy, P., & Mineau, G. W. (2015). Beyond TFIDF Weighting for Text Categorization in the Vector Space Model. In *Proceedings of the 19th International Joint Conference on Artificial Intelligence* (pp. 1130-1135).

Tamás, J., Podani, J., & Csontos, P. (2001). An extension of presence/absence coefficients to abundance data: A new look at absence. *Journal of Vegetation Science, 12*(3), 401–410. doi:10.2307/3236854

Tan, S., & Zhang, J. (2007). (2007). An empirical study of sentiment analysis for Chinese documents. *Expert Systems with Applications.* doi:10.1016/j.eswa.2007.05.028

Turney, P.D. & Littman, M.L. (2002). Unsupervised Learning of Semantic Orientation from a Hundred-Billion-Word Corpus.

Wan, X. (2009, August). Co-training for cross-lingual sentiment classification. In *Proceedings of the Joint Conference of the 47th Annual Meeting of the ACL and the 4th International Joint Conference on Natural Language Processing of the AFNLP* (Vol. 1, pp. 235-243). Association for Computational Linguistics.

Wang, G., & Araki, K. (2007). Modifying SO-PMI for Japanese Weblog Opinion Mining by Using a Balancing Factor and Detecting Neutral Expressions. In *Proceedings of NAACL HLT 2007* (pp. 189–192).

Zhang, Z., Ye, Q., Zheng, W., & Li, Y. (2010). Sentiment Classification for Consumer Word-of-Mouth in Chinese: Comparison between Supervised and Unsupervised Approaches. In *The 2010 International Conference on E-Business Intelligence*.

Chapter 10
Privacy Information Leakage Prevention in Cognitive Social Mining Applications:
Causes and Prevention Measures

Suriya Murugan
Bannari Amman Institute of Technology, India

Anandakumar H.
Sri Eshwar College of Engineering, India

ABSTRACT

Online social networks, such as Facebook are increasingly used by many users and these networks allow people to publish and share their data to their friends. The problem is user privacy information can be inferred via social relations. This chapter makes a study and performs research on managing those confidential information leakages which is a challenging issue in social networks. It is possible to use learning methods on user released data to predict private information. Since the main goal is to distribute social network data while preventing sensitive data disclosure, it can be achieved through sanitization techniques. Then the effectiveness of those techniques is explored, and the methods of collective inference are used to discover sensitive attributes of the user profile data set. Hence, sanitization methods can be used efficiently to decrease the accuracy of both local and relational classifiers and allow secure information sharing by maintaining user privacy.

INTRODUCTION TO SOCIAL MINING

A social networking service is an online service, platform, site that focuses on facilitating the building of social networks or social relations among people share their interests, activities, backgrounds, or real-life connections. A social network service consists of a representation of each user, his/her social links, and a variety of additional services. Most social network services are web-based and provide means for users to interact over the Internet, such as e-mail and instant messaging. Online community services are

DOI: 10.4018/978-1-5225-7522-1.ch010

sometimes considered as a social network service usually means an individual-centered service whereas online community services are group-centered.

Social networking sites allow users to share ideas, activities, events, and interests within their individual networks. When it comes to online social networking, websites are commonly used. These websites are known as social sites. Social networking websites function like an online community of internet users. Depending on the website in many of these online community members share common interests in hobbies, religion, politics and alternative lifestyles. Once user can grant access to a social networking website they can begin to socialize. This socialization may include reading the profile pages of other members and possibly even contacting them.

One of the benefits includes diversity because the internet gives individuals from all around the world access to social networking sites. Social networking often involves grouping specific individuals or organizations together. While there are a number of social networking websites that focus on particular interests, there are others that do not. The websites without a main focus are often referred to as traditional social networking websites and usually have open memberships. This means that anyone can become a member, no matter what their hobbies, beliefs, or views. However, once users inside this online community, they can begin to create your own network of friends and eliminate members that do not share common interests or goals.

TYPES OF SOCIAL NETWORKS

There are many types of social networks available as depicted in Figure 1 and Figure 2 in detail. This examines the privacy and security implication. Most social networks combine elements of more than one of these types of networks, and the focus of a social network may change over time. While does not address every type of social network, many of the security and privacy recommendations are applicable to other types of networks.

Figure 1. Social networking

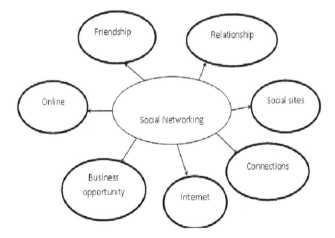

- **Personal Networks**: These networks allow users to create detailed online profiles and connect with other users, with an emphasis on social relationships such as friendship. For example, Facebook, Friendster and MySpace are platforms for communicating with contacts. These networks often involve users sharing information with other approved users, such as one's gender, age, interests, educational background and employment, as well as files and links to music, photos and videos. These platforms may also share selected information with individuals and applications that are not authorized contacts.

- **Status Update Networks:** These types of social networks are designed to allow users to post short status updates in order to communicate with other users quickly. For example, Twitter focuses its services on providing instantaneous, short updates. These networks are designed to broadcast information quickly and publicly, though there may be privacy settings to restrict access to status updates.

- **Location Networks:** With the advent of GPS-enabled cellular phones, location networks are growing in popularity. These networks are designed to broadcast one's real-time location, either as public information or as an update viewable to authorized contacts. Many of these networks are built to interact with other social networks; so that an update made to a location network could (with proper authorization) post to one's other social networks. Time for a Privacy Check-in and their Comparison Chart evaluating the privacy features of six location networks.

- **Content-Sharing Networks:** These networks are designed as platforms for sharing content, such as music, photographs and videos. When these websites introduce the ability to create personal profiles, establish contacts and interact with other users through comments, they become social networks as well as content hubs. Some popular content sharing networks include YouTube and Flickr.

Figure 2. Types of social networks

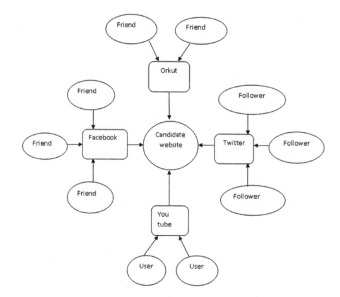

- **Shared-Interest Networks:** Some social networks are built around a common interest or geared to a specific group of people. These networks incorporate features from other types of social networks but are slanted toward a subset of individuals, such as those with similar hobbies, educational backgrounds, political affiliations, ethnic backgrounds, religious views, sexual orientations or other defining interests.

SOCIAL NETWORK ANALYSIS AND MINING

Social Network Analysis and Mining (SNAM) is a multidisciplinary journal serving researchers and practitioners in academia and industry. It is the main venue for a wide range of researchers and readers from computer science, network science, social sciences, mathematical sciences, medical and biological sciences, financial, management and political sciences. The solicit experimental and theoretical work on social network analysis and mining using a wide range of techniques from social sciences, mathematics, statistics, physics, network science and computer science.

Levels of Analysis

In general, social networks are self-organizing, emergent, and complex, such that a globally coherent pattern appears from the local interaction of the elements that make up the system. These patterns become more apparent as network size increases. However, a global network analysis of all interpersonal relationship in the world is not feasible and is likely to contain so much information as to be uninformative. Practical limitations of computing power, ethics and participant recruitment and payment also limit the scope of a social network analysis.

Social networks are analyzed at the scale relevant to the researcher's theoretical question. Although levels of analysis are not necessarily mutually exclusive, there are three general levels into which networks may fall:

- Micro-level
- Meso-level
- Macro-level

Micro Level

At the micro-level as shown in Figure 3, social network research typically begins with an individual, snowballing as social relationships are traced, or may begin with a small group of individuals in a particular social context.

- **Dyadic Level**: Dyad is a social relationship between two individuals. Network research on dyads may concentrate on structure of the relationship social equality, and tendencies toward reciprocity/mutuality.
- **Triadic Level:** Add one individual to a dyad, and you have a triad. Research at this level may concentrate on factors such as balance and transitivity, as well as social equality and tendencies toward reciprocity/mutuality.

Figure 3. Micro Level

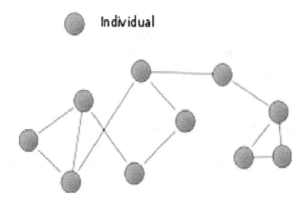

- **Actor Level**: The smallest unit of analysis in a social network is an individual in their social setting, i.e., an "actor" or "ego". Ego network analysis focuses on network characteristics such as size, relationship strength, density, centrality, prestige and roles such as isolates, liaisons, and bridges.
- **Subset Level:** Subset levels of network research problems begin at the micro-level, but may cross over into the meso-level of analysis. Subset level research may focus on distance and reachability, cliques, cohesive subgroups, or other group actions or behavior.

Meso Level

In general, meso-level theories begin with a population size that falls between the micro and macro-levels. However, meso-level may also refer to analyses that are specifically designed to reveal connections between micro and macro-levels. Meso-level networks are shown in Figure 4 which have low density and may exhibit causal processes distinct from interpersonal micro-level networks.

Figure 4. Meso level

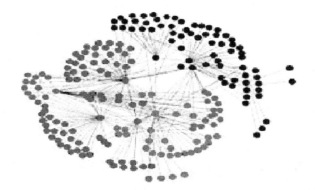

Organizations Formal

Organizations are social groups that distribute tasks for a collective goal. Network research on organizations may focus on either intra-organizational or inter-organizational ties in terms of formal or informal relationships. Intra-organizational networks themselves often contain multiple levels of analysis, especially in larger organizations with multiple branches, franchises or semi-autonomous departments. In these cases, research is often conducted at a workgroup level and organization level, focusing on the interplay between the two structures.

Randomly-Distributed Networks

Exponential random graph models of social networks became state-of-the-art methods of social network analysis in the 1980s. This framework has the capacity to represent social-structural effects commonly observed in many human social networks, including general degree-based structural effects commonly observed in many human social networks as well as reciprocity and transitivity, and at the node-level, homophily and attribute-based activity and popularity effects, as derived from explicit hypotheses about dependencies among network ties. Parameters are given in terms of the prevalence of small subgraph configurations in the network and can be interpreted as describing the combinations of local social processes from which a given network emerges. The probability models for networks on a given set of actors allow generalization beyond the restrictive dyadic independence assumption of micro-networks, allowing models to be built from theoretical structural foundations of social behavior. Examples of a random network and a scale-free network. Each graph has 32 nodes and 32 links.

Scale-Free Networks

A scale-free network is a network whose degree distribution follows a power law, at least asymptotically. In network theory a scale-free ideal network is a random network with a degree distribution that unravels the size distribution of social groups. Specific characteristics of scale-free networks vary with the theories and analytical tools used to create them, however, in general, scale-free networks have some common characteristics.

One notable characteristic in a scale-free network is the relative commonness of vertices with a degree that greatly exceeds the average. The highest-degree nodes are often called "hubs", and may serve specific purposes in their networks, although this depends greatly on the social context. Another general characteristic of scale-free networks is the clustering coefficient distribution, which decreases as the node degree increases.

Macro Level

Rather than tracing interpersonal interactions, macro-level analyses generally trace the outcomes of interactions, such as economic or other resource transfer interactions over a large population.

Large-Scale Networks

Large-scale network is a term somewhat synonymous with "macro-level" as used, primarily, in social and behavioral sciences, in economics. Originally, the term was used extensively in the computer sciences.

Complex Networks

Most larger social networks display features of social complexity, which involves substantial non-trivial features of network topology, with patterns of complex connections between elements that are neither purely regular nor purely random as do biological, and technological networks. Such complex network features include a heavy tail in the degree distribution, a high clustering coefficient among vertices, community structure, and hierarchical structure. In the case of agency-directed networks these features also include reciprocity, triad significance profile (TSP) and other features. In contrast, many of the mathematical models of networks that have been studied in the past, such as lattices and random graphs, do not show these features.

PRIVACY ISSUES OF SOCIAL NETWORKING

Cyber Stalking and Location Disclosure

With the creation of Facebook and the continued popularity of MySpace, many people are giving their personal information out on the internet. Most users are not aware that they can modify the privacy settings and unless they modify them, their information is open to the public. Sites such as Facebook, Myspace, and Twitter have grown popular by broadcasting status updates featuring personal information such as location. Some applications border on "cyberstalking." This has redefined the role of Internet privacy as overlapping with that of security.

Some applications are explicitly centered on "cyberstalking." An application named "Creepy" can track a person's location on a map using photos uploaded to Twitter or Flickr. When a person uploads photos to a social networking site, others are able to track their most recent location. Some smart phones are able to embed the longitude and latitude coordinates into the photo and automatically send this information to the application. Anybody using the application can search for a specific person and then find their immediate location. This poses many potential threats to users who share their information with a large group of followers.

Facebook "Places," is a Facebook service, which publicizes user location information to the networking community. Users are allowed to "check-in" at various locations including retail stores, convenience stores, and restaurants. Also, users are able to create their own "place," disclosing personal information onto the Internet. This form of location tracking is automated and must be turned off manually. Various settings must be turned off and manipulated in order for the user to ensure privacy. According to epic.org,

Facebook users are recommended to: (1) disable "Friends can check me in to Places," (2) customize "Places I Check In," (3) disable "People Here Now," and (4) uncheck "Places I've Visited.". Moreover, the Federal Trade Commission has received two complaints in regard to Facebook's "unfair and deceptive" trade practices, which are used to target advertising sectors of the online community. "Places" tracks user location information and is used primarily for advertising purposes. Each location tracked allows third party advertisers to customize advertisements that suit one's interests. Currently, the Federal Trade Commissioner along with the Electronic Privacy Information Center are shedding light on the issues of location data tracking on social networking sites.

Social Profiling and 3rd Party Disclosure

Social profiling allows for Facebook and other social networking media websites of filtering through the advertisements, assigning specific ones to specific age groups, gender groups, and even ethnicities. Data aggregation sites like Spokeo have highlighted the feasibility of aggregating social data across social sites as well as integrating it with public records. Study highlighted these issues by measuring the amount of unintended information leakage over a large number of users with varying number of social networks identified and measured information that could be used in attacks against what-you-know security. Studies have also pointed to most social networks unintentionally providing 3rd party advertising and tracking sites with personal information. Social network raises the issue of private information inadvertently being sent to 3rd party advertising sites via Referrer strings or cookies.

Invasive Privacy Agreements

Another privacy issue with social networks is the privacy agreement. The privacy agreement states that the social network owns all of the content that users upload. This includes pictures, videos, and messages are all stored in the social networks database even if the user decides to terminate his or her account.

Preteens and Early Teenagers

The most vulnerable victims of private-information-sharing behavior are preteens and early teenagers. There have been age restrictions put on numerous websites but how effective they are is debatable. Findings have discovered that informative opportunities regarding internet privacy as well as concerns from parents, teachers, and peers, play a significant role on impacting the internet user's behavior towards online privacy.

Additionally, other studies have also found that the heightening of adolescents' concern towards their privacy will also lead to a greater probability that they will utilize privacy-protecting behaviors. In the technological culture that society is developing into, not only adolescents' and parent's awareness should be risen, but society as a whole should acknowledge the importance of online privacy.

Law Enforcement Prowling the Networks

The FBI has dedicated undercover agents on Facebook, Twitter, MySpace, LinkedIn. The rules and guidelines to the privacy issue is internal to the Justice Department and details aren't released to the public. Agents can impersonate a friend, a long lost relative, even a spouse and child. This raises real issues regarding privacy. Although people who use Facebook, Twitter, and other social networking sites are aware of some level of privacy will always be compromised, but, no one would ever suspect that the friend invitation might be from a federal agent whose sole purpose of the friend request was to snoop around.

Furthermore, Facebook, Twitter, and MySpace have personal information and past posts logged for up to one year; even deleted profiles, and with a warrant, can hand over very personal information. One example of investigators using Facebook to nab a criminal is the case of Maxi Sopo. Charged with bank fraud, and having escaped to Mexico, he was nowhere to be found until he started posting on Facebook. Although his profile was private, his list of friends was not, and through this vector, they eventually caught him.

LITERATURE SURVEY

Anonymizing Social Network

In social network focus on the problem of private information leakage for individuals as a direct result of their actions. Backstrom, Dwork, and Kleinberg (2007) considers an attack against an anonymized network. In their model, the network consists of only nodes and edges. The goal of the attacker is simply to identify people. Further, their problem is very different than the one considered they ignore details and do not consider the effect of the existence of details on privacy. Here they work attacks on anonymized social networks it includes

- Walk-based attack
- Cut-based attack

The Nature of the Attack

Assume the social network is an n-node graph G= (V, E), representing interactions in an on-line system. Nodes correspond to user accounts, and an edge(U, V)indicates that U has communicated with Vagain, consider the example of an e-mail or instant messaging network. The attacks become easier to carry out if the released graph data is directed.

Parameters of the Active Attacks

To produce a sub graph likely to be unique in the network, an active attacker can use random generation: it creates k user accounts, and produces links by creating an edge between each pair independently at random.

Walk-Based Attack

Let G= (V, E) be then-node graph representing the anonymized social network that is released. As noted above, consider the undirected case, in which there is an undirected edge (U, V) if at least one of the directed edges (U, V) or (V, V) is present. So, focus on the undirected case because the attack becomes easier if the graph is directed. Let us consider the problem from the perspective of the attacker. For ease of presentation, begin with a slightly simplified version of the attack, and then show how to extend it to the attack really use.

First choose a set of K named users, $W = \{w1, ..., w_k\}$, that wish to target in the network want to learn all the pairs (w_i, w_j) for which there are edges in G. To find each w in the anonymized graph use the following strategy. First create a set of K new user accounts, $X = \{x1, ..., x_k\}$, which will appear as nodes in the system include each undirected edge (x_i, x_j) independently with probability 1/2. This produces a random graph H on X.

Then create an edge (xi, w_i) for each I as discussed above, this involves having x_i send w_i a message, or include w_i in an address book, or some other activity depending on the nature of the social network. For describing the basic version of the attack also assume that, because the account x_i corresponds to a fake identity, it will not receive messages from any node in G−H other than potentially w_i, and thus will have no link to any other node in G−H, see later that the attack can be made to work even when this latter assumption does not hold. When the anonymized graph G is released, need to find our copy of H, and to correctly label its nodes as $x_1, ..., x_k$. Having found these nodes, find w_i as the unique node in G−H that is linked to x_i. Thus, identify the full labeled set W in G, and can simply read off the edges between its elements by consulting G.

Thus, the construction of H succeeds if

1. There is no S=X such that G[S] and G[X] =Hare isomorphic
2. The subgraph H can be efficiently found, given G
3. The subgraph H has no non-trivial automorphisms

If (i) holds, then any copy of H find in G must in fact be the one constructed; if (ii) holds, then can in fact find the copy of H quickly; and if (iii) holds, then once find H, correctly label its nodes as $x_1, ..., x_k$, and hence find w_1, w_k.

Cut-Based Attack

In the walk-based attack just presented, one needs to construct algorithmic number of nodes in order to begin compromising privacy. On the other hand, show that at least $\Omega(\sqrt{\log n})$ nodes are needed in any active attack that requires a subgraph H to be uniquely identifiable with high probability, independent of both the structure of G−H and the choice of which users to target. It is therefore natural to try closing this gap between the O(logn) number of nodes used by the first attack, and the $\Omega(\sqrt{\log n})$ lower bound required in any attack. The cut-based attack; it matches the lower bound by compromising privacy using a subgraph H constructed on only $O(\sqrt{\log n})$ nodes. While the bound for the cut-based attack is appealing from a theoretical perspective, there are several important respects in which the walk-based attack that saw earlier is likely to be more effective in practice. First, the walk-based attack comes with a much more efficient recovery algorithm; and second, the walk-based attack appears to be harder for the curator of the data to detect (as the cut-based attack produces a densely connected component attached weakly to the rest of the graph, which is uncommon in many settings).

Hay, Miklau, Jensen, Weis, and Srivastava (2007) specifies several ways of anonymizing social networks work focuses on inferring details from nodes in the network, not individually identifying individuals. Here presents a framework for assessing the privacy risk of sharing anonymized network data.

This includes a model of adversary knowledge, for which consider several variants and make connections to known graph theoretical results. On several real-world social networks show that simple anonymization techniques are inadequate, resulting in substantial breaches of privacy for even modestly informed adversaries.

Propose a novel anonymization technique based on perturbing the network and demonstrate empirically that it leads to substantial reduction of the privacy threat. Also analyze the effect that anonymizing the network has on the utility of the data for social network analysis. The main objective is to enable the useful analysis of social network data while protecting the privacy of individuals (Anandakumar & Umamaheswari, 2018). Formalize the threat of re-identification and various kinds of adversary external information.

Advantage

- One cannot rely on anonymization to ensure individual privacy in social network data, in the presence of parties, who may be trying to compromise this privacy.
- One natural reaction is to try inventing methods of thwarting the particular attacks

Disadvantage

- The design of non-interactive mechanisms for ensuring reasonable notions of privacy in social network data is an open question, and potential results here are constrained by these existing impossibility results.
- The only techniques of which aware at the present time for simultaneously ensuring individual privacy and permitting accurate analysis.

NODE CLASSIFICATION IN SOCIAL NETWORKS

Clifton (2000) includes classification in network data based on a node-centric frame work in which classifiers comprise a Local classifier, a relational classifier and a collective inference procedure.

Non-Relational ("Local") Model

This component consists of a (learned) model, which uses only local information about (attributes of) the entities whose target variable is to be estimated. The local models can be used to generate priors that comprise the initial state for the relational learning and collective inference components. They also can be used as one source of evidence during collective inference. These models typically are produced by traditional machine learning methods.

Relational Model

In contrast to the non-relational component, the relational model makes use of the relations in the network as well as the values of attributes of related entities, possibly through long chains of relations. Relational models also may use local attributes of the entities.

Collective Inference

The collective inferencing component determines how the unknown values are estimated together, possibly influencing each local and relational model.

SmritiBhagat (2007) proposed for core problem is to use this information to extend the labeling so that all nodes are assigned a label consider two broad categories: methods based on iterative application of traditional classifiers using graph information as features, and methods which propagate the existing labels via random walks. Adopt a common perspective on these methods to highlight the similarities between different approaches within and across the two categories. So also describe some extensions and related directions to the central problem of graph labeling (Anandakumar & Umamaheswari, 2017).

There are many new applications that can make use of these kinds of labels:

- Suggesting new connections or contacts to individuals, based on finding others with similar interests, demographics, or experiences.
- Recommendation systems to suggest objects (music, movies, and activities) based on the interests of other individuals with overlapping characteristics.
- Question answering systems which direct questions to those with most relevant experience to a given question.
- Advertising systems which show advertisements to those individuals most likely to be interested and receptive to advertising on a particular topic
- Sociological study of communities, such as the extent to which communities form around particular interests or affiliations.
- Epidemiological study of how ideas and "memes" spread through communities over time.

The Graph Labeling Problem This leads to the central problem of given a social network (or more generally, any network structure) with labels on some nodes, how to provide a high quality labeling for every node. Refer to this as the "graph labeling problem", with the understanding that the basic problem can be abstracted as providing a labeling for a graph structure. Variations on this problem might work over generalized graph structures, such as hypergraphs, graphs with weighted, labeled, or time stamped edges, multiple edges between nodes, and so on (Haldorai & Ramu, 2018).

A first approach to this problem is to engage experts to provide labels on nodes, based on additional data about the corresponding individuals and their connections or individuals can be incentivized to provide accurate labels, via financial or other inducements. Indeed, historically this is exactly what sociologists have done when studying social groups of the order of tens to a hundred nodes.

Representing Data as a Graph

For consider data from social networks such as Facebook and LinkedIn, as well as other online networks for content access and sharing, such as Netflix, YouTube and Flickr. As is standard in this area, choose to represent these networks as graphs of nodes connected by edges. In our setting, consider graphs of the form G (V, E, W) from this data, where V is the set of n nodes E is the set of edges and W is the edge weight matrix. let Y be a set of labels that can be applied to nodes of the graph.

Consider Facebook as an example of a modern, complex social network. Users of Facebook have the option of entering a variety of personal and demographic information into their Facebook profile. In addition, two Facebook users may interact by (mutually) listing each other as friends, sending a message, posting on a wall, engaging in an IM chat, and so on. Create a graph representation of the Facebook social network in the form G (V, E, W), where

- **Nodes V:** The set of nodes V represents users of Facebook.
- **Edges E:** An edge $(i, j) \in E$ between two nodes v_i, v_j could represent a variety of possibilities: a relationship (friendship, sibling, partner), an interaction (wall post, private message, group message), or an activity (tagging in a photo, playing games). To make this example concrete, consider only edges which represent declared "friendships."
- **Node Labels Y:** The set of labels at a node may include the user's demographics (age, location, gender, occupation), interests (hobbies, movies, books, music) etc. Various restrictions may apply to some labels: a user is allowed to declare only one age and gender, whereas they can be a fan of an almost unlimited number of bands.
- **Edge Weights W:** The weight w_{ij} on an edge between nodes v_i, v_j can be used to indicate the strength of the connection. In our example, it may be a function of interactions among users, e.g., the number of messages exchanged, number of common friends etc. or it may simply be set to 1 throughout when the link is present

An example of a different kind of a network, consider the video sharing website, YouTube. Let graphG(V, E, W) represent the YouTube user network, where NodesV: A node $v_i \in V$ represents a user.

- **Edges E:** An edge $(i, j) \in E$ between two nodes v_i, v_j could be an explicit link denoting subscription or friend relation; alternately, it could be a derived link where v_i, v_j are connected if the corresponding users have co-viewed more than a certain number of videos.
- **Node Labels Y:** The set of labels at a node may include the user's demographics (age, location, gender, occupation), interests (hobbies, movies, books, music), a list of recommended videos extracted from the site, and so on.
- **Edge Weights W:** The weight on an edge could indicate the strength of the similarity by recording the number of co-viewed videos.

LINK BASED CLASSIFICATION

Friedman and Schuster (2010) specifies the traditional machine learning classification algorithms attempt to classify data organized as a collection of independent and identically distributed samples. Most real-world data, on the other hand, is relational where different samples are related to each other. Classification in the presence of such relationships requires that we exploit correlations present in them. Link-based classifications the task of classifying samples using the relations or links present amongst them. In link-based classification, the hypothesis is that the classifications of linked entities are correlated. This creates a problem since when classifying entity 1 need the classification of entity 2 and when classifying entity 2 need the classification of entity 1, where entities 1 and 2 are two linked entities. Such interactions render most traditional classification algorithms ineffective. A prime objective of link-based classification has been the development of novel inference methods or collective classification algorithms that allow us to classify multiple entities.

The link-based classification using Collective Classification Algorithms (CCA) assumes some organization of the input. The input to a CCA can roughly be divided into a qualitative part and a quantitative part. The qualitative part consists of the graph of random variables $G = (V, E)$. The quantitative part consists of a set of parameters. All three approximate collective classification algorithms (ACCAs) we discuss share the property of being iterative. In each iteration, the ACCA goes through G performing computations involving the G and the set of parameters. Each ACCA assumes a different set of parameters with various assumptions and semantics.

Collective Classification Methods is the most important step in link-based classification is to determine the set of labels y to the target random variables Y which minimizes the zero-one loss or error-rate, in other words, the number of incorrect classifications. Any algorithm which does this using the links E in G is called a collective classification algorithm (CCA). Link-based classification usually involves data with large graphs and exact inference is seldom tractable. Any algorithm which finds the optimal set of labels approximately is called an approximate collective classification algorithm (ACCA).

Belief propagation also known as sum-product message passing. I tis a message passing algorithm for performing inference on graphical models, such as Bayesian networks and Markov random fields. It calculates the marginal distribution for each unobserved node, conditional on any observed nodes. Belief propagation is commonly used in artificial intelligence and information theory and has demonstrated empirical success in numerous applications including low-density parity-check codes, turbo codes, free energy approximation.

INFERRING PRIVACY INFORMATION

Jianming He et al (2008) specifies the causal relations among friends in social networks can be modeled by a Bayesian network, and personal attribute values can be inferred with high accuracy from close friends in the social network. So, they propose schemes to protect private information by selectively hiding or falsifying information based on the characteristics of the social network. In this section propose an approach to map social networks into Bayesian networks, and then illustrate how to use this for attribute inference. The attribute inference is used to predict the private attribute value of a particular individual, referred to as the target node Z, from his social network which consists of the values of the same attribute of his friends. The attribute inference involves two steps. Before predicting the target attribute value of Z, first construct a Bayesian network from Z's social network, and then apply a Bayesian inference and obtain the probability that Z has a certain attribute value. It includes

- Multi-hop Inference
- Single hop inference

Privacy Protection in this section that private attribute values can be inferred from social relations. One way to prevent such inference is to alter an individual's social network, which means changing his social relations or the attribute values of his friends Causal Effect between Friends' Attribute Values

Theorem

Given a social network with a chain topology, let Z be the target node, Zn be Z's descendant at nhops away. Assuming the attribute value of Zn0 is the only evidence observed in this chain, and the prior probability Ptsatisfies 0 <Pt< 1, we have P(Z = t | Zn0 = t) > P(Z = t) (Ptlt- Ptlf)n> 0, and P(Z = t | Zn0 = f) > P(Z = t) (Ptlt- Ptlf) n<0, where Ptlt and Ptlf are the inheritance strength and mutation strength of the network respectively.

Privacy Protection Rule

Propose a privacy protection rule as follows. Assume the protection goal is to reduce others' belief that the target node has the attribute value t. We alter the nodes in the social network with attribute value t when Ptlt>Ptlf. The alteration could be:

- Hide or falsify the attribute values of friends who satisfy the above conditions
- Hide relationships to friends who satisfy the above conditions or add fraudulent relationships to friends who do not.

On the other hand, when Ptlt<Ptlf, alter nodes with attribute value t when that node is even hops away from the target node; otherwise, alter nodes with attribute value f. To mislead people into believing the target node possesses an attribute value t, can apply these techniques in the opposite way.

Advantage

- Inference accuracy increases as the influence strength increases between friends.
- Bayesian inference provides higher inference accuracies than naïve inference.
- Large variations of alterations can be provided by falsifying attribute values; this yields the most effective privacy protection among all the proposed methods.

Wesley Chu et al. (2010) specifies privacy information can be inferred via social relations, the privacy confidentiality problem becomes increasingly challenging as online social network services are more popular. Using a Bayesian network approach to model the causal relations among peoples in social networks, So the impact of prior probability, influence strength, and society openness to the inference accuracy on a real online social network. In experimental results reveal that personal attributes can be inferred with high accuracy especially when people are connected with strong relationships. Further, even in a society where most people hide their attributes, it is still possible to infer privacy information.

Bayesian Networks

A Bayesian network is a graphic representation of the joint probability distribution over a set of variables. It consists of a network structure and a collection of conditional probability tables (CPT). The network structure is represented as a Directed Acyclic Graph (DAG) in which each node corresponds to a random variable and each edge indicates a dependent relationship between connected variables. In addition, each variable (node) in a Bayesian network is associated with a CPT, which enumerates the conditional probabilities for this variable, given all the combinations of its parents' value. Thus, for a Bayesian network, the DAG captures causal relationships among random variables, and CPTs quantify these relationships.

Bayesian networks have extensively applied to fields such as medicine, image processing, and decision support systems. Since Bayesian networks include the consideration of network structure, so use inference model. Individuals in a social network can be represented as nodes and the relations between individuals can be modeled as edges in Bayesian networks.

Bayesian Inference via Social Relations

Intuitively, friends often share common attributes (e.g., hobbies and professions) thus, it is possible to predict someone's attributes by looking at the types of friends and want to investigate the effect of social relations on privacy inference. However, in the real world, people are acquainted with each other via all types of relations, and a personal attribute may only be sensitive to certain types of relations.

For example, in order to predict someone's age, it is more appropriate to consider the ages of his/her classmates. Therefore, to infer people's privacy from social relations, one must be able to alter out other types of relations between two connected people. To simplify this problem, investigate privacy inference in homogeneous societies where individuals are connected by a single type of social relations and the impact of every person on his/her friends is the same.

Homogenous societies reflect small closely related groups (such as offices, classes or clubs), where people are connected by a relatively pure relationship. Real social networks can be regarded as the combinations of many homogeneous societies. To perform inference, use Bayesian networks to model the causal relations among people in social networks. Specifically, if we want to infer the value of attribute A for a person (referred to asquery nodeX), first construct a Bayesian network from X's social network, and then analyze the Bayesian network to obtain the probability that X has attribute A.

INFORMATION REVELATION AND PRIVACY

Gross, Acquisti, and Heinz (2005), proposed patterns of information revelation in online social networks and their privacy implications. Patterns of Personal Information revelation is the information available depends on the purpose of the network. The Use of real names, Identifiable Personal photos. The use of real names to represent an account profile to the rest of the online community may be encouraged through technical specifications, registration requirements, or social norms in college websites like the Facebook, that aspire to connect participants' profiles to their public identities.

The use of real names may be tolerated but filtered in dating/connecting sites like Friendster, that create a thin shield of weak pseudonymity between the public identity of a person and her online persona by making only the first name of a participant visible to others, and not her last name. Or, the use of real names and personal contact information could be openly discouraged, as in pseudonymous-based dating websites like Match.com, that attempt to protect the public identity of a person by making its linkage to the online persona more difficult. However, notwithstanding the different approaches to identifiability, most sites encourage the publication of personal and identifiable personal photos such as clear shots of a person's face the type of information revealed or elicited often orbits around hobbies and interests but can stride from there in different directions.

Social Network Theory and Privacy

Suriya, Anandakumar, and Arulmurugan (2016) the relation between privacy and a person's social network is multi-faceted. In certain occasions want information about us to be known only by a small circle of close friends, and not by strangers. In other instances, willing to reveal personal information to anonymous strangers, but not to those who know us better. However, the application of social network theory to the study of information revelation and implicitly, privacy choices in online social networks highlights significant differences between the offline and the online scenarios

First, offline social networks are made of ties that can only be loosely categorized as weak or strong ties, but in reality are extremely diverse in terms of how close and intimate a subject perceives a relation to be. Online social networks, on the other side, often reduce these nuanced connections to simplistic binary relations: "Friend or not". Observing online social networks nodes that there is no way to determine what metric was used or what the role or weight of the relationship. While some people are willing to indicate anyone as Friends, and others stick to a conservative definition, most users tend to list anyone who they know and do not actively dislike. This often means that people are indicated as Friends even though the user does not particularly know or trust the person.

Second, while the number of strong ties that a person may maintain on a social networking site may not be significantly increased by online networking technology note that "the number of weak ties one can form and maintain may be able to increase substantially, because the type of communication that can be done more cheaply and easily with new technology is well suited for these ties".

Third, while an offline social network may include up to a dozen of intimate or significant ties and 1000 to 1700 "acquaintances" or "interactions," an online social network can list hundreds of direct "friends" and include hundreds of thousands of additional friends within just three degrees of separation from a subject.

Privacy Implications

Privacy implications associated with online social networking depend on the level of identifiability of the information provided, it's possible recipients, and its possible uses. Even social networking websites that do not openly expose their users' identities may provide enough information to identify the profile's owner. This may happen through face re-identification.

While privacy may be at risk in social networking sites, information is willingly provided. Different factors are likely to drive information revelation in online social networks. The list includes signaling because the perceived benefit of selectively revealing data to strangers may appear larger than the perceived costs of possible privacy invasions; peer pressure and herding behavior; relaxed attitudes towards (or lack of interest in) personal privacy; incomplete information (about the possible privacy implications of information revelation); faith in the networking service or trust in its members; myopic evaluation of privacy risks or also the service's own user interface, that may drive the unchallenged acceptance of permeable default privacy settings.

Advantage

- Users may be pragmatically publishing personal information because the benefits they expect from public disclosure surpass its perceived costs.

- Peer pressure and herding behavior may also be influencing factors, and so also myopic privacy attitudes.
- The sense of protection offered by the bounds of a campus community.

Disadvantage

- Possible for somebody's profile to be connected to hundreds of peers directly, and thousands of others through the network's ties.
- In fact, many may be complete strangers. And yet, personal and often sensitive information is freely and publicly provided.

PRESERVING THE PRIVACY OF SENSITIVE RELATIONSHIPS

Tasker, Abbeel, and Daphne (2010) consider the problem of inferring sensitive relationships from anonymized graph data as link re-identification and propose five different privacy preservation strategies, which vary in terms of the amount of data removed and the amount of privacy preserved. So assume the adversary has an accurate predictive model for links, and show experimentally the success of different link re-identification strategies under varying structural characteristics of the data.

Link Re-Identification Attacks

The extent of a privacy breach is often determined by data domain knowledge of the adversary. The domain knowledge can influence accurate inference in subtle ways. The goal of the adversary is to determine whether a sensitive relationship exists. There are different types of information that can be used to infer a sensitive relationship: node attributes, edge existence, and structural properties. Based on the domain knowledge of the adversary can construct rules for finding likely sensitive relationships.

Assume that the adversary has an accurate probabilistic model for link prediction describes the sensitive friendship link may be re-identified based on node attributes, edge existence or structural properties. This inference is based on node attributes.

Re-identification based on edge existence is two students in the same research group who are more likely to be friends compared to if they are in different research groups. A re-identification that is based on a structural property such as node degree would say that two students are more likely to be friends if they are likely to correspond to high degree nodes in the graph. A more complex observation is one which uses the result of an inferred relationship. For example, if each of two students is highly likely to be a friend with a third person based on other observations, then the two students are more likely to be friends too.

Link Re-Identification in Anonymized Data

In the first two types of link anonymization intact and partial the noisy-or model can be used directly to compute the probability of a sensitive edge. In the other two cases, one has to consider the probability that an observed edge exists between two nodes, and apply the noisy

Link Re-Identification in Cluster Edge Anonymization

In the case of keeping edges between equivalence classes, the probability of an observation existing between two nodes is not given and it needs to be estimated. The noisy-or function will need to take into consideration the probability associated with each observation in order to compute the likelihood of a sensitive relationship.

When the number of relationships of each type (e.g., course, research group, etc.) between two equivalence classes is given, the distribution is not uniform, and the probability of an observation $P(o)=P(observation(v_i, v_j))$ existing between two students can be computed directly from the counts of relationships between their equivalence classes. $P(classmates(v_i, v_j, c))$ expresses the probability that there exists a class edge between any two students v_i and v_j from two equivalence classes $C(v_i)$ and $C(v_j)$, i.e., the students take a course c together. It is equal to the number of possible student pairs from the two equivalence classes who take a course together $classmates(C(v_i), C(v_j))$ as a fraction of the number of possible relationships in the graph $|V|_2$.

Link Re-Identification in Cluster-Edge Anonymization With Constraints

In the constrained cluster-edge anonymization approach, the number of relationships between equivalence classes is not given. Therefore, the probability of an observation existing between any two edges has to be taken into account in the noisy-or model. To estimate this probability, an adversary can assume a uniform distribution, meaning that the probability of an observation existing between any two edges is the same for all edges in the graph. This estimate is worse than the cluster-edge anonymization method. Using the constraints on the data, it is possible to get estimates of this probability.

For example, if it is known that there are 50 pairs of students who take courses together, and there are 100 possible pairs, then the probability of any two students taking any class c together is $P(classmates(v_i, v_j, c)) = 0.5$. If the adversary knows the number of offered courses c, the number of courses per person n, the number of students $s = |V|$, and assumes that all courses have the same number of people $p = s*nc$, then the number of possible pairs who take courses together can be calculated as $n * (p-1)$. This number can be used to compute in a manner similar to the cluster-edge anonymization method $P(classmates(v_i, v_j, c)) = n * (p-1)|V|_2$.

Automatic Sanitization

It is generally accepted that social networks are both growing larger and becoming more important. The data contained in these diverse networks is useful for many reasons. Advertisers want access to this data so that they can know their audience better and thus target ads more effectively. Governments may want access to be able to track the habits and behaviors of its citizens or of potential terror threats. However, privacy concerns prevent many data owners from being able to release at least some of the data that they hold. When we deal with attacks on privacy in social networks, generally consider two threats.

Identification Attack

This is a situation where an attacker attempts to determine the real-world identity from examining a social network's data. The authors used various techniques to anonymize the link structure of the social network to prevent identification attacks, assuming that the links are the extent of the network released.

Inference Attack

This method of attack assumes that there is some hidden data within the social network's data. The attacker's goal is to use various machine learning techniques in an attempt to predict this hidden data. In other words, an attacker tries to build a highly accurate classifier to predict hidden sensitive data. So, focus on the inference problem. Here, it solves the problem of inference attacks on social network privacy through a novel generalization approach to network sanitization.

Mainly, all data contained within the graph is accurate. That is, do not generate false data to replace details with similar, yet unrelated traits. Additionally, unlike other anonymization techniques and do not alter the edge set of the graph in any way. Benefit is that our model specifically acknowledges a utility/privacy tradeoff. Since there is no option of perfect privacy with a data release, believe that this corresponds to a valid real-world data release.

Individuals who joined Facebook identified themselves as being a part of a then regional network. This data set is comprised of approximately 167,000 nodes with 3million links and 4.5 million details listed. Each of those details fell into one of several categories: Religion, Political Affiliation, Activities, Books, Music, Quotations, Shows/Movies, and Groups. Due to the lack of a reliable subject authority, Quotations were discarded from all experiments. To generate the DGH for each Activity, Book, and Show/Movie, we used Google Directories. To generate the DVD for Music. To generate the hierarchy for Groups used the classification criteria from the Facebook page of that group. Method of generalization do indeed decrease the accuracy of classification on the data set.

PRIVATE INFORMATION LEAKAGE PREVENTION SYSTEM

In the proposed work focus on the problem of private information leakage for individuals as a direct result of their actions as being part of an online social network. Model an attack scenario as follows: Suppose Facebook wishes to release data to electronic arts for their use in advertising games to interested people. However, once an electronic art has this data, they want to identify the political affiliation of users in their data for lobbying efforts.

Because they would not only use the names of those individuals who explicitly list their affiliation, but also through inference could determine the affiliation of other users in their data, this would obviously be a privacy violation of hidden details. So explore how the online social network data could be used to predict some individual private detail that a user is not willing to disclose such as political or religious affiliation, sexual orientation and explore the effect of possible data sanitization approaches on preventing such private information leakage, while allowing the recipient of the sanitized data to do inference on non-private details.

This chapter addresses two issues with respect to an inference attack:

1. First, need to have some understanding of the potential prior information (i.e. background knowledge) the adversary can use to launch an inference attack.
2. Second, need to analyze the potential success of inference attack given the adversary's background information.

Advantages

- Easy to remove details to decrease classification accuracy on sensitive attributes.
- To combat inference attacks on privacy, attempt to provide detail anonymization for social networks. By doing this, believe that will be able to reduce the value of to an acceptable threshold value that matches the desired utility/privacy tradeoff for a release of data.

Sharing Information

The social network peoples want to share their information to their friends and related peoples. User's each and every detail are stored in their profile database. Before posting the message, filtering rules checking the relation between the message creator and receiver and also the profile creation date etc. Some users are temporary blacklist because of their activities. With the Machine learning output and experts analyzing results regarding to a user's unwanted message, the message will be blocked and display the results in the message creator wall's in our system with the content-based message filtering by Machine Learning and profile checking process we prevent unwanted messages in a social network. It is important to note that for any detail type, the expected response can either be single or multivalve, and that a user has the option of listing no detail values for any given detail. Consider Face book's "home town" and "activities" detail type. A user can only have one home town, but can list multiple activities (for instance, soccer, reading, video games). However, a user also has the option of listing no detail values for these.

The detail value of "video games" for the detail type "activities" will be listed as activities, video games, to distinguish it from other details that may have the same detail value such as groups, video games. Further, even if a user lists multiple activities, store each independently in a detail with the corresponding detail name.

Naïve Bayes Algorithm

Using naive Bays as learning algorithm allowed us to easily scale implementation to the large size and diverseness of the Face book data set. It also has the added advantage of allowing simple selection techniques to remove detail and link information when trying to hide the class of a network node. Finally, it has shown itself to be extremely effective in these classification tasks.

- Given a node n_i with m details and pPotential classification labels, $C_{1,...,}C_p, C_x^i$, the probability of n_i being in class C_x, is given by the equation

$$\frac{argmax}{1 \le x \le p}\left[P\left(C_x^i | D_i^1, ..., D_i^m\right)\right] \qquad (1)$$

here argmax $1 \leq x \leq p$ represents the possible class label.

- or any given value of x is unknown by applying Bayes theorem the equation is

$$\frac{argmax}{1 \leq x \leq p} \left[\frac{P\left(C_x^i\right) \times P\left(D_i^1, \ldots\ldots D_i^m \mid C_x^i\right)}{P\left(D_i^1, \ldots, D_i^m\right)} \right] \tag{2}$$

- Further, equations (1), (2) by assuming that all details are independent that are left with the simplified equation is

$$\frac{argmax}{1 \leq x \leq p} \left[\frac{P\left(C_x^i\right) \times P(D_i^1 \mid C_x^i) \times, \ldots\ldots \times P(D_i^m \mid C_x^i)}{P\left(D_i^1, \ldots, D_i^m\right)} \right] \tag{3}$$

$P\left(D_i^1, \ldots D_i^m\right)$ is equivalent for all values of $\left(C_x^i\right)$.

Collective inference attempts to make up for these deficiencies by using both local and relational classifiers in a precise manner to attempt to increase the classification accuracy of nodes in the network. By using a local classifier in the first iteration, collective inference ensures that every node will have an initial probabilistic classification, referred to as a prior.

Protect Private Information

In order to protect privacy, sanitize both details and the underlying link structure of the graph. That is, delete some information from a user's profile and remove some links between friends and also examine the effects generalizing detail values to more generic values. To evaluate the effect of changing a person's details over privacy, first requires creating a learning method that could predict a person's private details. To private information leakage in social networks Using both friendship links and details together gives better predictability than details alone. In addition, it is the effect of removing details and links in preventing sensitive information leakage. In the process, we discovered situations in which collective inference does not improve on using a simple local classification method to identify nodes. The work has been implemented in java1.6, then loaded a user's profile, parsed the details out of the HTML, and store the details inside a MySQL database. All friends from the current profile are loaded and stored the friends inside the database both as friendship links and as possible profile given in Table 1. It shows the general information about the data which includes the number of nodes, friendship links, total number of listed details and unique details.

The classification result after considering the most liberal or conservative details are shown in Table 2.

Table 1. General information about the data in test data

Name	Count
Number of nodes in the graph	150
Number of friendship links in the graph	450
Total number of listed details in the graph	670
Total number of unique details in the graph	2230

Table 2. Liberal details

Detail Name	Detail Value	Likelihood
Group member	Equal rights	46.160667
Favourite books	The mideman	39.685994
Favourite movies	Life of pie	43.999900
interests	Dancing and swimming	1.6389999

Figure 5. Number of details in test set

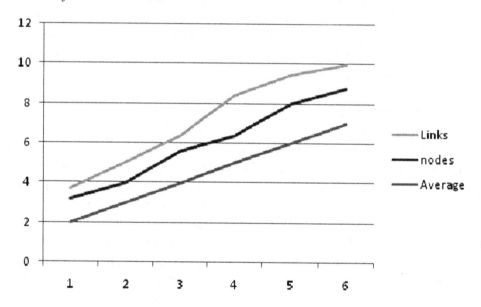

The study explains in the existing system, the accuracy of finding the nodes is easier. Because the links of the nodes are findable and can easily access the nodes by using these links. To avoid this, the classifier accuracy must be reduced. In the proposed system the links of the nodes are being reduced, so that the nodes cannot be found. The accuracy of classifier is being successfully reduced by sanitization method which is shown in Figure 5 and Figure 6 based on number on details.

Figure 6. Number of details removed in test set

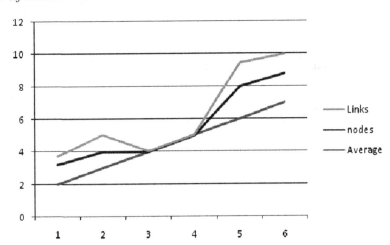

SUMMARY

In order to protect private information leakage using both friendship links and details together gives better predictability than details alone. By using collective inference, the identification of simple classification nodes can be reduced. This chapter analyses and concludes combining the results from the collective inference implications with the individual results, by removing details and friendship links together is the best way to reduce classifier accuracy. However, it also shown that by removing only details and hiding the image downloading process in social network and also filter the commenting text in wall can greatly reduce the accuracy of local and relational classifiers.

REFERENCES

Anandakumar, H., Umamaheswari, K., & Arulmurugan, R. (2019). A Study on Mobile IPv6 Handover in Cognitive Radio Networks. In *International Conference on Computer Networks and Communication Technologies* (pp. 399-408). Springer Singapore. doi:10.1007/978-981-10-8681-6_36

Anandakumar, H. & Umamaheswari, K. (2018). Cooperative Spectrum Handovers in Cognitive Radio Networks. In *Cognitive Radio, Mobile Communications and Wireless Networks* (pp. 47–63). Springer. doi:10.1007/978-3-319-91002-4_3

Backstrom, L., Dwork, C., & Kleinberg, J. (2007). Wherefore Art Thou r3579x?: Anonymized Social Networks, Hidden Patterns, and Structural Steganography. In *Proc. 16th Int'l Conf. World Wide Web (WWW '07)* (pp. 181-190). 10.1145/1242572.1242598

Clifton, C. (2000). Using Sample Size to Limit Exposure to Data Mining. J. Computer Security, 8, 281-307.

Dwork, C. (2006). Differential Privacy. In M. Bugliesi, B. Preneel, V. Sassone et al. (Eds.), Automata, Languages and Programming. Springer. doi:10.1007/11787006_1

Friedman, A., & Schuster, A. (2010). Data Mining with Differential Privacy. In *Proc. 16th ACM SIGKDD Int'l Conf. Knowledge Discovery and Data Mining* (pp. 493-502).

Fukunaga, K., & Hummels, D. M. (2006). Bayes Error Estimation Using Parzen and K-nn Procedures. IEEE Trans. Pattern Analysis and Machine Intelligence, 9(5), 634-643. doi:28809.28814.

Gross, R., Acquisti, A., & Heinz, H. (2005). Information Revelation and Privacy in Online Social Networks. In *Proc. ACM Workshop Privacy in the Electronic Soc. (WPES '05)* (pp. 71-80). doi:10.1145/1102199.1102214

Haldorai, A., & Ramu, A. (2018). An Intelligent-Based Wavelet Classifier for Accurate Prediction of Breast Cancer. In *Intelligent Multidimensional Data and Image Processing* (pp. 306–319). doi:10.4018/978-1-5225-5246-8.ch012

Hay, M., Miklau, G., Jensen, D., Weis, P., & Srivastava, S. (2007). Anonymizing Social Networks [Technical Report]. Univ. of Massachusetts Amherst.

He, J., Chu, W., & Liu, V. (2006). *Inferring Privacy Information from Social Networks*. Proc. Intelligence and Security Informatics. doi:10.1007/11760146_14

Heussne, K. M. (2009). "Gaydar" Facebook: Can Your Friends Reveal Sexual Orientation. ABC News. Retrieved from http://abcnews.go.com/Technology/gaydar-facebook

Lindamood, H.R., Kantarcioglu, M. & Thuraisingham, B. (2009). Inferring Private Information Using Social Network Data. In *Proc. 18th Int'l Conf. World Wide Web (WWW)*.

Machanavajjhala, A., Kifer, D., Gehrke, J., & Venkitasubramaniam, M. (2009). L-Diversity: Privacy Beyond K-Anonymity. *ACM Transactions on Knowledge Discovery from Data*, 1(1), 3. doi:10.1145/1217299.1217302

Macskassy, S. A., & Provost, F. (2007). Classification in networked data: A toolkit and a univariate case study. *Journal of Machine Learning Research*, 8(May), 935–983.

Sen, P., & Getoor, L. (2007). Link-Based Classification [Technical Report]. Univ. of Maryland.

Suriya, M., Anandakumar, H., & Arulmurugan, R. (2016). Social Aware Cognitive Radio Networks: Effectiveness of Social Networks as a Strategic Tool for Organizational Business Management. In *Social Network Analytics for Contemporary Business Organizations*. Hershey, PA: IGI Global.

Sweeney, L. (2002). k-anonymity: A model for protecting privacy. *International Journal of Uncertainty, Fuzziness and Knowledge-based Systems*, 10(5), 557–570.

Tasker, B., Abbeel, P., & Daphne, K. (2010). Discriminative Probabilistic Models for Relational Data. In *Proc. 18th Ann. Conf. Uncertainty in Artificial Intelligence (UAI '02)* (pp. 485-492).

Van Rijsbergen, C. J., Robertson, S. E., & Porter, M. F. (1980). *New models in probabilistic information retrieval*. London: British Library Research and Development Department.

Zheleva, E., & Getoor, L. (2008). Preserving the Privacy of Sensitive Relationships in Graph Data. In *Proc. First ACM SIGKDD Int'l Conf. Privacy, Security, and Trust in KDD* (pp. 153-171). 10.1007/978-3-540-78478-4_9

Chapter 11
Study of Efficient Hybrid Wireless Networks Using QoS–Oriented Distributed Routing Protocol:
QoS–Oriented Distributed Routing Protocol

Suriya Murugan
Bannari Amman Institute of Technology, India

Anandakumar H.
Sri Eshwar College of Engineering, India

ABSTRACT

Hybrid networks are next generation of wireless networks that are increasingly used in wireless communications that highly support real time transmission with a limited quality of service. The study proves that existing systems use QoS-oriented distributed routing protocols to enhance the QoS support capability of hybrid networks and it transforms the packet routing problem to a resource scheduling problem which has five algorithms. They are (1) QoS-guaranteed neighbor election algorithm, (2) distributed packet scheduling algorithm, (3) mobility-based segment resizing algorithm, (4) traffic redundant elimination algorithm, and (5) data redundancy elimination-based transmission algorithm. To increase the performance of hybrid networks in a real mobility model, this chapter analyses and devises a method to authenticate data streams for transmission. Data transparent authentication without communication overhead is an approach which reduces breakdown of original data or sends out-of-band authentication information.

DOI: 10.4018/978-1-5225-7522-1.ch011

INTRODUCTION TO WIRELESS NETWORKS

Wireless network enables people to communicate and access applications and information without wires. This provides freedom of movement and the ability to extend applications to different parts of a building, city, or nearly anywhere in the world. Wireless networks allow people to interact with e-mail or browse the Internet from a location that they prefer.

Wireless networks have been developed with various wireless applications, which have been used in areas of commerce, emergency, services, military, education and entertainment (Wu & Jia, 2009). The rapid improvement of Wi-Fi capable mobile devices including laptops and handheld devices, for example the purpose of wireless internet users of smart phone in last three years. The usage of people watching video, playing games and making long distance video or audio conferencing through wireless mobile devices and video streaming applications on infrastructure wireless networks which connects directly to mobile users for video playing and interaction in real time are increased. The evolution and the anticipate future of real time mobile multimedia streaming services are extensively expanded, so the networks are in need of high Quality of Service (QoS) to support wireless and mobile networking environment.

Infrastructure Mode

In the case of wireless networking in Infrastructure mode the connected devices uses a central device, namely a wireless access point. To join the WLAN, the Access Points (AP) and all wireless clients must be configured to use the same SSID. The AP is then cabled to the wired network to allow wireless clients access to, for example, Internet connections or printers. Additional APs can be added to the WLAN to increase the reach of the infrastructure and support any number of wireless clients.

Compared to the alternative, ad-hoc wireless networks, infrastructure mode networks offer the advantage of scalability, centralized security management and improved reach (Jawhar & Wu, 2005). The disadvantage of infrastructure wireless networks is simply the additional cost to purchase AP hardware.

As opposed to Ad Hoc mode networks, which make wireless connections directly between computers, Infrastructure mode wireless networks use networking infrastructure. In this case, *infrastructure* refers to switches, routers, firewalls, and APs. Infrastructure mode wireless networking is the mode that you most often encounter in your work as a networking professional supporting network for clients or in a

Figure 1. Infrastructure networks
Source: http://media.wiley.com/Lux/03/298503.image0.jpg

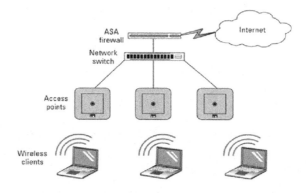

corporate environment. At a minimum, the only network infrastructure component that is required for Infrastructure mode is an access point, but if an AP is all you have, you have no more than you would have had when using Ad Hoc mode. However, most Infrastructure mode implementations include other components from your traditional network infrastructure.

Infrastructure Less Wireless Networks

An infrastructure less wireless network does not contain any centralized infrastructure, and thus, wireless client stations communicate with each other directly in a peer-to-peer manner. These types of networks are also known as wireless ad hoc networks. The network topology of the wireless ad hoc network is dynamic and changes constantly and the participating wireless stations adapt to changes in topology on the fly.

Subcategories of wireless networks under centralized infrastructure-based and infrastructure-less wireless networks are depicted in Cellular networks are for voice communications but also carry data. WiMAX, on the other hand, is for last-mile Internet delivery for a larger coverage area. WLANs are for data communication within smaller areas, typically for office and residential use. However, voice-over-Wi-Fi is also part of WLANs. Recent advancements have shown that infrastructure-based wireless networks support both voice and data communications.

Mobile Node (MN)

See Figure 2.

TYPES OF WIRELESS NETWORK

WLANS: Wireless Local Area Networks

WLANS allow users in a local area, such as a university campus or library, to form a network or gain access to the internet. A temporary network can be formed by a small number of users without the need of an access point; given that they do not need access to network resources.

Figure 2. Wireless infrastructures less networks

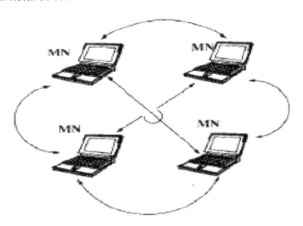

WPANS: Wireless Personal Area Networks

The two current technologies for wireless personal area networks are infrared (IR) and Bluetooth (IEEE 802.15). These will allow the connectivity of personal devices within an area of about 30 feet. However, IR requires a direct line of site and the range is less.

WMANS: Wireless Metropolitan Area Networks

This network allows the connection of multiple networks in a metropolitan area such as different buildings in a city, which can be an alternative or backup to laying copper or fibre cabling.

WWANS: Wireless Wide Area Networks

The networks can be maintained over large areas, such as cities or countries, via multiple satellite systems or antenna sites looked after by an ISP. These types of systems are referred to as 2G (2nd Generation) systems.

Space Network

The networks used for communication between spacecraft, usually in the vicinity of the Earth. The example of this is NASA's Space Network.

Wireless Mesh Network

It is a wireless network made up of radio nodes organized in a mesh topology. Each node forwards messages on behalf of the other nodes. Mesh networks can "self-heal," automatically re-routing around a node that has lost power. Table 1 highlights the comparison of wireless networks based on various parameters.

Table 1. Comparison of wireless network types

Type	Coverage	Performance	Standards	Applications
Wireless PAN	Within reach of a person	Moderate	Wireless PAN Within reach of a person Moderate Bluetooth, IEEE 802.15, and IrDA Cable replacement for peripherals	Cable replacement for peripherals
Wireless LAN	Within a building or campus	High	IEEE 802.11, Wi-Fi, and Hyper LAN	Mobile extension of wired networks
Wireless MAN	Within a city	High	Proprietary, IEEE 802.16, and WIMAX	Fixed wireless between homes and businesses and the Internet
Wireless WAN	Worldwide	Low	CDPD and Cellular 2G, 2.5G, and 3G	Mobile access to the Internet from outdoor areas

Cellular Network

A cellular network or mobile network is a radio network distributed over land areas called cells, each served by at least one fixed-location transceiver, known as a cell site or base station. In a cellular network, each cell characteristically uses a different set of radio frequencies from all their immediate neighbouring cells to avoid any interference.

When joined together these cells provide radio coverage over a wide geographic area. This enables a large number of portable transceivers (e.g., mobile phones, pagers, etc.) to communicate with each other and with fixed transceivers and telephones anywhere in the network, via base stations, even if some of the transceivers are moving through more than one cell during transmission.

Global Area Network

A Global Area Network (GAN) is a network used for supporting mobile across an arbitrary number of wireless LANs, satellite coverage areas, etc. The key challenge in mobile communications is handing off user communications from one local coverage area to the next. In IEEE Project 802, this involves a succession of terrestrial wireless LANs.

MOBILE ADHOC NETWORK

A Mobile Adhoc Network (MANET) is a collection of independent mobile nodes that can communicate to each other via radio waves. The mobile nodes that are in radio range of each other can directly communicate, whereas others need the aid of intermediate nodes to route their packets. Each of the nodes has a wireless interface to communicate with each other. These networks are fully distributed, and can work at any place without the help of any fixed infrastructure as access points or base stations (Wei & Yu, 2010). Figure 3 shows a simple ad-hoc network with 3 nodes. Node 1 and node 3 are not within range of each other; however, the node 2 can be used to forward packets between node 1and nodes 2. The node 2 will act as a router and these three nodes together form an ad-hoc network.

Figure 3. Mobile ADHOC network

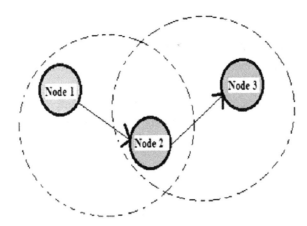

Characteristics

- **Distributed Operation:** There is no background network for the central control of the network operations; the control of the network is distributed among the nodes. The nodes involved in a MANET should cooperate with each other and communicate among themselves and each node acts as a relay as needed, to implement specific functions such as routing and security.
- **Multi Hop Routing:** When a node tries to send information to other nodes which is out of its communication range, the packet should be forwarded via one or more intermediate nodes.
- **Autonomous Terminal:** In MANET, each mobile node is an independent node, which could function as both a host and a router.
- **Dynamic Topology:** Nodes are free to move arbitrarily with different speeds; thus, the network topology may change randomly and at unpredictable time. The nodes in the MANET dynamically establish routing among themselves as they travel around, establishing their own network.
- **Light-Weight Terminals:** In maximum cases, the nodes at MANET are mobile with less CPU capability, low power storage and small memory size.
- **Shared Physical Medium:** The wireless communication medium is accessible to any entity with the appropriate equipment and adequate resources. Accordingly, access to the channel cannot be restricted.

Applications

Some of the typical applications include:

- **Military Battlefield:** Ad-Hoc networking would allow the military to take advantage of common-place network technology to maintain an information network between the soldiers, vehicles, and military information head quarter.
- **Collaborative Work:** For some business environments, the need for collaborative computing might be more important outside office environments than inside and where people do need to have outside meetings to cooperate and exchange information on a given project.
- **Local Level:** Ad-Hoc networks can autonomously link an instant and temporary multimedia network using notebook computers to spread and share information among participants at an e.g. conference or classroom. Another appropriate local level application might be in home networks where devices can communicate directly to exchange information.
- **Personal Area Network and Bluetooth:** A personal area network is a short range, localized network where nodes are usually associated with a given person. Short-range MANET such as Bluetooth can simplify the inter communication between various mobile devices such as a laptop, and a mobile phone.
- **Commercial Sector:** Ad hoc can be used in emergency/rescue operations for disaster relief efforts, e.g. in fire, flood, or earthquake. Emergency rescue operations must take place where non-existing or damaged communications infrastructure and rapid deployment of a communication network is needed.

Challenges

- **Limited Bandwidth:** Wireless link continue to have significantly lower capacity than infrastructure networks. In addition, the realized throughput of wireless communication after accounting for the effect of multiple access, fading, noise, and interference conditions, etc., is often much less than a radio's maximum transmission rate.
- **Dynamic Topology:** Dynamic topology membership may disturb the trust relationship among nodes. The trust may also be disturbed if some nodes are detected as compromised.
- **Routing Overhead:** In wireless adhoc networks, nodes often change their location within network. So, some stale routes are generated in the routing table which leads to unnecessary routing overhead.
- **Hidden Terminal Problem:** The hidden terminal problem refers to the collision of packets at a receiving node due to the simultaneous transmission of those nodes that are not within the direct transmission range of the sender, but are within the transmission range of the receiver.
- **Packet Losses Due to Transmission Errors:** Ad hoc wireless networks experience a much higher packet loss due to factors such as increased collisions due to the presence of hidden terminals, presence of interference, uni-directional links, and frequent path breaks due to mobility of nodes.
- **Mobility-Induced Route Changes:** The network topology in an ad hoc wireless network is highly dynamic due to the movement of nodes; hence an on-going session suffers frequent path breaks. This situation often leads to frequent route changes.
- **Security Threats:** The wireless mobile ad hoc nature of MANETs brings new security challenges to the network design. As the wireless medium is vulnerable to eavesdropping and ad hoc network functionality is established through node cooperation, mobile ad hoc networks are intrinsically exposed to numerous security attacks.

HYBRID WIRELESS NETWORK

The next-generation wireless networks face new challenges within the sort of increasing volume of traffic with the increase in the range of users and also the average traffic generated by users. The increasing attention of the analysis community on these problems has resulted in Hybrid Wireless Network (HWN) architectures that mix mulch-hop radio relaying and infrastructure support to supply high-capacity wireless networks (Zeng, Yang & Lou, 2010). The Figure 4 shows the hybrid wireless network diagram.

Features

Flexible

A hybrid network is one that supports multiple services, protocols, hardware platforms and in operation systems. Hybrid networks are versatile and designed to handle the varied usage necessities of their users (Lu et al., 2002). They're customized and built when a radical assessment of user and structure network necessities and therefore the resources out there.

Figure 4. Hybrid wireless network
Source: www.conceptdraw.com/picture/Hybrid-network-diagram.png

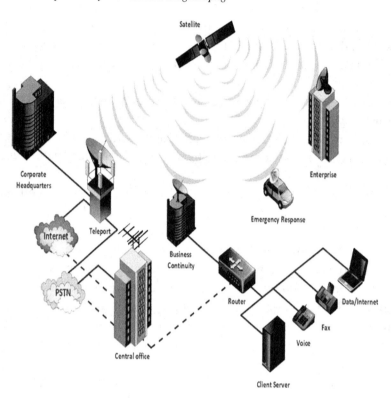

Effective

Network engineers are able to design economical hybrid systems by assessing and utilizing the strengths and ignoring the weaknesses of their parent network topologies (Haldorai & Ramu, 2018). Hybrid networks mix the best options of their parent topologies and are nearly always more practical than either, or each of them.

Practical

Hybrid networks are designed during a way to totally optimize the best options of their networks. They're seen as a practical various to single-topologies, that are related to various disadvantages.

QUALITY OF SERVICE

To improve the QoS support capability of hybrid network that are supported resource reservation-based routing. Once the transmission link breaks between source node and destination node invalid reservation problem occurs, and once same resource is allotted to two totally different QoS methods race condition problem occurs (He, Stankovic, Lu & Abdelzaher, 2003). However, very little effort has been dedicated to support QoS routing in hybrid networks. Most of the present works in hybrid networks concentrate on increasing network capability or routing dependability however cannot provide QoS-guaranteed services (Anandakumar & Umamaheswari, 2017). Direct adoption of the reservation-based QoS routing protocols of MANETs into hybrid networks inherits the invalid reservation and race condition issues. Some of factors of quality of service are:

Low Throughput

Due to varying load from disparate users sharing the same network resources, the bit rate (the maximum throughput) that can be provided to a certain data stream may be too low for real time multimedia services if all data streams get the same scheduling priority (Anandakumar & Umamaheswari, 2018).

Dropped Packets

The routers might fail to deliver (drop) some packets if their data is corrupted or they arrive when their buffers are already full. The receiving application may ask for this information to be retransmitted, possibly causing severe delays in the overall transmission.

Latency

It might take a long time for each packet to reach its destination, because it gets held up in long queues, or takes a less direct route to avoid congestion. This is different from throughput, as the delay can build up over time, even if the throughput is almost normal. In some cases, excessive latency can render an application such as VoIP or online gaming unusable.

Jitter

Packets from the source will reach the destination with different delays. A packet's delay varies with its position in the queues of the routers along the path between source and destination and this position can vary unpredictably. This variation in delay is known as jitter and can seriously affect the quality of streaming audio and/or video.

Out-of-Order Delivery

When a collection of related packets is routed through a network, different packets may take different routes, each resulting in a different delay. The result is that the packets arrive in a different order than they were sent. This problem requires special additional protocols responsible for rearranging out-of-order packets to an asynchronous state once they reach their destination. This is especially important for video and VoIP streams where quality is dramatically affected by both latency and lack of sequence.

QoS-Oriented Distributed (QoD) routing protocol is used in hybrid network for data transmission, which has extensive base station with two main features. An Access Point (AP) can be a source or destination and the number of transmission hops between mobile node and access points is small. Access point to any mobile nodes allows data streams to have any cast transmission along with multiple transmission paths to its destination through base stations. It enables a source node to connect through an intermediate node in all access point. Thus, having two features QOD transforms the packet routing problem into a dynamic resource scheduling problem. If a source node is not within the transmission range of the AP, a source node selects nearby neighbours that can provide QoS services to forward its packets to base stations in a distributed manner. The source node schedules the packet streams to neighbours based on their queuing condition, channel condition, and mobility, the purpose is to reduce transmission time and increase network capacity. But still the guarantee of QoS remains an open problem (Deb, Bhatnagar & Nath, 2003).

At present QoS-Oriented Distributed routing protocol is used to enhance the QoS support capability of hybrid networks, it transforms the packet routing problem to resource scheduling problem which has five algorithms.

- QoS guaranteed neighbour selection algorithm. The rule selects qualified neighbours and employs deadline-driven programming mechanism to ensure QoS routing.
- Distributed packet scheduling algorithm. After qualified neighbours are known, this algorithmic program schedules packet routing. It assigns earlier generated packets to forwarders with higher queuing delays, while assigns a lot of recently generated packets to forwarders with lower queuing delays to decrease total transmission delay.
- Mobility based segment resizing algorithm. The source node adaptively resizes every packet in its packet stream for every neighbour node in line with the neighbour's quality so as to extend the programming feasibility of the packets from the source node.
- Traffic redundant elimination algorithm. An intermediate node forwards the packet with the first smallest amount time allowed to attend before being forwarded to resolute succeed fairness in packet forwarding.
- Data redundancy elimination-based transmission algorithm. Due to the broadcasting feature of the wireless networks, the access point and mobile nodes will cache packets. This algorithmic rule eliminates the redundant data to boost the QoS of the packet transmission.

REVIEW OF WIRELESS NETWORKS PROTOCOL

Real Time Communication Architecture Protocol (RAP)

RAP provides convenient, high-level query and event services for distributed micro- sensing applications. Novel location-addressed communication models are supported by a scalable and light-weight network stack. Which provides a high delivering priority to the packets with longer distance/delay to the destination? However, each strategy needs every device to grasp its own location, so they are not appropriate for extremely dynamic surroundings. RAP provides a set of convenient, high-level query and event services to real-time distributed micro-sensing applications. Query and event services are based on novel location-addressed communication models supported by a scalable and lightweight network stack. RAP is a novel Velocity Monotonic Scheduling (VMS) policy suitable for packet scheduling in sensor networks. VMS is based on a notion of packet requested velocity. Each packet is expected to make its end-to-end deadline if it can move toward the destination at its requested velocity, which reflects its local urgency. Compared with non-prioritized packet scheduling, VMS improves the deadline miss ratios of sensor networks by giving higher priority to packets with higher requested velocities. VMS can outperform deadline-based packet scheduling because velocity more accurately reflects the local urgency at each hop when packets with the same deadline have different distances to their destinations (Perkins, Royer & Das, 2001).

The goal of RAP includes the following:

- Provide general service APIs that are suitable for distributed micro-sensing and control in sensor networks.
- Maximize the number of packets meeting their end-to-end deadlines.

Stateless Protocol End-to-End Deadlines (SPEED)

The protocol provides three types of real-time communication services, namely, real-time unicast, real-time area-multicast and real-time area-any cast. SPEED is specifically tailored to be a stateless, localized algorithm with minimal control overhead. End-to-end soft real-time communication is achieved by maintaining a desired delivery speed across the sensor network through a novel combination of feedback control and non-deterministic geographic forwarding. SPEED is a highly efficient and scalable protocol for sensor networks where the resources of each node are scarce. The performance results show that SPEED reduces the number of packets that miss their end-to-end deadlines reacts to transient congestion in the most stable manner, and efficiently handles voids with minimal control overhead. In view of this, the key design goal of the SPEED algorithm is to support a soft real-time communication service with a desired delivery speed across the sensor network, so that end-to-end delay is proportional to the distance between the source and destination (Venataramanan, Lin, Ying & Shakkottai, 2010). It should be noted that delivery speed refers to the approaching rate along a straight line from the source toward the destination. Unless the packet is routed exactly along that straight line, delivery speed is smaller than the actual speed of the packet in the network. Felemban et al. (2006) and Debutante et al. projected to boost routing dependableness by multipath routing. However, the redundant transmission of the packets might result in high power consumption.

Integrated Services (Intserv)

Intserv could be a state full model that uses resource reservation for individual flow and uses admission management and computer hardware to take care of the QoS of traffic flows. The integrated services model provides the ability for applications to choose among multiple classes of service. This means that all network nodes, such as the routers along the path of a flow, must be informed of the requested class of service and the respective parameters. The latter mechanism can be implemented by use of a resource reservation protocol, such as Resources Reservation Protocol (RSVP). The design of RSVP lends itself to be used with a variety of QoS control services. RSVP specification does not define the internal format of the RSVP protocol fields, or objects.

It treats these objects as opaque and deals only with the setup mechanism. RSVP was designed to support both unicast and multicast applications. RSVP supports heterogeneous QoS. Heterogeneous QoS means that different receivers in the same multicast group can request different QoS. This heterogeneity allows some receivers to have reservations while there could be others receiving the same traffic using the best-effort service.

Differentiated Service (DiffServ)

DiffServ could be an unsettled model that uses coarse-grained class-based mechanism for traffic management. DiffServ is a coarse-grained, class-based mechanism for traffic management. In contrast, IntServ is a fine-grained, flow-based mechanism. DiffServ relies on a mechanism to classify and mark packets as belonging to a specific class. DiffServ-aware routers implement Per-Hop Behaviours (PHBs), which define the packet-forwarding properties associated with a class of traffic. Different PHBs may be defined to offer, for example, low-loss or low-latency.

DiffServ operates on the principle of traffic classification, where each data packet is placed into a limited number of traffic classes, rather than differentiating network traffic based on the requirements of an individual flow. Each router on the network is configured to differentiate traffic based on its class. Each traffic class can be managed differently, ensuring preferential treatment for higher-priority traffic on the network. The premise of DiffServ is that complicated functions such as packet classification and policing can be carried out at the edge of the network by edge routers who then mark the packet to receive a particular type of per-hop behaviour. Core router functionality can then be kept simple. No classification and policing are required. Such routers simply apply PHB treatment to packets based on the marking. PHB treatment is achieved by core routers using a combination of scheduling policy and queue management policy.

REVIEW OF MANET

A majority of QoS routing protocols area unit supported resource reservation, within which a supply node sends probe messages to a destination to get and reserve ways satisfying a given QoS demand. Perkins, Royer, and Das, (2001) extended the AODV routing protocol by adding information of the most delay and minimum out their bandwidth of every neighbour during a node's routing table. Venataramanan, Lin, Ying, and Shakkottai (2010) projected a planning algorithm to make sure the tiniest buffer usage of the nodes in the forwarding path to BS. These works specialise in increasing network capability supported scheduling however fail to ensure QoS delay performance. Some works think about providing multipart routing to increase the strength of QoS routing.

Dynamic Source Routing Protocol (DSR)

DSR is one of the most well-known routing algorithms for ad hoc wireless networks. DSR uses source routing, which allows packet routing to be loop free. It increases its efficiency by allowing nodes that are either forwarding route discovery requests or overhearing packets through promiscuous listening mode to cache the routing information for future use. DSR is also on demand, which reduces the bandwidth use especially in situations where the mobility is low. It is a simple and efficient routing protocol for use in ad hoc networks. It has two important phases, route discovery and route maintenance.

The main algorithm works in the following manner. A node that desires communication with another node first searches its route cache to see if it already has a route to the destination. If it does not, it then initiates a route discovery mechanism. This is done by sending a Route Request message.

When the node gets this route request message, it searches its own cache to see if it has a route to the destination. If it does not, it then appends its id to the packet and forwards the packet to the next node;

this continues until either a node with a route to the destination is encountered (i.e. has a route in its own cache) or the destination receives the packet. In that case, the node sends a route reply packet which has a list of all of the nodes that forwarded the packet to reach the destination.

This constitutes the routing information needed by the source, which can then send its data packets to the destination using this newly discovered route. Although DSR can support relatively rapid rates of mobility, it is assumed that the mobility is not so high as to make flooding the only possible way to exchange packets between nodes.

Review of Hybrid Networking Protocol

Very few ways are planned to produce QoS secured routing for hybrid networks. Most of the routing protocols solely attempt to improve the network capability and dependableness to indirectly give QoS service however bypass the constraints in QoS routing that need the protocols to produce secured service. Sung, Lund, Lyn, Rao, and Sen, (2009) introduced relay selection scheme for improving the performance of hybrid wireless network to improve network life time, error propagation and spectral efficiency.

Unlike the on top of works, QOD aims to supply QoS secure routing. QOD totally takes advantage of the widely deployed APs, and novelty treats the packet routing problem as a resource programming drawback between nodes and APs. To limit the throughput in wireless networks the two major factors are co-channel inference and unreliability. Zeng, Yang, and Lou (2010) proposed Multi radio Multi Channel Opportunistic Routing scheme to improve the network throughput capacity to eliminating the limitation of the above factors.

This process can be done by optimizing the end-to-end throughput in linear programming using feasible scheduling of resources for achieving network capacity. The various comparisons of issues in Hybrid Networks, the architecture is a Hybrid Wireless Network (HWN); Multi-Power Architecture for Cellular networks (MuPAC), Throughput enhanced Wireless in Local Loop (TWiLL), and Mobile Assisted Data Forwarding (MADF) is stated in the Table.2.

Hybrid routing protocols are a new generation of protocols that are each proactive and reactive in nature. These protocols are designed to extend salability by allowing nodes in dose proximity to figure along to create some variety of backbone and to reduce the route discovery overhead. This can be primarily achieved by proactively maintaining routes to near nodes and determinative routes to distant nodes employing a route discovery strategy. Most hybrid protocols projected to date are zone primarily

Table 2. Comparison of hybrid wireless architectures

Issue	HWN	MuPAC	TWiLL	MADF
Routing Efficiency	Low	High	High	High
Routing Complexity	High	Low	Low	High
Connection or Packet based	Packet	Both	Connection	Both
Real-Time Traffic Support	Cellular Mode	Yes	Yes	Yes
Multiple Interfaces	Yes	Yes	Yes	No
Control Overhead	High	High	Low	High
Technology Dependent	No	No	No	No

based, which implies that the network is partitioned off or seen as variety of zones by every node. Others cluster nodes into trees or clusters.

Zone Routing Protocol (ZRP)

In ZRP the nodes have a routing zone that defines a variety (in hops) that every node uses to maintain proactive network connectivity. Therefore, for nodes inside the routing zone, routes are now available. For nodes that lie outside the routing zone, routes are determined on-demand (i.e., reactively), and might use any on demand routing protocol to work out a route to the desired destination. The advantage of this protocol is that it's considerably reduced the number of communication overhead when put next to pure proactive protocols. It also has reduced the delays related to pure reactive protocols, like DSR, by allowing routes to be discovered quicker. this is often because, to determine a route to a node outside the routing zone, the routing only has to pass to a node that lies on the boundaries (edge of the routing zone) of the desired destination—because the boundary node would proactively maintain routes to the destination (i.e., the boundary nodes will complete the route from the source to the destination by causing a reply back to the source with the desired routing address).

Zone Based Hierarchical Link State (ZHLS)

Unlike ZRP, ZHLS the routing protocol employs hierarchical structure. In ZHLS, the network is divided into non-overlapping zones, and each node has a node ID and none 113, which are calculated using a GPS. The hierarchical topology is made up of two levels:

1. Node level topology
2. Zone level topology

   As described previously. In ZHLS, location management has been simplified. This is because no cluster head or location manager is used to coordinate data transmission. This means that there is no processing overhead associated with duster head or location manager selection when compared to the HSR, MMWN, and CGSR protocols. This also means that a single point of failure and traffic bottlenecks can be avoided. Another advantage of ZHLS is that it has reduced the communication overhead when compared to pure reactive protocols such as DSR and AODV. In ZHLS, when a route to a remote destination is required (i.e., the destination is in another zone), the source node broadcasts a zone-level location request to all other zones. That way, it generates significantly lower overhead when compared to the flooding approach in reactive protocols.

Scalable Location Update Routing Protocol (SLURP)

Similar to ZHLS, In SLURP the nodes are organized into a number of non-overlapping zones. However, SLURP further reduces the cost of maintaining routing information by eliminating a global route discovery. This is achieved by assigning a home region for each node in the network.

   The home region for each node is one specific zone (or region), which is determined using a static mapping function, f (Node! D) Region D, where f is a many-to-one function that is static and known to all nodes. An example of a function that can perform the static zone mapping is f(Node I D) = g(Node I

D)rood C. where g(Node I 0) is a random number generating function that uses the node ID as the seed and output a large number and k is the total number of home regions in the network. Now, because the node ID of each node is constant (i.e., a MAC address), the mapping function always calculates the same home region. Therefore, all nodes are determining the home region for each node using this function, provided they have their node IDs. Each node maintains its current location (current zone) with the home region by unit casting a location update message toward its home region.

Distributed Spanning Trees Based Routing Protocol (DST)

In DST the nodes in the network are grouped into a number of trees. Each tree has two types of nodes: (I) route node and (2) Internal node. The root controls the structure of the tree and whether the tree can merge with another tree, and the rest of the nodes within each tree are the regular nodes. Each node can be in one of three different states: (1) router, (2) merge or (3) configure, depending on the type of task that it tries to perform.

To determine a route, DST proposes two different routing strategies: (I) hybrid tree-flooding (HTF) and (2) distributed spanning tree shuttling (DST). In HTF, control packets are sent to all the neighbors and adjoining bridges in the spanning tree, where each packet is held for a period of time called the holding time. The idea behind the holding time is that as connectivity increases, and the network becomes more stable, it might be useful to buffer and route packets when the network connectivity is increased over time.

Distributed Dynamic Routing (DDR)

DDR is also a tree-based routing protocol. However, unlike in DST, in DDR the trees do not require a root node. In this strategy, trees are constructed using periodic beaconing messages that are exchanged by neighboring nodes only. The trees in the network form a forest that is connected together via gateway nodes (i.e., nodes that are in transmission range but belong to different trees). Each tree in the forest forms a zone that is assigned a zone ID by running a zone naming algorithm. Furthermore, because each node can only belong to a single zone (or tree), the network can also be seen as a number of non-overlapping zones. Once the zones are created, a hybrid routing strategy, called the Hybrid Ad hoc Routing Protocol (HARP) which is built on top of DDR to determine routes. HARP uses the intro-zone and inter-zone routing tables created by DDR to determine a stable path between the source and the destination. This section describes variety of various hybrid routing protocols planned for MANETs. Furthermore, the efficiency comparison between the represented routing protocols are highlighted in detail and given in Table 3.

To understand the table the following notations are needed

I=periodic update interval
N=number of nodes in the network
M=number of zones or cluster in the network
Z_N=number of nodes in a zone, cluster or tree
Z_D=diameter of a zone, cluster or tree
Y=number of nodes in the path to the home region
V=number of nodes on the route reply path

Table 3. Comparison of routing protocols

PROTOCOL	ZRP	ZHLS	SLURP	DST	DDR
Routing Structure	Flat	Hierarchical	Hierarchical	Hierarchical	Hierarchical
Routing Metric	Shortest Path	Shortest Path	Zone Forwarding	Neighbor tree Forwarding	Stable routing
Multiple routes	No	Yes	Yes	Yes	Yes
Route Maintenance	Zone tables	Zone tables	Location Cache	Routing table	Zone tables
Route Reconfiguration strategy	Point of Failure	Location request	Source notification	Holding time or shuttling	source notification
Time complexity — Route Discovery	$Intra\ O(I)$ $Inter\ O(2D)$	$Intra\ O(I)$ $Inter\ O(D)$	$Intra\ O(2z_2)$ $Inter\ O(2D)_t$	$Intra\ O(z_2)$ $Inter\ O(D)$	$Intra\ O(I)$ $Inter\ O(2D)$
Time complexity — Route maintenance	$\dfrac{O(I)}{O(2D)}$	$\dfrac{O(I)}{O(D)}$	$\dfrac{O(2z_2)}{O(2D)}$	$\dfrac{O(z_2)}{O(D)}$	$\dfrac{O(I)}{O(2D)}$
Communication complexity — Route Discovery	$O(ZN)/O(N+V)$	$O(N/M)/O(N+V)$	$O(2N/M)/O(2\Gamma)$	$O(ZN)/O(N)$	$O(ZN)/O(N+V)$
Communication complexity — Route maintenance	$O(ZN)/O(N+V)$	$O(N/M)a/\ O(N+V)$	$O(2N/M)/O(2\Gamma)$	$O(ZN)/O(N)$	$O(ZN)/O(N+V)$

OVERVIEW OF QOS-ORIENTED DISTRIBUTED ROUTING PROTOCOL (QOD)

Taking advantage of fewer transmission hops and any cast transmission features of the hybrid networks, based on the random way-point model and the real human mobility model show that QOD can provide high QoS performance in terms of overhead, transmission delay, mobility-resilience, and scalability. QOD transforms the packet routing problem to a resource scheduling problem is given in Table 4.

Scheduling feasibility is the ability of a node to guarantee a packet to arrive at its destination within QoS requirements. As mentioned, when the QoS of the direct transmission between a source node and an AP cannot be guaranteed, the source node sends a request message to its neighbour nodes. After receiving a forward request from a source node, a neighbour node n_i with space utility less than a threshold replies the source node.

The reply message contains information about available resources for checking packet scheduling feasibility, packet arrival interval Ta, transmission delay T_{ID}, and packet deadline Dp of the packets in each flow being forwarded by the neighbour for queuing delay estimation and distributed packet scheduling and the node's mobility speed for determining packet size. Based on this information, the source node chooses the replied neighbours that can guarantee the delay QoS of packet transmission to APs. The selected neighbour nodes periodically report their statuses to the source node, which ensures their scheduling feasibility and locally schedules the packet stream to them. The individual packets are forwarded to the neighbour nodes that are scheduling feasible in a round-robin fashion from a longer delayed node to a shorter delayed node, aiming to reduce the entire packet transmission delay.

Table 4. QOD algorithm

ALGORITHM	FUNCTION
QOS granted neighbor selection	Manages Transmission Delay Requirement.
Distributed packet switching	Reduce Transmission delay.
Mobility-based segment resizing	Optimizes Transmission Time.
Traffic redundant elimination	Improves the Transmission throughput.
Data redundancy elimination-based transmission	Eliminate Redundant data & Increase transmission QOS.

QOD Based Application-DaTA

Data- Transparent Authentication (DaTA) without Communication Overhead, to authenticate data streams, is based on the timing correlation of data packets between the sender and the receiver. Particularly, the Interpacket delays are utilized and some selected packet delays are slightly adjusted (in a range). The Interpacket delay increase and decrease represent different bits (0 or 1), and thus, transparently embed the digest. Since the limit of delay adjustment in a small range and the delay adjustment is not cumulative, the application's performance is hardly affected.

In DaTA, the authentication unit is a data block and the authentication code is generated based on the content of the data block, thus called Block Authentication Code (BAC). DaTA works as follows: At the sender side, the authentication information BAC is generated based on a selected hash function with the packet content and a commonly agreed key as the input. Based on the value of each bit (0/1) of BAC, some packets are scheduled to be sent out with additional delays.

At the receiver side, the receiver extracts the embedded BAC based on the relative packet delay and compares the extracted BAC with the BAC generated based on the received content for authentication. Thus, the proposed model consists of five modules namely packet selection and generation, mobility-based packet resizing, redundant packet elimination, packet authentication and transmission, efficient estimation and retransmission.

BAC GENERATION ALGORITHM

The proposed scheme uses the following notations:

1. The stream packets are clustered to blocks, denoted as block[p], with c packets in each block, where $0 < p < $ [tot_packet_no/ctotal-packet-number/b]. Padding is used when necessary to generate the last block.
2. The length (in terms of bits) of the BAC for each data block is m.
3. A hash function, denoted as H(Y), is a one-way hash, using an algorithm such as MD5 or SHA.
4. Q, R represents the concatenation of Q with R.
5. A secret key S is only known to the communicating parties.
6. The origin of the data stream can be identified by a flag, which is g bits, where $0 \leq g \leq m$.

In this BAC generation algorithm, if the values vary of & while keeping & +g=m, they have different strategies.

- &=0, When & is 0, the strategy becomes easy and straight forward. There is no chain at all. It only demands a fixed sized buffer of c packets at the sender side and the receiver side. The strategy can detect packet alteration or addition and can locate changes in the granularity of a block. However, it cannot detect block deletion and block (burst packet) loss, which are very important in some stream-based applications, such as streaming media delivery, since streaming media data delivery normally runs on UDP.

Figure 5. BAC generation

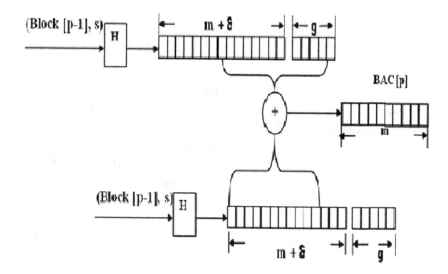

- &=m, When & is m, the strategy cannot authenticate the source. With more bits (2m) in the authentication code, the strategy reduces the collision rate since the number of bits in the hash result is larger. However, it has a problem due to chaining. For example, if the verification of the current data block indicates that the current block is changed, it means that the hash value of the current block cannot be used to authenticate the next block. Thus, the authentication of the next block and all its subsequent blocks will be uncertain. In addition, the protocol cannot distinguish the change of a data block and the deletion (or loss) of a data block. The choices of & and g have the trade-off between authenticating the source and chaining to determine if the preceding block is lost. In most of existing hash-chain-based strategies, & is m, or the hash function takes the two consecutive blocks as the input. This causes their authentication deficiency. Thus, an appropriate & should satisfy 0 < & < m.

PACKET SELECTION AND GENERATION

In sender, the authentication information Block Authentication Code (BAC) is generated based on a selected hash function with the packet content and a commonly agreed key as the input. Based on the value of each bit (0/1) of BAC, some packets are scheduled to be sent out with additional delays.

The BAC generation for data block i involve three steps:

1. The concatenation of data block i and the secret key k is used as input to hash function H to generate a binary string of n + & bits, where & = n - f.
2. The source flag, denoted as f, is concatenated to the generated bit in the previous step to get a binary string of 2n bits.
3. The first n bits of the binary string are XORed with the last n bits of the block i- first binary string, the result, BAC[i], is the final BAC for data blocks i.

Figure 6. Packet generation

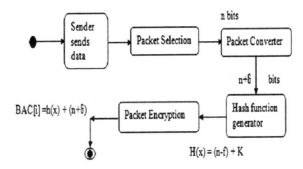

MOBILITY BASED PACKET RESIZING

After the Packet is generated with BAC, the next step is to resize the packet, which is different from existing strategies where the packet information is sent out-of-band or resized into the original data before data transmission. The BAC is filtered by adjusting the inter packet delay. The BAC bits can be resized and filtered without touching the content of the packet.

Take packet flow $P_1, P_2, P_3... P_m$ with time stamps $t_1, t_2, t_3 ..., t_m$, respectively ($t_i < t_j$ for $1 \leq i < j \leq m$), independently and randomly choose 2r (r > 0) distinct packets: $P_{z1}, P_{z2} ..., P_{z2r}$ ($1 \leq zk \leq m$ -d for $1 \leq k \leq 2r$) Create 2r packet pair (p_{zk}, p_{2krd}) (d ≥ 1, k=1, 2, ..., 2r) where d is packet pair distance. The Inter Packet Delay (IPD) between P_{zkrd} and P_{zk} is defined as $Ipd_{zk,d} = t_{zk+d} - t_{zk}$

The BAC Packet is resized and defined as $Y_{k,d} = \dfrac{\left(ipd1, k, d - ipd2, k, d \right)}{2}$

Then the packets for transmission is defined as $\mathbf{Y}_{t, d} = \dfrac{1}{r} \sum_{k=1}^{\infty} y_{k,d}$

Figure 7. Packet resizing

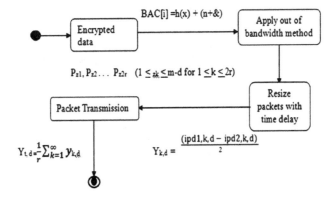

REDUNDANT PACKET ELIMINATION

In receiver side the receiver calculates $Y_{r,d}$ as it receives the data packets. Which is defined as $Y_{r,d} = \dfrac{1}{r}$ $\sum_{k=1}^{\infty} y_{k,d}$, the authentication information Block Authentication Code (BAC) is generated based on a selected hash function with the packet content and a commonly agreed key as the input. Based on the value of each bit (0/1) of BAC, some packets are scheduled to be sent out with additional delays.

To eliminate redundant packet same hash function is extracted from the received BAC bits. The BAC generation for data block i involve three steps:

1. The concatenation of data block i and the secret key k is used as input to hash function H to generate a binary string of n + & bits, where & = n - f.
2. The source flag, denoted as f, is concatenated to the generated bit in the previous step to get a binary string of 2n bits.

PACKET AUTHENTICATION AND TRANSMISSION

With the Resized BAC bits and received data packets, the receiver applies the same hash function (H) on the received data packets with the same secret key (k) to generate the content-based BAC following the same procedure used for BAC generation at the sender side, Then, the extracted BAC is compared with the generated BAC. The comparisons consist of two parts: the first part is on the first & bits, while the second is on the rest f= (n - &) bits. Every received data block is authenticable independently, which is based on the f-bit matching in the BAC packet comparisons.

1. Where the extracted and generated BAC packets are completely matched, the current data block is authenticated to be genuine.
2. The authentication failure on both parts strongly suggests that the current data block has been changed.

Figure 8. Packet elimination

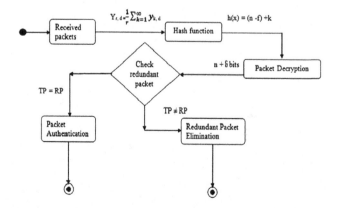

EFFICIENT ESTIMATION AND RETRANSMISSION

The authentication information is generated based on the content of the data block, which we call content BAC packet. The BAC packet resized in (or extracted from) the inter packet timing is called the reference BAC packet. At the receiver side, when the receiver receives the stream flow, the reference BAC extracted from the inter packet timing will be used as a reference for the content BAC packet calculated from the packet content. Let $C = b_1, b_2 ..., b_n$ be the original content BAC and the original reference BAC (they are always equal $C_1 = b_1, b_2 ..., b_n$ be the reference BAC of the received stream flow, and $C_2 = b_1, b_2 ..., b_n$ be the content BAC of the received streaming flow. The process is to find whether $C = C_1 = C_2$ for BAC packet retransmission.

SUMMARY

Data streams have been used in many Internet applications, such as grid computing and streaming media. More and more applications like these demand a reliable and effective authentication mechanism to ensure the genuineness of data streams transferred over the Internet. Although plenty of research work has been conducted, existing work shares the characteristics of either slightly changing the original data or sending the authentication information out-of-band, neither of which is desirable when the data carry sensitive information or when the data are transmitted to mobile devices. To increase the performance of hybrid networks in real mobility model a method to authenticate data streams for transmission has been studied in this chapter. Data Transparent Authentication without Communication overhead is an approach which reduces breakdown of original data or sends out of band authentication information.

REFERENCES

Anandakumar, H., & Umamaheswari, K. (2018). Cooperative Spectrum Handovers in Cognitive Radio Networks. In Cognitive Radio, Mobile Communications and Wireless Networks (pp. 47–63). Springer. doi:10.1007/978-3-319-91002-4_3

Anandakumar, H., Umamaheswari, K., & Arulmurugan, R. (2019). A Study on Mobile IPv6 Handover in Cognitive Radio Networks. In *International Conference on Computer Networks and Communication Technologies* (pp. 399-408). Springer Singapore. doi:10.1007/978-981-10-8681-6_36

Braden, R., Clark, D. & Shenker, S. (1994). Integrated Services in the Internet Architecture: An Overview.

Deb, B., Bhatnagar, S., & Nath, B. (2003). ReInForm: Reliable Information Forwarding Using Multiple Paths in Sensor Networks. In *Proc. IEEE 28th Ann. International Conference Local Computer Networks.*

Felemban, E., Lee, C., & Ekici, E. (2006, June). MMSPEED: Multipath multi-speed protocol for QoS Guarantee of reliability and timeliness in wireless sensor networks. *IEEE Transactions on Mobile Computing, 5*(6), 738–754. doi:10.1109/TMC.2006.79

Haldorai, A., & Ramu, A. (2018). An Intelligent-Based Wavelet Classifier for Accurate Prediction of Breast Cancer. In Intelligent Multidimensional Data and Image Processing (pp. 306–319). doi:10.4018/978-1-5225-5246-8.ch012

He, T., Stankovic, J., Lu, C., & Abdelzaher, T. (2003). SPEED: A Stateless Protocol for Real-Time Communication in Sensor Networks. In *Proc. 23rd International Conference Distributed Computing Systems*.

Hong, X., Xu, K., & Gerla, M. (2002). Scalable routing protocols for mobile ad hoc networks. *IEEE Network*, *14*(4), 11–21.

Jawhar, I., & Wu, J. (2005). Quality of Service Routing in Mobile Ad Hoc Networks. In M. Cardei, I. Cardei, & D. Z. Du (Eds.), *Resource Management in Wireless Networking. Network Theory and Applications* (Vol. 16). Boston, MA: Springer; doi:10.1007/0-387-23808-5_14

Jawhar, I., & Wu, J. (2005). Quality of service routing in mobile ad hoc networks. In *Resource Management in Wireless Networking* (pp. 365–400). Boston, MA: Springer.

Joa-Ng, M., & Lu, I.-T. (1999). A peer-to-peer zone-based two-level link state routing for mobile ad hoc networks. *IEEE Journal on Selected Areas in Communications*, *17*(8).

Kodialam, M., & Lakshman, T. V. (2000). Dynamic routing of bandwidth guaranteed tunnels with restoration. *IEEE/ACM Transactions on Networking*, *11*(3), 399–410. doi:10.1109/TNET.2003.813044

Kurose, J., & Ross, K. (2004). *Computer networking: A top-down approach featuring the internet*. Addison Wesley.

Lu, C., Blum, B., Abdelzaher, T., Stankovic, J., & He, T. (2002). RAP: A Real-Time Communication Architecture for Large-Scale Wireless Sensor Networks. In *Proc. IEEE Real-Time and Embedded Technology Applications Systems*.

Nikaein, N., Bonnet, C., & Nikaein, N. (2001, September). Harp-hybrid ad hoc routing protocol. In *Proceedings of international symposium on telecommunications (IST)* (pp. 56-67).

Pearlman, M. R., & Haas, S. J. (1999). Determining the optimal configuration for the zone routing protocol. *IEEE Journal on Selected Areas in Communications*, *17*(8).

Perkins, C., Belding-Royer, E., & Das, S. (2003). Ad Hoc on Demand Distance Vector (AODV) Routing.

Perkins, C.E., Royer, E.M. & Das, S.R. (2001) Quality of service in ad hoc on-demand distance vector routing.

Radhakrishnan, S., Racherla, G., Sekharan, C. N., Rao, N. S. V., & Batsell, S. G. (1999) DST-A routing protocol for ad hoc networks using distributed spanning trees. In *1999 IEEE Wireless Communications and Networking Conference*.

Stoica, I., & Zhang, H. (1999). Providing guaranteed services without per flow management. *Computer Communication Review*, *29*(4), 81–94.

Sung, Y. E., Lund, C., Lyn, M., Rao, S., & Sen, S. (2009) Modeling and understanding end-to-end class of service policies in operational networks. In *Proc. ACM Special Interest Group Data Comm. (SIGCOMM)*.

Suriya, M., Anandakumar, H., & Arulmurugan, R. (2016). Social Aware Cognitive Radio Networks: Effectiveness of Social Networks as a Strategic Tool for Organizational Business Management. In *Social Network Analytics for Contemporary Business Organizations*. Hershey, PA: IGI Global.

Venkataramanan, V. J., Lin, X., Ying, L., & Shakkottai, S. (2010, March). On scheduling for minimizing end-to-end buffer usage over multihop wireless networks. In INFOCOM, 2010 Proceedings IEEE (pp. 1-9). IEEE.

Wei, Y., Yu, F. R., & Song, M. (2010). Distributed Optimal Relay Selection in Wireless Cooperative Networks with Finite-State Markov Channels. IEEE Trans. Veh. Technology, 59(5).

Wu, H., & Jia, X. (2009). QoS Multicast Routing by Using Multiple Paths/Trees in Wireless Ad Hoc Networks. *Ad Hoc Networks*, 5(5), 600–612. doi:10.1016/j.adhoc.2006.04.001

Zeng, K., Yang, Z., & Lou, W. (2010). Opportunistic routing in multi-radio multi-channel multi-hop wireless networks. *IEEE Trans. Wireless Comm.*, 9(11).

Chapter 12

Machine Learning Techniques for Healthcare Applications:
Early Autism Detection Using Ensemble Approach and Breast Cancer Prediction Using SMO and IBK

Rajamohana S. P.
PSG College of Technology, India

Dharani A.
PSG College of Technology, India

Anushree P.
PSG College of Technology, India

Santhiya B.
PSG College of Technology, India

Umamaheswari K.
PSG College of Technology, India

ABSTRACT

Autism spectrum disorder (ASD) is one of the common disorders in brain. Early detection of ASD improves the overall mental health, which is very important for the future of the child. ASD affects social coordination, emotions, and motor activity of an individual. This is due to the difficulties in getting self-evaluation results and expressive experiences. In the first case study in this chapter, an efficient method to automatically detect the expressive states of individuals with the help of physiological signals is explored. In the second case study of the chapter, the authors explore breast cancer prediction using SMO and IBK. Breast cancer is the second leading cause of cancer deaths in women worldwide and occurs in nearly one out of eight. In this proposed system, the tumor is the feature that is used to identify the breast cancer presence in women. Tumors are basically of two types (i.e., benign or malignant). In order to provide appropriate treatment to the patients, symptoms must be studied properly, and an automatic prediction system is required that will classify the tumor into benign or malignant using SMO and IBK.

DOI: 10.4018/978-1-5225-7522-1.ch012

INTRODUCTION

An automated analysis of a complex organ brain would be very useful to neurologists to detect disorders. Autism spectrum disorder (ASD) is one of the common disorders in brain. Early detection of Autism Spectrum Disorder improves the overall mental health, which is very important for the future of child. ASD affects social coordination, emotions and motor activity of an individual. This is due to the difficulties in getting self-evaluation results and expressive experiences. It is an efficient method to automatically detect the expressive states of individuals with the help of physiological signals. The efficiency of ensemble classifiers over the other classifiers is measured and compared. Electroencephalogram a record of electrical activity of brain is used in ASD detection. Autism is an impairment of development in the central nervous system. Children affected by autism will have less social coordination, swinging emotions, impaired motor activity and repeated actions. The major cause behind Autism is still a mystery. The various factor that causes autism is genetic, which is predominant and environmental to which parents are exposed. Autism Spectrum Disorder (ASD) prevails in different forms like very severe to very mild.

OVERVIEW OF ASD

Autism spectrum disorder is a neuro-develop mental disorder identified by the difficulties in social interactions and repetitive and restricted behaviours and interests. An individual's communal impairments and emotional processing deficits are interconnected (Honkalampi, Hintikka, Tanskanen, Lehtonen & Viinamäki, 2000). An analysis on this subject suggests that individuals with ASD always face obscurity in ascertaining their own mental and expressive states (Baron-Cohen, Tager-Flusberg & Cohen, 1994). The persons affected by ASD are also affected by alexithymia. The probability of occurrence of alexithymia is very less. The underlying factor of alexithymia in ASD patients is apparent disassociation between expressive arousal and conscious awareness of the response. The result of challenges in emotional processing is psychiatric disorders such as depression (Frith, 2004). Early detection and diagnosis is important in preventing unnecessary delays in providing behavioural therapies and rehabilitating speech. There are various types of Autism spectrum disorder. They are High functioning Autism, Asperger's syndrome, Rett Syndrome, pervasive developmental disorderetc (Baron-Cohen, Tager-Flusberg & Lombardo, 2013).

Table 1. Types OF ASD

Autism Types	Description
Asperger's syndrome	This is on the milder end of the autism spectrum.
Pervasive developmental disorder, not otherwise specified (PDD-NOS)	Diagnosis included most children whose autism was more severe than Asperger's syndrome, but not as severe as autistic disorder.
Autistic disorder	It includes the same types of symptoms, but at a more intense level.
Childhood disintegrative disorder	This was the rarest and most severe part of the spectrum.
High-functioning autism	It is an informal one, people who can speak, read, write, and handle basic life skills like eating and getting dressed.
Rett syndrome	A rare, severe neurological disorder that affects mostly girls.

Table 2.ASD factors with symptom

Autism Spectrum Disorder-Risk Factors	Autism Spectrum Disorder - Symptoms
Child SEX	• A learning disability
Family History	• Attention deficit hyperactivity disorder (ADHD) • Tourette's syndrome or other tic disorders
Extremely preterm babies.	• Epilepsy • Dyspraxia
Parents' ages	• Obsessive compulsive disorder (OCD)
	• Generalised anxiety disorder • Depression • Bipolar disorder • Sleep problems • Sensory difficulties • are some of the common symtoms for children which can be treated by separate medication or cognitive based therapy(CBT) in addition to treatment of ASD.

The problem in malfunctioning of brain due to various conditions is termed as Autism spectrum disorder. Some of the characteristics of ASD are problems in social interaction with others, great variation in abilities, need for sameness, unusual interest in objects, under or over reaction to one or more of the five senses: touch, sight, smell, taste, or hearing, repeated actions or body movements. There are different symptoms to predict the disorder, each type will have its own symptoms. Some of the most common ASD symptoms and its types are listed in the Table 1 and Table 2.

DATASOURCE

The autism dataset consists of 705 instances with 10 input attributes and 1 output attribute (whether the presence or absence of the disease). The data set consists of 2 types of attributes:

- Input attributes
- Predictable attributes

Various research works on detection of Autism spectrum disorder using machine learning techniques are discussed in the following section:

Sharmistha Bardhan et al. A new programmed approach is suggested to screen autism using smart device in children called Autism Barta. There is a tool called M-CHAT which is used for screening Autism and it is integrated with the application with pictorial representation. With the help of the representation the parents can easily identify the interactive questions and use it effectively. ASD child is identified by the applicaion and the user updates the responses in the online database. Those data can be used by medical centers for further action.

Prediction of the clinical diagnosis with EEG measurements willgive (result) the outcome as ASD or not ASD (Bosl, Tager-Flusberg, & Nelson, 2018). It was highly accurate from as early as 3 months of age. The severity of ASD symptoms, as determined by the CSS, was predicted and the score is correlated with the actual CSS scores. Nonlinear measures are computed to find the significant difference between ASD and LRC groups. The proposed method is a promising technology for monitoring neural development in a broad population of children by using EEG measurements.

In this system, data consisted of Autism Diagnostic Interview-Revised (ADI-R) and Social Responsiveness Scale (SRS) scores for both ASD and non ASD individuals (Bone, Bishop, Black, Goodwin, Lord & Narayanan, 2016). ML-based Classifier is used, which consists of training phase that maps Instrument code to BEC-Diagnoses. In the testing phase, BEC-Diagnose which are predicted from the instrument code and are compared to existing instrument code. The proposed, ML fusion: ADI-R-C/SRS codes gave 89.2% Sensitivity (1.0) and 59.0% (Specificity 2.8) for Age group (10-20).

ASD can be detected from children at their earlier ages through behavioral metrics and neuroimaging techniques (Ramani & Sivaselvi, 2017). The knowledge of disorder is obtained from a new perspective of analysis (performed on the neuroimage). The major features are chosen by using feature selection methods like Random forest, SVM, CS-CRT, Naïve Bayes and C4.5. The above mentioned algorithms are implemented and their results are analyzed. Random tree classifier gives an accuracy of 88.46%.

In this paper, author suggests a method for assessment of Identification of ASD cases in EI (Early intervention records) (Liu, An, Hu, Langer, Newschaffer & Shea, 2013). Various classification methods like Bayes, Bayesian Logistic Regression and SVM are used. The system uses Ontology based feature extraction technique. Various performance metrics used in this system are recall, precision, F-score for both unigram and bigram features. As a result of analysis, SVM performs efficiently.

In this paper, Autism is detected using Discrete Sine Transform in EEG signal (Ganesh & Menaka, 2014). The system involves the processes like Data acquisition, Preprocessing, signal processing, Thresholding, Artificial Neural network. The accuracy of the system is 80%.

A fuzzy expert system is used to detect the severity level of Autism in children (Isa, Yusoff, Khalid, Tahir & Binti Nikmat, 2014). It involves the processes like data acquisition, fuzzy system architecture, fuzzification, rule evaluation, rules aggregation, defuzzification.

The Figure 1 describes the flow of steps involved in a classification process. The dataset consists of training data, testing data and validation data. Initially the training data is fed into the classifier and the model is built. Then the new data or testing data is fed to verify the accuracy of the system.

IMPLEMENTATION AND RESULTS

To analyze the performance of various machine learning techniques some evaluation metrics are used. Confusion Matrix is also computed to measure the performance. The various measures used for evaluation are precision, recall, ROC and F-measure.

1. Precision is also called as positive predictive value. It is used in various applications like pattern recognition, information retrieval and binary classification. It is defined as the ratio of relevant values to retrieved values.
2. Recall is defined as the ratio of relevant instances retrieved to the total amount of relevant instances. Recall is also called as sensitivity. It is a measure of relevance.
3. F-measure is defined as the Harmonic mean of precision and recall along with assigned weights. It is mainly in applications of information retrieval. It is considered as a measure of accuracy.

The following are the algorithms used to detect Autism Spectrum Disorder.

Figure 1. Steps in classification

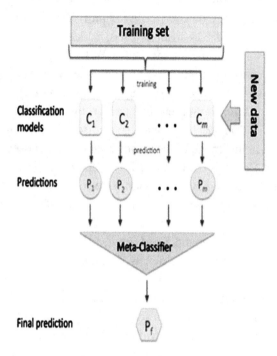

Naïve Bayes

It is a probabilistic random classifier that calculates a group of possibilities. It investigates frequency and combination of values on a given knowledge set. In this algorithm Bayes theorem is applied with naïve assumption of independence. Classification in Bayes network is NP-complete problem. But Naïve Bayes is a linear time algorithm.

The accuracy of the system using Naïve Bayes technique is 85.80%

Random Forest

Random Forest is an ensemble algorithm which was shaped from trees algorithm and Bagging algorithm. It is developed to improve the classification accuracy of the algorithm. It also works well with a data set with an enormous range of input variables. The algorithm begins by making a combination of trees which every tree will vote for a class. The accuracy of this method is 91.23%.

Table 3.

PRECISION	RECALL	FMEASURE	ROC	CLASS
0.971	0.984	0.978	0.996	NO
0.956	0.921	0.938	0.996	YES

Table 4.

PRECISION	RECALL	FMEASURE	ROC	CLASS
0.947	0.942	0.944	0.9	NO
0.844	0.857	0.85	0.899	YES

Bagging

Bagging is an ensemble technique which is used to improve the accuracy of the algorithm. Bagging is a parallel approach where the there are multiple classifiers involved in prediction and the results of each classifier are made to undergo a voting process. The prediction with higher accuracy is considered as the final result. The accuracy is 93.18%

MultiboostAB Algorithm

Boosting is a technique which trains classifiers in sequential manner. The output of one classifier is fed as input to another classifier. All the classifier outputs are made to undergo a voting process where the best output is selected as the prediction result.

MultiBoost approach is similar to Adaboost with wagging technique in addition. Wagging is a form of bagging where the weights of training values generated during boosting are used in selection of the bootstrap samples. Multiboost is more accurate than wagging or adaboost.The accuracy of Multiboost is 93.18% which is more than Bagging accuracy.

CONCLUSION

In this paper various machine learning Algorithms are compared using the performance metrics like precision, recall, F-score, etc. Confusion matrix is also computed to measure the true positive, true negative, false positive and false negatives. The various Ensemble methods are also included to measure

Table 5.

PRECISION	RECALL	FMEASURE	ROC	CLASS
0.948	0.959	0.954	0.981	NO
0.885	0.857	0.871	0.981	YES

Table 6.

PRECISION	RECALL	FMEASURE	ROC	CLASS
0.924	0.87	0.896	0.929	NO
0.694	0.804	0.745	0.932	YES

the performance of various algorithms. The implementation results show that Ensemble methods like Bagging and Multiboosts have higher accuracy than Naïve Bayes algorithm. Bagging has an accuracy of 91.23%. Multiboost has an accuracy of 93.18%.

CASE STUDY: BREAST CANCER PREDICTION USING SMO AND IBK

Data mining is a technique which retrieves the meaningful information from the available huge data. The useful information are extracted from the organized data (http://www.euroasiapub.org/IJRIM/June2011/10.pdf). Some consistent patterns or similar relationships are found using this process to explore large amounts of data. The analysis of Classification and Prediction of data mining techniques are discussed in this paper. Breast cancer is the commonly found cancer in women. It is found in both men and women(http://www.nationalbreastcancer.org/). 12% of new cancer cases are represented as breast cancer. Among all the countries breast cancer is found to be the second most common cancer. If breast cancer is detected in early stage is very helpful to identify the type of tumor. The tumor is defined as the abnormal growth of extra cells. Malignant and benign are the two types of tumor. The tumor which is known as non-cancerous and which sticks to one part of the body is called as Benign tumor. The tumor which is cancerous and which will spread to all parts of the body is known as Malignant. The Breast Cancer dataset is chosen for the experiment. The classification algorithms based on data mining techniques such as SMO, and IBK which provides accurate results.

Data Mining in Health Care

The term data mining has a different meaning when different peoples are describing it. But the actual and basic definition is analyzing a large data in order to predict the future events. Recently, data mining has played a vital role in the medical field to make the medical industry more efficient.

Data Mining for Breast Cancer Recurrence

Nowadays a lot of real-world problems are solved using data mining concepts. Data mining techniques are highly used to convert the raw data into more meaning information. Breast cancer can affect both the gender male and female. According to the world breast cancer statistics female have a high probability of occurrence of breast cancer than males. The symptoms of this disease should be taken serious by both patients and doctors. After the treatment of breast cancer if it comes again, then it is said to be recurred. Local recurrence, Distance recurrence and Regional recurrence are the three types of breast cancer recurrence.

OVERVIEW OF BREAST CANCER

Breast Cancer is the second leading cause of cancer deaths in women world wise and occurs in nearly one out of eight women. In this proposed system the tumor is the feature which is used to identify the breast cancer presence in women. Tumors are basically of two types i.e. benign or malignant. In order to provide appropriate treatment to the patients, symptoms must be studied properly and an automatic prediction system is required which will classify the tumor into benign or malignant. The main aim of this system is to develop more cost – effective and easy to use systems for supporting clinicians. The comparison between three algorithms with help of WEKA (The Waikato Environment for Knowledge Analysis), which is an open source software is conducted. It contains different type's data mining algorithms such as and Sequential Minimal Optimization (SMO). Here, the parameters like kappa statistic, relative absolute error, and root relative squared error, correctly classified instances, incorrectly classified instances, time taken, are used for comparing the result.

The breast cancer starts in the breast tissue. Any type of Cancer will begin in the cells. The building blocks of tissues and organs of the body constitute to breast cancer cells. Normal cells in the breast are divided to form new cells which includes other parts of the body are grown. Once the normal cells die or damaged a new cell can be grown in that place. This process is not suitable for each case. In some cases, the old or damaged cells doesn't die instead a new cell can be grown in that place (Chen, Han & Yu, 1996). The extra cells are bind together to form a mass of tissue which is known as lump, tumor, or growth. The breast tumors are of two types they are benign (not cancer) and malignant (cancer).

Benign Tumors

Benign tumors are usually harmless. They won't spread to other parts of the body and it can be removed and usually it won't grow back again. The tissues around them are invaded rarely.

Malignant Tumors

Malignant tumors are harmful and it may cause threat to life. They can spread to other parts of the body. It can be removed but it can grow back sometimes. The tissues and nearby organs can invade which forms a chest wall.

Risk Factors

A risk factor is an attribute, or a characteristic that increases the likelihood of developing a disease. Some of the risk factors related to breast cancer are listed below.

- **Gender:** Breast cancer is more common in women than men about 100 times.
- **Age:** As woman gets older, the chance of getting breast cancer increases.
- **Genetic Risk Factors:** The genes like BRCA1 and BRCA2 can increase the risk of getting breast cancer due to some inherited changes (mutations).
- **Family History:** If the blood relatives have this disease then there is a chance of getting Breast cancer. It is higher among women.
- **Personal History of Breast Cancer:** A woman who had cancer in one breast has a greater chance of getting cancer in the other breast or in another part of the same breast.
- **Race:** Women from breast cancer a lower risk of dying is more likely to be seen in white women rather than Asian, Hispanic, and Native-American women.
- **Dense Breast Tissue:** More gland tissue and less fatty tissue may lead to dense breast tissue. Women with such tissue may have a higher risk of breast cancer.

- **Certain Benign (Not Cancer) Breast Problems:** Women who had changes in benign breast may have an increased risk of getting breast cancer. The breast cancer risk is more closely linked to benign problems than others.

- **Menstrual Periods:** Women who reached puberty early (before age 12) or who went through the change of life (menopause) after the age of 55 have an increased risk of breast cancer.

- **Breast Radiation Early in Life:** A child or young adult have an increased risk of breast cancer when Women had radiation treatment to the chest area (as treatment for another cancer) During the teenage, the risk of breast cancer is high due to chest radiation when the breasts were still developing.

- **Treatment With DES:** During pregnancy the women who were given the drugs DES (diethylstil-bestrol) have an increased risk of getting breast cancer.

- **Not Having Children or Having Them Later in Life:** Women who had no children, or who had their first child after the age of 30, have higher risk of breast cancer. During young age, the pregnancy can reduce the breast cancer risk.

- **Certain Kinds of Birth Control:** The women who are using birth control pills or an injectable form of birth control can increase the risk of getting breast cancer than women who have never used them.

- **Using Hormone Therapy After Menopause:** After menopause, taking estrogen and progesterone increases the risk of getting breast cancer.

- **Not Breastfeeding:** The breastfeeding may lower the risk of breast cancer, especially if breastfeeding lasts from 1½ to 2 years.

- **Alcohol:** The use of alcohol is directly proportional to an increased risk of getting breast cancer. Even if one drink a day can increase the risk.

- **Being Overweight or Obese:** After menopause, being overweight or obese may leads to breast cancer.

RELATED WORKS

For survivability analysis there are many papers about applying machine learning techniques. In the field of medical diagnosis several studies have been reported that they have focused on the importance of new techniques. These studies have applied different approaches to the given problem and achieved high classification accuracies. Different techniques are stated in the study provided by Bittern, Dolgobrodov, Marshall, Moore, Steele, and Cuschieri (2007) stated the prediction of the survivability for the breast cancer patients, the artificial neural network is used. The test was made upon a limited data set for their approach to be evaluated, but their results show a good agreement with actual survival.

Chaurasia and Pal (2017) stated the prediction of the survivability for the breast cancer patients the algorithms like RepTree, RBF Network and Simple Logistics are used.

Djebbari, Liu, Phan, and Famili (2008) to predict the survival time in breast cancer the effect of ensemble of machine learning techniques are considered. Better accuracy on the breast cancer data set is achieved using this technique comparing to the other previously achieved results. Liu, Wang, and Zhang (2009) stated the prediction of the breast cancer survivability which was experimented on the breast cancer data using C5 algorithm with bagging. Bellaachia and Guven, (2006) stated the prediction of the breast cancer survivability which uses the Naive Bayes, decision tree and back-propagation neural network. Good results (about 90% accuracy), are achieved the results were not significant. It is because the whole dataset is divided into two groups, one for the patients who survived more than 5 years and the other for those patients who died before 5 years.

Li, Liu, Ng, and Wong (2003) proposed the prediction of the breast cancer survivability which uses the ovarian tumor data by using C4.5 algorithm with and without bagging. Chaurasia and Pal (2014) developed the prediction of the breast cancer survivability which uses the Naive Bayes, J48 Decision Tree and Bagging algorithms.

Chaurasia and Pal (2013). implemented the prediction of the breast cancer survivability which uses the CART (Classification and Regression Tree), ID3 (Iterative Dichotomized 3) and decision table (DT) algorithms. Wen, P. (2009). stated the prediction of the breast cancer survivability which uses the ECG data to identify the abnormal high frequency electrocardiograph using the decision tree algorithm and C4.5 algorithm with bagging.

Tu, Shin, and Shin (2009) stated the prediction of the breast cancer survivability which uses the bagging with C4.5 algorithm, and also bagging with Naïve Bayes algorithm. Cao, Xu, Liang, Chen, and Li (2010) stated the prediction of the breast cancer survivability which uses a new decision tree-based ensemble method combined with feature selection method.

Vijayaran, (2013) stated the prediction of the breast cancer survivability which uses different classification function techniques in data mining. The classification function algorithms are used. And the performance factors used are accuracy and error rate. Tsirogiannis, Frossyniotis, Stoitsis, Golemati, Stafylopatis, and Nikita (2004) stated the prediction of the breast cancer survivability which uses the applied bagging algorithm, neural networks, SVMs and decision trees. Accuracy of bagging is efficient than without bagging.

Tu, Shin, and Shin (2009) stated the prediction of the breast cancer survivability which uses the bagging algorithm, decision tree induction algorithm with and without bagging. Kaewchinporn, Vongsuchoto, and Srisawat (2011) stated the prediction of the breast cancer survivability which uses a new classification algorithm TBWC combination of decision tree with bagging and clustering. Harish, Guru, and Manjunath (2010) stated the prediction of the breast cancer survivability which uses various text representation schemes with different classifiers and compared it to the predefined classes.

CLASSIFICATION TECHNIQUES

In data mining the frequently used technique is Classification. The process of identifying a set of functions in which the data classes or concepts are separated and explained. The derived function is based on the analysis of a set of training data in which the class value is known. The main aim of classification is to precisely predict the target class for each case in the data. For example, a classification model can be used to identify the salary details of each citizen (applicants) as low, medium, or high credit risks.

The one of the essential tasks of data mining and machine learning research is building accurate and efficient classifiers for large databases. In Classification usually, classification the preliminary data analysis step is examining a set of cases. As a result of examining we can conclude that based on similarity to each other we can group them. To increase understanding of the domain or to improve predictions compared to unclassified data is the ultimate reason for doing classification technique in them. The central task of data mining is building effective classification systems. Based on user's domain knowledge and also the departure of constructing new models for given a classification and a partial observation, always the classification is used to compute the statistical estimate of the unobserved attribute values. The different types of classification technique includes Decision Trees, Naive- Bayesian methods, Sequential Minimal Optimization (SMO), random forest, support vector machine etc. The classification technique used now is sequential Minimal optimization (SMO) and IBK (K- Nearest neighbours classifier).

Sequential Minimal Optimization (SMO)

For training Support Vector machines (SVMs) a new algorithm is proposed, which is known as Sequential Minimal Optimization (SMO). John Platt in 1998, proposed this sequential minimal optimization which is a simple and fast method for training a SVM. The main idea is derived for solving dual quadratic optimization problem. For which to solve at each iteration the optimization is done for the minimal subset including two elements. Simply and Analytically the SMO can be implemented that is the main advantage of SMO. The solution of a very large quadratic programming optimization problem is required for training a support vector machine problem. SMO involves a series of smallest possible quadratic programming problems which is broken down from the large quadratic programming problem. Without using a time-consuming numerical quadratic programming optimization as an inner loop analytically these small quadratic programming problems are solved. SMO can handle very large training set because of the amount of memory which is required for the training set size is linear. For various test problems, SMO scales somewhere between linear and quadratic in the training set size because matrix computation is avoided. SVM algorithm scales somewhere between linear and cubic in the training set size as other standard chunking. SMOs computation time is dominated by SVM evaluation hence SMO is fastest for linear SVMs and sparse data sets.

IBK (K Nearest Neighbours Classifier)

Based on the similarity the K-Nearest Neighbour (KNN) classification classifies instances. In multi-dimensional space each case is considered as a point and based on the nearest neighbours classification is done. For nearest neighbours the value of k can vary. The value of k determines how many cases are to be considered as neighbours. And also, it decides how to classify an unknown instance. A k-nearest neighbour classifier searches the pattern space for the k training samples that are closest to the unknown sample when given an unknown sample. Among its k nearest neighbours the unknown sample is assigned to the most common class. The unknown sample is assigned the class of the training sample that is closest to it in pattern space when k=1. With the number of training instances that are kept in the classifier, the time taken to classify the test instance with nearest-neighbour classifier increases linearly. The storage requirement is very large. With increasing noise levels its performance degrades quickly. When different attributes affect the outcome to different extents it performs badly. The number of nearest neighbours to be used is one of the parameters which can affect the performance of the IBK algorithm. By default, it uses just one nearest neighbour.

BREAST-CANCER-WISCONSIN DATA SET SUMMARY

The data used in this study are provided by the UC machine learning repository. The dataset comprises of 699 instances, 2 classes which are malignant and benign, and also 9 integer-valued attributes. The

16 instances with missing values from the dataset are removed to construct a new dataset with 683 instances. The percentage of Class distribution for Benign is 458 (65.5%) and Malignant is 241 (34.5%).

Evaluation Methods

These three data mining algorithms are used in Weka toolkit to experiment with. Using libraries from Weka Machine learning environment all the experiments are performed. The Weka is an ensemble of tools for data classification, regression, clustering, association rules and visualization. To evaluate the performance and effectiveness of three breast cancer prediction models built from several techniques, the Weka version 3.6.9 was utilized as a data mining tool. That is because a well defined framework is offered by the Weka Program for experimenters and developers to build and evaluate their models. Compared to other similar methods, the results clearly depicts that the proposed methods performs well by concluding that the attributes which are considered for the analysis are not the direct indicators of breast cancer in the patients.

Experimental Results

This section summarizes the results of our algorithms. Initially it describes the final data set, and then the results of the modelling from classification are provided. Here the 10-fold cross validation for all the classifiers is experimented. For predicting the breast cancer patients some experiments are computed in order to evaluate its performance and usefulness of different classification algorithms. The following subsection summarizes the results of our experiment as shown in the Table 7. From the table the conclusion made is that Sequential Minimal Optimization (SMO) is more accurate classifier in comparison to IBK. And also, it can be easily seen that it has highly classified correct instances than incorrectly classified instances than any other classifiers.

SUMMARY

Various data mining techniques can be applied for identification and prevention of breast cancer among patients. For Medical applications there is an important challenge in data mining and machine learning. The challenge is to build precise and computationally efficient classifiers. In this paper, the use of two

Table 7. Performance study of algorithms

Classifier	Time Taken (Sec)	Correctly classified instances (%)	Incorrectly classified instance (%)	Coefficient correlation	Mean absolute error	Root mean squared error	Relative absolute error (%)	Root relative squared error (%)
SMO	0.47	96.19%	3.81%	0.9582	0.003	0.0052	22.0251 %	28.7786 %
K-Nearest Neighbor (IBK)	0.02	95.90	4.1%	0.7733	0.0086	0.0118	63.7239 %	65.4299 %

Figure 2. Performance result for SMO algorithm

Figure 3. Performance result for IBK algorithm

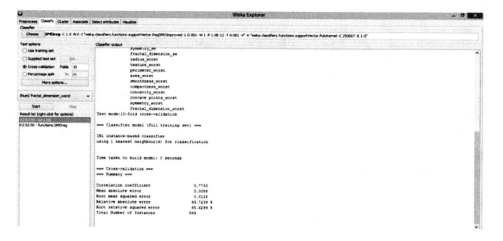

different data mining classification methods is used for the prediction of breast cancer. The classification methods such as SMO and IBK are used. The comparison is done based on the different parameters for predicting the breast cancer. Based on the selected classifier algorithm the accuracy of classification techniques is evaluated. Accuracy and lowest computing time are compared for prediction. This proposal study filtered all the algorithms based on their lowest computing time and accuracy. After all the comparison study the conclusion made is that the performance of SMO is efficient when compared with other classifiers. Therefore, SMO classifier is suggested for diagnosis of breast cancer disease-based classification to get better results with accuracy, low error rate and performance.

REFERENCES

American Psychiatric Association. (2000). *Diagnostic and Statistical Manual of Mental Disorders* (4th ed.). American Psychiatric Association.

Anurekha, G., & Geetha, P. (2017). Performance Analysis of Supervised Approaches for Autism Spectrum Disorder Detection. *International Journal of Trend in Research and Development.*

Baron-Cohen, S., Tager-Flusberg, H., & Lombardo, M. (Eds.). (2013). *Understanding other minds: Perspectives from developmental social neuroscience.* Oxford University Press. doi:10.1093/acprof:oso/9780199692972.001.0001

Baron-Cohen, S. E., Tager-Flusberg, H. E., & Cohen, D. J. (1994). Understanding other minds: Perspectives from autism. In *Workshop in Seattle, April 1991.* Oxford University Press.

Bellaachia, A., & Guven, E. (2006). Predicting breast cancer survivability using data mining techniques. *Age*, *58*(13), 10–110.

Bittern, R., Cuschieri, A., Dolgobrodov, S. G., Marshall, R., & Moore, P. (2007) A. artificial neural networks in cancer management. *e-Science All Hands Meeting*, *19*, 251-263.

Bone, D., Bishop, S. L., Black, M. P., Goodwin, M. S., Lord, C., & Narayanan, S. S. (2016). Use of machine learning to improve autism screening and diagnostic instruments: Effectiveness, efficiency, and multi-instrument fusion. *Journal of Child Psychology and Psychiatry, and Allied Disciplines*, *57*(8), 927–937. doi:10.1111/jcpp.12559 PMID:27090613

Bosl, W. J., Tager-Flusberg, H., & Nelson, C. A. (2018). EEG analytics for early detection of autism spectrum disorder: A data-driven approach. *Scientific Reports*, *8*(1), 6828. doi:10.103841598-018-24318-x PMID:29717196

Bosl, W. J., Tager-Flusberg, H., & Nelson, C. A. (2018). EEG analytics for early detection of autism spectrum disorder: A data-driven approach. *Scientific Reports*, *8*(1), 6828. doi:10.103841598-018-24318-x PMID:29717196

Cao, D. S., Xu, Q. S., Liang, Y. Z., Chen, X., & Li, H. D. (2010). Automatic feature subset selection for decision tree-based ensemble methods in the prediction of bioactivity. *Chemometrics and Intelligent Laboratory Systems*, *103*(2), 129–136. doi:10.1016/j.chemolab.2010.06.008

Chaurasia, V., & Pal, S. (2013). Early prediction of heart diseases using data mining techniques. *Caribbean Journal of Science and Technology*, *1*, 208–217.

Chaurasia, V., & Pal, S. (2014). Data mining approach to detect heart diseases. *International Journal of Advanced Computer Science and Information Technology.*, *2*(4), 56–66.

Chaurasia, V., & Pal, S. (2017). Data mining techniques: To predict and resolve breast cancer survivability. *International Journal of Computer Science and Mobile Computing.*, *3*(1), 10–22.

Chen, M. S., Han, J., & Yu, P. S. (1996). Data mining: An overview from a database perspective. *IEEE Transactions on Knowledge and Data Engineering*, *8*(6), 866–883. doi:10.1109/69.553155

Dell. (n.d.). Data mining techniques. Retrieved from http://documents.software.dell.com/Statistics/Textbook/Data-Mining-Techniques

Djebbari, A., Liu, Z., Phan, S., & Famili, A. N. D., F. (2008) International journal of computational biology and drug design (IJCBDD). In *21st Annual Conference on Neural Information Processing Systems.*

EuroAsia. (2011). Retrieved from http://www.euroasiapub.org/IJRIM/June2011/10.pdf

Frith, U. (2004). Emanuel Miller lecture: Confusions and controversies about Asperger syndrome. *Journal of Child Psychology and Psychiatry, and Allied Disciplines, 45*(4), 672–686. doi:10.1111/j.1469-7610.2004.00262.x PMID:15056300

Ganesh, P., & Menaka, R. (2014). Use of Discrete Sine Transform in EEG signal classification for early Autism detection. In *2014 International Conference on Advanced Communication Control and Computing Technologies (ICACCCT)* (pp. 1507-1510). IEEE.

Geetha Ramani, R., & Sahayamary Jabarani, R. (2017). Detection of autism spectrum disorder and typically developing brain from structural connectome through feature selection and classification. *International Journal of Innovations & Advancement in Computer Science, 6*(8).

Geetha Ramaniand, R. & Sivaselvi; K. (2017). Autism Spectrum Disorder Identification using Data mining techniques. *International Journal of Pure and Applied Mathematics, 117*(16), 427–436.

Harish, B. S., Guru, D. S., & Manjunath, S. (2010). Representation and classification of text documents: A brief review. *IJCA, (2),* 110-119.

Honkalampi, K., Hintikka, J., Tanskanen, A., Lehtonen, J., & Viinamäki, H. (2000). Depression is strongly associated with alexithymia in the general population. *Journal of Psychosomatic Research, 48*(1), 99–104. doi:10.1016/S0022-3999(99)00083-5 PMID:10750635

Isa, N. R. M., Yusoff, M., Khalid, N. E., Tahir, N., & binti Nikmat, A. W. (2014). Autism severity level detection using fuzzy expert system. In *2014 IEEE International Symposium on Robotics and Manufacturing Automation (ROMA)* (pp. 218-223). IEEE.

Kaewchinporn, C., Vongsuchoto, N., & Srisawat, A. (2011, May). A combination of decision tree learning and clustering for data classification. In *2011 Eighth International Joint Conference on Computer Science and Software Engineering* (pp. 363-367). IEEE.

Li, J., Liu, H., Ng, S. K., & Wong, L. (2003). Discovery of significant rules for classifying cancer diagnosis data. *Bioinformatics (Oxford, England), 19*(Suppl. 2), ii93–ii102.

Liu, M., An, Y., Hu, X., Langer, D., Newschaffer, C., & Shea, L. (2013). An evaluation of identification of suspected autism spectrum disorder (ASD) cases in early intervention (EI) records. In *2013 IEEE International Conference on Bioinformatics and Biomedicine (BIBM)* (pp. 566-571). IEEE.

Liu, Y. Q., Wang, C., & Zhang, L. (2009). Decision tree based predictive models for breast cancer survivability on imbalanced data. In *3rd International Conference on Bioinformatics and Biomedical Engineering ICBBE 2009* (pp. 1-4). IEEE.

Motlagh, S. H. R. E., Moradi, H., & Pouretemad, H. (2013, June). Using general sound descriptors for early autism detection. In *2013 9th Asian Control Conference (ASCC)* (pp. 1-5). IEEE.

National Breast Cancer. (n.d.). Retrieved from http://www.nationalbreastcancer.org/

Sarabadani, S., Schudlo, L. C., Samadani, A. A., & Kushki, A. (2018). *Physiological detection of affective states in children with autism spectrum disorder. IEEE Transactions on Affective Computing*.

Sarabadani, S., Schudlo, L. C., Samadani, A. A., & Kushki, A. (2018). *Physiological Detection of Affective States in Children with Autism Spectrum Disorder. IEEE Transactions on Affective Computing*.

Silani, G., Bird, G., Brindley, R., Singer, T., Frith, C., & Frith, U. (2008). Levels of emotional awareness and autism: An fMRI study. *Social Neuroscience, 3*(2), 97–112. doi:10.1080/17470910701577020 PMID:18633852

Tan, A. C., & Gilbert, D. (2003). Ensemble machine learning on gene expression data for cancer classification. *Applied Bioinformatics, 2*(3 Suppl.), S75–S83. PMID:15130820

Tsirogiannis, G. L., Frossyniotis, D., Stoitsis, J., Golemati, S., Stafylopatis, A., & Nikita, K. S. (2004). Classification of medical data with a robust multi-level combination scheme. In *Proceedings. 2004 IEEE International Joint Conference on Neural Networks* (Vol. 3, pp. 2483-2487). IEEE.

Tu, M. C., Shin, D., & Shin, D. (2009). Effective diagnosis of heart disease through bagging approach. In *2nd International Conference on Biomedical Engineering and Informatics BMEI '09* (pp. 1-4). IEEE.

Tu, M. C., Shin, D., & Shin, D. (2009, December). A comparative study of medical data classification methods based on decision tree and bagging algorithms. In *2009 Eighth IEEE International Conference on Dependable, Autonomic and Secure Computing* (pp. 183-187). IEEE. 10.1109/DASC.2009.40

van den Bekerom, B. (2017). Using Machine Learning for Detection of Autism Spectrum Disorder. Retrieved from https://pdfs.semanticscholar.org/65af/94822bcd64ed5365172ba6cf6fb6fc2a8fc6.pdf

Vijayaran, S. (2013). An Effective Classification Rule Technique for Heart Disease Prediction. *International Journal of Engineering Associates*.

Wen, P. (2009). Application of decision tree to identify abnormal high frequency electro-cardiograph. *Physics Experimentation, 11*.

World Cancer Research Fund International. (n.d.) *Cancer facts*. Retrieved from http://www.wcrf.org/int/cancer-facts figures/data-specific cancers/breast-cancer-statistics

Chapter 13

A Detailed Study on Security Concerns of VANET and Cognitive Radio VANETs

M. Manikandakumar
Thiagarajar College of Engineering, India

Sri Subarnaa D. K.
Thiagarajar College of Engineering, India

Monica Grace R.
Thiagarajar College of Engineering, India

ABSTRACT

Wireless ad hoc networks are dynamic networks in which nodes can move freely in the network. A new type of Vehicular Ad Hoc Network (VANET) that allows smart transport system to provide road security and reduces traffic jams through automobile-to-automobile and automobile-to-roadside communication. In this, vehicles rely on the integrity of received data for deciding when to present alerts to drivers. Because of wireless network the VANET messages are vulnerable to many attacks and the security concerns are also major issues. So, with respect to these methods, this article will discuss the Denial of Service (DoS) attack, masquerading, and their vulnerabilities. Also, it classifies the securities and their prevention mechanisms in overcoming these security issues in VANET and Cognitive Radio VANET perspectives.

INTRODUCTION

Nowadays VANET are the most important and upcoming recent technology which allow many vehicles to communicate with each other with in a network. In common, a VANET is formed from a number of vehicles which are in the same road to form ad-hoc network. In the presence of these networks will create the way for a wide range of applications such as travelling safely, mobility and connectivity for both driver and passengers to exploit the transport systems in a smoothly, efficiently and safer way. There are three most common component in VANET they are onboard unit (OBU), Road side unit (RSU) and

DOI: 10.4018/978-1-5225-7522-1.ch013

Application unit (AU) for communication among vehicles. And it is the challenging research area to provide an Intelligent Transportation System (ITS) services to every user in the network. Every vehicle with in that network will be installing (OBU), which will integrate the respective vehicles where the micro-sensors, embedded systems, wireless communications, and Global Positioning System (GPS) would be there in the vehicle (Al-Sultan et al., 2014; Jiang et al., 2006). In this VANET the Cognitive Radio (CR) is introduced and it is used as extended application in wireless communications. This Cognitive radio verifies the availability of electromagnetic spectrum and permits the waves for the transmission parameter. Here the communication takes places in open air medium. Wireless networks lack the complexities of infrastructure setup and administration, enabling devices to create and join networks "on the fly" – anywhere, anytime. A wireless ad hoc network is a type of computer-to-computer connection. In ad hoc mode, one can set up a wireless connection directly to another computer without having to connect to a Wi-Fi access point or router.

COMPONENTS

On Board Unit (OBU)

This OBU is the central processing power where the vehicular node is installed in vehicle. This unit can contain a variety of devices that are used for communication and information processing like:

- A processor that are processing the application to obtain the communication protocols.
- A wireless transceiver is used to transmit and receive data among itself, other vehicles and with road side units.
- A GPS is used here for viewing the vehicles location.
- A set of sensors is used to measure various parameters which can then be processed in a distributed network. Special sensors can also be used to measure driver's mental status.
- Network interfaces used for VANET are IEEE 802.11p card and other networks like Bluetooth and infrared for communication.

Mode of Operation

Once the data has been entered, the vehicle gets activated for automatic system by comparing the GPS signal and information from positioning sensors with the motor network information, the OBU automatically detects whether the vehicle is on a route segment, and determines which segments are used. Based on the route and vehicle data that has been saved automatically, OBU can calculate the toll charges, saves this information, and transmit it through radio signal (GSM) to the computing center.

Application Unit (AU)

The application layer of the network is intended to provide a safety measures and non-safety applications. AU is a device with input output interfaces like monitor, keypad, headphone jack, USB port etc (Anandakumar, Umamaheswari, & Arulmurugan, 2018). The AU is connected by either wired connection or wirelessly connected to OBU.

Road Side Unit (RSU)

This RSU is fixed device located on road side that helps in maintaining the network. It is also equipped with network interfaces like IEEE 802.11p. IEEE 802.11p is a standard to add wireless access in vehicular environments (WAVE), a vehicular communication system. This RSU requires a support Intelligent Transportation Systems (ITS) applications. This RSU includes data exchange between high-speed vehicles and the vehicles on the roadside infrastructure, so it is called as V2X communication. The RSU also facilitates the routing mechanism. The RSU receives the information and provide a warning message to the drivers about the accidents occurred in some area.

VANET

VANETs deal with movement of nodes. There are different types of VANET communications exist. Here a vehicle can contact another vehicle, known as Vehicle-to-Vehicle (V2V) communication. These vehicles can also transmit the information with roadside infrastructures, known as Vehicle to Infrastructure (V2I) communication. The road-side infrastructures at the roadside communicate with one another. Communication in VANET is a challenging fact due to its faster mobility. VANET has been classified into two categories and the one is comfort applications and other is safety related applications (Haldorai & Ramu, 2018).

COMFORT APPLICATIONS

The main objective of comfort applications is to improve the passenger comfort and traffic efficiency. These applications can be included in Value Added Services (VASs) which can be used by VANET. Passengers in a vehicle for a long period would be interested to use some applications from vehicular networks. Some of the applications are as follows:

- **Automatic Toll Collection:** By using this type of service, payment is done through automatic process. So, the vehicle does not need to stop to pay the fees.
- **Location Based Applications:** Information about the location of restaurants, shopping malls, ATMs, Gas and filling stations etc., can be uploaded to the vehicles. Vehicles can exchange this information through vehicular network to facilitate travelling.
- **Internet Connectivity:** Vehicle passengers can access the Internet to send or receive emails using internet. Distributing this information using vehicular networks reduces the cost of infrastructure installation along roadside.
- **Entertainment applications:** Movies, songs, games, etc., can be shared among vehicles using VANET Where one or more vehicles can store those data.
- **Safety Applications:** It aims to save human lives on the roads. The feature of these safety applications is to deliver the safety related data to the actual receiver in time. Safety related applications are as follows:
- **Assistance Messages (AM):** These messages include cooperative collision avoidance (CCA), navigating and lane switching messages. Preventing collisions is the main goal of CCA. If there is a possibility of a collision among the vehicles nearby, these applications will trigger automatically

to warn the driver to steer the vehicle or reduce the speed, thereby avoiding possible collision(s). Vehicles detecting an accident may start sending messages to other vehicles so that others may take a detour.

- **Warning Messages (WMs):** Some of the basic examples of WMs are obstacle, post-crash, toll point or road condition warnings; stop light ahead in a highway. Vehicles may start transmitting WMs to other vehicles in a certain zone after sensing it, thereby helping other subsequent vehicles reducing their speed to avoid accidents.
- **Information Messages (IMs):** Some of the basic examples of Information Messages are speed limit, work zone information in the highway, toll point ahead.

COGNITIVE RADIO (CR)

Cognitive radio will extend the spectral efficiency, with the available frequencies in a region. This CR monitors the available spectrum and when a spectral is identified it adapts the transceiver to operate in the same frequency channel when frequency is not occupied by users or even when the interference levels do not harm other users. This Spectrum will allow the users to classify as Primary Users (PU) or Licensed users else Secondary Users (SU) or Cognitive Users. Licensed users are authorized users those operate in a specific frequency band, while the secondary users do not have a permission to transmit and receive the frequency bands. Cognitive user should monitor the frequency spectrum to find out if there is any authorized user occupying the spectrum or if there is a spectral opportunity. Cognitive users verify the presence and absence of spectrum holes via spectrum sensing. Spectrum holes are defined as temporarily non-used spectrum bands that can be accessed by cognitive users. If a band is available, the cognitive user can opportunistically use that channel, although the priority will be given to authorized user if they are present, then the CR will not be allowed to benefit from that frequency band. Spectrum Sensing (SS) is fundamental in a cognitive radio network. Higher bandwidth and lower error rates in the transmission can be observed with the monitoring of channel occupancy. Different spectrum sensing techniques can be adopted by cognitive networks. There are some techniques which is used to improve spectral detection and they are Energy Detection Matched Filtering detection. Also, the combination of two or more spectrum sensing techniques sometimes referred as hybrid sensing is a new approach in recent researches. New applications in different scenarios are arising grace to cognitive radio. Some of the major applications of CR are:

- TV white spaces and regulation
- Smart grids
- Wireless sensor networks (WSN)
- Public safety and medical networks
- Power line communications
- Vehicular networks

COGNITIVE RADIO VEHICULAR AD HOC NETWORKS (CRVs)

Recently, almost all automatic vehicles are investing the dangers and traffic in road side and providing an infotainment solutions and new alternatives to drivers and passengers. Internet access or Bluetooth connections inside cars are already suffering interferences in heavy-traffic roads. So that this Cognitive radio has been introduced and inserted to vehicular communication. Cognitive radio for vehicular Ad hoc Networks (CRVs or CRVANETs) led the cars to monitor the available frequency bands and provide an opportunistically to operate only on these specified frequencies. CRVs can improve the throughput; also, these CR-VANETs enable more users to operate in high user density scenarios (Anandakumar & Umamaheswari, 2018).

Spectrum users are classified as primary users (Licensed) users or secondary user (Cognitive) users. Licensed users are authorized user that they can operate in a specific frequency band, while secondary users do not have a permission to transmit and receive in that frequency bands. Cognitive user should monitor the frequency spectrum to find out if there is any licensed user occupying the spectrum or if there is a spectral opportunity.

Spectrum sensing properly detect the presence or absence of PUs or SUs in a specific frequency band; this optimizes the usage of spectrum holes opportunistic. Spectrum sensing schemes are classified as:

- Per-vehicle sensing
- Spectrum database techniques
- Cooperation

In per-vehicle sensing method each car will performs the spectrum sensing mechanism automatically and be independent from others. The spectrum sensing is performed with traditional SS strategies as cyclostationary detection, matched filter, and energy detection. Spectrum database techniques are used to establish a centralized database for collecting the information from all PUs operating in a geographic region. This centralized database can reduce the limitations of observing the per-vehicle sensing, however the control of this database is complex and expensive. Based on the CR concept, the information collected from all vehicles are forwarded to a fusion center and transmitted to all users within the central node range.

Security Attacks in VANET

Security and privacy issues are most effective design for implementation of CR enabled VANETs due to potential threats like traffic flow, malicious attacks, or sending fake message by using the authorized user ID by which it leads to a traffic disruption and some accidents. This VANET provide a wireless access to random vehicles for transforming the information on the road sides, where else this CRNs enable an efficient sharing of available spectrum bandwidth between the random vehicles. Hence, guaranteeing security, privacy, anonymity, and liability in CR assisted vehicular networks. Due to open wireless nature of communication various security threats and attacks occurs in VANET network and disrupts the services provided. The attacks on VANET network in the different layer is presented and focused mainly on network layer attack, especially Denial of Service (DoS) attack.

The requirements for security in VANET are:

Authentication

Authentication is a process in which the credentials provided are compared to those on file in a database of authorized users' information on a local operating system or within an authentication server. Since the large volume of vehicular data has transmitted and need to be processed in big data environment, security of big vehicular data is essential (Manikandakumar & Ramanujam, 2018). If the credentials match, the process is completed, and the user is granted authorization for access. The permissions and folders returned define both the environment the user sees and the way he can interact with it, including hours of access and other rights such as the amount of allocated storage space. The process of granting an administrator rights and the process of checking user account for access specific resources are referred to as authorization. The privileges and preferences granted for the authorized account depend on the user's permissions, which are either stored locally or on the authentication server. The settings defined for all these environment variables are set by an administrator.

Integrity

It involves maintaining the consistency, accuracy, and trust worthiness of data over its entire life cycle. Data must not be changed in transit, and steps must be taken to ensure that data cannot be altered by unauthorized people. These measures include user access controls and file permissions. Version control is used to prevent accidental deletion or erroneous changes by authorized users becoming a problem. As with data confidentiality, cryptography plays a very major role in ensuring data integrity. The most commonly used methods are to protect the data integrity which includes hashing the data you receive and comparing it with the hash of the original message. However, this means that the hash of the original data must be provided to you in a secure fashion.

Confidentiality

The confidentiality ensures that no unauthorized gain of information is possible. Requirements regarding confidentiality are application specific in a VANET. It ensures that sensitive information is accessed only by an authorized person and kept away from those not authorized to possess them. It is implemented using security mechanisms such as access control lists (ACLs), usernames, passwords, and encryption method. It is also common for information to be categorized according to the extent of damage that could be done should it fall into unintended hands. Security measures can then be implemented accordingly.

Non-Repudiation

Non-repudiation is the assurance that someone cannot deny something. Typically, non-repudiation refers to the ability to ensure that a party to a contract or a communication cannot deny the authenticity of their signature on a document or the sending of a message that they originated. The email non-repudiation process which involves email tracking mechanism which is designed to ensure that the sender cannot deny having sent a message and/or that the recipient cannot deny having received it.

Possible Attacks in VANET

For a secured transformation of messages, a dissemination protocol has to provide cognitive security solution for a secure communication in vehicular networks through the usage of distributed sensor technology. This distributed sensor technology helps us to guarantee high reliability and priorities an efficient QoS, robustness against denial of service (DoS) security attacks, and the prevention of data aging. In general, wireless access in vehicular network like other wireless networks is highly vulnerable to both DoS and distributed DoS security attacks, such as radio jamming attack.

Then some of the possible attacks are:

Masquerade Attacks

A masquerade attack is a attack on network side which uses a fake identity, this false network identity will work as an authorized user to access their personal computer to gain information through legitimate access identification. If an authentication process is not fully protected, it will become extremely vulnerable to a masquerade attack. These attacks can be perpetrated using stolen passwords and logons, by locating gaps in programs, or by finding a way around the authentication process. These attacks can be triggered either by employees within the organization or by an outsider if the organization is connected to a public network. The amount of masquerade attackers will depend on the level of authorization that they have managed to attain. It allows one machine to act on behalf of other machines. That is one machine can pretend to be another and can misuse the information obtained via conversation. The problem of masquerading is also eliminated in our proposed algorithm by mutual authentication. As such, masquerade attackers can have a full smorgasbord of cybercrime opportunities if they've gained the highest access authority to a business organization. Personal attacks, although less common, can also be harmful.

DoS Attack

Due to the wireless medium in VANET, there are a number of possible DoS attacks will occur in VANET. Hence, there will be many chances for high attacks. The purpose of the denial of service attack is to create a problem for legitimate users, and as a result the user cannot access the services. Some of the DOS attacks are.

Sybil Attack

The Sybil attack is an attack where reputation system is subverted by forging identities in peer-to-peer networks. A Sybil attack happens when an insecure computer is hijacked to claim multiple identities. A Sybil attack is a type of network attack where the multiple nodes are controlled by single adversary Avoiding Sybil attacks is a difficult problem. In centralized systems they are typically avoided through heuristics that do not provide cryptographic assurance of Sybil resilience. In a Sybil attack, the attacker subverts the reputation system of a peer-to-peer network by creating a large number of pseudonymous identities, using them to gain a disproportionately large influence (Hasbullah, & Soomro, 2010). For example, in a centralized entity every time it will try to avoid this Sybil attacks by requiring an individual IP, but it cannot create to more user with a specific number for every user account in a given time interval.

Node Impersonation

It is an attempt by a node to send a modified version of a message received from the real originator for the wrong purpose and claim the message has come from the originator. In order to overcome these types of problems, a unique identifier is assigned to each vehicle node in VANET, which will be used to verify from where the message is originating (Hasbullah & Soomro, 2010).

Sending False Information

It is type of attack where it produces a wrong or fake information to the user which was purposely sent by a node to other nodes in the network to create a chaos traffic scenario, which it may lead to misinterpretation of the actual situation. With the falsified information, the users would likely to leave the road, thus it makes the road free for the attacker to use it for their own purposes (Hasbullah, & Soomro, 2010).

Impersonate

This attack happens when the adversaries pretend to be authenticated vehicles or RSUs. The adversaries use the legitimate identities they hacked into to insert malicious information in the network, which would not only fool other vehicles but also make the innocent drivers whose identities were taken be removed from the network and denied service.

Hardware Tampering

This attack happens when the sensors, other onboard hardware RSUs are manipulated by adversaries. For example, an adversary can relocate a tampered RSU to launch a malicious attack, such as tampering the traffic lights to always be green when the malicious attack is approaching an intersection.

Black Hole Attack

In this Black hole attack, data packets may get lost while travelling through the Black Hole because it does not have any nodes, so it refuses to transmit data packets to the next destination.

Deception

Some vehicles may pretend to another by its movement. For example, a private car may pretend itself as an emergency vehicle to clear the congestion ahead, thereby making its movement faster.

Malware and Spam

These types of attacks are caused by malicious insider nodes of the network rather than outsider. The attack is performed when the software is getting updated for both OBUs and RSUs. These attacks can be mitigated by centralized administration.

Timing Attack

One of the basic requirements of VANET is to broadcast VANET security messages at the right time and at right place. When a malicious car receives an emergency message, it may delay the forwarding and transmission of message. The neighboring vehicles don't receive the message at the proper time. In order to avoid a dangerous situation a malicious car receives a message "accident ahead" from neighbor but it doesn't transmit the message immediately.

Global Positioning System (GPS) Spoofing

Identifying the location based on the location table is carried out by the GPS satellites with the help of that uniqueness of the vehicle and geographic location in the network is found. A malicious vehicle may alter the information in the location table to some other random location. In that case, a vehicle will decide to think that it is in a different position by reading the false information, due to that there will be accidents to the vehicle. An attacker can also use a GPS simulator to produce signals stronger than the original satellite. Initially the attacks will take place on GPS receivers concentrated on GPS jamming to simply ban receivers from location information and acquiring time. A more powerful attack is given by GPS spoofing. This kind of attack allows the attacker to manipulate the received GPS signal inside the attacked area in an arbitrary way. Thus, receivers report time and location information as controlled by the attacker. An attacker can easily empower the original GPS signal, when it arrives at the earth surface with very low power i.e., about 10-20 dB below the receiver's noise floor. Thereby, GPS receivers of attacked ITS-S will synchronize to the spoofed time signal. Studies on countermeasures to GPS spoofing concentrate on detection of the attack. Thereby, usage of antennas or multi-antenna systems with well-known micro movement has been suggested. Both the systems are currently not used in the automotive domain. Instead, a fixed single antenna is typically used in vehicles. And the usage of the detection systems would significantly increase the costs of on VANET deployment as every ITS-S has to be equipped with them. And the use of classical GPS spoofing detection on the physical layer, by using a multi antenna system, with trustworthiness model on higher layers. This model is based in the fact that a smart grid can be controlled by a central entity VANET.

PREVENTION MEASURES OF DOS ATTACK IN VANET CRYPTOGRAPHIC SOLUTIONS

ECDSA (Elliptic Curve Digital Signature Algorithm)

In authentication process the VANET messages uses the public key cryptography (i.e) it uses both the private and public keys is achieved. This technique generates digital signatures for messages using elliptic curve parameters and sends the message along with digital signature and certificate issued by the central authority. This ECDSA achieves broadcast authentication and non-repudiation in VANET with computational overhead on the OBU and also it has to verify one ECDSA signature the OBU which lead to computational identify for computation-based DoS under highly dense VANET environment.

TESLA (Timed Efficient Stream Loss-Tolerant Authentication)

In TESLA it authenticates messages through symmetric key cryptography. The source authentication, it uses one-way hash chains with key and provide a source and destination time that are synchronized. To generate one-way hash chain, selects a random number An, apply hash to get a previous value An-1, repeatedly apply hash to get new values up to A0. To authenticate a message m in the time t_i, it uses hash a_i to create MAC (m), send it along with the message to the receiver. The receiver buffers the message along with the MAC until the key is communicate with each other. After some duration of time (d), the source will send the key, which the receiver uses to verify the message it buffered. TESLA achieves an coherent authentication with low communication and computation overhead since it uses hashing and single key cryptography.

FastAuth and SelAuth

This prevention mechanism defines another two efficient broadcast authentication techniques as a countermeasure for signature flooding. Fast Authentication (FastAuth), secures single-hop beam messages by predicting the future beam messages using chained Huffman hash trees, which is used to generate one-time signature scheme which is 50 times faster and generation time is 20 times faster than ECDSA. Selective Authentication (SelAuth), this also secures the multi-hop messages. It provides fast isolation of malicious vehicles due to which invalid signatures are constrained to a small area without impacting the whole network and uses forwarder identification mechanism to distinguish between original and misbehaving vehicles.

ID-Based Cryptography

By implementing this ID-based cryptography the computing cost is reduced. ID-based cryptography will make use of online/offline signature (IBOOS) scheme for verification purpose. Online process is performed during V2V communications among the vehicles. Offline method is performed first in the vehicles or in the RSUs. IBOOS is a best method for Verification process than IBS. Using IBS and IBOOS proposed an ID-based scheme. This scheme does not provide a vehicle privacy using real-world IDs rather it uses self-constructed pseudonyms. In this approach, IBOOS is used during V2V authentications and IBS is used for V2I authentication. This approach will provide the privacy of VANET in an efficiently manner.

Symmetric and Hybrid Methods

In symmetric and hybrid methods, vehicles can contact each other when they both share a secret key. Security methods use either symmetric key or public key. Recently a new method is proposed which uses both symmetric key and public key. This method is known as hybrid system. Two types of communications are used in this approach: group communication and pair wise communication. The key pair is used to reduce overhead; symmetric key is used for pair wise communication in hybrid system.

Certificate Revocation Methods

This certificate revocation will invalidate the association of a vehicle by using centralized and decentralized certification process. In centralized system certificate authority (CA) will start revocation. In decentralized approach, revocation decision is taken by the neighboring vehicles. CA transmits messages to the RSU when an invalid certificate is detected. When vehicles get the message from RSU, then the vehicles will cancel that certificate and no longer communicate with it.

Ant-Colony Optimization

In an Ant-Colony Optimization (ACO) algorithm is proposed to provide an efficient, optimized and secure technique for securing routing process by isolating the malicious attacker in the path to the destination. It defends against a Blackhole attack, a form of DoS attack, ACO based routing algorithm creates the path with trust and pheromone value, to detect the malicious node. The main goal is to maintain the maximum lifetime of network, during data transmission in an efficient manner. The node with low trust and pheromone value are identified as malicious and any route through the node is cancelled. This ACO is one of the bio-inspired mechanisms. ACO is a dynamic and reliable protocol. It provides data gathering structure and aware-of-energy in wireless network. It can avoid network congestion and fast consumption of energy of individual node. Then it can prolong the life cycle of the whole network. ACO algorithm reduces the energy consumption. It optimizes the routing paths, and provides an effective multi-path data transmission structure to obtain a reliable communications in the case of fault node.

Applications

The main objectives of VANETs and CR-VANETs are public safety. The primary concern is the improvement of safety for drivers and passengers by optimization technique. Driving Safety Support Systems (DSSS) is a development process to reduce traffic accidents and to increase drivers' awareness. Vehicle-to-Person applications aim to provide security measures to pedestrians, motorcycles and bicycles. To eliminate V2P collisions, the pedestrian will use of Dedicated Short-Range Communications (DSRC) and enable the Smartphone to sends a navigation screen alert and audible warning to the vehicle. On the side, the system detects a vehicle close to the person or motorcycle or bicycle, and alerts are forwarded to the walker. Company like Honda also develops these solutions for the named Vehicle-to-Motorcycle (V2M) safety.

SUMMARY

This Vehicular Adhoc Networks is an emerging technology with many features to offer. Only if the security hazards in these types of networks are taken care of, VANET can be integrated with the upcoming automobile technology that is essential for VANET. Here the authors have discussed about VANET security via digital certificate and attempted to secure the network against the most common form of network attacks like DOS and Masquerade. The main focus is to do the task with minimum overhead on network and using the available resources.

REFERENCES

Al Hasan, A. S., Hossain, M. S., & Atiquzzaman, M. (2016, September). Security threats in vehicular ad hoc networks. In *2016 International Conference on Advances in Computing, Communications and Informatics (ICACCI)* (pp. 404-411). IEEE.

Al-Sultan, S., Al-Doori, M. M., Al-Bayatti, A. H., & Zedan, H. (2014). A comprehensive survey on vehicular ad hoc network. *Journal of Network and Computer Applications*, *37*, 380–392. doi:10.1016/j.jnca.2013.02.036

Anandakumar, H., & Umamaheswari, K. (2018). Cooperative Spectrum Handovers in Cognitive Radio Networks. In Cognitive Radio, Mobile Communications and Wireless Networks (pp. 47–63). Springer. doi:10.1007/978-3-319-91002-4_3

Anandakumar, H., Umamaheswari, K., & Arulmurugan, R. (2019). A Study on Mobile IPv6 Handover in Cognitive Radio Networks. In *International Conference on Computer Networks and Communication Technologies* (pp. 399-408). Springer Singapore. doi:10.1007/978-981-10-8681-6_36

Biglieri, E., Goldsmith, A. J., Greenstein, L. J., Mandayam, N. B., & Poor, H. V. (2013). *Principles of cognitive radio*. Cambridge University Press.

Bouabdallah, F., Bouabdallah, N., & Boutaba, R. (2009). On balancing energy consumption in wireless sensor networks. *IEEE Transactions on Vehicular Technology*, *58*(6), 2909–2924. doi:10.1109/TVT.2008.2008715

Haldorai, A., & Ramu, A. (2018). An Intelligent-Based Wavelet Classifier for Accurate Prediction of Breast Cancer. In *Intelligent Multidimensional Data and Image Processing* (pp. 306–319). doi:10.4018/978-1-5225-5246-8.ch012

Hasbullah, H., & Soomro, I. A. (2010). Denial of service (dos) attack and its possible solutions in VANET. *International Journal of Electrical, Computer, Energetic, Electronic and Communication Engineering*, *4*(5), 813–817.

Haykin, S. (2005). Cognitive radio: Brain-empowered wireless communications. *IEEE Journal on Selected Areas in Communications*, *23*(2), 201–220. doi:10.1109/JSAC.2004.839380

Jiang, D., Taliwal, V., Meier, A., Holfelder, W., & Herrtwich, R. (2006). Design of 5.9 GHz DSRC-based vehicular safety communication. *IEEE Wireless Communications*, *13*(5), 36–43. doi:10.1109/WC-M.2006.250356

Li, H., & Irick, D. K. (2010, May). Collaborative spectrum sensing in cognitive radio vehicular ad hoc networks: belief propagation on highway. In 2010 IEEE 71st Vehicular technology conference (VTC 2010-spring) (pp. 1-5). IEEE.

Manikandakumar, M., & Ramanujam, E. (2018). Security and Privacy Challenges in Big Data Environment. In Handbook of Research on Network Forensics and Analysis Techniques (pp. 315-325). Hershey, PA: IGI Global.

Naik, M. (2015). Early Detection and Prevention of DDOS attack on VANET [Doctoral dissertation].

Patel, K. N., & Jhaveri, R. H. (2015). Isolating Packet Dropping Misbehavior in VANET using Ant Colony Optimization. *International Journal of Computers and Applications, 120*(24).

Petit, J. (2009, December). Analysis of ecdsa authentication processing in vanets. In *2009 3rd International Conference on New Technologies, Mobility and Security (NTMS)* (pp. 1-5). IEEE.

Qian, Y., & Moayeri, N. (2008, May). Design of secure and application-oriented VANETs. In *IEEE Vehicular Technology Conference VTC Spring 2008* (pp. 2794-2799). IEEE. 10.1109/VETECS.2008.610

Shabbir, M., Khan, M. A., Khan, U. S., & Saqib, N. A. (2016, December). Detection and Prevention of Distributed Denial of Service Attacks in VANETs. In *2016 International Conference on Computational Science and Computational Intelligence (CSCI)* (pp. 970-974). IEEE.

Singh, K. D., Rawat, P., & Bonnin, J. M. (2014). Cognitive radio for vehicular ad hoc networks (CR-VANETs): Approaches and challenges. *EURASIP Journal on Wireless Communications and Networking, 2014*(1), 49. doi:10.1186/1687-1499-2014-49

Thilak, K. D., & Amuthan, A. (2016, February). DoS attack on VANET routing and possible defending solutions-A survey. In *2016 International Conference on Information Communication and Embedded Systems (ICICES)* (pp. 1-7). IEEE.

Varshney, N., Roy, T., & Chaudhary, N. (2014, April). Security protocol for VANET by using digital certification to provide security with low bandwidth. In *2014 International Conference on Communications and Signal Processing (ICCSP)* (pp. 768-772). IEEE.

Vijay, G., Bdira, E. B. A., & Ibnkahla, M. (2011). Cognition in wireless sensor networks: A perspective. *IEEE Sensors Journal, 11*(3), 582–592. doi:10.1109/JSEN.2010.2052033

Chapter 14
Application of Cognitive Computing in Healthcare

Sabarmathi K. R.
Bannari Amman Institute of Technology, India

Leelavathi R.
Bannari Amman Institute of Technology, India

ABSTRACT

Cognitive systems mimic the functions of the human brain and improves decision-making to harness the power of big data in multiple application areas. It generates a model that reacts by sensing, understanding natural language, and providing a response to stimulus naturally rather than traditional programmable systems. Cognitive computing is trained to process large unstructured datasets imposing machine learning techniques to adapt to different context and derive value from big data. Using a custom chat box or search assistant to interact with human in natural language which can understand queries and explains data insights. This chapter also touches on the challenges of cognitive computing to demonstrate insights that are similar to those of humans.

INTRODUCTION

Cognitive computing depicts innovation stages that, extensively, depend on the logical orders of artificial intelligence and signal processing. These stages envelop machine learning, reasoning, natural language processing, speech recognition and vision, human– PC communication, among other technologies. At current scenario, there is no broadly settled upon definition for cognitive computing in either the scholarly community or industry.

As a wide range, the term cognitive computing has been utilized to allude to new equipment or potentially programming that impersonates the working of the human mind and enhances human basic leadership. In this sense, cognitive computing is another kind of computing with the objective of more exact models of how the human cerebrum/mind detects, reasons, and reacts to every stimulus. Cognitive computing applications connect information investigation and versatile page displays (AUI) to change content for a specific kind of group of onlookers. All things considered, Cognitive computing applications endeavor to be more emotional and more prominent by plan (Anandakumar & Umamaheswari, 2018).

DOI: 10.4018/978-1-5225-7522-1.ch014

Drawn out to future, the expanding multifaceted nature of medication and wellbeing, administrations raise wellbeing costs overall significantly. Progressions in pervasive processing applications in blend with the utilization of modern wise sensor systems may give a premise to help. While the keen wellbeing idea can possibly encourage the idea of the rising P4-solution (preventive, participatory, prescient, and customized), such innovative prescription delivers a lot of high-dimensional, pitifully organized informational indexes and monstrous measures of unstructured data. All these innovative methodologies alongside "enormous information" are transforming the therapeutic sciences into an information concentrated science. To keep pace with the developing measures of complex information, brilliant healing center methodologies are a rule without bounds, requiring setting mindful reckoning alongside cutting edge communication ideal models in new physical-advanced biological communities. In such a framework the restorative specialists are reinforced by their keen versatile therapeutic collaborators on dealing with their surges of information semi-naturally by following the human-on top of it idea. In the meantime, patients are upheld by their health assistants to encourage a more beneficial life, health and prosperity.

RELATED WORKS

The intense increase of population worldwide is challenging the existing healthcare systems. With the advancement of new technology, smart home environments are used for monitoring the patients and also enabling patients to remain in the home for their comfort. In this paper, a Cloud-Based Smart Home Environment (CoSHE) for home human services is proposed. CoSHE gathers physiological, movement and audio signals through wearable sensors and gives information about patients' daily activities. This allows healthcare experts to think about day by day activities, behavioral changes and monitor rehabilitation. A smart home environment is set up with natural sensors to give related information. The sensor information is captured and sent to a private cloud, which gives ongoing information access to remote healthcare experts. Our contextual analysis demonstrates that we can effectively coordinate relevant data to human wellbeing information and this thorough data can help betterment of human wellbeing (Pham, Mengistu, Do & Sheng, 2018).

In the recent decades, the advancement in medical and computer technologies provided a great interest for both academia and industry. But most healthcare systems fail in emergency situations of patients and are incapable to give a customized resource services for users. To address this issue, the Edge-Cognitive-Computing-based (ECC-based) smart-healthcare framework is proposed in this paper. This framework uses cognitive computing to observe and examine the user's physical health. It additionally modifies the computing resource allocation of the entire edge computing network extensively as per the risk hazard of each user. The investigations demonstrate that the ECC-based healthcare framework gives a better user experience and simplifies the computing resources sensibly, and in addition altogether enhancing in the survival rates of patients in a sudden crisis (Chen, Li, Hao, Qian & Humar, 2018).

Human context recognition (HCR) from wearable sensor networks plays an important role for many healthcare applications since it offers consistent monitoring capability of both individual and natural parameters. In any case, these frameworks still face a major energy issue (Haldorai & Ramu, 2018). In reality, in healthcare applications, sensors are utilized to catch information about daily activities of patients for monitoring the health issues. Therefore, persistent sampling and communication tasks quickly reduce sensors' battery reserves, and regular battery substitution are not advantageous. Accordingly, there is a need to create energy-efficient solutions for long-term observing applications to increase the acceptance of these technologies by the patients. In this paper, existing energy-efficient methodologies intended for HCR based on wearable sensor systems. A new classification of the energy-efficient mechanisms is proposed for health-related human context recognition applications. Also, given a qualitative correlation of the solutions based on energy-consumption, recognition accuracy and latency (Rault, Bouabdallah, Challal & Marin, 2017).

Improvements and new innovations in medical field have provided numerous individuals more advantageous. But, there are still expansive design inadequacies because of the imbalanced appropriation of medical resources, particularly in developing nations. To address this issue, a video conference-based telemedicine framework is prepared to break the confinements of medical resources in terms of time and space (Röcker, Ziefle & Holzinger, 2014). By outsourcing medical resources from big clinics to rural and remote ones, centralized and high-quality medical resources can be shared to accomplish a higher rescue rate while enhancing the use of medical resources. In spite of the fact that viable, existing telemedicine frameworks just treat patients' physiological diseases, leaving another testing issue unsolved: How to remotely distinguish patients' passionate state to analyze mental ailments (Anandakumar & Umamaheswari, 2017). In this paper, a novel healthcare framework based on 5G Cognitive System (5G-Csys) is proposed. The 5G-Csys comprises of a resource cognitive engine and a data cognitive engine. Resource cognitive engine, based on learning of system settings, aims at ultra-low latency and ultra-high reliability for cognitive applications. Data cognitive engine, based on the investigation of healthcare big data, is utilized to deal with a patient's well-being status physiologically and mentally. In this chapter, the design of 5G-Csys is first displayed, and after that the key innovations and application situations are discussed. A prototype platform of 5G-Csys, incorporating speech emotion recognition is developed to monitor the human safety (Chen, Yang, Hao, Mao & Hwang, 2017).

PROPOSED WORK

The proposed model comprises of four noteworthy parts: an environmental setup, a wearable unit, a private cloud framework, and a mobile unit. Natural sensors are utilized for gathering movement and action data of the human subject (Courtney, 2008). The wearable unit is utilized to gather physiological and body action data through non-intrusive, wearable sensors. Information from the natural sensors and wearable sensors are handled by a gateway where pre-preparing, indoor confinement and action acknowledgment algorithms are executed. The extensive physiological information with relevant data is then sent to the private cloud for remote access purposes (Wilson, Hargreaves & Hauxwell-Baldwin, 2014). The mobile unit receives the data from the cloud to get comprehension of the human setting, and therefore it can connect appropriately with the human.

ENVIRONMENT SETUP

A brilliant environment condition gives abundant relevant information identified with an occupant's wellbeing, which permits more exact wellbeing checking than just utilizing physiological signs. Obviously the setting of inhabitants, for example, what they do, or where they are in the home, can give vital data to wellbeing evaluation.

Figure 1. System architecture

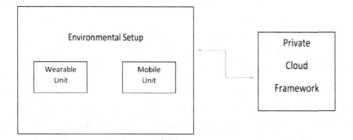

Motion sensors can have consolidated highlights trying to decrease false alerts. For instance, a passive infrared (PIR) sensor could be joined with a microwave sensor. Since each works in various regions of the range, and one is passive, and one is dynamic. Dual Technology motion sensors are not as likely as different kinds to cause false cautions. On the grounds all together for the alert to be activated, the two sensors must be stumbled. This does not imply that they never cause false alerts (Patel, Park, Bonato, Chan & Rodgers, 2012). This brings down the likelihood of a false alert since warmth and light changes may trip the PIR yet not the microwave. On the off chance that an interloper can trick either the PIR or microwave, nonetheless, the sensor won't recognize it. Frequently, PIR innovation is matched with another model to boost accuracy level and diminish energy consumption. PIR draws less vitality than emissive microwave identification, thus numerous sensors are adjusted with the goal that when the PIR sensor is stumbled, it initiates a microwave sensor. On the off chance, microwave sensor also grabs an interloper, and initiates the alarm.

WEARABLE UNIT

Wearable sensors have turned out to be extremely famous in numerous applications, such as medical, entertainment, security, commercial fields and education fields. They are tremendously valuable in giving precise and trustworthy data on individuals' activities and behaviors, thus ensuring a safe life. In sports field, there is an expanding pattern of utilizing different wearable sensors. There are numerous gadgets as of now available for wellness and wellbeing of patients for better utilization of applications that can be effectively incorporated into clinical practice. A few years back, the estimation of sweat rate was possible only in the laboratory but now it's possible using wearable sensor. Wearable sensors sense abnormal and/or unanticipated situations by checking physiological parameters along with other symptoms. Most sensors can either be worn or set on garments. Some wearable gadgets can be put on the any piece of the body: wrist, lower leg, abdomen, chest, arm, legs, etc. (Chan, Campo, Estève, & Fourniols, 2009).

The utilization of wearable sensors has made it possible to have the important treatment at home for users after an assault of infections, for example, heart-attacks, sleep apnea, Parkinson disease etc., Patients after an operation follow the strict schedule for recovery process. All these physiological signs and physical activities of the patient are likely to be checked with the assistance of wearable sensors (Varshney, 2007). The framework can be tuned to the needs of individual patients. The entire action can be observed remotely by specialists, medical attendants or guardians. A lot of sensors are now available in market with lower energy consumption and less processing time.

Few years back, the checking of cardiac activity is performed during a visit to the hospital by recording electrocardiograph (ECG) signals. Checking the heart movement through ECG signals is an extremely basic method, performed by setting at least three terminals to the skin to gauge the electrical action of heart. Generally, Holter monitors are utilized for ambulatory monitoring after cardiovascular medical surgery. A Holter monitor is a battery-worked compact gadget that measures and records your heart's movement (ECG) consistently for 24 to 48 hours or longer relying upon the kind of checking utilized (Rantz, Skubic, Koopman, Phillips, Alexander, Miller & Guevara, 2011). The gadget is the measure of a little camera. Holter monitor is bulky and it disturbs the daily routine of the patient and is not feasible for continuous monitoring. In the recent years, with the progression in remote advancements, Holter monitor have been scaled down and wireless gadgets have been incorporated in the market.

Nowadays, Heart attack is the main source of death for both men and women. This paper exhibits a model for observing the Heartbeat rate even if the person is at home. A Heart Beat (HB) sensor is used to monitor/sense the heartbeat of a person and transforms it in the form of electrical signals and pulses. For a patient who have already diagnosed with heart disease, their heart rate condition must be checked continuously (Chernbumroong, Atkins & Hongnian, 2011). The user may set the high and also low levels of heart beat limit. Subsequent to setting these limits, the framework begins checking and when persistent heart beat goes over a specific farthest point, the framework sends an alarm to the mobile unit and also transmits this over the web to alert the specialists as well as to the concerned user. Likewise, the framework alerts for lower heartbeats and additionally shows the live heart rate of the patient. In this manner, the user may monitor heart rate and the individuals time can be saved.

Mobile Unit

Classification algorithm retrieves data from the cloud platform initially. Features are extracted from the sensors and feature selection is performed. Here, Pulse rate is the feature being extracted. Number of times per minute that the heart contracts is read as pulse rate. A mobile device is connected to the application which alerts the client when he/she is prone to a heart attack. This alert is made as a notification to the registered mobile number which can be client's number, guardian's number and the doctor.

Artificial Neural Network

Artificial Neural Network (ANN) has been broadly utilized in many fields. An ANN is the recreation of the human mind. The utilization of an artificial neural network algorithm is to track the progress periodically. ANN contains supervised and unsupervised learning strategies. Both supervised and unsupervised taking in, an artificial neural network can be perfected to make a precise forecast. Supervised learning intends to prepare the machine to make an interpretation of the information into a desired output value. ANN of supervised learning method is used here for prediction of coronary illness. It gives accurate result as compare to the decision trees and Naive-Bayes framework.

Private Cloud Framework

The Smart Home Healthcare Cloud uses Private Cloud Infrastructure. This framework is set up utilizing the open source Cloud Orchestration Software, OpenStack Juno. Storage server provides a persistent storage for Non-structured database MongoDB (NoSQL) is utilized to store sensor information (Chen,

King, Thomaz, & Kemp, 2011). So as to have quick access to this information for real-time applications, NoSQL furnishes the ability to adjust with distributed storage which is taken care the Hadoop File System (HDFS) and MapReduce in the cloud. Likewise, all raw data from the PIR sensor, Microwave sensor and Heat Beat Sensor are transferred to the cloud database each 24 hour for accurate results. Infrastructure-as-a-Service (IaaS) is used in this framework for storing huge data generated from sensors. The private cloud is used to provide better security and privacy for health data.

METHODOLOGY

The client wears a heartbeat (HB) sensor as a smart watch, that periodically records the client's pulse rate. The client is monitored using a motion sensor and location sensor. PIR Sensor captures the motion of the client. Microwave sensor tracks the location of the client in the given environmental setup. The generated sensor data is stored into a private cloud ensuring data confidentiality (Revetria, Catania, Cassettari, Guizzi, Romano, Murino, Fujita, 2012). The data are fed into an ANN classifier, which classifies the abnormal functioning from normal functioning of heart using the pulse rate fluctuation. The threshold limit for normal pulse rate is 70-84. When the reading exceeds given threshold limit, a notification is pop-up for registered users.

CONCLUSION AND FUTURE WORK

This paper helps the client to be alerted with signs of heart attack being occurred using pulse rate recorded by HB -Heart Beat sensor. The system also measures the client movement (PIR sensor) and location (microwave sensor). When the PIR sensor gets down, microwave sensor presides to be on active state. Either the motion or location of the client is kept monitored and recorded in a private cloud platform. This Dual technology sensor allows the system to be in stable state. Artificial Neural Network provides higher accuracy in classifying the pulse rate on exceeding the given threshold value. Once the pulse rate is shooted above or below the given threshold limit, a notification message is given to the registered mobile number. It can be multiple mobile numbers like guardian, doctor, hospital helpline.

This work can be extended to detect few more disorder occurrences in the human body. The wearable unit may be added with sensors that detect abnormal cell growth, tuberculosis, respiration problem. Yet more efficient storage mechanisms are introduced to utilize the cloud storage. Medicine can be prescribed to avoid worsen situation at times of emergency.

Figure 2. Cardiac arrest alert system

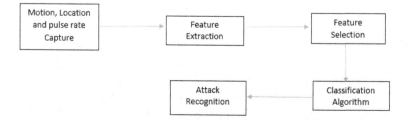

REFERENCES

Anandakumar, H., & Umamaheswari, K. (2018). Cooperative Spectrum Handovers in Cognitive Radio Networks. In Cognitive Radio, Mobile Communications and Wireless Networks (pp. 47–63). Springer. doi:10.1007/978-3-319-91002-4_3

Anandakumar, H., Umamaheswari, K., & Arulmurugan, R. (2019). A Study on Mobile IPv6 Handover in Cognitive Radio Networks. In *International Conference on Computer Networks and Communication Technologies* (pp. 399-408). Springer Singapore. doi:10.1007/978-981-10-8681-6_36

Chan, M., Campo, E., Estève, D., & Fourniols, J.-Y. (2009). Smart homes — Current features and future perspectives. *Maturitas*, *64*(2), 90–97. doi:10.1016/j.maturitas.2009.07.014 PMID:19729255

Chen, M., Li, W., Hao, Y., Qian, Y., & Humar, I. (2018). Edge cognitive computing based smart healthcare system. *Future Generation Computer Systems*, *86*, 403–411. doi:10.1016/j.future.2018.03.054

Chen, M., Yang, J., Hao, Y., Mao, S., & Hwang, K. (2017). A 5G Cognitive System for Healthcare. *Big Data and Cognitive Computing*, *1*(1), 2. doi:10.3390/bdcc1010002

Chen, T. L., King, C.-H., Thomaz, A. L., & Kemp, C. C. (2011). Touched by a robot. In *Proceedings of the 6th international conference on Human-robot interaction - HRI '11*. ACM Press. 10.1145/1957656.1957818

Chernbumroong, S., Atkins, A. S., & Yu, H. (2011). Activity classification using a single wrist-worn accelerometer. In *2011 5th International Conference on Software, Knowledge Information, Industrial Management and Applications (SKIMA) Proceedings*. IEEE. 10.1109kima.2011.6089975

Courtney, K. L. (2008). Privacy and Senior Willingness to Adopt Smart Home Information Technology in Residential Care Facilities. *Methods of Information in Medicine*. doi:10.3414/ME9104 PMID:18213432

Haldorai, A., & Ramu, A. (2018). An Intelligent-Based Wavelet Classifier for Accurate Prediction of Breast Cancer. In Intelligent Multidimensional Data and Image Processing (pp. 306–319). doi:10.4018/978-1-5225-5246-8.ch012

Patel, S., Park, H., Bonato, P., Chan, L., & Rodgers, M. (2012). A review of wearable sensors and systems with application in rehabilitation. *Journal of Neuroengineering and Rehabilitation*, *9*(1), 21. doi:10.1186/1743-0003-9-21 PMID:22520559

Pham, M., Mengistu, Y., Do, H., & Sheng, W. (2018). Delivering home healthcare through a Cloud-based Smart Home Environment (CoSHE). *Future Generation Computer Systems*, *81*, 129–140. doi:10.1016/j.future.2017.10.040

Rantz, M. J., Skubic, M., Koopman, R. J., Phillips, L., Alexander, G. L., Miller, S. J., & Guevara, R. D. (2011). Using sensor networks to detect urinary tract infections in older adults. In *2011 IEEE 13th International Conference on e-Health Networking, Applications and Services*. IEEE. 10.1109/health.2011.6026731

Rault, T., Bouabdallah, A., Challal, Y., & Marin, F. (2017). A survey of energy-efficient context recognition systems using wearable sensors for healthcare applications. *Pervasive and Mobile Computing*, *37*, 23–44. doi:10.1016/j.pmcj.2016.08.003

Revetria, R., Catania, A., Cassettari, L., Guizzi, G., Romano, E., Murino, T., & Fujita, H. (2012). Improving Healthcare Using Cognitive Computing Based Software: An Application in Emergency Situation. In Advanced Research in Applied Artificial Intelligence (pp. 477–490). Springer Berlin Heidelberg. doi:10.1007/978-3-642-31087-4_50

Röcker, C., Ziefle, M., & Holzinger, A. (2014). From Computer Innovation to Human Integration: Current Trends and Challenges for Pervasive Health Technologies. In Pervasive Health (pp. 1–17). Springer London. doi:10.1007/978-1-4471-6413-5_1

Varshney, U. (2007). Pervasive Healthcare and Wireless Health Monitoring. *Mobile Networks and Applications*, *12*(2–3), 113–127. doi:10.100711036-007-0017-1

Wilson, C., Hargreaves, T., & Hauxwell-Baldwin, R. (2014). Smart homes and their users: A systematic analysis and key challenges. *Personal and Ubiquitous Computing*, *19*(2), 463–476. doi:10.100700779-014-0813-0

Chapter 15
Cognitive Social Exchange:
A Case Study

Sampoornam K. P.
Bannariamman Institute of Technology, India

ABSTRACT

This book chapter presents the role of telecommunications network in voice and data transmission. Switching, signaling and transmission are the technologies used to carry out this process. In landline call establishment, calls are routed from subscriber handset to a remote switching unit (RSU), a main switching unit (MSU), and to the internet protocol trunk automated exchange (IPTAX). Then, it is directed to the National Internet Backbone (NIB). On the receiver side, the IPTAX receives this signal from the NIB and directs to it to the MSU and RSU, respectively. The receiver side RSU delivers the information to the destination subscriber. In order to transmit the information from one place to other, it undergoes various process like modulation, demodulation, line coding, equalization, error control, bit synchronization and multiplexing, digitizing an analog message signal, and compression. This chapter also discusses the various services provided by BSNL and agencies governing the internet. Finally, it focuses on the National Internet Backbone facility of BSNL, India.

INTRODUCTION

Telecommunication networks have been evolving in the last 150 years and would continue to evolve to provide wider services in a more convenient form in the coming century. We seem to be entering an era of 'Sophisticated' telecommunications. The term Telecommunications means long-distance connection. In 1876, Alexander Graham Bell demonstrated his own telephone set and the possibility of long-distance communication.

Initially this is suitable for both long-distance telephone network and to the television industry's worldwide network. But these two networks use very different technologies to transmit voice or video. Now, it has been expanded to data transmission due to INTERNET revolution. In 1989, the tele-density in India is only 0.6% and it is moved to 2.8% in 1999. It leads to 700 million active mobile phone connections as of October 2012 which increases the telecom penetration rate from less than 3% in 1999 to over 70% in 2012.

DOI: 10.4018/978-1-5225-7522-1.ch015

According to Global Sector Leader for Telecommunications Mr. Prashant Singhal in August 2016, out-off 2,355 megahertz (MHz) total spectrum, only 40% of the spectrum got sold. But there was no activity seen in 700MHz and 900MHz band. Telecom operators utilize this band especially for 4G services.

The ubiquitous aim of telecommunications network is to transmit user information to another user of the network. The technologies required to carry out this transmission are

1. Switching & Signaling
2. Transmission

LITERATURE SURVEY

The authors Chih-Hsiu Zeng and Kwang-Cheng Chen estimated the clustering coefficient for eqiping the network nodes along with topological cognition (Zeng & Chen, 2018). If Multiple-Input-Multiple-Output (MIMO) radar and a Full-Duplex (FD) MIMO cellular communication system with FD Base Station (BS) which simultaneously serves multiple downlink and uplink are collocated, the spectrum sharing between them is discussed by Keshav Singh et.al (2018). They designed a transceiver required for cellular BS. To maximize the radar detection probability of uplink users they developed power allocation vectors. Beibei Wang and K.J. Ray Liu (2018) surveyed about spectrum sharing of cognitive radio network and also discussed how the spectrum is allocated dynamically.

Thanh-Dat Le and Oh-Soon Shin (2016) proposed a relay selection scheme by considering the harvested energy and also analyzed the power shut down probability in wireless sensor networks. Oluwatayo Y. Kolawole et al. (2017) investigated the function of cognitive satellite terrestrial network with multibeam. The primary satellite network shares resources with a mobile terrestrial system. In a multi-hop cooperative relay network, if the distance between source and destination is too long, a topology based on clustering mechanism is proposed by Javad Zeraatkar Moghaddam et al. (2018). They analyzed the issues related to power allocation and relay selection in different secondary units of different clusters (Javad Zeraatkar Moghaddam, 2018).

Alireza Shams Shafigh (2017) proposed a Semi-Cognitive Radio Network (SCRN) paradigm which allow the primary user to use all free channels until occupying the channels which is currently used by secondary user. They adopted game-theoretic analysis and derived adaptive algorithms to control the process (Shafigh, 2017). Satyam Agarwal and Swades De (2016) proposed a model called Cognitive Multihoming (CM), in which the licensed cellular band is used by cognitive radio (CR)-enabled base station for simultaneous transmission.

SWITCHING AND SIGNALLING

In telecommunication networks connectivity is achieved through switching systems. In olden days, the switches were manual and operator oriented. Then the automatic switching systems came into existence. The primary function of a switching system is to establish an electrical path between a given inlet-outlet pair. The station which maintains this switching system is called as an Exchange. These Exchanges are operating at -48 volts. The reason for giving more negative voltage is to protect the system from lightning. The Exchanges are classified as

1. OCB
2. EWSD
3. CDOT
4. ETOP
5. AXE

Electronic Worldwide Switch Digital (EWSD) performs switching for over 160 million lines. Carriers using EWSD can provide Automatic Call Distributor services for customers with call centres.

As shown in Figure 1 switching can be mainly classified as manual and automatic switching. Automatic switching can be performed by either using electro mechanical switches or electronic switches. Step-by – step and crossbar are two types of electro mechanical switching (Thiagarajan Viswanathan, 1992).

A modern telecommunication network may be viewed as an aggregate of a large number of point–to-point electrical or optical communication systems. A medium is required to carry the signals. This medium, called the channel may be a free space, a copper cable, Optical Fiber cable or the free space in conjunction with a satellite in the case of an electrical communication system. Accordingly, the information signals should be properly processed before transmission (Anandakumar, 2014).

Signal processing requires amplification, filtering, band-limiting, multiplexing and de-multiplexing (Tarmo Anttalainen, 2003).

Connection between subscribers can be established in four ways.

1. Local call connection between two subscribers in the system
2. Outgoing call connection between a subscriber and an outgoing trunk
3. Incoming call connection between an incoming trunk and a local subscriber
4. Transit call connection between an incoming trunk and outgoing trunk

Figure 1. Classification of switching systems

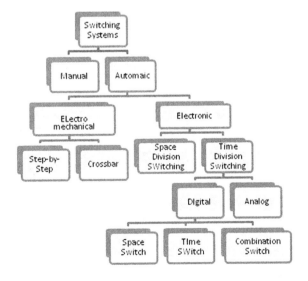

Land Line Call Establishment

The major units involved in this landline call establishment are Main Switching Unit (MSU), Remote Switching Unit (RSU), Internet Protocol Trunk Automated Exchange (IPTAX), National Internet Backbone (NIB) and International Long Distance (Haldorai & Ramu, 2018) Trunk Automated Exchange (ILDTAX). These units are connected through simple telephone network as shown in Figure 2 and the detailed connection between Telephone handset, LJU (Line Jack Unit) and RSU units are shown in the Figures 2 and 3.

The two major sections of telephone handsets are mouth piece and ear piece.

Figure 2. Simple telephone network

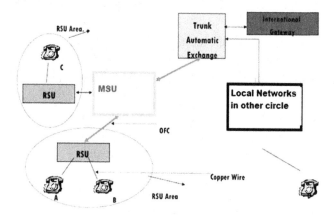

Figure 3. Connection establishments between handset and line jack unit

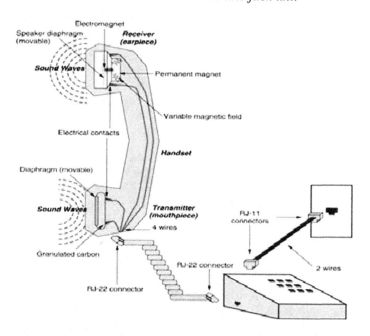

Figure 4. Connection establishments between handset and rsu

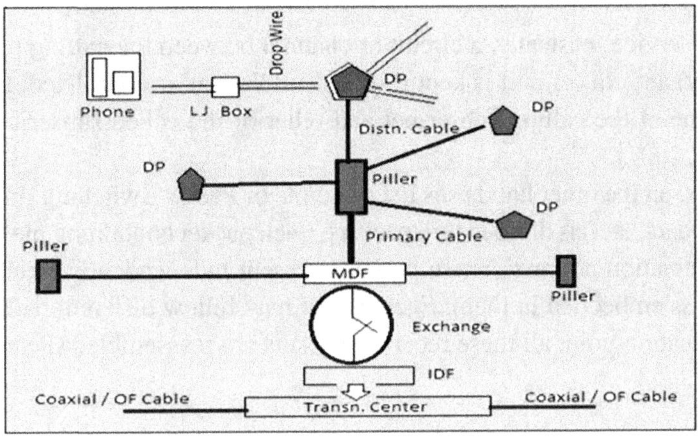

- **Mouthpiece**: It consists of Microphone sensitive to both amplitude and frequency. It converts the audio signals into corresponding electrical signal and send out into the voice network.
- **Earpiece**: It performs the reverse operation of the mouthpiece. It produces varying levels of magnetism for the varying levels of received electric signal, which in turn cause the diaphragm to move in direct proportion and produces the sound. Pulse and Dual Tone Multi-Frequency (DTMF) dialing modes are available. Telephone numbers are decided by the ITU internationally (Anandakumar & Umamaheswari, 2018).

How to Route the STD and ISD Calls?

The STD calls are routed from subscriber hand set to Remote Switching Unit (RSU) of subscriber area. From RSU, it is routed to MSU with which the subscriber's RSU is connected and from MSU to their IPTAX. Then it is directed to NIB. It directs the signals to receiver side IPTAX, MSU and to RSU. This RSU is responsible for delivering the information to the destination subscriber. In addition to the above said units, ILDTAX unit is to be required for routing ISD calls after IPTAX unit.

In India ILDTAX unit is installed only in Chennai, Cochin, Kolkata and Mumbai. But each state is equipped with one IPTAX. The connectivity between each unit is having more cut points for easy shifting and fault rectification

DATA TRANSMISSION

In telecommunication networks, Transmission (Tx) is the process of sending and propagating an analog or digital information signal over a transmission medium either wired, optical fibre or wireless. The technologies involved in this transmission are modulation, demodulation, line coding, equalization, error control, bit synchronization and multiplexing, digitizing an analog message signal, and compression (Anandakumar, Umamaheswari & Arulmurugan, 2018).

Due to the long distances involved, the bearer circuits need amplifiers or repeaters at appropriate intervals to boost the signals.

Circuit Switching and Packet Switching

In normal telephone service, basically, a circuit or channel between the calling party and Called party is set up (temporarily) and this circuit is kept reserved till the call is completed. Here two speech time slots are involved -one of the calling subscriber and other of the called subscriber. It is called circuit switching (Forouzan, 2007).

The data networks, on the other hand uses the principle of Packet Switching. In Packet switching the information (speech, data, etc.) is divided into packets. Each packet containing piece of information also bears source and destination address. These packets are sent independently through the network with the destination address embedded in them. Each packet may follow different path depending upon the network. At the destination point all these received packets are reassembled (Peterson & Davie, 2011).

BSNL Services

The service offered by BSNL can be categorised as follows

- Land line services
- Mobile communication services
- Internet services
- Data communication services

Land Line Services

In addition to telephone services, other services like Fax, ISDN (for voice, data and video) and PCO are possible by establishing a dedicated connection between each subscriber unit and its exchange. For intercom services, PBX (Private Branch Exchange) and EPBAX (Electronic Private Board Automatic Exchange) units are available (Anandakumar & Umamaheswari, 2017))

Other Land line services are

- Call waiting, call forwarding, call transfer, call hunting
- Abbreviated dialing
- Hot line
- Backup call
- Wakeup alarm
- Video calling

Mobile Communication Services

Based on the technology adopted, the mobile communication services can be classified as GSM technology and CDMA technology. Mostly all service providers are using GSM technology, but only limited operators are using CDMA technology. BSNL, Reliance Communications, Tata Indicom are some of the service providers adopting CDMA technology. Though the coverage area of GSM is only 20km when compared to 80 km coverage area of CDMA technology, the GSM is having high mobility with good quality voice. This is the reason for universal acceptability of GSM technology by all network operators.

Internet Services

As per TRAI: Broadband is "An always-on data connection that is able to support interactive services and has the capability of minimum download speed of 512 kbps".

BSNL provides the following types of connections to access Internet to customer (Figure 5). BSNL Telecom Office or Customer Care Centre of the city is responsible for providing connections to the customer of that city.

Every internet session should have an IP address allotted for the source by the ISP (Internet Service Provider). There are two methods of IP allotment. In the first method, Dynamic IP allotted and maintained till the end of the session and the same IP can be allotted for another customer for other sessions. In the second method, Static IP is allotted permanently for a customer and for all sessions the IP remains same, generally, for mail servers, web servers, etc. (Freeman, 1996)

Wired Internet Services

Dial Up

Dial up internet works under Direct Internet Access Services (DIAS) technology. The data transfer rate of this service is 56kbps. The DIAS services shall be offered to the PSTN subscribers of BSNL, on the same copper pair as is being used for their DELs (Direct Exchange Line) at present.

In ISDN single copper line can be used to carry voice, data and video. ISDN networks are most suitable for video conferencing applications (Stallings, 2010). ISDN service can be accessed in two ways. One is Basic Rate Access (2B+D) and the other is Primary Rate Access (30 B+D). In Basic Rate Access two 64 Kbps Channels are used for carrying speech & data and one Channel of 16 Kbps is used for Signaling. On the other hand, 30 Channels of 64 Kbps are used for speech & data and one Channel of 64 Kbps is used for Signaling in Primary Rate Access (O'Reilly, 1989). At present BSNL provide ISDN services to and from India to 19 countries. Various services offered by ISDN are

- Normal Telephone & Fax
- Digital Telephone -with a facility to identify the calling subscriber number and other facilities.
- Fax

Figure 5. Internet services

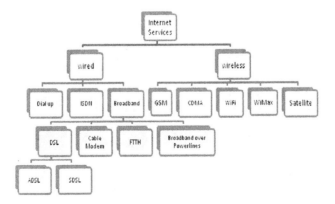

- Data Transmission at 64 Kbps with ISDN controller card
- Video Conferencing at 128 Kbps
- Video Conferencing at 384 Kbps (Possible with 3 ISDN lines)
- ATM (Asynchronous Transfer Mode) or PVC (Permanent Virtual Circuit) (Acampora, 1994)

Wired Broadband

In the broadband wired architecture core routers and aggregation switches of Tier1 are connected to Tier2 switches through gigabit Ethernet. This architecture utilizes dark fibre for providing services to several hundred service providers who provide various alternative services to end user as shown in Figure 6

Definitions framed by ITU for wired broadband

- 512 kbps minimum download speed (2 mbps in BSNL)
- Always ON
- Simultaneous Voice and Data

Broadband Services in the wire line technologies include

- Digital Subscriber Lines (DSL) on copper loop
- Optical Fiber Technologies
- Cable TV Network
- PLC (Power Line Communication)

Digital Subscriber Line (DSL)

DSL technology provides an internet access over traditional copper telephone lines, which is already installed to homes and business places. The connection established between home and telephone exchange is described in Figure 7. The data transmission speeds ranging from several hundred Kilobits per second (Kbp)s to Millions of bits per second (Mbps). The availability and speed of your DSL service may

Figure 6. Broadband connectivity in a city

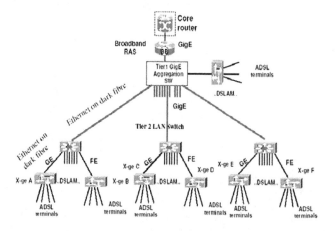

Figure 7. DSL broadband connection diagram

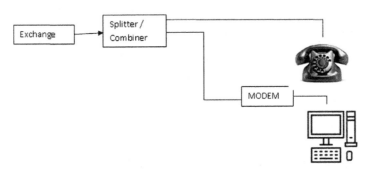

depends upon the distance from your home or business place to the closest telephone company facility. If the number of joints in the copper cable increases, the quality will decrease.

There are two types of DSL transmission technologies:

- **Asymmetrical Digital Subscriber Line (ADSL):** It provides faster speed in the downstream direction than the upstream direction. Hence it is suitable for the customers who receive a lot of data but do not send much.
- **Symmetrical Digital Subscriber Line (SDSL):** This technique is suitable for the application which require high speed in both upstream and downstream direction. Example: Video conferencing

Cable Modem

This service allows the cable TV operators to provide broadband connection. The coaxial cables are used to carry picture and sound information to subscriber TV set. In cable modems, one terminal is connected to the cable wall outlet and the other to a computer. The data can be transmitted at a rate of 1.5Mbps. Both TV signals and data can be transmitted simultaneously over the same network. By simply turning on the computer, subscriber can access the service.

FTTH

FTTH (Fibre To The Home) is the deployment of triple play services through fibre optic cable from a central office to an individual home. In India BSNL installed a technology called FTTH. The fibre connectivity having unlimited bandwidth and able to deliver the high-speed broadband from 256 Kbps to 100 Mbps.

In 1980's wideband WDM (Wave Division Multiplexing) technique occupied only two channels with 1310nm and 1550nm spacing in the fibre. In the early 1990's, each fibre accommodated 2 to 4 channels with 3 – 5 nm spacing with the help of passive WDM components. By using Densed WDM (DWDM) technique 16+ Channels with 0.8 nm spacing was accommodated in the year 1996.

As shown in Figure 8 optical termination joint box is available for the distribution and termination connection for various kinds of fibre optic systems, especially suitable for mini-network terminal distribution, in which pigtails are connected. This box can also be applied to joint fibre pigtail, protect fibre optic splices and share out the connectivity to individual customers. The cable taken out from OTJB is deployed under the ground in the depth of 165cm. These cables are inserted into the pipe coated with

Figure 8. FTTH broadband connection diagram

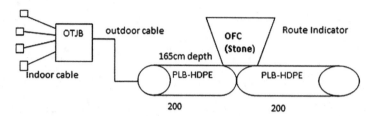

Pre-lubricated High Density Poly Ethylene (PLB-HDPE) using air blowing method. This PLB-HDPE pipe is having 200meter length and route indicator (red stone) is placed at every pipe joint. At the same time yellow stone can be used as a route indicator for every cable joint. In the river area, these cables are covered by Galvanised Iron Pipe. Electronic Route Marker is used to survey the route and find the distance. Joint man hole is provided in the path for every 2km distance.

Broadband over Power Lines (BPL)

BPL is an emerging technology that is implemented only in very few areas. This technology uses the existing low and medium voltage electric power distribution network for internet services. Subscriber can access the service using existing electrical connections and outlets.

Wireless Services

This section describes the following wireless technologies (Tomasi, 2007)

1. GSM
2. CDMA
3. Wi-Fi (Wireless Fidelity)
4. WiMax
5. Satellite Media

4GSM

The GSM standards are defined by the 3GPP collaboration and implemented in hardware and software by equipment manufacturers and mobile phone operators. In GSM mobile, the following technologies with different data transmission rate are adopted to access the internet as given in Table 1

CDMA

BSNL CDMA mobile connection provides voice, SMS, 1X data, EVDO data, STD, ISD, etc., services with good quality and strong network coverage. The data can be transmitted at a rate of 2.4Mbps.

WiMAX

WiMAX (Worldwide Interoperability for Microwave Access) technology being deployed by BSNL for the first time in India. This technology provides fixed as well as fully mobile high-speed broadband con-

Table 1. GSM mobile technologies

S.N.	Technology	Data Rate
1	GPRS	171kbps
2	EDGE	384 kbps
3	HSPN	2 mbps
4	4G - LTE	10mbps
5	5G	100mbps

nectivity along with roaming feature. 50 km radial coverage can be achieved by using this technology. As in the 4G technology, this technique also provides 10mbps speed (Dodd, 2013).

WiFi

WiFI (Wireless Fidelity) provides high speed internet access at convenient public locations. Wi-Fi technology allows the people to access very affordable high-speed Broadband services anywhere & anytime, while on the move. BSNL has provided Wi-Fi services over 600 locations with more than 2000 Hotspots in more than 114 cities. It can cover up to 100-meter distance with the speed of 1GB/1000 mbps.

Satellite

Satellite broadband operates by sending and receiving information to/from a satellite about 22,000 miles in space. Because of that height, it can provide equal quality of coverage to every home or business in its footprint.

Data Communication Services

A network can consist of two or more computers are connected together by a medium and they are sharing the resources. The resources can be Files, Printers, Fax and Hard drives. Modem is mostly used as an interface between end equipment and a transport medium. Hub and Switch are used for aggregating input packets to the next stage in the network based on MAC address. Bridge is used for regeneration of weak signals, retiming and routing decisions as per table configuration. Router is used for interconnecting two networks of same type separated apart with necessary routing tables. The router will behave as a Gateway router when a router functions as an entrance to another network / a network with different protocol (Kurose & Ross, 2012).

Agencies Governing the Internet

To have a uniform standard on internet policies and technical requirements, many committees are established as shown in the Figure 9. Broadly, one for controlling IP addresses and others for standardizing all technical parameters related to data transaction over the internet

The Internet Assigned Numbers Authority (IANA) is a non-profit private American corporation that oversees global IP address allocation, autonomous system number allocation, root zone management in the Domain Name System (DNS), media types, and other Internet Protocol-related symbols and Internet numbers.

Figure 9. Agencies governing the Internet

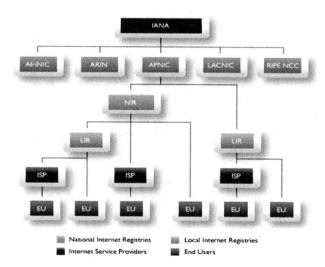

A Regional Internet Registry (RIR) is an organization that manages the allocation and registration of Internet number resources within a particular region of the world. Internet number resources include IP addresses and Autonomous System (AS) numbers.

The Regional Internet Registry system evolved over time, eventually dividing the world into five RIRs:

- African Network Information Centre (AFRINIC) for Africa
- American Registry for Internet Numbers (ARIN) for the United States, Canada, several parts of the Caribbean region, and Antarctica.
- Asia-Pacific Network Information Centre (APNIC) for Asia, Australia, New Zealand, and neighbouring countries
- Latin America and Caribbean Network Information Centre (LACNIC) for Latin America and parts of the Caribbean region
- Réseaux IP Europeans Network Coordination Centre (RIPE NCC) for Europe, Russia, the Middle East, and Central Asia

NATIONAL INTERNET BACKBONE

The National Internet Backbone (NIB) has been developed to provide Nation-wide connectivity to ISPs as well as customers. NIB consists of 550 nodes available at almost all the district headquarters. NIB is connected to VSNL Gateways at 6 locations i.e. Mumbai, Kolkata, New Delhi, Bangalore, Chennai and Ernakulam. Routers, Remote Access server, LAN Switch and Server /Storage are the major equipments available with the NIB. Figure 10 shows the location of core routers in different part of our country. Routers are located in such a way that any customer can access the service from any part of the nation (Wu, 2010).

For international connection Level 1 Trunk Automatic Exchange (L1 TAX) is available in state headquarters. In India, twenty-four such L1TAX exchanges are available. Similarly, Level II type exchanges are located in every district headquarters. In order to provide successful connectivity, 306 level II type exchanges and 4000 to 5000 local exchanges are functioning in India.

NIB has been grouped into following three major projects

Project 1: Multiprotocol Label Switching (MPLS) based IP Network infrastructure covering 71 cities along with associated NMS, PMS, Firewall and caching platforms.

Project 2.1: Access Gateway platform using Dialup comprising of narrow band RAS and DSL equipment.

Project 2.2: Access Gateway platform comprising of Broadband RAS and DSL equipment.

Project 3: Messaging, Storage platform, Provisioning, Billing, Customer care and Enterprise Management System.

NIB – II Broadband DSL can be deployed using DSLAM (Digital Subscriber Line Access Multiplexer), MDF and switches as shown in Figure 11. DSLAM is used to split voice and data. Voice directed through the normal line over exchange. Data is aggregated and up linked through Ethernet Port. Switches aggregate multiple DSLAM and provide a common uplink to the core (Robertazzi, 1993). A Main Distribution Frame (MDF) is used to connect the equipment in the system. An uplink of DSLAM is on Gigabit Ethernet (GE)/Fast Ethernet (FE).

Figure 10. NIB 2 – IP MPLS Core Backbone locations (courtesy: BSNL, India)

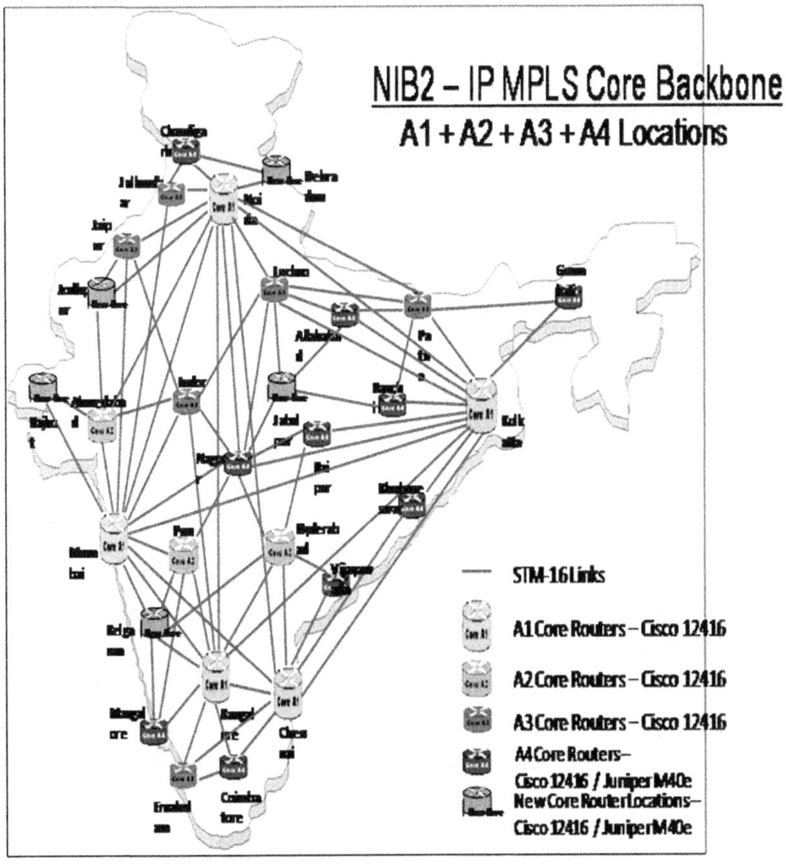

Figure 11. NIB-II Broadband DSL Deployment (courtesy: BSNL, India)

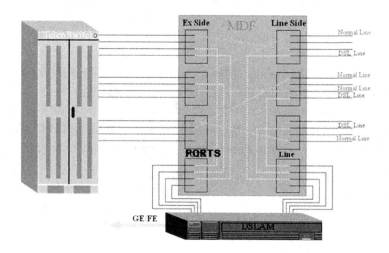

The core router CISCO 12000 series is connected to NOC (Network Operation Centre) at Bangalore, Chennai and Ernakulum on STM 16 backbone. For emergency services Disaster Recovery NOC is deployed at Pune. In addition to that, NOC has DNS Server, Mail Server & Billing server etc.

Other Services Provided By NIB: Internet Leased Lines

- Internet access can be given on leased line also starting from 64kbps up to 100Mbps
- 64kbps to 2Mbps - with copper in last mile and with necessary line drivers / modems
- 2Mbps and above – with fiber / TX systems in last mile with necessary interface devices
- Leased line is given to 8 static IPs at free of cost. More than 8 IPs also given free, based on customer's network requirements
- MPLS VPN, VPN o BB, FTTH-GPON, and VVoBB (De Ghein, 2006)
- Wi-Max, web hosting, web co-location services are provided
- Associated services with broadband on revenue sharing basis with content providers – games on demand, web conferencing, e-learning
- IPTV (TV channels, VOD, MOD, FM radio)

SUMMARY

In a telecommunication system, switching provides an electrical path between sending and receiving device. In order to protect the system from lightening, exchanges are operating with -48 volts. Before transmission, signal should undergo amplification, filtering, band-limiting, and multiplexing. Circuit Switching and Packet Switching techniques are used for transmitting voice and data respectively. This chapter described about land line call establishment procedure. Several committees are formed to standardize the internet policies. Internet Service Providers and Customers will get nationwide internet connectivity through National Internet Backbone (NIB). In India NIB is connected to VSNL Gateways at 6 locations.

REFERENCES

Acampora, A. S. (1994). *An introduction to broadband networks: LANs, MANs, ATM, B-ISDN, and optical networks for integrated multimedia telecommunications.* Plenum Press New York.

Agarwal, S., & De, S. (2016). Cognitive multihoming system for energy and cost aware video transmission. In IEEE Transactions on Cognitive Communications and Networking (pp. 316-329). IEEE.

Anandakumar. (2014, May). Energy Efficient Network Selection Using 802.16g Based GSM Technology. *Journal of Computational Science, 10*(5), 745–754. doi:10.3844/jcssp.2014.745.754

Anandakumar, H., & Umamaheswari, K. (2017). A bio-inspired swarm intelligence technique for social aware cognitive radio handovers. *Computers & Electrical Engineering,* (Sep). doi:10.1016/j.compeleceng.2017.09.016

Anandakumar, H., & Umamaheswari, K. (2018). Cooperative Spectrum Handovers in Cognitive Radio Networks. In Cognitive Radio, Mobile Communications and Wireless Networks (pp. 47–63). Springer. doi:10.1007/978-3-319-91002-4_3

Anandakumar, H., Umamaheswari, K., & Arulmurugan, R. (2019). A Study on Mobile IPv6 Handover in Cognitive Radio Networks. In *International Conference on Computer Networks and Communication Technologies* (pp. 399-408). Springer Singapore. doi:10.1007/978-981-10-8681-6_36

Anttalainen, T. (2003). *Introduction to Telecommunications Network Engineering.* Artech House.

De Ghein, L. (2006). *MPLS Fundamentals.* Cisco Press.

Dodd, A. Z. (2013). *The Essential Guide to Telecommunications* (5th ed.). Pearson India Publications.

Forouzan, B. A. (2007). *Data Communications and* (4th ed.). McGraw Hill Publication.

Freeman, R. L. (1996). *Telecommunication System Engineering.* Wiley-Interscience Publications.

Haldorai, A., & Ramu, A. (2018). An intelligent-based wavelet classifier for accurate prediction of breast cancer. In Intelligent Multidimensional Data and Image Processing (pp. 306-319). doi:10.4018/978-1-5225-5246-8.ch012

Kolawole, O. Y., Vuppala, S., Sellathurai, M., & Ratnarajah, T. (2017). *On the performance of cognitive satellite-terrestrial networks.* IEEE Transactions on Cognitive Communications and Networking.

Kurose, J., & Ross, K. (2012). *Computer Networking: A Top-Down Approach* (5th ed.). Pearson India Publications.

Le, T.-D., & Shin, O.-S. (2016). Optimal relaying scheme with energy harvesting in a cognitive wireless sensor network. In *2016 International Conference on Information and Communication Technology Convergence (ICTC)* (pp. 82-84).

Moghaddam, J. Z., Usman, M., & Granelli, F. (2018). *A device-to-device communication based disaster response network.* IEEE Transactions on Cognitive Communications and Networking.

O'Reilly, J. J. (1989). *Telecommunication Principles.* Van Nostrand Reinhold Publications.

Osborne, E., & Simha, A. (2002). *Traffic Engineering with MPLS*. Cisco Press.

Peterson, L., & Davie, B. (2011). *Computer Networks A Systems Approach* (5th ed.). Morgan Kaufmann Publishers.

Robertazzi, T. G. (1993). *Broadband ISDN, And MAN Technology*. Wiley-IEEE Press.

Shafigh, A. S., Mertikopoulos, P., Glisic, S., & Michae, Y. (2017). Semi-cognitive radio networks: A novel dynamic spectrum sharing mechanism. *IEEE Transactions on Cognitive Communications and Networking*, *3*(1), 97–111.

Singh, K., Biswas, S., Ratnarajah, T., & Khan, F. A. (2018). *Transceiver design and power allocation for full-duplex MIMO communication systems with spectrum sharing radar*. IEEE Transactions on Cognitive Communications and Networking.

Stalling, W. (2010). *ISDN and Broadband ISDN with Frame Relay and ATM. Knopf Doubleday Publishing Group*.

Tomasi, W. (2007). *Introduction to Data communication and Networking*. Pearson India Publications.

Viswanathan, T. (1992). *Telecommunication Switching Systems and Networks*. New Delhi: Prentice Hall of India Private Limited.

Wang, B., & Liu, K. J. R. (2011). Advances in cognitive radio networks: A survey. *IEEE Journal of Selected Topics in Signal Processing*, *5*(1), 5–23.

Wu, T. (2010). *The Master Switch: The Rise and Fall of Information Empires*. New York: Knopf.

Zeng, C. H., & Chen, K. C. (2018). *Social network analysis facilitates cognition in large wireless networks: clustering coefficient aided geographical routing*. IEEE Transactions on Cognitive Communications and Networking.

Compilation of References

Abbas, A. T., Pimenov, D. Y., Erdakov, I. N., Taha, M. A., Soliman, M. S., & El Rayes, M. M. (2018). ANN surface roughness optimization of AZ61 magnesium alloy finish turning: Minimum machining times at prime machining costs. *Materials (Basel)*, *11*(5), 808. doi:10.3390/ma11050808 PMID:29772670

Abbas, N., Nasser, Y., & El Ahmad, K. (2015). Recent advances on artificial intelligence and learning techniques in cognitive radio networks. *EURASIP Journal on Wireless Communications and Networking*, *174*(1). doi:10.118613638-015-0381-7

Acampora, A. S. (1994). *An introduction to broadband networks: LANs, MANs, ATM, B-ISDN, and optical networks for integrated multimedia telecommunications*. Plenum Press New York.

Adedoyin-Olowe, M., Gaber, M., & Stahl, F. (2013). A Methodology for Temporal Analysis of Evolving Concepts in Twitter. In *Proceedings of the 2013 ICAISC, International Conference on Artificial Intelligence and Soft Computing*. 10.1007/978-3-642-38610-7_13

Adedoyin-Olowe, M., Gaber, M., & Stahl, F. (2013). A Survey of Data Mining Techniques for Social Media Analysis. *Journal of Data Mining and Digital Humanities*, *9*(2).

Adomavicius, G., & Tuzhilin, A. (2005). Toward the next generation of recommender systems: A survey of the state-of-the-art and possible extensions. *IEEE Transactions on* Knowledge and Data Engineering, *17*(6), 734–749.

Agarwal, S., & De, S. (2016). Cognitive multihoming system for energy and cost aware video transmission. In IEEE Transactions on Cognitive Communications and Networking (pp. 316-329). IEEE.

Aggarwal, C. (2011). *An introduction to social network data analytics*. Springer. doi:10.1007/978-1-4419-8462-3

Aggarwal, N., & Liu, H. (2008). Blogosphere: Research issues, tools, applications. *SIGKDD Explorations*, *10*(1), 20. doi:10.1145/1412734.1412737

Agosta, G., Barenghi, A., Pelosi, G., & Scandale, M. (2015). Trace-based schedulability analysis to enhance passive side-channel attack resilience of embedded software. *Information Processing Letters*, *115*(2), 292–297. doi:10.1016/j.ipl.2014.09.030

Agrawal, A., Rajput, R. S., & Shrivastava, N. (2017). Operation sequencing and machining parameter selection in CAPP for cylindrical part using hybrid feature based genetic algorithm and expert system. *International Research Journal of Engineering and Technology*, *4*(6), 858–863.

Ahire, J. B. (2018, January 8). Cognitive computing: everything you should know. *Buzzrobot*. Retrieved from https://buzzrobot.com/cognitive-computing-everything-you-should-know-8896590bb1

Ahmed, M.N., Toor, A.S., Neil, K. & Friedland, D (2017, May 17). Cognitive Computing and the Future of Health Care, The cognitive power of IBM Watson has the potential to transform global personalized medicine. *IEEE Pulse*. Retrieved from https://pulse.embs.org/may-2017/cognitive-computing-and-the-future-of-health-care/

Aiello, L. M., Petkos, G., Martin, C., Corney, D., Papadopoulos, S., Skraba, R., ... Jaimes, A. (2013). Sensing trending topics in Twitter. *IEEE Transactions on Multimedia*, *15*(6), 1268–1282.

Al Hasan, A. S., Hossain, M. S., & Atiquzzaman, M. (2016, September). Security threats in vehicular ad hoc networks. In *2016 International Conference on Advances in Computing, Communications and Informatics (ICACCI)* (pp. 404-411). IEEE.

Al Hazza, M. H., & Adesta, E. Y. (2013). Investigation of the effect of cutting speed on the surface roughness parameters in CNC end milling using artificial neural network. *IOP Conference Series. Materials Science and Engineering*, *53*(1), 012089. doi:10.1088/1757-899X/53/1/012089

Alakali, T. T., Sambe, I. I., Adekole, F. E., & Tarnongo, M. O. (2013). The impact of social Media on information dissemination and challenges of national insecurity in Nigeria: An overview of BokoHaram Insurgence in Northern Nigeria. *Journal of Management and Entrepreneurial Development*, *3*(2), 1–11.

Alharthi, N. H., Bingol, S., Abbas, A. T., Ragab, A. E., El-Danaf, E. A., & Alharbi, H. F. (2017). Optimizing Cutting Conditions and Prediction of Surface Roughness in Face Milling of AZ61 Using Regression Analysis and Artificial Neural Network. *Advances in Materials Science and Engineering*.

Al-Sahib, N. K. A., & Abdulrazzaq, H. F. (2014). Selection of optimum cutting speed in end milling process using fuzzy logic. *Innovative Systems Design and Engineering*, *5*(2), 14–30.

Al-Sultan, S., Al-Doori, M. M., Al-Bayatti, A. H., & Zedan, H. (2014). A comprehensive survey on vehicular ad hoc network. *Journal of Network and Computer Applications*, *37*, 380–392. doi:10.1016/j.jnca.2013.02.036

American Psychiatric Association. (2000). Diagnostic and Statistical Manual of Mental Disorders (4th ed.). American Psychiatric Association.

An, N. T. T., & Hagiwara, M. (2014). Adjective-Based Estimation of Short Sentence's Impression. In *Proceedings of the 5th Kanesi Engineering and Emotion Research International Conference (KEER2014)*, Sweden.

Anandakumar, H., & Umamaheswari, K. (2014, May). Energy Efficient Network Selection Using 802.16g Based GSM Technology. *Journal of Computational Science*, *10*(5), 745–754. doi:10.3844/jcssp.2014.745.754

Anandakumar, H., & Umamaheswari, K. (2017). An Efficient Optimized Handover in Cognitive Radio Networks using Cooperative Spectrum Sensing. *Intelligent Automation & Soft Computing*, 1–8. doi:10.1080/10798587.2017.1364931

Anandakumar, H., & Umamaheswari, K. (2018). Cooperative Spectrum Handovers in Cognitive Radio Networks. In Cognitive Radio, Mobile Communications and Wireless Networks (pp. 47–63). Springer. doi:10.1007/978-3-319-91002-4_3

Anandakumar, H., Umamaheswari, K., & Arulmurugan, R. (2019). A Study on Mobile IPv6 Handover in Cognitive Radio Networks. In *International Conference on Computer Networks and Communication Technologies* (pp. 399-408). Springer Singapore. doi:10.1007/978-981-10-8681-6_36

Anandakumar, H., & Umamaheswari, K. (2017). A bio-inspired swarm intelligence technique for social aware cognitive radio handovers. *Computers & Electrical Engineering*, (Sep). doi:10.1016/j.compeleceng.2017.09.016

Anandakumar, H., & Umamaheswari, K. (2017). Supervised machine learning techniques in cognitive radio networks during cooperative spectrum handovers. *Cluster Computing*, *20*(2), 1505–1515. doi:10.100710586-017-0798-3

Andréia da Silva, M., Antonio, A. F. G., Pereira de Souza, A., & Lopes de Souza, C. Jr. (2004). Comparison of similarity coefficients used for cluster analysis with dominant markers in maize (Zea maysL). *Genetics and Molecular Biology*, *27*(1), 83–91. doi:10.1590/S1415-47572004000100014

Anttalainen, T. (2003). *Introduction to Telecommunications Network Engineering*. Artech House.

Anurekha, G., & Geetha, P. (2017). Performance Analysis of Supervised Approaches for Autism Spectrum Disorder Detection. *International Journal of Trend in Research and Development*.

Anwar, S., Inayat, Z., Zolkipli, M. F., Zain, J. M., Gani, A., Anuar, N. B., ... Chang, V. (2017). Cross-VM cache-based side channel attacks and proposed prevention mechanisms: A survey. *Journal of Network and Computer Applications*, *93*, 259–279. doi:10.1016/j.jnca.2017.06.001

Apache. (2017). Retrieved from http://apache.org

Arigela, A. K., & Bansal, V. (2014). *Value decomposition and dimension selection in multi-dimensional datasets using map-reduce operation.* Paper presented at the International Conference on Recent Trends in Computer Science Engineering (ICRTCSE'14).

Ash, M. (2016, December 9). Security intelligence, augmented intelligence: making the case for cognitive security. *Security Intelligence.* Retrieved from https://securityintelligence.com/augmented-intelligence-making-the-case-for-cognitive-security/

Asur, S., & Huberman, B. (2010). Predicting the future with social network. In *2010 IEEE/WIC/ACM International Conference on Web Intelligence and Intelligent Agent Technology (WI-IAT)* (Vol. 1). IEEE.

Au Yeung, C. M., & Iwata, T. (2011). Strength of social influence in trust networks in product review sites. In *Proceedings of the fourth ACM international conference on Web search and data mining* (pp. 495-504). ACM. 10.1145/1935826.1935899

Babu, K. A., Kumar, G. V., & Venkataramaiah, P. (2015). Prediction of surface roughness in drilling of Al 7075/10%-SiCp composite under MQL condition using fuzzy logic. *Indian Journal of Science and Technology*, *8*(12).

Backstrom, L., Dwork, C., & Kleinberg, J. (2007). Wherefore Art Thou r3579x?: Anonymized Social Networks, Hidden Patterns, and Structural Steganography. In *Proc. 16th Int'l Conf. World Wide Web (WWW '07)* (pp. 181-190). 10.1145/1242572.1242598

Bai, A., & Hammer, H. (2014). Constructing sentiment lexicons in Norwegian from a large text corpus. *2014 IEEE 17th International Conference on Computational Science and Engineering*.

Bakshy, E., Hofman, J. M., Mason, W. A., & Watts, D. J. (2011). Identifying influencers on twitter. In *Fourth ACM International Conference on Web Search and Data Mining (WSDM)*.

Balachander, J., & Ramanujam, E. (2017). Rule based Medical Content Classification for Secure Remote Health Monitoring. *International Journal of Computers and Applications*, *165*(4).

Bannister, K. (2015, January 26). Understanding sentiment analysis: what it is & why it's used. *Brand Watch.* Retrieved from https://www.brandwatch.com/blog/understanding-sentiment-analysis/

Baron-Cohen, S. E., Tager-Flusberg, H. E., & Cohen, D. J. (1994). Understanding other minds: Perspectives from autism. In *Workshop in Seattle, April 1991.* Oxford University Press.

Baron-Cohen, S., Tager-Flusberg, H., & Lombardo, M. (Eds.). (2013). *Understanding other minds: Perspectives from developmental social neuroscience.* Oxford University Press. doi:10.1093/acprof:oso/9780199692972.001.0001

Barzani, M. M., Zalnezhad, E., Sarhan, A. A., Farahany, S., & Ramesh, S. (2015). Fuzzy logic based model for predicting surface roughness of machined Al–Si–Cu–Fe die casting alloy using different additives-turning. *Measurement, 61*, 150–161. doi:10.1016/j.measurement.2014.10.003

Baziz, M., Boughanem, M., & Traboulsi, S. (2005). A concept-based approach for indexing documents in IR. In INFORSID (pp. 489-504).

Becker, H., Chen, F., Iter, D., Naaman, M., & Gravano, L. (2011). *Automatic Identification and Presentation of Twitter Content for Planned Events.*

Becker, H., Iter, D., Naaman, M., & Gravano, L. (2012). Identifying content for planned events across social media sites. In *Proceedings of the fifth ACM international conference on Web search and data mining* (pp. 533-542). ACM. 10.1145/2124295.2124360

Becker, H., Naaman, M., & Gravano, L. (2011). Beyond trending topics: Real-world event identification on Twitter. *ICWSM, 11*, 438–441.

Beig, E. F. G. M. (2015). Data Mining Techniques for Web Mining: A Review. *Applied mathematics in Engineering Management and Technology, 3*(5), 81–90.

Bekkerman, R., & McCallum, A. (2005). Disambiguating web appearances of people in a social network. In *Proceedings of the 14th international conference on World Wide Web* (pp. 463-470). ACM. 10.1145/1060745.1060813

Bellaachia, A., & Guven, E. (2006). Predicting breast cancer survivability using data mining techniques. *Age, 58*(13), 10–110.

Bethard, S., Yu, H., Thornton, A., & Hatzivassiloglou, V. Jurafsky. D. (2004). Automatic Extraction of Opinion Propositions and their Holders. In *Proceedings of the AAAI Spring Symposium on Exploring Attitude and Affect in Text.*

Bhatia, N., & Rana, M. C. (2015). Deep Learning Techniques and its Various Algorithms and Techniques. *International Journal of Engineering Innovation & Research, 4*(5).

Biglieri, E., Goldsmith, A. J., Greenstein, L. J., Mandayam, N. B., & Poor, H. V. (2013). *Principles of cognitive radio.* Cambridge University Press.

Bittern, R., Cuschieri, A., Dolgobrodov, S. G., Marshall, R., & Moore, P. (2007) A. artificial neural networks in cancer management. *e-Science All Hands Meeting, 19*, 251-263.

Boiy, E., & Moens, M. (2009). A Machine Learning Approach to Sentiment Analysis in Multilingual Web Texts. *Information Retrieval, 12*(5), 526–558. doi:10.100710791-008-9070-z

Bollen, J., Mao, H., & Pepe, A. (2011). *Modelling public mood and emotion: Twitter sentiment and socio-economic phenomena.*

Bone, D., Bishop, S. L., Black, M. P., Goodwin, M. S., Lord, C., & Narayanan, S. S. (2016). Use of machine learning to improve autism screening and diagnostic instruments: Effectiveness, efficiency, and multi-instrument fusion. *Journal of Child Psychology and Psychiatry, and Allied Disciplines, 57*(8), 927–937. doi:10.1111/jcpp.12559 PMID:27090613

Borgatti, S. P. (2009). 2-Mode concepts in social network analysis. In Encyclopedia of Complexity and System Science (pp. 8279-8291). doi:10.1007/978-0-387-30440-3_491

Borgatti, S. P., & Everett, M. G. (2006). A graph-theoretic perspective on centrality. *Social Networks, 28*, 466–484.

Bosl, W. J., Tager-Flusberg, H., & Nelson, C. A. (2018). EEG analytics for early detection of autism spectrum disorder: A data-driven approach. *Scientific Reports, 8*(1), 6828. doi:10.103841598-018-24318-x PMID:29717196

Bouabdallah, F., Bouabdallah, N., & Boutaba, R. (2009). On balancing energy consumption in wireless sensor networks. *IEEE Transactions on Vehicular Technology, 58*(6), 2909–2924. doi:10.1109/TVT.2008.2008715

Bozdemir, M. (2018). Prediction of surface roughness considering cutting parameters and humidity condition in end milling of polyamide materials. *Computational Intelligence and Neuroscience,* 1–7. doi:10.1155/2018/5850432 PMID:30050565

Braden, R., Clark, D. & Shenker, S. (1994). Integrated Services in the Internet Architecture: An Overview.

Brooke, J., Tofiloski, M., & Taboada, M. (2009). Cross-Linguistic Sentiment Analysis: From English to Spanish. In *International Conference RANLP 2009,* Borovets, Bulgaria (pp. 50-54).

Burke, R. (2002). Hybrid recommender systems: Survey and experiments. *User Modeling and User-Adapted Interaction, 12*(4), 331–370. doi:10.1023/A:1021240730564

Burre, P. (2018, February 28). Power up IT operations with Cognitive Technologies. Retrieved from https://blog.csscorp.com/power-up-it-operations-with-cognitive-technologies

Burt, R. S. (2005). *Brokerage and closure: An introduction to social capital.* Oxford University Press.

Cai, J., Liu, Y., & Yin, J. (2007). An improved semantic smoothing model for model-based document clustering. In *Proceedings of the Eighth ACIS International Conference on Software Engineering, Artificial Intelligence, Networking, and Parallel Distributed Computing* (Vol. 3, pp. 670–675).

Cambridge English Dictionary. (2017). Retrieved from http://dictionary.cambridge.org/

Campbell, J. Y., & Shiller, R. J. (2005). *Valuation Ratios and the Long Run Stock Market Outlook: An Update.*

Cao, D. S., Xu, Q. S., Liang, Y. Z., Chen, X., & Li, H. D. (2010). Automatic feature subset selection for decision tree-based ensemble methods in the prediction of bioactivity. *Chemometrics and Intelligent Laboratory Systems, 103*(2), 129–136. doi:10.1016/j.chemolab.2010.06.008

Carafano, J. (2007, July 5). Future computing and cutting edge national security. Heritage. Retrieved from https://www.heritage.org/defense/report/future-computing-and-cutting-edge-national-security

Carrera-Trejo, V., Sidorov, G., Miranda-Jiménez, S., Ibarra, M. M., & Cadena Martínez, R. (2015). Latent Dirichlet Allocation complement in the vector space model for Multi-Label Text Classification. *International Journal of Combinatorial Optimization Problems and Informatics, 6*(1), 7–19.

Castellanos, M., Dayal, M., Hsu, M., Ghosh, R., & Dekhil, M. (2011). LCI: A Social Channel Analysis Platform for Live Customer Intelligence. In *Proceedings of the 2011 international Conference on Management of Data.*

Celler, B., De Chazal, P., & Lovell, N. (1997). A comparison of expert systems for the automated interpretation of the ECG: regulatory implications of the use of neural networks. In *APAMI-HIC 1997: Managing Information for Better Health Outcomes in Australia and the Asia Pacific Region: 11 to 13 August 1997, Asia Pacific Association of Medical Informatics, HISA: Conference Proceedings* (p. 492). Health Informatics Society of Australia.

Chandrasekaran, M., Muralidhar, M., Krishna, C. M., & Dixit, U. S. (2010). Application of soft computing techniques in machining performance prediction and optimization: A literature review. *International Journal of Advanced Manufacturing Technology, 46*(5-8), 445–464. doi:10.100700170-009-2104-x

Chan, M., Campo, E., Estève, D., & Fourniols, J.-Y. (2009). Smart homes — Current features and future perspectives. *Maturitas, 64*(2), 90–97. doi:10.1016/j.maturitas.2009.07.014 PMID:19729255

Chaskar, P. R., Lad, A. S., Mane, J. K., Sangre, A., & Kirkire, M. S. (2017). Optimization of CNC Milling Parameters Using "Artificial Neural Network." *Imperial Journal of Interdisciplinary Research, 3*(2).

Chaurasia, V., & Pal, S. (2013). Early prediction of heart diseases using data mining techniques. *Caribbean Journal of Science and Technology, 1*, 208–217.

Chaurasia, V., & Pal, S. (2014). Data mining approach to detect heart diseases. *International Journal of Advanced Computer Science and Information Technology., 2*(4), 56–66.

Chaurasia, V., & Pal, S. (2017). Data mining techniques: To predict and resolve breast cancer survivability. *International Journal of Computer Science and Mobile Computing., 3*(1), 10–22.

Chelmis, C. Prasanna. VK. (2011). Social networking analysis: A state of the art and the effect of semantics. In *2011 IEEE third international conference on Privacy, security, risk and trust (PASSAT), and 2011 IEEE third international conference on social computing (Socialcom)*. IEEE.

Chen, S., Wang, R., Wang, X., & Zhang, K. (2010, May). Side-channel leaks in web applications: A reality today, a challenge tomorrow. In *2010 IEEE Symposium on Security and Privacy (SP)* (pp. 191-206). IEEE.

Chen, T. L., King, C.-H., Thomaz, A. L., & Kemp, C. C. (2011). Touched by a robot. In *Proceedings of the 6th international conference on Human-robot interaction - HRI '11*. ACM Press. 10.1145/1957656.1957818

Chenji, H., Stewart, G., Wu, Z., Javaid, A., Devabhaktuni, V., Bhasin, K., & Wang, B. (2016). An architecture concept for cognitive space communication networks. In *34th AIAA International Communications Satellite Systems Conference* (p. 5728).

Chen, M. S., Han, J., & Yu, P. S. (1996). Data mining: An overview from a database perspective. *IEEE Transactions on Knowledge and Data Engineering, 8*(6), 866–883. doi:10.1109/69.553155

Chen, M., Li, W., Hao, Y., Qian, Y., & Humar, I. (2018). Edge cognitive computing based smart healthcare system. *Future Generation Computer Systems, 86*, 403–411. doi:10.1016/j.future.2018.03.054

Chen, M., Yang, J., Hao, Y., Mao, S., & Hwang, K. (2017). A 5G Cognitive System for Healthcare. *Big Data and Cognitive Computing, 1*(1), 2. doi:10.3390/bdcc1010002

Chen, Y., & Lee, K. (2011). *User-centred sentiment analysis on customer product review. World Applied Sciences Journal, 12*, 32-38.

Chen, Z. S., Kalashnikov, D. V., & Mehrotra, S. (2009). Exploiting context analysis for combining multiple entity resolution systems. In *Proceedings of the 2009 ACM International Conference on Management of Data (SIGMOD'09)*.

Chernbumroong, S., Atkins, A. S., & Yu, H. (2011). Activity classification using a single wrist-worn accelerometer. In *2011 5th International Conference on Software, Knowledge Information, Industrial Management and Applications (SKIMA) Proceedings*. IEEE. 10.1109kima.2011.6089975

Chim, H., & Deng, X. (2008). Efficient phrase-based document similarity for clustering. *IEEE Transactions on Knowledge and Data Engineering, 20*(9), 1217–1229. doi:10.1109/TKDE.2008.50

Choi, S.S., Cha, S-H & Tappert, C.C. (2010). A Survey Of Binary Similarity And Distance Measures. *Systemics, Cybernetics And Informatics, 8*(1).

Chou, W. Y. S., Hunt, Y. M., Beckjord, E. B., Moser, R. P., & Hesse, B. W. (2009). Social media use in the United States: Implications for health communication. *Journal of Medical Internet Research, 11*(4), e48. doi:10.2196/jmir.1249 PMID:19945947

Cica, D., Sredanovic, B., Borojevic, S., & Kramar, D. (2017). An Integration of Bio-inspired Algorithms and Fuzzy Logic for Tool Wear Estimation in Hard Turning. In *International Conference on Advanced Manufacturing Engineering and Technologies* (pp. 1-12). Cham: Springer.

Cilio, W., Linder, M., Porter, C., Di, J., Thompson, D. R., & Smith, S. C. (2013). Mitigating power-and timing-based side-channel attacks using dual-spacer dual-rail delay-insensitive asynchronous logic. *Microelectronics Journal, 44*(3), 258–269. doi:10.1016/j.mejo.2012.12.001

Cirak, B. (2017). Mathematically Modeling and Optimization by Artificial Neural Network of Surface Roughness in CNC Milling–A Case Study. *World Wide Journal of Multidisciplinary Research and Development, 3*(8), 299–307.

Clifton, C. (2000). Using Sample Size to Limit Exposure to Data Mining. J. Computer Security, 8, 281-307.

Cloudera. (2017). Retrieved from http://www.cloudera.com

Conover, M. D., Gonçalves, B., Ratkiewicz, J., Flammini, A., & Menczer, F. (2011, October). Predicting the political alignment of twitter users. In *2011 IEEE Third International Conference on Privacy, Security, Risk and Trust (PASSAT) and 2011 IEEE Third International Conference on Social Computing (SocialCom)* (pp. 192-199). IEEE.

Cordeiro, M. (2012). Twitter event detection: Combining wavelet analysis and topic inference summarization. In *Doctoral Symposium on Informatics Engineering, DSIE.*

Cortizo, J., Carrero, F., Gomez, J., Monsalve, B., & Puertas, E. (2009). Introduction to Mining SM. In *Proceedings of the 1st International Workshop on Mining SM* (pp. 1 – 3).

Courtney, K. L. (2008). Privacy and Senior Willingness to Adopt Smart Home Information Technology in Residential Care Facilities. *Methods of Information in Medicine.* doi:10.3414/ME9104 PMID:18213432

D'addona, D. M., & Teti, R. (2013). Genetic algorithm-based optimization of cutting parameters in turning processes. *Procedia CIRP, 7*, 323–328. doi:10.1016/j.procir.2013.05.055

Daquilla. M & Shirer. M (2017, April 3). Worldwide spending on cognitive and artificial intelligence systems forecast to reach $12.5 billion this year, according to new idc spending guide. *IDC.* Retrieved from https://www.idc.com/getdoc.jsp?containerId=prUS42439617

Das, B., Roy, S., Rai, R. N., & Saha, S. C. (2016). Application of grey fuzzy logic for the optimization of CNC milling parameters for Al–4.5% Cu–TiC MMCs with multi-performance characteristics. *Engineering Science and Technology, an International Journal, 19*(2), 857-865.

Das, B., Roy, S., Rai, R. N., & Saha, S. C. (2014). Surface Roughness of Al-5Cu Alloy using a Taguchi-Fuzzy Based Approach. *Journal of Engineering Science & Technology Review, 7*(2).

Das, S., & Chen, M. (2001). Yahoo! for Amazon: Extracting M arket Sentiment from Stock Message Boards. In *Proceedings of the Asia Pacific Finance Association Annual Conference (APFA).*

Dat, N. D., Phu, V. N., Tran, V. T. N., Chau, V. T. N., & Nguyen, T. A. (2017). STING Algorithm used English Sentiment Classification in A Parallel Environment. *International Journal of Pattern Recognition and Artificial Intelligence, 31*(7). doi:10.1142/0218001417500215

Dave, K. L., & Pennock, D. (2003). Mining the peanut gallery: Opinion Extraction and Semantic Classification of Product Re views. In *Proceedings of WWW* (pp. 519-528).

De Ghein, L. (2006). *MPLS Fundamentals.* Cisco Press.

De Lathauwer, L., De Moor, B., & Vandewalle, J. (2000). A Multilinear Singular Value Decomposition. *SIAM Journal on Matrix Analysis and Applications*, *21*(4), 1253–1278. doi:10.1137/S0895479896305696

Deb, B., Bhatnagar, S., & Nath, B. (2003). ReInForm: Reliable Information Forwarding Using Multiple Paths in Sensor Networks. In *Proc. IEEE 28th Ann. International Conference Local Computer Networks*.

Dell. (n.d.). Data mining techniques. Retrieved from http://documents.software.dell.com/Statistics/Textbook/Data-Mining-Techniques

Deng, Z., Zhang, H., Fu, Y., Wan, L., & Lv, L. (2018). Research on intelligent expert system of green cutting process and its application. *Journal of Cleaner Production*, *185*, 904–911. doi:10.1016/j.jclepro.2018.02.246

Depolli, M., Konc, J., Rozman, K., Trobec, R., & Janežič, D. (2013). Exact parallel maximum clique algorithm for general and protein graphs. *Journal of Chemical Information and Modeling*, *53*(9), 2217–2228. doi:10.1021/ci4002525

Ding, X., Liu, B., & Yu, P. (2008). A Holistic Lexicon-based Approach to Opinion Mining. In *Proceedings of the Conference on Web Search and Web Data Mining (WSDM-2008)*. 10.1145/1341531.1341561

Dinh, D., Tamine, L., & Boubekeur, F. (2013). Factors affecting the effectiveness of biomedical document indexing and retrieval based on terminologies. *Artificial Intelligence in Medicine*, *57*(2), 155–167. doi:10.1016/j.artmed.2012.08.006 PMID:23092678

Djapic, M., Lukic, L., Fragassa, C., Pavlovic, A., & Petrovic, A. (2017). Multi-agent team for engineering: A machining plan in intelligent manufacturing systems. *International Journal of Machining and Machinability of Materials*, *19*(6), 505–521. doi:10.1504/IJMMM.2017.088893

Djebbari, A., Liu, Z., Phan, S., & Famili, A. N. D., F. (2008) International journal of computational biology and drug design (IJCBDD). In *21st Annual Conference on Neural Information Processing Systems*.

Dodd, A. Z. (2013). *The Essential Guide to Telecommunications* (5th ed.). Pearson India Publications.

Doley, K. (2016, December). Financial express. Move over artificial intelligence, 'cognitive technology' is the future. *Financial Express*. Retrieved from http://www.financialexpress.com/lifestyle/science/move-over-artificial-intelligence-cognitive-technology-is-the-future/470711/

Drinić, S. M., Nikolić, A., & Perić, V. (2008). Cluster analysis of soybean genotypes based on RAPD markers. In *Proceedings. 43rd Croatian And 3rd International Symposium On Agriculture*, Opatija. Croatia (pp. 367-370).

Du, W., Tan, S., Cheng, X., & Yun, X. (2010). Adapting Information Bottleneck Method for Automatic Construction of Domain-oriented Sentiment Lexicon. In WSDM'10, New York, USA.

Dwork, C. (2006). Differential Privacy. In M. Bugliesi, B. Preneel, V. Sassone et al. (Eds.), Automata, Languages and Programming. Springer. doi:10.1007/11787006_1

Elaakil, R., Ahmed, R., El Mesbahi, A., & Jaider, O. (2017). Technical Data Extraction and Representation in Expert CAPP System. *Transactions on Machine Learning and Artificial Intelligence, 5*(4).

Engelmore, R. S., & Feigenbaum, E. (1993). Expert systems and artificial intelligence. *Expert Systems: International Journal of Knowledge Engineering and Neural Networks*, *100*, 2.

English Dictionary of Lingoes. (2017). Retrieved from http://www.lingoes.net/

Esuli, A. Sebastiani. F. (2005). Determining the semantic orientation of terms through gloss classification. In *Proceedings of ACM International Conference on Information and Knowledge Management (CIKM-2005)*.

EuroAsia. (2011). Retrieved from http://www.euroasiapub.org/IJRIM/June2011/10.pdf

Fang, N., Fang, N., Pai, P. S., & Edwards, N. (2016). Neural Network Modeling and Prediction of Surface Roughness in Machining Aluminum Alloys. *Journal of Computer and Communications, 4*(5), 1–9. doi:10.4236/jcc.2016.45001

Fang, R., Pouyanfar, S., Yang, Y., Chen, S. C., & Iyengar, S. S. (2016). Computational health informatics in the big data age: A survey. *ACM Computing Surveys, 49*(1), 12. doi:10.1145/2932707

Fearn, N. (2017). Firms look to security analytics to keep pace with cyber threats. *Computer Weekly*. Retrieved from https://www.computerweekly.com/feature/Firms-look-to-security-analytics-to-keep-pace-with-cyber-threats

Felemban, E., Lee, C., & Ekici, E. (2006, June). MMSPEED: Multipath multi-speed protocol for QoS Guarantee of reliability and timeliness in wireless sensor networks. *IEEE Transactions on Mobile Computing, 5*(6), 738–754. doi:10.1109/TMC.2006.79

Feng, S., Zhang, L., Li Daling Wang, B., Yu, G., & Wong, K.-F. (2013). Is Twitter A Better Corpus for Measuring Sentiment Similarity? In *Proceedings of the 2013 Conference on Empirical Methods in Natural Language Processing* (pp. 897–902).

Flair, D. (2018 February 9). Datamining tutorials. Disadvantages of data mining-data mining issues. *Data Flair*. Retrieved from https://data-flair.training/blogs/disadvantages-of-data-mining/

Forouzan, B. A. (2007). *Data Communications and* (4th ed.). McGraw Hill Publication.

Fortunato, S. (2010). Community detection in graphs. *Physics Reports, 486*(3), 75–174. doi:10.1016/j.physrep.2009.11.002

Freeman, R. L. (1996). *Telecommunication System Engineering*. Wiley-Interscience Publications.

Friedman, A., & Schuster, A. (2010). Data Mining with Differential Privacy. In *Proc. 16th ACM SIGKDD Int'l Conf. Knowledge Discovery and Data Mining* (pp. 493-502).

Frith, U. (2004). Emanuel Miller lecture: Confusions and controversies about Asperger syndrome. *Journal of Child Psychology and Psychiatry, and Allied Disciplines, 45*(4), 672–686. doi:10.1111/j.1469-7610.2004.00262.x PMID:15056300

Fromont, E., Prado, A., & Robardet, C. (2009). Constraint-Based Subspace Clustering. In *Proc. SIAM Int'l Conf. Data Mining (SDM)* (pp. 26-37).

Fukunaga, K., & Hummels, D. M. (2006). Bayes Error Estimation Using Parzen and K-nn Procedures. IEEE Trans. Pattern Analysis and Machine Intelligence, 9(5), 634-643. doi:28809.28814.

Funk, M. E., & Reid, C. A. (1983). Indexing consistency in MEDLINE. *Bulletin of the Medical Library Association, 71*(2), 176–183. PMID:6344946

Fu, Q., & Banerjee, A. (2009). Bayesian Overlapping Subspace Clustering. In *Proc. IEEE Ninth Int'l Conf. Data Mining (ICDM)* (pp. 776-781).

Gamon, M., Aue, A., Corston-Oliver, S., & Ringger, E. (2005). Pulse: Mining Customer Opinions from Free Text. In *International symposium on intelligent data analysis* (pp. 121-132). Springer.

Ganesh, P., & Menaka, R. (2014). Use of Discrete Sine Transform in EEG signal classification for early Autism detection. In *2014 International Conference on Advanced Communication Control and Computing Technologies (ICACCCT)* (pp. 1507-1510). IEEE.

Geetha Ramaniand, R. & Sivaselvi; K. (2017). Autism Spectrum Disorder Identification using Data mining techniques. *International Journal of Pure and Applied Mathematics, 117*(16), 427–436.

297

Geetha Ramani, R., & Sahayamary Jabarani, R. (2017). Detection of autism spectrum disorder and typically developing brain from structural connectome through feature selection and classification. *International Journal of Innovations & Advancement in Computer Science, 6*(8).

Gharibi, W., & Shaabi, M. (2012). Cyber threats in social networking websites. *International Journal of Distributed and Parallel Systems, 3*(1). doi:10.5121/ijdps.2012.3109

Ghosh, R., & Lerman, K. (2011). Parameterized centrality metric for network analysis. *Physical Review. E, 83*(6), 066118. doi:10.1103/PhysRevE.83.066118 PMID:21797452

Girimonte, D., & Izzo, D. (2007). Artificial Intelligence for Space Applications. In A. J. Schuster (Ed.), *Intelligent Computing Everywhere*. London: Springer. doi:10.1007/978-1-84628-943-9_12

Girvan, M., & Newman, M. E. (2002). Community structure in social and biological networks. *Proceedings of the National Academy of Sciences of the United States of America, 99*(12), 7821–7826. doi:10.1073/pnas.122653799 PMID:12060727

Godbole, N., Srinivasaiah, M., & Steven, S. (2007). Large Scale Sentiment Analysis for News and Blogs. In *Proceedings of the International Conference on Weblogs and SM (ICWSM)*.

Goldberg, A., & Zhu, X. (2004). Seeing stars when there aren't many stars: Graph-based semi supervised learning for sentiment categorization. In *HLT-NAACL 2006 Workshop on Textgraphs: Graph-based Algorithms for Natural Language Processing*.

Golden, D. & Johnson, T. (2017, June 8). AI-augmented cybersecurity How cognitive technologies can address the cyber workforce shortage. *Deloitte*. Retrieved from https://www2.deloitte.com/insights/us/en/industry/public-sector/addressing-cybersecurity-talent-shortage.html

Gomes, J. B., Adedoyin-Olowe, M., Gaber, M. M., & Stahl, F. (2013). Rule type identification using TRCM for trend analysis in twitter. In *Research and Development in Intelligent Systems XXX* (pp. 273–278). Springer International Publishing. doi:10.1007/978-3-319-02621-3_20

Graffigna, G., & Riva, G. (2015). Social media monitoring and understanding: An integrated mixed methods approach for the analysis of social media. *International Journal of Web Based Communities, 11*(1), 57–72. doi:10.1504/IJWBC.2015.067083

Gross, R., Acquisti, A., & Heinz, H. (2005). Information Revelation and Privacy in Online Social Networks. In *Proc. ACM Workshop Privacy in the Electronic Soc. (WPES '05)* (pp. 71-80). doi:10.1145/1102199.1102214

Guiotoko, E. H., Aoyama, H., & Sano, N. (2017). Optimization of hole making processes considering machining time and machining accuracy. *Journal of Advanced Mechanical Design, Systems, and Manufacturing, 11*(4).

Hadoop. (2017). Retrieved from http://hadoop.apache.org

Haldorai, A., & Ramu, A. (2018). An Intelligent-Based Wavelet Classifier for Accurate Prediction of Breast Cancer. In *Intelligent Multidimensional Data and Image Processing* (pp. 306–319). doi:10.4018/978-1-5225-5246-8.ch012

Haldorai, A., & Ramu, A. (2018). The Impact of Big Data Analytics and Challenges to Cyber Security. In Handbook of Research on Network Forensics and Analysis Techniques (pp. 300–314). Hershey, PA: IGI Global. doi:10.4018/978-1-5225-4100-4.ch016

Hansen, D. L., Nielsen, S. B., & Lykke-Andersen, H. (2000). The post-Triassic evolution of the Sorgenfrei–Tornquist Zone —results from thermo-mechanical modelling. *Tectonophysics, 328*(3–4), 245–267. doi:10.1016/S0040-1951(00)00216-X

Harinath Gowd, G., Theja, K. D., Rayudu, P., Goud, M. V., & Roa, M. S. (2014). Modeling & Analysis of End Milling Process Parameters Using Artificial Neural Networks. *Applied Mechanics and Materials, 592*, 2733–2737. doi:10.4028/www.scientific.net/AMM.592-594.2733

Harish, B. S., Guru, D. S., & Manjunath, S. (2010). Representation and classification of text documents: A brief review. *IJCA*, (2), 110-119.

Hasbullah, H., & Soomro, I. A. (2010). Denial of service (dos) attack and its possible solutions in VANET. *International Journal of Electrical, Computer, Energetic, Electronic and Communication Engineering, 4*(5), 813–817.

Hatzivassiloglou, V., & McKeown, K. (1997). Predicting the Semantic Orientation of Adjectives. In *Proc. 8th Conf. on European chapter of the Association for Computational Linguistics*, Morristown, NJ (pp. 174-181). Association for Computational Linguistics.

Hay, M., Miklau, G., Jensen, D., Weis, P., & Srivastava, S. (2007). Anonymizing Social Networks [Technical Report]. Univ. of Massachusetts Amherst.

Haykin, S. (2005). Cognitive radio: Brain-empowered wireless communications. *IEEE Journal on Selected Areas in Communications, 23*(2), 201–220. doi:10.1109/JSAC.2004.839380

He, J., Chu, W., & Liu, V. (2006). *Inferring Privacy Information from Social Networks*. Proc. Intelligence and Security Informatics. doi:10.1007/11760146_14

Hernández-Ugalde, J. A., Mora-Urpí, J., & Rocha, O. J. (2011). Genetic relationships among wild and cultivated populations of peach palm (Bactris gasipaes Kunth, Palmae): Evidence for multiple independent domestication events. *Genetic Resources and Crop Evolution, 58*(4), 571–583. doi:10.100710722-010-9600-6

Hersh, W. (2008). *Information Retrieval: A Health and Biomedical Perspective: A Health and Biomedical Perspective*. Springer Science & Business Media.

He, T., Stankovic, J., Lu, C., & Abdelzaher, T. (2003). SPEED: A Stateless Protocol for Real-Time Communication in Sensor Networks. In *Proc. 23rd International Conference Distributed Computing Systems*.

Heussne, K. M. (2009). "Gaydar" Facebook: Can Your Friends Reveal Sexual Orientation. ABC News. Retrieved from http://abcnews.go.com/Technology/gaydar-facebook

Hoffman, T. (2008). Online Reputation Management is Hot — but is it Ethical? *Computerworld*.

Honavar, V. (1995). Symbolic artificial intelligence and numeric artificial neural networks: towards a resolution of the dichotomy. In *Computational Architectures integrating Neural and Symbolic Processes* (pp. 351–388). Boston, MA: Springer.

Hong, X., Xu, K., & Gerla, M. (2002). Scalable routing protocols for mobile ad hoc networks. *IEEE Network, 14*(4), 11–21.

Honkalampi, K., Hintikka, J., Tanskanen, A., Lehtonen, J., & Viinamäki, H. (2000). Depression is strongly associated with alexithymia in the general population. *Journal of Psychosomatic Research, 48*(1), 99–104. doi:10.1016/S0022-3999(99)00083-5 PMID:10750635

Hou, T. H., & Lin, L. (1995). Using neural networks for the automatic monitoring and recognition of signals in manufacturing processes. In *Design and implementation of intelligent manufacturing systems* (pp. 141–160). Prentice-Hall, Inc.

Htait, A., Fournier, S., & Bellot, P. (2016). LSIS at SemEval-2016 Task 7: Using Web Search Engines for English and Arabic Unsupervised Sentiment Intensity Prediction. In *Proceedings of SemEval-2016* (pp. 481–485).

Huang, A. (2008). Similarity measures for text document clustering. In *Proceedings of the sixth New Zealand computer science research student conference (NZCSRSC2008),* Christchurch, New Zealand (pp. 49-56).

Hu, M., & Liu, B. (2004). Mining and Summarizing Customer Reviews. In *Proceedings of the tenth ACM SIGKDD International Conference KDD '04.*

Hunter, E. (2018, January 20). Cognitive computing takes on cyber-security. *The Innovation Enterprise.* Retrieved from https://channels.theinnovationenterprise.com/articles/cognitive-computing-takes-on-cyber-security

Hu, P., Han, Z., Fu, Y., & Fu, H. (2016). Implementation of Real-Time Machining Process Control Based on Fuzzy Logic in a New STEP-NC Compatible System. *Mathematical Problems in Engineering, 2016.*

IBM. (2017). Arm security analysts with the power of cognitive security. Retrieved from https://www-01.ibm.com/common/ssi/cgi-bin/ssialias?htmlfid=WGS03087GBEN

IBM. (2017). Ponemon cost of data breach study. Retrieved from https://www.ibm.com/security/data-breach

IBM. (n.d.). Evolve your defenses with security that understands, reasons and learns [white paper]. Retrieved from https://cognitivesecuritywhitepaper.mybluemix.net/

IBM. (n.d.). Products and services. Retrieved from https://www.ibm.com/watson/products-services/

Ighravwe, D. E., & Oke, S. A. (2015). Machining performance analysis in end milling: Predicting using ANN and a comparative optimisation study of ANN/BB-BC and ANN/PSO. *Engineering Journal (New York), 19*(5), 121–137.

Imambi, S. S., & Sudha, T. (2013). Extraction of biomedical information from MEDLINE documents – A text mining approach. *International journal of Science Environmental Technology, 2*(2), 267–274.

Iqbal, A., & Al-Ghamdi, K. A. (2017). Incorporating Energy Efficiency in Performance Measures of Machining: Experimental Investigation and Optimization. In *Sustainable Machining* (pp. 47–65). Cham: Springer. doi:10.1007/978-3-319-51961-6_3

Isa, N. R. M., Yusoff, M., Khalid, N. E., Tahir, N., & binti Nikmat, A. W. (2014). Autism severity level detection using fuzzy expert system. In *2014 IEEE International Symposium on Robotics and Manufacturing Automation (ROMA)* (pp. 218-223). IEEE.

Jackson, M. O. (2010). *Social and economic networks.* Princeton University Press.

Jawhar, I., & Wu, J. (2005). Quality of Service Routing in Mobile Ad Hoc Networks. In M. Cardei, I. Cardei, & D. Z. Du (Eds.), *Resource Management in Wireless Networking. Network Theory and Applications* (Vol. 16). Boston, MA: Springer; doi:10.1007/0-387-23808-5_14

Jawhar, I., & Wu, J. (2005). Quality of service routing in mobile ad hoc networks. In *Resource Management in Wireless Networking* (pp. 365–400). Boston, MA: Springer.

Jhajj, H. K., Garg, R., & Saluja, N. (2018). Aspects of Machine Learning in Cognitive Radio Networks. In *Progress in Advanced Computing and Intelligent Engineering* (pp. 553–559). Springer Singapore.

Jiang, D., Taliwal, V., Meier, A., Holfelder, W., & Herrtwich, R. (2006). Design of 5.9 GHz DSRC-based vehicular safety communication. *IEEE Wireless Communications, 13*(5), 36–43. doi:10.1109/WC-M.2006.250356

Jiang, T., Jiang, J., Dai, Y., & Li, A. (2015). Micro–blog Emotion Orientation Analysis Algorithm Based on Tibetan and Chinese Mixed Text. In *International Symposium on Social Science (ISSS 2015).* 10.2991/isss-15.2015.39

Ji, L., Tan, K. L., & Tung, A. K. H. (2006). Mining Frequent Closed Cubes in 3D Data Sets. In *Proc. 32nd Int'l Conf. Very Large Databases (VLDB)* (pp. 811-822).

Jindal, N. Liu. B. (2006). Mining Comparative Sentences and Relations. In *Proceedings of National Conf. on Artificial Intelligence (AAAI-2006)*.

Ji, W., Wang, L., Haghighi, A., Givehchi, M., & Liu, X. (2018). An enriched machining feature based approach to cutting tool selection. *International Journal of Computer Integrated Manufacturing, 31*(1), 1–10.

Ji, X., Chun, S. A., Wei, Z., & Geller, J. (2015). Twitter sentiment classification for measuring public health concerns. *Social Network Analysis and Mining, 5*(1), 13. doi:10.100713278-015-0253-5

Joa-Ng, M., & Lu, I.-T. (1999). A peer-to-peer zone-based two-level link state routing for mobile ad hoc networks. *IEEE Journal on Selected Areas in Communications, 17*(8).

Jogendra, J., Amit, K. V., & Sanjay, V. (2018). Experimental Investigation of Machining Parameters on Milling Machine using Grey-Fuzzy Logic Method. *International Journal of Mechanical and Production Engineering, 6*(2).

Jovanoski, D., Pachovski, V., & Nakov, P. (2015). Sentiment Analysis in Twitter for Macedonian. Proceedings of Recent Advances in Natural Language Processing, Bulgaria (pp. 249-257).

Kaewchinporn, C., Vongsuchoto, N., & Srisawat, A. (2011, May). A combination of decision tree learning and clustering for data classification. In *2011 Eighth International Joint Conference on Computer Science and Software Engineering* (pp. 363-367). IEEE.

Kagdi, H., Collard, M. L., & Maletic, J. I. (2007). A survey and taxonomy of approaches for mining software repositories in the context of software evolution. Journal of software maintenance and evolution: Research and practice, *19*(2), 77–131. doi:10.1002mr.344

Kailing, K., Kriegel, H. P., Kroger, P., & Wanka, S. (2003). *Ranking Interesting Subspaces for Clustering High Dimensional Data. In Proc. Practice of Knowledge Discovery in Databases* (pp. 241–252). PKDD.

Kaji, N., & Kitsuregawa, M. (2006). Automatic construction of polarity-tagged corpus from HTML documents. In *Processing of the COLING, ACL Main Conference Poster Sessions*.

Kalaichelvi, V., Karthikeyan, R., Sivakumar, D., & Srinivasan, V. (2012). Tool wear classification using fuzzy logic for machining of al/sic composite material. *Modeling and Numerical Simulation of Material Science, 2*(02), 28–36. doi:10.4236/mnsms.2012.22003

Kamaljeet, S. V., & Bhattacharyya, P. (2009). Context-Sensitive Semantic Smoothing using Semantically Relatable Sequences. In *Proceedings of International Joint conference on Artificial Intelligence (IJCAI'09)* (pp. 1580-1585).

Kandeepan, S., De Nardis, L., Di Benedetto, M., Guidotti, A., & Corazza, G. E. (2010). Cognitive Satellite Terrestrial Radios. In *Global Telecommunications Conference*.

Kannan, T. D. B., Kumar, B. S., & Baskar, N. (2014). Application of artificial neural network modeling for machining parameters optimization in drilling operation. *Procedia Materials Science, 5*, 2242–2249. doi:10.1016/j.mspro.2014.07.433

Kaplan, A.M. & Haenlein, M. (2010). Users of the world unite! The challenges and opportunities of social media. *Science direct, 53*(1), 59-68.

Kaschesky, M., Sobkowicz, P., & Bouchard, G. (2011). Opinion Mining in Social network: Modelling, Simulating, and Visualizing Political Opinion Formation in the Web. In *The Proceedings of 12th Annual International Conference on Digital Government Research*.

Kaur, G. (2013). Social network evaluation criteria and influence on consumption behaviour of the youth segment.

Kaur, R., & Singh, S. (2016). A survey of data mining and social network analysis based anomaly detection techniques. *Egyptian Informatics Journal, 17*(2), 199-216. doi:10.1016/j.eij.2015.11.004

Kaur, R., & Singh, S. (2016). A survey of data mining and social network analysis based anomaly detection techniques. *Egyptian Informatics Journal, 17*(2), 199–216.

Kemp, S. (2018, January). 11 New People Join Social Media Every Second (And Other Impressive Stats). *Hootsuite.* Retrieved from https://blog.hootsuite.com/11-people-join-social-every-second/

Keshtkar, F., & Inkpen, D. (2009). Using sentiment orientation features for mood classification in blogs. In *Proceedings of the IEEE International Conference on Natural Language Processing and Knowledge Engineering (IEEE NLP-KE 2009).*

Khare, A., & Jadhav, A. N. (2010). An efficient concept-based mining model for enhancing text clustering. *International Journal of Advances in Engineering and Technology, 2*(4), 196–201.

Khorasani, A., & Yazdi, M. R. S. (2017). Development of a dynamic surface roughness monitoring system based on artificial neural networks (ANN) in milling operation. *International Journal of Advanced Manufacturing Technology, 93*(1-4), 141–151. doi:10.100700170-015-7922-4

Kilickap, E., Yardimeden, A., & Celik, Y. H. (2017). Mathematical modelling and optimization of cutting force, tool wear and surface roughness by using artificial neural network and response surface methodology in milling of Ti-6242S. *Applied Sciences, 7*(10), 1064. doi:10.3390/app7101064

Kim, P. (2006). The Forrester Wave: Brand Monitoring, Q3 2006 [white paper]. Forrester.

Kim, H., Han, D. G., & Hong, S. (2011). First-order side channel attacks on Zhang's countermeasures. *Information Sciences, 181*(18), 4051–4060. doi:10.1016/j.ins.2011.04.049

Kim, S., & Hovy, E. (2004). Determining the Sentiment of Opinions. In *Proceedings of Intentional Conference on Computational Linguistics (COLING-2004).*

Kim, T. H., Kim, C., & Park, I. (2012). Side channel analysis attacks using AM demodulation on commercial smart cards with SEED. *Journal of Systems and Software, 85*(12), 2899–2908. doi:10.1016/j.jss.2012.06.063

Kim, Y., Hsu, S.-H., & de Zuniga, H. G. (2013). Influence of social network use on discussion network heterogeneity and civic engagement: The moderating role of personality traits. *Journal of Communication, 63*(3), 498–516. doi:10.1111/jcom.12034

Kodialam, M., & Lakshman, T. V. (2000). Dynamic routing of bandwidth guaranteed tunnels with restoration. *IEEE/ACM Transactions on Networking, 11*(3), 399–410. doi:10.1109/TNET.2003.813044

Kolawole, O. Y., Vuppala, S., Sellathurai, M., & Ratnarajah, T. (2017). *On the performance of cognitive satellite-terrestrial networks.* IEEE Transactions on Cognitive Communications and Networking.

Koppel, M., & Schler, J. (2006). The importance of neutral examples for learning sentiment computational intelligence. *Computational Intelligence, 22*(2), 100–109.

Korda, H., & Itani, Z. (2013). Harnessing social network for health promotion and behaviour change. *Health Promotion Practice, 14*(1), 15–23. doi:10.1177/1524839911405850 PMID:21558472

Kowarschik, M., & Weiß, C. (2003). An overview of cache optimization techniques and cache-aware numerical algorithms. In *Algorithms for Memory Hierarchies* (pp. 213–232). Springer. doi:10.1007/3-540-36574-5_10

Kriegel, H. P., Borgwardt, K. M., Kröger, P., Pryakhin, A., Schubert, M., & Zimek, A. (2007). Future Trends in Data Mining. *Data Mining and Knowledge Discovery, 15*(1), 87–97. doi:10.100710618-007-0067-9

Kroger, P., Kriegel, H. P., & Kailing, K. (2004). Density-Connected Subspace Clustering for High-Dimensional Data. In *Proc. SIAM Int'l Conf. Data Mining (SDM)* (pp. 246-257).

Ku, L.-W., Liang, Y.-T., & Chen, H.-H. (2006). Opinion extraction, summarization and tracking in news and blog corpora. In *Proc. of the AAAI-CAAW'06.*

Kulkarni, P. (2018, May 8). Analytics. pros and cons of datamining social interactions. *The Innovation Enterprise.* Retrieved from https://channels.theinnovationenterprise.com/articles/pros-and-cons-of-datamining-social-interactions

Kumari, N., & Chugh, S. (2015). Reduction Of Noise From Audio Signals Using Wavelets. *International Journal For Advance Research In Engineering And Technology, 3.*

Kumudha, S., Srinivasa, Y. G., & Krishnamurthy, R. (1998). Estimation of Tool Status Using Artificial Neural Network in Face Milling Operation. *Journal for Manufacturing Science and Production, 1*(3), 189–198. doi:10.1515/IJMSP.1998.1.3.189

Kurose, J., & Ross, K. (2004). *Computer networking: A top-down approach featuring the internet.* Addison Wesley.

Kurose, J., & Ross, K. (2012). *Computer Networking: A Top-Down Approach* (5th ed.). Pearson India Publications.

Le, T.-D., & Shin, O.-S. (2016). Optimal relaying scheme with energy harvesting in a cognitive wireless sensor network. In *2016 International Conference on Information and Communication Technology Convergence (ICTC)* (pp. 82-84).

Lefki, K., & Dormans, J. G. M. (1998). Measurement of piezoelectric coefficients of ferroelectric thin films. *Journal of Applied Physics, 76*(3), 1764–1767. doi:10.1063/1.357693

Lewis, T. (2006, November 20). Future Aircraft Jet Engines Will Think for Themselves. *AFRL Horizons.* Retrieved from www.afrlhorizons.com/Briefs/Dec01/PR0105.html

Li, H., & Irick, D. K. (2010, May). Collaborative spectrum sensing in cognitive radio vehicular ad hoc networks: belief propagation on highway. In 2010 IEEE 71st Vehicular technology conference (VTC 2010-spring) (pp. 1-5). IEEE.

Li, J., Liu, H., Ng, S. K., & Wong, L. (2003). Discovery of significant rules for classifying cancer diagnosis data. *Bioinformatics (Oxford, England), 19*(Suppl. 2), ii93–ii102.

Lindamood, H.R., Kantarcioglu, M. & Thuraisingham, B. (2009). Inferring Private Information Using Social Network Data. In *Proc. 18th Int'l Conf. World Wide Web (WWW).*

Lin, Y. S., Jiang, J. Y., & Lee, S. J. (2013). A similarity measure for text classification and clustering. *IEEE Transactions on Knowledge and Data Engineering, 26*(7), 1–15.

Lipiński, D., Bałasz, B., & Rypina, Ł. (2018). Modelling of surface roughness and grinding forces using artificial neural networks with assessment of the ability to data generalisation. *International Journal of Advanced Manufacturing Technology, 94*(1-4), 1335–1347. doi:10.100700170-017-0949-y

Li, Q., & Wu, Y. F. B. (2006). Identifying important concepts from medical documents. *Journal of Biomedical Informatics, 39*(6), 668–679. doi:10.1016/j.jbi.2006.02.001 PMID:16545986

Liu, B. (2011). Sentiment analysis and opinion Mining. In AAAI-2011, San Francisco, CA. doi:10.1007/978-3-642-19460-3_11

Liu, H. (2014, April 29). Challenges in Mining Social Media Data. *Carlson School of Management, University of Minnesota*. Retrieved from http://sobaco.umn.edu/content/challenges-mining-social-media-data

Liu, M., An, Y., Hu, X., Langer, D., Newschaffer, C., & Shea, L. (2013). An evaluation of identification of suspected autism spectrum disorder (ASD) cases in early intervention (EI) records. In *2013 IEEE International Conference on Bioinformatics and Biomedicine (BIBM)* (pp. 566-571). IEEE.

Liu, Y. Q., Wang, C., & Zhang, L. (2009). Decision tree based predictive models for breast cancer survivability on imbalanced data. In *3rd International Conference on Bioinformatics and Biomedical Engineering ICBBE 2009* (pp. 1-4). IEEE.

Liu, D., & Nocedal, J. (1989). On the Limited Memory BFGS Method for Large Scale Optimization. *Mathematical Programming*, *45*(1), 503–528. doi:10.1007/BF01589116

Liu, F., & Lee, H. J. (2010). Use of social network information to enhance collaborative filtering performance. *Expert Systems with Applications*, *37*(7), 4772–4778. doi:10.1016/j.eswa.2009.12.061

Liu, G., Sim, K., Li, J., & Wong, L. (2009). Efficient Mining of Distance-Based Subspace Clusters. *Statistical Analysis and Data Mining*, *2*(5/6), 427–444. doi:10.1002am.10062

Li, Y., Chung, S. M., & Holt, J. D. (2008). Text document clustering based on frequent word meaning sequences. *Data & Knowledge Engineering*, *64*(1), 381–404. doi:10.1016/j.datak.2007.08.001

Lu, C., Blum, B., Abdelzaher, T., Stankovic, J., & He, T. (2002). RAP: A Real-Time Communication Architecture for Large-Scale Wireless Sensor Networks. In *Proc. IEEE Real-Time and Embedded Technology Applications Systems*.

Lyudmyla, K., Tamara, R., & Anders, C. (2017). Detecting cyber threats through social network analysis: Short survey. *SocioEconomic Challenges*, *1*(1), 20–34.

Machanavajjhala, A., Kifer, D., Gehrke, J., & Venkitasubramaniam, M. (2009). L-Diversity: Privacy Beyond K-Anonymity. *ACM Transactions on Knowledge Discovery from Data*, *1*(1), 3. doi:10.1145/1217299.1217302

Macskassy, S. A., & Provost, F. (2007). Classification in networked data: A toolkit and a univariate case study. *Journal of Machine Learning Research*, *8*(May), 935–983.

Madhava Reddy, S., Chennakesava Reddy, A., & Sudhakar Reddy, K. (2012). Latest Developments in Condition Monitoring of Machining Operations. *Journal of Applied Sciences (Faisalabad)*, *12*(10), 938–946. doi:10.3923/jas.2012.938.946

Mahesh, T. P., & Rajesh, R. (2014). Optimal selection of process parameters in CNC end milling of Al 7075-T6 aluminium alloy using a Taguchi-fuzzy approach. *Procedia Materials Science*, *5*, 2493–2502. doi:10.1016/j.mspro.2014.07.501

Makhfi, S., Haddouche, K., Bourdim, A., & Habak, M. (2018). Modeling of machining force in hard turning process. *Mechanics*, *24*(3), 367–375. doi:10.5755/j01.mech.24.3.19146

Malghan, R. L., Rao, K., Shettigar, A. K., Rao, S. S., & D'Souza, R. J. (2018). Forward and reverse mapping for milling process using artificial neural networks. *Data in Brief*, *16*, 114–121. doi:10.1016/j.dib.2017.10.069 PMID:29188231

Malouf, R., & Mullen, T. (2017). Graph-based user classification for informal online political discourse. In *Proceedings of the 1st Workshop on Information Credibility on the Web*.

Manafi, D., Nategh, M. J., & Parvaz, H. (2017). Extracting the manufacturing information of machining features for computer-aided process planning systems. *Proceedings of the Institution of Mechanical Engineers. Part B, Journal of Engineering Manufacture*, *231*(12), 2072–2083. doi:10.1177/0954405415623487

Manikandakumar, M., & Ramanujam, E. (2018). Security and Privacy Challenges in Big Data Environment. In Handbook of Research on Network Forensics and Analysis Techniques (pp. 315-325). Hershey, PA: IGI Global.

Manikandakumar, M., & Ramanujam, E. (2018). Security and Privacy Challenges in Big Data Environment. In Handbook of Research on Network Forensics and Analysis Techniques (pp. 315–325). Hershey, PA: IGI Global. doi:10.4018/978-1-5225-4100-4.ch017

Man, K. F., Tang, K. S., & Kwong, S. (1996). Genetic algorithms: Concepts and applications. *IEEE Transactions on Industrial Electronics, 43*(5), 519–534. doi:10.1109/41.538609

Mansour, A., Mesleh, R., & Abaza, M. (2016). New challenges in wireless and free space optical communications. *Optics and Lasers in Engineering, 89, 95-108.* doi:10.1016/j.optlaseng.2016.03.027

Mao, H., Gao, P., Wang, Y., & Bollen, J. (2014). Automatic Construction of Financial Semantic Orientation Lexicon from Large-Scale Chinese News Corpus. In *7th Financial Risks International Forum*, Institut Louis Bachelier.

Marutitech. (n.d.). What is cognitive computing? Features, Scope & Limitations. Retrieved from https://www.marutitech.com/cognitive-computing-features-scope-limitations/

Mathioudakis, M., & Koudas, N. (2010). Twittermonitor: trend detection over the twitter stream. In *Proceedings of the 2010 ACM SIGMOD International Conference on Management of data* (pp. 1155-1158). ACM. 10.1145/1807167.1807306

Mathur, K. (2016). Online social network mining. *International Journal of Computer Trends and Technology, 35*(4), 202–206.

Matthews, A. (2006). Side-channel attacks on smartcards. *Network Security,* (12), 18–20. doi:10.1016/S1353-4858(06)70465-2

McCreesh, C., & Prosser, P. (2013). Multi-Threading a State-of-the-Art Maximum Clique Algorithm. *Algorithms, 6*(4), 618–635. doi:10.3390/a6040618

Mcneese, M. (2012). Perspectives on the role of cognition in cyber security. In *Proceedings of the human factors and ergonomics society 56th annual meeting*, Boston, MA. Human Factors and Ergonomics Society.

McPherson, M., Smith-Lovin, L., & Cook, J. M. (2001). Birds of a feather: Homophily in social networks. *Annual Review of Sociology, 27*(1), 415–444. doi:10.1146/annurev.soc.27.1.415

Miller, S. D. (2015). *The internet as a tool for terrorism*. Waco, TX: Baylor University.

Minsky, M. (1974). *A framework for representing knowledge.*

Mishra, R., Malik, J., Singh, I., & Davim, J. P. (2010). Neural network approach for estimating the residual tensile strength after drilling in uni-directional glass fiber reinforced plastic laminates. *Materials & Design, 31*(6), 2790–2795. doi:10.1016/j.matdes.2010.01.011

Moghaddam, J. Z., Usman, M., & Granelli, F. (2018). *A device-to-device communication based disaster response network.* IEEE Transactions on Cognitive Communications and Networking.

Moise, G., & Sander, J. (2008). Finding non-redundant, statistically significant regions in high dimensional data: A novel approach to projected and subspace clustering. In *Proc. 14th ACM SIGKDD Int'l Conf. Knowledge Discovery and Data Mining (KDD)* (pp. 533-541).

Morinaga, S., Yamanishi, K., Tateishi, K., & Fukushima, T. (2002). Mining product reputations on the web. In ACM SIGKDD (pp. 341–349).

Motlagh, S. H. R. E., Moradi, H., & Pouretemad, H. (2013, June). Using general sound descriptors for early autism detection. In *2013 9th Asian Control Conference (ASCC)* (pp. 1-5). IEEE.

Murthy, D., Gross, A., Takata, A., & Bond, S. (2013). Evaluation and Development of Data Mining Tools for Social Network Analysis. In *Mining Social Networks and Security Informatics* (pp. 183–202). Springer Netherlands. doi:10.1007/978-94-007-6359-3_10

Nafeez, A., Tomohisha, T., & Yoshio, S. (2014). Machining parameter optimisation by genetic algorithm and artificial neural network. *International Journal of Data Analysis Techniques and Strategies, 6*(3), 261–274. doi:10.1504/IJDATS.2014.063061

Naik, M. (2015). Early Detection and Prevention of DDOS attack on VANET [Doctoral dissertation].

Namdari, M., Jazayeri-Rad, H., & Hashemi, S. J. (2014). Process fault diagnosis using support vector machines with a genetic algorithm based parameter tuning. *Journal of Automation and Control, 2*(1), 1–7.

Naresh, N., (2014). Modeling and Analysis of Machining GFRP Composites Using Fuzzy Logic and ANOVA. *IUP Journal of Mechanical Engineering, 7*(4).

Nasir, J. A., Varlamis, I., Karim, A., & Tsatsaronis, G. (2013). Semantic smoothing for text clustering. *Knowledge-Based Systems, 54*, 216–229. doi:10.1016/j.knosys.2013.09.012

Nassehi, A., Essink, W., & Barclay, J. (2015). Evolutionary algorithms for generation and optimization of tool paths. *CIRP Annals, 64*(1), 455–458. doi:10.1016/j.cirp.2015.04.125

Nathan, R. D., Vijayaraghavan, L., & Krishnamurthy, R. (2001). Intelligent estimation of burning limits to aid in cylindrical grinding cycle planning. *International Journal of Heavy Vehicle Systems, 8*(1), 48–59. doi:10.1504/IJHVS.2001.001154

National Breast Cancer. (n.d.). Retrieved from http://www.nationalbreastcancer.org/

Netzer, O., Feldman, R., Goldenberg, J., & Fresko, M. (2012). Mine Your Own Business: Market-Structure Surveillance Through Text Mining. *Marketing Science, 31*(3), 521–543. doi:10.1287/mksc.1120.0713

Newman, M. (2010). *Networks: An introduction*. Oxford University Press. doi:10.1093/acprof:oso/9780199206650.001.0001

Niekerk, B. V. (2013). Social media and information conflict. *International Journal of Communication, 7*, 1162–1184.

Nikaein, N., Bonnet, C., & Nikaein, N. (2001, September). Harp-hybrid ad hoc routing protocol. In *Proceedings of international symposium on telecommunications (IST)* (pp. 56-67).

Nsude, I., & Onwe, E. C. (2017). Social Media and Security Challenges in Nigeria: The Way Forward. *World Applied Sciences Journal, 35*(6), 993–999. doi:10.5829/idosi.wasj.2017.993.999

O'Reilly, J. J. (1989). *Telecommunication Principles*. Van Nostrand Reinhold Publications.

Olowe, A., Gaber, M.M., & Stahl, F. (2013). A survey of data mining techniques for social media analysis. Retrieved from http://arxiv.org/abs/1312.4617v1

Omar, N., Albared, M., Al-Shabi, A. Q., & Al-Moslmi, T. (2013). Ensemble of classification algorithms for subjectivity and sentiment analysis of Arabic customers' reviews. *International Journal of Advancements in Computing Technology, 5*.

Osborne, E., & Simha, A. (2002). *Traffic Engineering with MPLS*. Cisco Press.

Osborne, M., Petrovic, S., McCreadie, R., Macdonald, C., & Ounis, I. (2012). Bieber no more: First story detection using twitter and wikipedia. In *Proceedings of the Workshop on Time-aware Information Access*.

Oxford English Dictionary. (2017). Retrieved from http://www.oxforddictionaries.com/

Page, D. (2003). Defending against cache-based side-channel attacks. *Information Security Technical Report, 8*(1), 30–44. doi:10.1016/S1363-4127(03)00104-3

Pak, A., & Paroubek, P. (2010). *Twitter as a Corpus for Sentiment Analysis and Opinion Mining. In Proceedings of the international conference on language resources and evaluation (LREC 2010).* Valletta, Malta: ELRA.

Pang, B., & Lee, L. (2008). Opinion mining and sentiment analysis. Foundations and trends in information Retrieval, 2(1–2), 1–135.

Pang, B., & Lee, L. (2008). Using very simple statistics for review search: An exploration. In *Proceedings of the International Conference on Computational Linguistics (COLING)* [Poster paper].

Pang, B., Lee, L., & Vaithyanathan, S. (2002). Thumbs up? Sentiment classification using machine learning techniques. In *Proceedings of Conference on Empirical methods in natural Language Processing (EMNLP)*, Philadelphia, PA, July (pp. 79 – 86). Association for Computational Linguistics. 10.3115/1118693.1118704

Pang, B., & Lee, L. (2005). Seeing stars: Exploiting class relationships for sentiment categorization with respect to rating scales. In *Proceedings of the Association for Computational Linguistics (ACL)* (pp. 115–124).

Papadopoulos, S., Kompatsiaris, Y., Vakali, A., & Spyridonos, P. (2012). Community detection in social media. *Data Mining and Knowledge Discovery, 24*(3), 515–554. doi:10.100710618-011-0224-z

Papageorgiou, E. I. (2011). A new methodology for decisions in medical informatics using fuzzy cognitive maps based on fuzzy rule-extraction techniques. *Applied Soft Computing, 11*(1), 500–513. doi:10.1016/j.asoc.2009.12.010

Park, J. Y., Han, D. G., Yi, O., & Kim, J. (2014). An improved side channel attack using event information of subtraction. *Journal of Network and Computer Applications, 38*, 99–105. doi:10.1016/j.jnca.2013.05.001

Patel, K. N., & Jhaveri, R. H. (2015). Isolating Packet Dropping Misbehavior in VANET using Ant Colony Optimization. *International Journal of Computers and Applications, 120*(24).

Patel, S., Park, H., Bonato, P., Chan, L., & Rodgers, M. (2012). A review of wearable sensors and systems with application in rehabilitation. *Journal of Neuroengineering and Rehabilitation, 9*(1), 21. doi:10.1186/1743-0003-9-21 PMID:22520559

Pawar, S. C., & Solapur, R. S. (2016). Research Issues and Future Directions in Web Mining: A Survey. In *Proceedings on National Seminar on Recent Trends in Data Mining (RTDM 2016)*, Periye, India.

Pearlman, M. R., & Haas, S. J. (1999). Determining the optimal configuration for the zone routing protocol. *IEEE Journal on Selected Areas in Communications, 17*(8).

Pendokhare, D. G., & Quazi, T. Z. (2012). Fuzzy Logic Based Drilling Control Process. *Int. J. Scientific and Engg. Research, 5*(12), 61–65.

Perkins, C.E., Royer, E.M. & Das, S.R. (2001) Quality of service in ad hoc on-demand distance vector routing.

Perkins, C., Belding-Royer, E., & Das, S. (2003). Ad Hoc on Demand Distance Vector (AODV) Routing.

Peterson, L., & Davie, B. (2011). *Computer Networks A Systems Approach* (5th ed.). Morgan Kaufmann Publishers.

Petit, J. (2009, December). Analysis of ecdsa authentication processing in vanets. In *2009 3rd International Conference on New Technologies, Mobility and Security (NTMS)* (pp. 1-5). IEEE.

Pham, M. C., Cao, Y., Klamma, R., & Jarke, M. (2011). A clustering approach for collaborative filtering recommendation using social network analysis. *J. UCS, 17*(4), 583–604.

Pham, M., Mengistu, Y., Do, H., & Sheng, W. (2018). Delivering home healthcare through a Cloud-based Smart Home Environment (CoSHE). *Future Generation Computer Systems, 81*, 129–140. doi:10.1016/j.future.2017.10.040

Phu, V. N., Dat, N. D., Vo, T. N. T., Vo, T. N. C., & Nguyen, T. A. (2017a). Fuzzy C-means for English sentiment classification in a distributed system. *International Journal of Applied Intelligence, 46*(3), 717–738. doi:10.100710489-016-0858-z

Phu, V. N., Vo, T. N. C., Dat, N. D., Vo, T. N. T., & Nguyen, T. A. (2017e). *A Valences-Totaling Model for English Sentiment Classification. International Journal of Knowledge and Information Systems*. doi:10.1007/S13115-017-1054-0

Phu, V. N., Vo, T. N. C., & Vo, T. N. T. (2017b). SVM for English Semantic Classification in Parallel Environment. *International Journal of Speech Technology*. doi:10.100710772-017-9421-5

Phu, V. N., Vo, T. N. C., & Vo, T. N. T. (2017f). *Shifting Semantic Values of English Phrases for Classification. International Journal of Speech Technology*. doi:10.1007/S13772-017-9420-6

Phu, V. N., Vo, T. N. C., Vo, T. N. T., & Dat, N. D. (2017d). *A Vietnamese adjective emotion dictionary based on exploitation of Vietnamese language characteristics. International Journal of Artificial Intelligence Review*. doi:10.1007/S13462-017-9538-6

Phu, V. N., Vo, T. N. C., Vo, T. N. T., Dat, N. D., & Khanh, L. D. D. (2017g). *A Valence-Totaling Model for Vietnamese Sentiment Classification. International Journal of Evolving Systems*. doi:10.100712530-017-9187-7

Phu, V. N., Vo, T. N. C., Vo, T. N. T., Dat, N. D., & Khanh, L. D. D. (2017h). *Semantic Lexicons of English Nouns for Classification. International Journal of Evolving Systems*. doi:10.100712530-017-9188-6

Phu, V. N., & Vo, T. N. T. (2017c). A STING Algorithm and Multi-dimensional Vectors Used for English Sentiment Classification in a Distributed System. *American Journal of Engineering and Applied Sciences*. doi:10.3844/ajeassp.2017

Phu, V. N., & Vo, T. N. T. (2018a). English sentiment classification using a Gower-2 coefficient and a genetic algorithm with a fitness-proportionate selection in a parallel network environment. *Journal of Theoretical and Applied Information Technology, 96*(4), 1–50.

Phu, V. N., & Vo, T. N. T. (2018b). English sentiment classification using a Fager & MacGowan coefficient and a genetic algorithm with a rank selection in a parallel network environment. *International Journal of Computer Modelling and New Technologies, 22*(1), 57–112.

Phu, V. N., & Vo, T. N. T. (2018c). Latent Semantic Analysis using A Dennis Coefficient for English Sentiment Classification in A Parallel System. *International Journal of Computers, Communications & Control, 13*(3), 390–410.

Phu, V. N., & Vo, T. N. T. (2018e). English Sentiment Classification using A BIRCH Algorithm and The Sentiment Lexicons-Based One-dimensional Vectors in a Parallel Network Environment. *International Journal of Computer Modelling and New Technologies, 22*(1).

Phu, V. N., & Vo, T. N. T. (2018f). A Fuzzy C-Means Algorithm and Sentiment-Lexicons-based Multi-dimensional Vectors Of A SOKAL & SNEATH-IV Coefficient Used For English Sentiment Classification. *International Journal of Theoretical and Applied Information Technology, 96*(10).

Phu, V. N., & Vo, T. N. T. (2018g). A Self-Training - Based Model using A K-NN Algorithm and The Sentiment Lexicons - Based Multi-dimensional Vectors of A S6 coefficient for Sentiment Classification. *International Journal of Theoretical and Applied Information Technology, 96*(10).

Phu, V. N., & Vo, T. N. T. (2018h). The Multi-dimensional Vectors and An Yule-II Measure Used for A Self-Organizing Map Algorithm of English Sentiment Classification in A Distributed Environment. *Journal of Theoretical and Applied Information Technology, 96*(10).

Phu, V. N., & Vo, T. N. T. (2018i). Sentiment Classification using The Sentiment Scores Of Lexicons Based on A Kuhns-II Coefficient in English. *International Journal of Tomography & Simulation, 31*(3).

Phu, V. N., & Vo, T. N. T. (2018j). K-Medoids algorithm used for english sentiment classification in a distributed system. *Computer Modelling and New Technologies, 22*(1), 20–39.

Phu, V. N., & Vo, T. N. T. (2018k). A Reformed K-Nearest Neighbors Algorithm for Big Data Sets. *Journal of Computational Science.* doi:10.3844/jcssp.2018

Phuvipadawat, S., & Murata, T. (2010). Breaking news detection and tracking in twitter. In *2010 IEEE/WIC/ACM International Conference on Web Intelligence and Intelligent Agent Technology (WI-IAT)* (Vol. 3, pp. 120-123). IEEE.

Pleinis, J. (2006, November 20). Advanced adaptive autopilot. Retrieved from www.afrlhorizons.com/Briefs/Jun03/MN0213.html

Pohokar, N., & Bhuyar, L. (2014). Neural Networks Based Approach for Machining and Geometric Parameters optimization of a CNC End Milling. *Neural Networks, 3*(2).

Ponomarenko, J. V., Bourne, P. E., & Shindyalov, I. N. (2002). Building an automated classification of DNA-binding protein domains. *Bioinformatics (Oxford, England), 18*(Suppl. 2), S192–S201. doi:10.1093/bioinformatics/18.suppl_2.S192 PMID:12386003

Prabhakar, A., Kingsley, D., Singh, J., & Jebaraj, C. (2004). Creating process plan sheet from a feature based model. In *Proceedings of the National Conference on Advanced Manufacturing and Robotics* (pp. 247-254).

Preethi, V., & Suriya, M. (2013). A survey on mining actionable clusters from high dimensional datasets. *International Journal of Advanced Research in Computer Science and Software Engineering, 3*(11).

Purdy, M., & Daugherty, P. (2016). Why Artificial Intelligence is the Future of Growth.

Qian, Y., & Moayeri, N. (2008, May). Design of secure and application-oriented VANETs. In *IEEE Vehicular Technology Conference VTC Spring 2008* (pp. 2794-2799). IEEE. 10.1109/VETECS.2008.610

Qi, F., Zhihui, Y., & Keqin, S. (2012). Spectrum Environment Machine Learning in Cognitive Radio. *Procedia Engineering, 29*, 4181–4185. doi:10.1016/j.proeng.2012.01.640

Radhakrishnan, S., Racherla, G., Sekharan, C. N., Rao, N. S. V., & Batsell, S. G. (1999) DST-A routing protocol for ad hoc networks using distributed spanning trees. In *1999 IEEE Wireless Communications and Networking Conference.*

Rahayu, D. A., Krishnaswamy, S., Alahakoon, O., & Labbe, C. (2010). RnR: Extracting rationale from online reviews and ratings. In *2010 IEEE International Conference on Data Mining Workshops (ICDMW)* (pp. 358-368). IEEE.

Raimond, K. (2008). Effective tool wear estimation through multisensory information fusion using Artificial Neural Network. *Journal of EEA, 25*, 33–42.

Raja, C., & Saravanan, M. (2018). Tool path optimization by genetic algorithm for energy efficient machining. *TAGA Journal of Graphic Technology, 14*, 1670–1679.

Rajasekhar, K., & Naresh, N. (2014). Modeling and analysis of process parameters in machining Aisi 304 stainless steel using fuzzy logic. *i-Manager's Journal on Mechanical Engineering, 4*(2), 18.

Rajeck, J. (2016, December 13). Three ways brands will use cognitive marketing. *Econsultancy.* Retrieved from https://econsultancy.com/blog/68634-three-ways-brands-will-use-cognitive-marketing/

Raju, E., & Sravanthi, K. (2012). Analysis of social networks using the techniques of web mining. *International Journal of Advanced Research in Computer Science and Software Engineering, 2*(10), 443–450.

Rantz, M. J., Skubic, M., Koopman, R. J., Phillips, L., Alexander, G. L., Miller, S. J., & Guevara, R. D. (2011). Using sensor networks to detect urinary tract infections in older adults. In *2011 IEEE 13th International Conference on e-Health Networking, Applications and Services.* IEEE. 10.1109/health.2011.6026731

Rao, D., & Ravichandran, D. (2009). Semi-supervised polarity lexicon induction. In *Proceedings of the European Chapter of the Association for Computational Linguistics (EACL).* 10.3115/1609067.1609142

Rault, T., Bouabdallah, A., Challal, Y., & Marin, F. (2017). A survey of energy-efficient context recognition systems using wearable sensors for healthcare applications. *Pervasive and Mobile Computing, 37,* 23–44. doi:10.1016/j.pmcj.2016.08.003

Ren, Y., Kaji, N., Yoshinaga, N., & Kitsuregaw, M. (2014). Sentiment classification in under-resourced languages using graph-based semi-supervised learning methods. *IEICE Transactions on Information and Systems, E97–D*(4), 790–797. doi:10.1587/transinf.E97.D.790

Ren, Y., Kaji, N., Yoshinaga, N., Toyoda, M., & Kitsuregawa, M. (2011). Sentiment Classification in Resource-Scarce Languages by using Label Propagation. In *Proceedings of the 25th Pacific Asia Conference on Language, Information and Computation* (pp. 420-429). Institute of Digital Enhancement of Cognitive Processing, Waseda University.

Revetria, R., Catania, A., Cassettari, L., Guizzi, G., Romano, E., Murino, T., & Fujita, H. (2012). Improving Healthcare Using Cognitive Computing Based Software: An Application in Emergency Situation. In Advanced Research in Applied Artificial Intelligence (pp. 477–490). Springer Berlin Heidelberg. doi:10.1007/978-3-642-31087-4_50

Riloff, E., Wiebe, J., & Wilson, T. (2003). Learning subjective nouns using extraction pattern bootstrapping. In *Proceedings of the Conference on Natural Language Learning (CoNLL)* (pp. 25–32).

Rishi, K., Pradhan, M. K., & Rajesh, K. 2014. Modeling and optimization of milling parameters on Al-6061 alloy using multi- objective genetic algorithm. In *Proc. of 26th AIMTDR Conference,* IIT Guwahati, India, December 12-14.

Robertazzi, T. G. (1993). *Broadband ISDN, And MAN Technology.* Wiley-IEEE Press.

Röcker, C., Ziefle, M., & Holzinger, A. (2014). From Computer Innovation to Human Integration: Current Trends and Challenges for Pervasive Health Technologies. In Pervasive Health (pp. 1–17). Springer London. doi:10.1007/978-1-4471-6413-5_1

Roy, A., & Bhagat, K. (2015). An application of Artificial Neural Network to predict surface roughness during drilling of AISI1020 steel. *International Journal of Scientific Research Engineering and Technology, 4*(8).

Ruan, X. H., Hu, X., & Zhang, X. (2014). Research on Application Model of Semantic Web-Based Social Network Analysis. In *Proceedings of the 9th International Symposium on Linear Drives for Industry Applications* (Vol. 2, pp. 455-460). Springer Berlin Heidelberg. 10.1007/978-3-642-40630-0_59

Ruedinger, J. (2006). The complexity of DPA type side channel attacks and their dependency on the algorithm design. *Information security technical report, 11*(3), 154-158.

Sadique, U. M., & James, D. (2016). A Novel Approach to Prevent Cache-Based Side-Channel Attack in the Cloud. *Procedia Technology, 25,* 232–239. doi:10.1016/j.protcy.2016.08.102

Salimi, A., Özdemir, A., & Erdem, A. (2015). Simulation and monitoring of the machining process via fuzzy logic and cutting forces. *Iranian Journal of Materials Science and Engineering, 12*(3), 14–26.

Santorini, B. (1995). *Part-of-speech tagging guidelines for the Penn treebank project (3rd revision, 2nd printing) [Technical Report]*. Department of Computer and Information Science, University of Pennsylvania.

Sarabadani, S., Schudlo, L. C., Samadani, A. A., & Kushki, A. (2018). *Physiological detection of affective states in children with autism spectrum disorder. IEEE Transactions on Affective Computing*.

Sarabadani, S., Schudlo, L. C., Samadani, A. A., & Kushki, A. (2018). *Physiological Detection of Affective States in Children with Autism Spectrum Disorder. IEEE Transactions on Affective Computing*.

Saraswathi, A. T., Kalaashri, Y. R. A., & Padmavathi, S. (2015). Dynamic resource allocation scheme in cloud computing. *Procedia Computer Science, 47*, 30–36. doi:10.1016/j.procs.2015.03.180

Sarhan, A. A., Sayuti, M., & Hamdi, M. (2012). A Fuzzy Logic Based Model to Predict Surface roughness of a machined surface in glass milling operation using CBN grinding tool. *World Academy of Science, Engineering and Technology, 6*, 564–570.

Šarić, T., Šimunović, G., Lujić, R., Šimunović, K., & Antić, A. (2016). Use of soft computing technique for modelling and prediction of CNC grinding process. *Technical Gazette, 23*(4), 1123–1130.

Scheible, C. (2010). Sentiment Translation through Lexicon Induction. In *Proceedings of the ACL 2010 Student Research Workshop*, Sweden (pp. 25–30).

Scott, J. (2011). Social network analysis: Developments, advances, and prospects. *Social Network Analysis and Mining, 1*(1), 21–26. doi:10.100713278-010-0012-6

Scozzari, A., & Tardella, F. (2008). A clique algorithm for standard quadratic programming. *Discrete Applied Mathematics, 156*(13), 2439–2448. doi:10.1016/j.dam.2007.09.020

Sebastiani, F. (2002). Machine learning in automated text categorization. *ACM Computing Surveys, 34*(1), 1–47. doi:10.1145/505282.505283

Segundo, P. S., Matia, F., Rodriguez-Losada, D., & Hernando, M. (2013). An improved bit parallel exact maximum clique algorithm. *Optimization Letters, 7*(3), 467–479. doi:10.100711590-011-0431-y

Self-Regenerative Systems. Mission (2006, November 15). Retrieved from www.darpa.mil/ipto/programs/srs/index.htm

Sen, P., & Getoor, L. (2007). Link-Based Classification [Technical Report]. Univ. of Maryland.

Senthilkumar, N., Sudha, J., & Muthukumar, V. (2015). A grey-fuzzy approach for optimizing machining parameters and the approach angle in turning AISI 1045 steel. *Advances in Production Engineering & Management, 10*(4), 195–208. doi:10.14743/apem2015.4.202

Sequeira, K., & Zaki, M. J. (2004). SCHISM: A new approach for interesting subspace mining. In *Proc. IEEE Fourth Int'l Conf. Data Mining (ICDM)* (pp. 186-193). 10.1109/ICDM.2004.10099

Shabbir, M., Khan, M. A., Khan, U. S., & Saqib, N. A. (2016, December). Detection and Prevention of Distributed Denial of Service Attacks in VANETs. In *2016 International Conference on Computational Science and Computational Intelligence (CSCI)* (pp. 970-974). IEEE.

Shafigh, A. S., Mertikopoulos, P., Glisic, S., & Michae, Y. (2017). Semi-cognitive radio networks: A novel dynamic spectrum sharing mechanism. *IEEE Transactions on Cognitive Communications and Networking, 3*(1), 97–111.

Shaik, J. H., & Srinivas, J. (2017). Optimal selection of operating parameters in end milling of Al-6061 work materials using multi-objective approach. *Mechanics of Advanced Materials and Modern Processes, 3*(1), 5. doi:10.118640759-017-0020-6

Sharma, A., Sharma, M. K., & Dwivedi, R. K. (2017). Literature Review and Challenges of Data Mining Techniques for Social Network Analysis. *Advances in Computational Sciences and Technology, 10*(5), 1337–1354.

Shih, W.-K., & Hsu, W.-L. (1989). An O(n log n + m log log n) maximum weight clique algorithm for circular-arc graphs. *Information Processing Letters, 31*(3), 129–134. doi:10.1016/0020-0190(89)90220-2

Shikalgar, N. R., & Dixit, A. M. (2014). JIBCA: Jaccard Index based Clustering Algorithm for Mining Online Review. *International Journal of Computers and Applications, 105*(15).

Silani, G., Bird, G., Brindley, R., Singer, T., Frith, C., & Frith, U. (2008). Levels of emotional awareness and autism: An fMRI study. *Social Neuroscience, 3*(2), 97–112. doi:10.1080/17470910701577020 PMID:18633852

Sim, K., Aung, Z., & Gopakrishnan, V. (2010). Discovering correlated subspace clusters in 3D continuous-valued data. In *Proc. IEEE Int'l Conf. Data Mining (ICDM)* (pp. 471-480).

Sim, K., Poernomo, A. K., & Gopalkrishnan, V. (2010). Mining actionable subspace clusters in sequential data. In *Proc. SIAM Int'l Conf. Data Mining (SDM)* (pp. 442-453).

Sindhwani, V., & Melville, P. (2008). Document-word co-regularization for semi-supervised sentiment analysis. In *8th IEEE International Conference on Data Mining*.

Singh, D. (2017). An Effort to Design an Integrated System to Extract Information Under the Domain of Metaheuristics. *International Journal of Applied Evolutionary Computation, 8*(3), 13–52. doi:10.4018/IJAEC.2017070102

Singh, D. (2018). A Modified Bio Inspired: BAT Algorithm. *International Journal of Applied Metaheuristic Computing, 9*(1), 60–77. doi:10.4018/IJAMC.2018010105

Singh, K. D., Rawat, P., & Bonnin, J. M. (2014). Cognitive radio for vehicular ad hoc networks (CR-VANETs): Approaches and challenges. *EURASIP Journal on Wireless Communications and Networking, 2014*(1), 49. doi:10.1186/1687-1499-2014-49

Singh, K., Biswas, S., Ratnarajah, T., & Khan, F. A. (2018). *Transceiver design and power allocation for full-duplex MIMO communication systems with spectrum sharing radar*. IEEE Transactions on Cognitive Communications and Networking.

Singh, V. K., & Singh, V. K. (2015). Vector Space Model: An Information Retrieval System. *Int. J. Adv. Engg. Res., 141*, 143.

Smith, M., Hansen, D. L., & Gleave, E. (2009). *Analyzing enterprise social media networks. In proceedings of the international symposium on social computing applications (SCA09)*. Vancouver, Canada: IEEE Computer Society.

Soucy, P., & Mineau, G. W. (2015). Beyond TFIDF Weighting for Text Categorization in the Vector Space Model. In *Proceedings of the 19th International Joint Conference on Artificial Intelligence* (pp. 1130-1135).

Stalling, W. (2010). *ISDN and Broadband ISDN with Frame Relay and ATM. Knopf Doubleday Publishing Group*.

Stoica, I., & Zhang, H. (1999). Providing guaranteed services without per flow management. *Computer Communication Review, 29*(4), 81–94.

Subhadra, K., Shashi, M., & Ap, V. (2012). Hybrid distance based document clustering with keyword and phrase indexing. *International Journal of Computer Science Issues, 9*(2), 345–350.

Sudhir, K., & Rajagopalan, R. (1992). An artificial intelligence approach to precedence network generation for assembly line balancing. *Computers in Industry, 18*(2), 177–191. doi:10.1016/0166-3615(92)90112-Z

Sung, Y. E., Lund, C., Lyn, M., Rao, S., & Sen, S. (2009) Modeling and understanding end-to-end class of service policies in operational networks. In *Proc. ACM Special Interest Group Data Comm. (SIGCOMM)*.

Sun, J., Tao, D., & Faloutsos, C. (2006). Beyond streams and graphs: Dynamic tensor analysis. In *Proc. 12th ACM SIGKDD Int'l Conf. Knowledge Discovery and Data Mining (KDD)* (pp. 374-383). 10.1145/1150402.1150445

Suriya, M., Sugandhanaa, M., Vaishnavi, J. & Bharathy, P.D. (2016). A survey on cognitive handover between the terrestrial and satellite segments.

Suriya, M. M., Swathi, M. R., Scholar, R. U., Surya, M. P., Scholar, U. G., & Veeralakshmi, M. R. (2018). Enhancing energy in WBAN through cognitive radio networks. *International Journal of Advanced Information and Communication Technology*, *4*(11).

Suriya, M., Anandakumar, H., & Arulmurugan, R. (2016). Social Aware Cognitive Radio Networks: Effectiveness of Social Networks as a Strategic Tool for Organizational Business Management. In *Social Network Analytics for Contemporary Business Organizations*. Hershey, PA: IGI Global.

Suriya, M., Vaishnavi, J., Sugandhanaa, M., & Bharathy, P. D. (2016), A Survey on IEEE 802.16g Protocol Convergence between Terrestrial and Satellite Segments. In *International Conference on Explorations and Innovations in Engineering & Technology*.

Sweeney, L. (2002). k-anonymity: A model for protecting privacy. *International Journal of Uncertainty, Fuzziness and Knowledge-based Systems*, *10*(5), 557–570.

Symeonidis, P., Tiakas, E., & Manolopoulos, Y. (2011). Product recommendation and rating prediction based on multi-modal social networks. In *Proceedings of the fifth ACM conference on Recommender systems* (pp. 61-68). ACM. 10.1145/2043932.2043947

Tamás, J., Podani, J., & Csontos, P. (2001). An extension of presence/absence coefficients to abundance data: A new look at absence. *Journal of Vegetation Science*, *12*(3), 401–410. doi:10.2307/3236854

Tan, A. C., & Gilbert, D. (2003). Ensemble machine learning on gene expression data for cancer classification. *Applied Bioinformatics*, *2*(3 Suppl.), S75–S83. PMID:15130820

Tang, L., & Liu, H. (2010) Graph mining applications to social network analysis. In C. Aggarwal & H. Wang (Eds.), *Managing and mining graph data. Springer, New York The growing role of artificial intelligence in business*. Retrieved from http://www.livemint.com/Opinion/UKCvUCD1mVgVp8CcR62uvJ/The-growing-role-of-artificial-intelligence-in-business.html

Tang, H., Tan, S., & Cheng, X. (2009). A survey on sentiment detection of reviews. *Expert Systems with Applications*, *36*(7), 10760–10773. doi:10.1016/j.eswa.2009.02.063

Tanikić, D., Marinković, V., Manić, M., Devedžić, G., & Ranđelović, S. (2016). Application of response surface methodology and fuzzy logic based system for determining metal cutting temperature. *Bulletin of the Polish Academy of Sciences. Technical Sciences*, *64*(2), 435–445. doi:10.1515/bpasts-2016-0049

Tan, S., & Zhang, J. (2007). (2007). An empirical study of sentiment analysis for Chinese documents. *Expert Systems with Applications*. doi:10.1016/j.eswa.2007.05.028

Tar, H. H., & Nyaunt, T. T. S. (2011). Enhancing traditional text documents clustering based on Ontology. *International Journal of Computers and Applications*, *33*(10), 38–42.

Tasker, B., Abbeel, P., & Daphne, K. (2010). Discriminative Probabilistic Models for Relational Data. In *Proc. 18th Ann. Conf. Uncertainty in Artificial Intelligence (UAI '02)* (pp. 485-492).

Tepper, A. (2012). How much data is created every minute? [infographic]. *Mashable*. Retrieved from http://mashable.com/2012/06/22/data-created-every-minute/

The Manufacturer. (2018, February 26). *Power of artificial intelligence*. Retrieved from https://www.themanufacturer.com/articles/power-artificial-intelligence-manufacturing/

Thilak, K. D., & Amuthan, A. (2016, February). DoS attack on VANET routing and possible defending solutions-A survey. In *2016 International Conference on Information Communication and Embedded Systems (ICICES)* (pp. 1-7). IEEE.

Thompson, J. B. (2013). *Media and modernity: A social theory of the media*. John Wiley & Sons.

Titov, I., & McDonald, R. (2008). A joint model of text and aspect ratings for sentiment summarization. In *Proceedings of 46th Annual Meeting of the Association for Computational Linguistics (ACL'08)*.

Tomasi, W. (2007). *Introduction to Data communication and Networking*. Pearson India Publications.

Tong, R. (2001). An operational system for detecting and tracking opinions in on-line discussion. In *Proceedings of the Workshop on Operational Text Classification (OTC)*.

Tsirogiannis, G. L., Frossyniotis, D., Stoitsis, J., Golemati, S., Stafylopatis, A., & Nikita, K. S. (2004). Classification of medical data with a robust multi-level combination scheme. In *Proceedings. 2004 IEEE International Joint Conference on Neural Networks* (Vol. 3, pp. 2483-2487). IEEE.

Tu, M. C., Shin, D., & Shin, D. (2009). Effective diagnosis of heart disease through bagging approach. In *2nd International Conference on Biomedical Engineering and Informatics BMEI '09* (pp. 1-4). IEEE.

Tu, M. C., Shin, D., & Shin, D. (2009, December). A comparative study of medical data classification methods based on decision tree and bagging algorithms. In *2009 Eighth IEEE International Conference on Dependable, Autonomic and Secure Computing* (pp. 183-187). IEEE. 10.1109/DASC.2009.40

Tumuluru, J. S., & McCulloch, R. (2016). Application of hybrid genetic algorithm routine in optimizing food and bio-engineering processes. *Foods*, *5*(4), 76. doi:10.3390/foods5040076 PMID:28231171

Turney, P.D. & Littman, M.L. (2002). Unsupervised Learning of Semantic Orientation from a Hundred-Billion-Word Corpus.

Turney, P. (2001). Mining the web for synonyms: PMI-IR Versus LSA on TOEFL. In *Proceedings of the Twelfth European Conference on Machine Learning (pp. 491-*502). Springer-Verlag.

Turney, P. (2002). Thumbs Up or Thumbs Down? Semantic orientation applied to unsupervised Classification of Reviews. In *Proceedings of the Association for Computational Linguistics (ACL)* (pp. 417–424).

Underwood, J. (2018, March 28). IBM Watson cognitive computing. Retrieved from http://www.jenunderwood.com/2017/03/28/ibm-watson-cognitive-computing/

Van De Camp, M., & van den Bosch, A. (2011, June). A link to the past: constructing historical social networks. In *Proceedings of the 2nd Workshop on Computational Approaches to Subjectivity and Sentiment Analysis* (pp. 61-69). Association for Computational Linguistics.

van den Bekerom, B. (2017). Using Machine Learning for Detection of Autism Spectrum Disorder. Retrieved from https://pdfs.semanticscholar.org/65af/94822bcd64ed5365172ba6cf6fb6fc2a8fc6.pdf

Van Rijsbergen, C. J., Robertson, S. E., & Porter, M. F. (1980). *New models in probabilistic information retrieval*. London: British Library Research and Development Department.

Varshney, N., Roy, T., & Chaudhary, N. (2014, April). Security protocol for VANET by using digital certification to provide security with low bandwidth. In *2014 International Conference on Communications and Signal Processing (ICCSP)* (pp. 768-772). IEEE.

Varshney, U. (2007). Pervasive Healthcare and Wireless Health Monitoring. *Mobile Networks and Applications, 12*(2–3), 113–127. doi:10.100711036-007-0017-1

Venkataramanan, V. J., Lin, X., Ying, L., & Shakkottai, S. (2010, March). On scheduling for minimizing end-to-end buffer usage over multihop wireless networks. In INFOCOM, 2010 Proceedings IEEE (pp. 1-9). IEEE.

Verma, K. S., & Bhattacharyya, P. (2009). Context-Sensitive Semantic Smoothing using Semantically Relatable Sequences. In IJCAI (pp. 1580–1585).

Vijayaran, S. (2013). An Effective Classification Rule Technique for Heart Disease Prediction. *International Journal of Engineering Associates*.

Vijay, G., Bdira, E. B. A., & Ibnkahla, M. (2011). Cognition in wireless sensor networks: A perspective. *IEEE Sensors Journal, 11*(3), 582–592. doi:10.1109/JSEN.2010.2052033

Vijaykumar, K., Panneerselvam, K., & Sait, A. N. (2014). Machining Parameter Optimization of Bidirectional CFRP Composite Pipe by Genetic Algorithm. *Materials Testing, 56*(9), 728–736. doi:10.3139/120.110623

Vilic, V. M. (2017). Cyber terrorism on the internet and social networking: a threat to global security. In *Proceedings of international scientific conference on information technology and data related research (SINTEZA 2017)*, Belgrade, Serbia.

Viswanathan, T. (1992). *Telecommunication Switching Systems and Networks*. New Delhi: Prentice Hall of India Private Limited.

Wan, X. (2009, August). Co-training for cross-lingual sentiment classification. In *Proceedings of the Joint Conference of the 47th Annual Meeting of the ACL and the 4th International Joint Conference on Natural Language Processing of the AFNLP* (Vol. 1, pp. 235-243). Association for Computational Linguistics.

Wang, H., Lu, Y., & Zhai, C. (2010). Latent aspect rating analysis on review text data: A rating regression approach. In KDD '10, New York, NY (pp. 783-792).

Wang, M, Chen, X. & Gao, W. (2015), High Precision Uplink Time and Frequency Calibration in Cognitive Space Communications. In *IEEE 14th Int Conf. on Cognitive Informatics & Cognitive Computing*.

Wang, Y., Baciu, G., & Li, C. (2017). Cognitive exploration of regions through analyzing geo-tagged social media data. In *Proceedings of IEEE 16th International Conference on Cognitive Informatics & Cognitive Computing (ICCI*CC)*. UK: IEEE Computer Society.

Wang, B., & Liu, K. J. R. (2011). Advances in cognitive radio networks: A survey. *IEEE Journal of Selected Topics in Signal Processing, 5*(1), 5–23.

Wang, G., & Araki, K. (2007). Modifying SO-PMI for Japanese Weblog Opinion Mining by Using a Balancing Factor and Detecting Neutral Expressions. In *Proceedings of NAACL HLT 2007* (pp. 189–192).

Wang, K., Zhou, S., & Han, J. (2002). Profit mining: From patterns to actions. In *Proc. Eighth Int'l Conf. Extending Database Technology: Advances in Database Technology (EDBT)* (pp. 70-87).

Waqas. (2012, March 4). Hacking news. Six Automotive Giants: FORD, KIA, Subaru, Suzuki, Kawasaki, SsangYong Hacked and Defaced by Q8 Spy. Retrieved from https://www.hackread.com/six-automotive-giant-ford-kia-subaru-suzuki-kawasaki-ssangyong-hacked-and-defaced-by-q8-spy/

Watrous-deVersterre, L., Wang, C., & Song, M. (2012). Concept chaining utilizing meronyms in text characterization. In *Proceedings of the twelfth ACM/IEEE-CS joint conference on Digital Libraries* (pp. 241-248). ACM.

Wei, Y., Yu, F. R., & Song, M. (2010). Distributed Optimal Relay Selection in Wireless Cooperative Networks with Finite-State Markov Channels. IEEE Trans. Veh. Technology, 59(5).

Wen, P. (2009). Application of decision tree to identify abnormal high frequency electro-cardiograph. *Physics Experimentation, 11*.

Weng, J., & Lee, B.-S. (2011). Event detection in twitter. In ICWSM.

West, V. L., Borland, D., West, D., & Hammond, W. E. (2015). An evaluation of machine learning methods and visualization of results to characterize large healthcare document collections.

Wheaton, K. J., & Richey, M. K. (2014, January 9). The potential of Social Network Analysis in Intelligence. *E-international Relations*. Retrieved from http://www.e-ir.info/2014/01/09/the-potential-of-social-network-analysis-in-intelligence/

Wikipedia. (n.d.). Social network analysis Practical Applications. Retrieved March 17, 2018 from https://en.wikipedia.org/wiki/Social_network_analysis#Practical_applications

Wilson, C., Hargreaves, T., & Hauxwell-Baldwin, R. (2014). Smart homes and their users: A systematic analysis and key challenges. *Personal and Ubiquitous Computing, 19*(2), 463–476. doi:10.100700779-014-0813-0

Wong, J. C., & Solon, O. (2017, May 12). Massive ransomware cyber-attack hits nearly 100 countries around the world. *The Guardian*. Retrieved from https://www.theguardian.com/technology/2017/may/12/global-cyber-attack-ransomware-nsa-uk-nhs

World Cancer Research Fund International. (n.d.) Cancer facts. Retrieved from http://www.wcrf.org/int/cancer-facts figures/data-specific cancers/breast-cancer-statistics

Wu, H., & Jia, X. (2009). QoS Multicast Routing by Using Multiple Paths/Trees in Wireless Ad Hoc Networks. *Ad Hoc Networks, 5*(5), 600–612. doi:10.1016/j.adhoc.2006.04.001

Wu, T. (2010). *The Master Switch: The Rise and Fall of Information Empires*. New York: Knopf.

Younis, Y. A., Kifayat, K., Shi, Q., & Askwith, B. (2015, October). A new prime and probe cache side-channel attack for cloud computing. In *2015 IEEE International Conference on Computer and Information Technology; Ubiquitous Computing and Communications; Dependable, Autonomic and Secure Computing; Pervasive Intelligence and Computing (CIT/IUCC/DASC/PICOM)* (pp. 1718-1724). IEEE.

Zadeh, L. (1965). Fuzzy sets. *Information and Control, 8*(3), 338–353. doi:10.1016/S0019-9958(65)90241-X

Zadeh, L. A. (1973). Outline of a new approach to the analysis of complex systems and decision processes. *IEEE Transactions on Systems, Man, and Cybernetics, SMC-3*(1), 28–44. doi:10.1109/TSMC.1973.5408575

Zatari, T. (2015). Data Mining in Social Media. *International Journal of Scientific & Engineering Research, 6*(7), 152–154.

Zeng, K., Yang, Z., & Lou, W. (2010). Opportunistic routing in multi-radio multi-channel multi-hop wireless networks. *IEEE Trans. Wireless Comm., 9*(11).

Zeng, C. H., & Chen, K. C. (2018). *Social network analysis facilitates cognition in large wireless networks: clustering coefficient aided geographical routing*. IEEE Transactions on Cognitive Communications and Networking.

Zhang, Z., Ye, Q., Zheng, W., & Li, Y. (2010). Sentiment Classification for Consumer Word-of-Mouth in Chinese: Comparison between Supervised and Unsupervised Approaches. In *The 2010 International Conference on E-Business Intelligence.*

Zhang, C., Yao, X., Zhang, J., & Jin, H. (2016). Tool condition monitoring and remaining useful life prognostic based on a wireless sensor in dry milling operations. *Sensors (Basel)*, *16*(6), 795. doi:10.339016060795 PMID:27258277

Zhao, X., Guo, S., Zhang, F., Wang, T., Shi, Z., Liu, H., & Huang, J. (2013). Efficient Hamming weight-based side-channel cube attacks on PRESENT. *Journal of Systems and Software*, *86*(3), 728–743. doi:10.1016/j.jss.2012.11.007

Zheleva, E., & Getoor, L. (2008). Preserving the Privacy of Sensitive Relationships in Graph Data. In *Proc. First ACM SIGKDD Int'l Conf. Privacy, Security, and Trust in KDD* (pp. 153-171). 10.1007/978-3-540-78478-4_9

Zheng, N., Liu, Z., Ren, P., Ma, Y., Chen, S., Yu, S., ... Wang, F. (2017). Hybrid-augmented intelligence: Collaboration and cognition. *Frontiers of Information Technology & Electronic Engineering*, *18*(2), 153–179. doi:10.1631/FITEE.1700053

Zhou, X., Hu, X., Zhang, X., Lin, X., & Song, I. Y. (2006). Context-sensitive semantic smoothing for the language modeling approach to genomic IR. In *Proceedings of the 29th annual international ACM SIGIR conference on Research and development in information retrieval* (pp. 170-177).

Zhu, K., & Zhang, Y. (2018). A Cyber-Physical Production System Framework of Smart CNC Machining Monitoring System. *IEEE/ASME Transactions on Mechatronics*, 1. doi:10.1109/TMECH.2018.2834622

Zhu, S., Zeng, J., & Mamitsuka, H. (2009). Enhancing MEDLINE document clustering by incorporating MeSH semantic similarity. *Bioinformatics*, *25*(15), 1944–1951. doi:10.1093/bioinformatics/btp338 PMID:19497938

About the Contributors

Anandakumar Haldorai, Professor (Associate) and Research Head in Department of Computer Science and Engineering, Sri Eshwar College of Engineering, Coimbatore, Tamilnadu, India. He has received his Master's in Software Engineering from PSG College of Technology, Coimbatore. He has a PhD in Information and Communication Engineering from PSG College of Technology under, Anna University, Chennai. His research areas include cognitive radio networks, mobile communications and networking protocols. He has authored more than 45 research papers in reputed International Journals and IEEE, Springer Conferences. He has authored 5 books and many book chapters with reputed publishers such as Springer and IGI Global. He is an Editor-in-chief of the Inderscience IJISC Journal and has also served as a reviewer for IEEE, IET, Springer, Inderscience and Elsevier journals. He is also the guest editor of many journals with Wiley, Springer, Elsevier, Inderscience, etc. He has been the General chair, Session Chair, and Panelist in several conferences. He is senior member of IEEE, MIET, MACM and EAI research group.

Arulmurugan Ramu received his PhD degree in Information and Communication Engineering from Anna University, Chennai, Tamil Nadu, India. He is currently working as an Assistant Professor in the Department of Computer Science and Engineering, Presidency University, India. He received a Young Faculty Award in 2018. He has published many papers in Scopus indexed and SCI journals with a total of 61 Google scholar citations. His research interests include digital image processing, biomedical image processing computer vision, cognitive learning pattern recognition, and machine learning.

***

P. Anushree is a PG scholar in the Department of Information Technology at PSG College of Technology, Coimbatore, India. She completed her Bachelor's in Information Technology from KIT-Kalaignarkarunanidhi Institute of Technology and she is currently pursuing her MTech in Information Technology.

A. Dharani is a PG scholar in the Department of Information Technology at PSG College of Technology, Coimbatore, India. She completed her Bachelor's in Information Technology from the same institution and she is currently pursuing her MTech in Information Technology.

Sri Subarnaa D.K. received a bachelor's degree in Information Technology and pursuing master's degree in Computer Science and Information Security at Thiagarajar College of Engineering, Madurai, India. Her research interest includes wireless networks and Internet of Things.

Ramanujam Elangovan has received his M.E from Anna University, Chennai, Tamil Nadu. He is pursuing his research in the area of biomedical engineering. His current areas of interest are data mining, time series mining and biomedical processing. He has also published papers in national and international conferences and journals.

Premalatha K. is currently working as a Professor in the Department of Computer Science and Engineering at Bannari Amman Institute of Technology, Erode, Tamil Nadu, India. She completed her PhD in Computer Science and Engineering (CSE) at Anna University, Chennai, India. She did her Master of Engineering in CSE and Bachelor of Engineering in CSE at Bharathiar University, Coimbatore, Tamil Nadu, India. Her research interests include data mining, networking, information retrieval and soft computing.

Sampoornam K.P. completed UG (Electronics and Communication Engineering Department) in the year 1990, PG (VLSI Design) in the year 2005 and a PhD (Information and Communication Engineering) in the year 2013. At present, he is working as an Associate Professor in Bannari Amman Institute of Technology, Sathyamangalam.

R. Leelavathi is working as Assistant Professor at Bannari Amman Institute of Technology, Sathyamangalam, Tamil Nadu, India. She has received her Master of Engineering in Computer Science and Engineering on 2015 at Avinashilingam Institute for Home Science and Higher Education for Women, Coimbatore, Tamil Nadu, India. She completed her Bachelor of Technology in Information Technology during 2013 at Coimbatore Institute of Engineering and Technology, Coimbatore, Tamil Nadu, India. Her area of research & specialization is Data Mining, Data analytics and Big Data.

S. Logeswari received her Bachelor of Engineering in Computer Science and Engineering from Bharathiar University, Coimbatore in 1997, Master of Engineering in Computer Science and Engineering from Anna University, Chennai in 2007 and Doctor of Philosophy in Computer Science and Engineering from Anna University, Chennai in 2015. She has 20 years of teaching experience in the academic field. Presently, she is working as a Professor in the Department of Computer science and Engineering at Bannari Amman Institute of Technology, Sathyamangalam. Her professional activities include guiding PhDs in the field of CSE, published 12 papers in the national and international journals and presented more than 15 papers at international and national conferences.

Prianga M. is currently pursuing his master's in computer science engineering and information security at Thiagarajar college of engineering, Madurai. He did his bachelor's degree in stream of information technology at Velammal College of Engineering and Technology, Viraganoor. His areas of interest are cognitive science, cloud computing and ethical hacking. Currently, I am doing my research project in the area of cognitive science. Other than academics, he is doing online courses and has also volunteered for the national service scheme and the blood donation camp.

M. Manikandakumar received the master's degree in Computer Science and Engineering and pursuing research degree at Anna University, Chennai. He is currently an Assistant Professor with the department of Information Technology, Thiagarajar College of Engineering, Madurai, India. His research interest includes Security, Internet of Things and Big Data.

Suriya Murugan is an Assistant Professor (Senior Grade) in Department of Computer Science and Engineering, Bannari Amman Institute of Technology, Sathyamangalam, Erode (Dt), Tamilnadu, India has received her Master's in Computer Science and Engineering from Anna University of Technology, Coimbatore. She is pursuing a PhD in Information and Communication Engineering from Bannari Amman Institute of Technology under, Anna University, Chennai. Her research areas include soft computing, big data and cognitive radio networks. She has authored more than 25 research papers in reputed International Journals and IEEE conferences. She has published book chapters with reputed publishers such as IGI Global and has served as a reviewer for international journals like Inderscience and Taylor and Francis. She has recently obtained patent on the title "Spectrum Detection Methodology for Cognitive Radio System through Machine Learning." She is a member of IEEE, CSI and IAENG.

Deivanathan R. is an Associate Professor of the School of Mechanical and Building Sciences, VIT, Chennai. He earned a BE (Mechanical Engineering, 1991), an ME (Production Engineering, 1993), and a PhD (Grinding, 2005).

Monica Grace R. received a bachelor's degree in Information Technology and is pursuing a master's degree in Computer Science and Information Security at Thiagarajar College of Engineering, Madurai, India. Her research interest includes wireless networks and evolutionary computing.

S. P. Rajamohana is an Assistant Professor in the Department of Information Technology at the, PSG College of Technology, Coimbatore, India. She completed her Master's in Information Technology from the same institution and is currently pursuing her PhD in Information and Communication Engineering from PSG College of Technology, Anna University, Chennai. Her research interests include review spam classification and evolutionary algorithms.

K R. Sabarmathi is working as an Assistant Professor at Bannari Amman Institute of Technology, Sathyamangalam, Tamil Nadu, India. She has received her Master of Engineering in Software Engineering with a Gold medal in 2016 from Sri Ramakrishna Engineering College, Coimbatore, Tamil Nadu, India. She completed her Bachelor of Technology in Information Technology during 2014 at Sri Shakthi Institute of Engineering and Technology, Coimbatore, Tamil Nadu, India. Her areas of research and specialization is data mining, data analytics and big data.

B. Santhiya is an PG Scholar in the Department of Information Technology at the, PSG College of Technology, Coimbatore, India. She completed her Bachelor's in Information Technology from the Coimbatore Institute of Technology and she is currently pursuing her Master's in Information Technology in PSG College of Technology.

T. Senthilkumar received his B.Tech in Information Technology from Dr. Mahalingam College of Engineering and Technology, Pollachi and his M.Tech in Information Technology from Anna University, Coimbatore. He then joined the faculty of Tamil Nadu College of Engineering, where he is a Lecturer of Information Technology. In 2011, he became an Assistant professor in the Department of CSE in the Professional Group of Institutions. Now he is working as an Assistant professor in the Department of Information Technology, Hindusthan Institute of Technology. He has published over 50 papers on a wide range of topics in various areas.

Dharmpal Singh received his Bachelor of Computer Science and Engineering and Master of Computer Science and Engineering from West Bengal University of Technology. He has about eight years of experience in teaching and research. At present, he is with the JIS College of Engineering, Kalyani, and West Bengal, India as an Associate Professor. He completed his PhD at the University of Kalyani. He has about 26 publications in national and international journals and conference proceedings. He is also the editorial board members of many reputed/ referred journal.

M.G. Sumithra serves as Professor in Electronics and Communication Engineering, Bannari Amman Institute of Technology, Sathyamangalm, Erode, Tamil Nadu, India. She was born on 26 May 1973 at Salem, Tamil Nadu. She obtained a B.E. (Electronics and Commn. Engg.) from Govt. College of Engineering, Salem, India in 1994, received a M.E. (Medical Electronics) from the College of Engineering, Guindy, Anna University Chennai, India in 2001 and received a PhD (Information and Communication Engineering) from Anna University Chennai, India in 2011. Her areas of interest include signal processing, medical image processing, biomedical engineering and wireless communications. She has published 55 technical papers in refereed journals, 124 research papers in national and international conferences in India and abroad. She is a recognized supervisor of Anna University, Chennai and four research scholars are pursuing PhD under her supervision. She is an active member in various professional societies like ISTE, IEEE, IAENG, IACSIT, IET, IEEE Nanotechnology Council, IEEE Biometrics Council IEEE Computer Society Technical Committee, Cloud Computing Community, Green ICT Community and Fellow in IETE, India Bio-design. She has been contributing as a reviewer for 10 refereed journals which includes the Springer Journal of Signal, Image and Video Processing, the IEEE Communication Letters, Circuits, Systems & Signal Processing (CSSP), Signal & Image Processing: An International Journal (SIPIJ), the Journal of Engineering Science & Technology (JESTEC), etc. Further, she is also an Editorial Member of the Journal of Communication Engineering and Systems and an Associate Editorial Member of the South Asian Journal of Research in Engineering Science and Technology.

S. Uma is Professor and Head of the Department of Information Technology at Hindusthan Institute of Technology, Coimbatore, Tamil Nadu, India. She received her B.E., degree in Computer Science and Engineering in First Class with Distinction from P.S.G. College of Technology and the M.S., degree from Anna University, Chennai, Tamil Nadu, India. She received her Ph.D. in Computer Science and Engineering from Anna University, Chennai, Tamil Nadu, India with High Commendations. She has 27 years of academic experience. She has organized many national-level events like seminars, workshops and conferences. She has published many research papers in national and international conferences and journals. She is a reviewer of international journals and a member of professional bodies like the ISTE,

CSI, IEEE, and IAENG. She has earned several digital credentials from Google Adwords, IBM Certifications and IBM badges on the latest computer science and information technologies. She is a recipient of "Bharath Jyoti," Certificate of Excellence and Best Citizen of India Awards. Her research interests are pattern recognition and analysis of nonlinear time series data and digital analytics.

K. Umamaheswari, Professor & Head in the Department of Information Technology, at the PSG College of Technology, India and has completed her bachelor's and master's in Computer Science and Engineering in 1989 and 2000, respectively and a PhD degree from Anna University in 2010. She has 22 years of teaching experience and more than 100 Publications in international and national journals and conferences. Her research interests include data mining, cognitive networks and information retrieval.

Vijayaganth V. received his M.E in Software Engineering from Anna University-Chennai in 2010. In 2010, he became an Assistant Professor at the CSI College of Engineering and in the year 2017 he joined Bannari Amman Institute of Technology as an Assistant Professor. He has published 9 papers in International Journals. He has presented 3 papers at international conferences and 2 papers at national conferences. He has attended more than 15 training programs and has 8 years of teaching experience in engineering. His areas of expertise are data mining, data analytics and cryptography and network security.

Phu Ngoc Vo, Professor of Computer Science, his research includes work in natural language, computer science, artificial intelligence, parallel network environments, expert systems, intelligent systems, machine intelligence, data mining, machine learning, etc. He is a co-author of the book, Artificial Intelligence (ISBN 978-953-51-6129-5), edited by Dr. Marco Antonio Aceves-Fernandez in IntechOpen. I wrote Chapter 1, "The Today Tendency of Sentiment classification." He is a co-author of the book "Simulation for Industry 4.0 - Past, Present, and Future" edited by Dr. Murat M. Gunal from Springer. He is a co-author of the book ""Smart Data: State-of-the-Art and Perspectives in Computing and Applications" edited by Dr. Kuan-Ching Li, Dr. Qingchen Zhang, Dr. Laurence T. Yang and Dr. Beniamino Di Martino He is a co-author of the book ""Smart Data: Managerial Perspectives on Intelligent Big Data Analytics" edited by Prof. Dr. Zhaohao Sun. He is a co-author of the book " "Handbook of Research on Big Data and the IoT," edited by Dr. Gurjit Kaur and Dr. Pradeep Tomar. He is a co-author of the book "Handbook of Research on Deep Learning Innovations and Trends," edited by Dr. Aboul Ella Hassanien, Dr. Ashraf Darwish, and Dr. Chiranji Lal Chowdhary. He is a co-author of the book " Computational Intelligence in the Internet of Things," edited by Dr. Hindriyanto Dwi Purnomo . He is a co-author of the book "Encyclopedia of Organizational Knowledge, Administration, and Technologies, 1st Edition"," edited by Mehdi Khosrow-Pour. He is a co-author of the book "Artificial Intelligence and Information: A Multidisciplinary Perspective," edited by Steven S. Gouveia, and João de Fernandes Teixeira. He is a co-author of the book "EAI/Springer Innovations in Communications and Computing." He is an Editor-in-Chief of the book "The Unsupervised and Semi-Supervised Learning Models for Big Data Sets" He has written the book "The Unsupervised and Semi-Supervised Learning Models for Big Data Sets" from Springer. He has served as a peer reviewer for multiple ISI journals such as the Journal of Big Data; the Journal of Soft Computing; Cyberpsychology, Behavior, and Social Networking; the Journal of Computer Science; the Journal Issue on Information and Communications Technology; the Journal of Supercomputing (SUPE); the African Educational Research Journal; Information;

Data; Computers; etc. He has also served as a peer reviewer for many conferences: including the 4th International Conference on Fuzzy Systems and Data Mining (FSDM 2018); a Member of the Technical Program Committee (TPC) and a Reviewer of the 9th Annual International Conference on ICT: Big Data, Cloud and Security (ICT-BDCS 2018); 37th AIAA/IEEE Digital Avionics Systems Conference (DASC); the 22nd International Conference on Knowledge-Based and Intelligent Information & Engineering Systems (KES-2018); the 32nd ACM International Conference on Supercomputing; the 19th Computational Intelligence in Bioinformatics and Computational Biology; the 25th Anniversary of the European Community on Computational Methods in Applied Sciences (ECCOMAS), the 6th European Conference on Computational Mechanics (Solids, Structures, and Coupled Problems) (ECCM 6) and the 7th European Conference on Computational Fluid Dynamics (ECFD 7); QUORS: The 12th IEEE International Workshop on Quality Oriented Reuse of Software; RevOpiD-2018 Workshop on Opinion Mining, Summarization and Diversification; etc. He has joined the Editorial Boards of ISI journals. He has published over 50 ISI manuscripts.

Index

Ensure Quality Research is Introduced to the Academic Community

Become an IGI Global Reviewer for Authored Book Projects

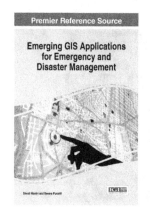

Premier Reference Source

Emerging GIS Applications for Emergency and Disaster Management

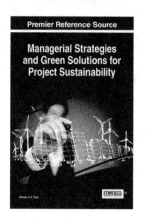

Premier Reference Source

Managerial Strategies and Green Solutions for Project Sustainability

Premier Reference Source

Comparative Approaches to Using R and Python for Statistical Data Analysis

Premier Reference Source

Solutions for High-Touch Communications in a High-Tech World

The overall success of an authored book project is dependent on quality and timely reviews.

In this competitive age of scholarly publishing, constructive and timely feedback significantly expedites the turnaround time of manuscripts from submission to acceptance, allowing the publication and discovery of forward-thinking research at a much more expeditious rate. Several IGI Global authored book projects are currently seeking highly qualified experts in the field to fill vacancies on their respective editorial review boards:

Applications may be sent to:
development@igi-global.com

Applicants must have a doctorate (or an equivalent degree) as well as publishing and reviewing experience. Reviewers are asked to write reviews in a timely, collegial, and constructive manner. All reviewers will begin their role on an ad-hoc basis for a period of one year, and upon successful completion of this term can be considered for full editorial review board status, with the potential for a subsequent promotion to Associate Editor.

If you have a colleague that may be interested in this opportunity, we encourage you to share this information with them.

Information Resources Management Association

Advancing the Concepts & Practices of Information Resources Management in Modern Organizations

Become an IRMA Member

Members of the **Information Resources Management Association (IRMA)** understand the importance of community within their field of study. The Information Resources Management Association is an ideal venue through which professionals, students, and academicians can convene and share the latest industry innovations and scholarly research that is changing the field of information science and technology. Become a member today and enjoy the benefits of membership as well as the opportunity to collaborate and network with fellow experts in the field.

IRMA Membership Benefits:

- **One FREE Journal Subscription**

- **30% Off Additional Journal Subscriptions**

- **20% Off Book Purchases**

- Updates on the latest events and research on Information Resources Management through the IRMA-L listserv.

- Updates on new open access and downloadable content added to Research IRM.

- A copy of the Information Technology Management Newsletter twice a year.

- A certificate of membership.

IRMA Membership $195

Scan code or visit **irma-international.org** and begin by selecting your free journal subscription.

Membership is good for one full year.

Printed in the United States
By Bookmasters